BUSINESS ORGANIZATIONS

CONTENTS:

CHAPTER 3: ENTITY SELECTION AND FORMATION   p. 37

Don't need to Know LP

BUSINESS ORGANIZATIONS: PRACTICAL APPLICATIONS

Christopher Gulinello

Northern Kentucky University, Chase College of Law

Business Organizations: Practical Applications

Gulinello, Christopher

Published by:

Vandeplas Publishing, LLC – April 2016

801 International Parkway, 5th Floor
Lake Mary, FL. 32746
USA

www.vandeplaspublishing.com

ISBN 978-1-60042-282-9

Dedications

To my family, here and in Taiwan.

To all the students at NKU-Chase who suffered through early drafts of this book.

BRIEF CONTENTS:

CHAPTER **8**: **L**ITIGATION p. 413

UNIT 8A **C**ORPORATIONS – **L**ITIGATION: p. 416

CHAPTER 1
INTRODUCTION

This book is a coursebook and a treatise. It is the coursebook I wish we had used in class when I was a law student. It is the resource I wanted on my shelf when I first started working as a corporate lawyer. It is the treatise and coursebook I lacked when I first became a law professor.

This book does not provide you with everything you need to know about business organizations. Instead, it helps you build the prerequisite foundation for further study. It provides you with a broad-based knowledge of the law and the context of the law, without which you would be at a disadvantage.

If you are a law student using this book as the main text for your business-organizations class, you should use the Companion Workbook to guide you. You cannot learn everything in this book in one semester. The Companion Workbook has one hundred and thirty exercises that will take you through the most important content of this book. The remaining content is there to round out your knowledge, satisfy your curiosity, and make connections that you would otherwise miss.

There are a few main resources that are referred to repeatedly throughout this book. I thought it would be convenient to list them here. Eventually, you will not need to refer to this list.

> **RMBCA:**   The Revised Model Business Corporation Act – prepared by the Committee on Corporate Laws of the Section of Business Law, American Bar Association.

> **MBCA:**   Earlier versions of the Model Business Corporation Act – prepared by the Committee on Corporate Laws of the Section of Business Law, American Bar Association.

> **RULLCA:**   The Revised Uniform Limited Liability Company Act – 2006 version of the Uniform Limited Liability Company Act, prepared by the National Conference of Commissioners on Uniform State Laws (now called the Uniform Law Commission).

> **ULLCA:**   The Uniform Limited Liability Company Act – 1995 version of the Uniform Limited Liability Company Act, prepared by the National Conference of Commissioners on Uniform State Laws (now called the Uniform Law Commission).

> **RUPA:** The Revised Uniform Partnership Act – 1997 version of the Uniform Partnership Act, prepared by the National Conference of Commissioners on Uniform State Laws (now called the Uniform Law Commission).

UPA: The Uniform Partnership Act – 1914 version of the Uniform Partnership Act, prepared by the National Conference of Commissioners on Uniform State Laws (now called the Uniform Law Commission).

DGCL: The Delaware General Corporation Law – found in Title 8, Chapter 1 of the Delaware Code.

DLLCA: The Delaware Limited Liability Company Act – found in Title 6, Chapter 18 of the Delaware Code.

Finally, an apology: There are mistakes in this book, I am sure, but I have already become blind to them. Unfortuntely, I am the king of typographical errors and careless mistakes. My sister thinks I have dysgraphia. I am not even sure what that means, but I am willing to blame my mistakes on any affliction I imagine I might have. My research assistants did a wonderful job, but they could not catch all of my errors.[1]

Please let me know how I can improve this book and the Companion Workbook.

Chris Gulinello

---

[1] Many students made comments and suggestions on earlier versions of the manuscript for this book. Several made herculean efforts, and I'd like to thank them here: Linda Long, Angela White, Mark Bernstein, Terrence Demery, and Matt Ryan.

CHAPTER 2

IMPORTANT TERMS AND CONCEPTS

2-100 BUSINESS ORGANIZATIONS – TERMS AND CONCEPTS:

Students without a formal education in business often approach a business organizations course with a defeatist attitude. They believe they can only suffer through the material and, at best, earn a respectable grade.

Admittedly, a deep understanding of business is useful in the study of business-organization law, but it is not crucial. With a good grasp of some basic business, economic, financial, and legal concepts, any good student can thrive in a business-organizations course, and even look forward to practicing business-organization law upon graduation.

This chapter introduces the basic terms and concepts necessary for the study of business-organization law.

2-101 WHAT IS A BUSINESS ORGANIZATION?

This text explores the legal and economic aspects of business organizations. This text is not a text on businesses; it is a text on business organizations. Businesses sell products, ideas, or services. A business organization, in contrast, is the legal structure the business takes.

For example, if Mary and Bob decide to create a business selling baked goods, they will take the steps they need to get the *business* going, such as raising capital, obtaining equipment, developing recipes, working on a business plan and marketing strategy, finding suppliers, getting proper business licenses, etc.

Bob and Mary have created a bakery business, but what *legal structure* will this business take? Bob and Mary effectively have four choices:

> **Corporation:** A corporation is a legal entity. It requires **approval of the state** for it to come into existence. Contrary to the perception of many laypersons, a corporation does not necessarily have many shareholders or a large amount of capital. In fact, in most U.S. states, you may "incorporate" a business with only one owner (an owner of a corporation is called a "**shareholder**") and with no significant capital investment.

> Bob and Mary could incorporate their business by paying a fee and filing certain documents with the secretary of state of their state.

> **Limited Liability Company:** A limited liability company, or "**LLC**," is very similar to a corporation. It is a legal entity and it requires **approval of the state** for it to come into existence. There are some differences between corporations and LLCs, which we will explore in detail in Chapter 3 and throughout the text. For now, it is sufficient for you to know that that the formation of an LLC is very similar to the formation of a corporation.

8

Bob and Mary could organize their business as an LLC by paying a fee and filing certain documents with the secretary of state of their state.

Sole proprietorship: The sole proprietorship is the default legal structure for a business owned by one person. In other words, if an individual creates a business where she is the only owner, and she does not organize it as an LLC or a corporation, the business is a sole proprietorship. Forming a sole proprietorship **requires no approval from the state** and no filing fees.

Bob and Mary's bakery could not be a sole proprietorship if they are both owners. By definition, a sole proprietorship has only one owner.

Partnership: The partnership is the default legal form for a business owned by more than one person. If two or more co-owners operate a business for profit without forming an LLC or corporation, the law considers their business to be a partnership. Forming a partnership **requires no state approval** and no filing fees.

Bob and Mary's bakery could be a partnership if they are co-owners and they do not form an LLC or corporation.

2-101(a) LIMITED LIABILITY:

You might be wondering why anyone would form a corporation or an LLC when these two business organizations require state approval and filing fees. The answer is **limited liability**.

The owners of an LLC or a corporation enjoy limited liability, which means they **will NOT be personally responsible for the debts of the business**. In contrast, the owners of sole proprietorships and partnerships will be personally responsible for debts of their businesses. Here is a simple illustration:

Bob and Mary set up a bakery business. They each contribute $10,000 capital for their ownership interests in the bakery. The bakery business does poorly. It has $15,000 in assets, all in the form of equipment and cash, and owes $75,000 to its suppliers and lenders. The business has a $60,000 deficiency.

If Bob and Mary have set up the business as a **corporation or LLC**, they would not be personally responsible for the business's debts. The creditors could not recover the $60,000 deficiency from Bob or Mary personally.

If Bob and Mary have set up the business as a **partnership** (or if either one of them had set it up as a **sole proprietorship**), they would be personally responsible for the debts of the partnership.

The creditors of the business could recover from Bob or Mary's personal assets.

However, the owners of LLCs and corporations, in fact, do bear some liability for the debts of the business. The owners risk whatever investment they have made in the company.

Illustration:

In the above example, Mary and Bob each contributed, or "invested" $10,000 in the business in exchange for their ownership stakes in the business. If the business has $75,000 in debt and only $15,000 in assets, Bob and Mary will not be able to recover the $10,000 they each invested in the business.

2-101(b) INCORPORATING VS. ORGANIZING:

We say that a person **organizes** an LLC. We do NOT say a person "incorporates" an LLC. If one **incorporates** a business, one creates a corporation. Of course, lawyers commonly use the terms **set up**, **form**, or **organize** for the creation of LLCs, corporations, or partnerships.

You may hear scholars, judges, and attorneys refer to "incorporated business organizations" and "unincorporated business organizations." An **incorporated business organization** is simply a fancy way of referring to a corporation. **Unincorporated business organizations** include every business organization that is not a corporation – e.g., LLCs, partnerships, sole proprietorship, etc.

2-101(c) BUSINESS LICENSES:

As previously discussed, setting up a corporation or LLC requires filing documents with the state's secretary of state along with a filing fee. In addition, corporations and LLCs might need to obtain business licenses. Partnerships and sole proprietorships are also required to obtain business licenses even though the formation of a partnership or sole proprietorship does not require state filings or fees.

Business licenses are usually issued by the city or county. The city or county may require a general business license that would apply to all businesses. There may also be licensing requirements for specific businesses, such as a liquor license for a business selling alcoholic beverages.

———————

Economists have questioned why people form firms (i.e., business organizations). To better understand the question, you need to understand what a firm is and what alternative exists.

A business requires inputs in the form of **capital** (i.e., cash or property) and labor. The business may acquire capital and labor through transactions **within a firm** or through transactions **across markets**.

As an illustration, let's go back to Bob and Mary and the bakery business. Assume that Bob wants to start a bakery business. He has some great family recipes and $10,000 in cash. Mary has several commercial-grade ovens.

Transaction across markets:

Bob would purchase the ovens from Mary. This is a transaction across markets because the input, the ovens, would not come from within the firm, it comes from an outside party. Nor would the provider of the input, Mary, become part of the business because of the transaction.

Transaction within the firm:

Bob would contribute his recipes and cash in exchange for an ownership interest in the business. Mary would also contribute her ovens in exchange for an ownership interest in the business. Both Bob and Mary would be part of the business because of the transactions.

Transactions across markets and within the firm also take place where services are involved. Imagine Bob and Mary's bakery needs to deliver its cakes and pastries around town.

Transaction across markets:

The bakery would pay Adam, an independent contractor, to deliver their goods for them. They might pay Adam per delivery, or on a weekly basis, etc. The transaction is across markets as long as Adam remains an independent contractor and does not become part of the business.

Transaction within the firm:

The bakery would hire Adam as an employee to deliver the bakery's goods.

The question economists have asked is, under what circumstances would the parties organize their transaction across markets and under what circumstances would they organize their transaction within the firm? The short answer is deceptively simple:

Parties will structure their transaction within the firm when they perceive that it will benefit them more than a transaction across markets. Similarly, they will structure their transaction across markets when they perceive it will benefit them more than a transaction within the firm.

2-103 NON-PROFIT ENTITIES:

The topic of this text is business organizations. Implicit in the term "business" is a profit motive. This text and most courses on business organizations do not cover non-profit entities.

Although this text does not address non-profit organizations, once you are familiar with business organizations, you will have the basic skills and general knowledge that will help you better understand the law of non-profit organizations.

Most states have a business corporation act that governs for-profit corporations, and a non-profit corporation act that governs non-profit corporations. The same holds true for LLCs. Once you have become familiar with the law of for-profit business organizations, you will have a good basis for understanding the law of non-profit organizations.

2-104 VARIATIONS IN THE SIZE OF BUSINESS ORGANIZATIONS:

Business-organization law provides rules for the **internal governance** of firms. Business organizations may have different governance issues depending on the number of owners.

For example, compare a corporation formed by Bob and Mary for their bakery business ("BM") to a large public corporation such as the General Electric Company ("GE"). Both BM and GE are corporations. The same statutory business corporation act applies to each, but let's consider how the structure of each of these firms affects the internal governance issues for that firm.

> *BM Bakery:* BM is a private company. Bob and Mary are the only owners, or "shareholders" of the company. They probably intend to be active participants in the business. Control of the corporation is in the hands of Bob and Mary. The corporation's governance issues will focus on the relationship between Bob and Mary.

> *GE:* GE is a public company. It has tens of thousands of shareholders. The shareholders are not really owners of the corporation in the same sense that Bob and Mary are owners of BM Bakery. Each shareholder in GE only owns a relatively small percentage of GE's total shares, which

means that no one shareholder has the financial incentive to monitor the executive officers and other employees to make sure they are performing their duties in an efficient and honest manner. In a large public corporation like GE, the shareholders elect a board of directors to monitor the performance of the corporation's executive officers and other employees. In the large public corporation, the governance issues focus on the relationship between the shareholders, the board, and the executive officers.

Lawyers, judges, and scholars use certain terms to refer to business organizations of different scopes and sizes. A student of corporate law should be familiar with the following terms and the concepts they represent.

"Closely-held business" or "closely-held company":

These terms refer to a business organization with a relatively few number of owners. The paradigm of the closely-held business is one where all or most of the owners are active participants in the business in some way.

Generally, most LLCs and partnerships are closely-held businesses because their default governance rules are particularly well suited for the governance of closely-held businesses.

There are also a large number of **closely-held corporations**. The default governance rules for corporations are not always well suited for the governance of closely-held businesses, but parties use contractual methods to tailor their corporations to fit the governance needs of a closely-held business.

"Publicly-held company" or "public company":

These terms refer to business organizations whose ownership interests are traded on active stock markets. The ownership interests of publicly-held corporations are often listed on centralized securities exchanges, like the New York Stock Exchange, making it easier for investors to buy and sell.

The paradigm of a public company is one where the shareholders are dispersed and passive, and control of the corporation is completely within the hands of the board of directors and the executive officers. Public companies are usually corporations because the corporate form is well suited for business organizations with dispersed ownership.

Chances are that you or one of your family members is a shareholder (i.e., owner) in a public corporation. When someone says *"I have stock in XYZ Company"* or *"I sold stock in Zed*

13

Company," it is likely that she is referring to a public company. If you do not own stock in a public company, you can open an account with an online broker to purchase shares in any of the thousands of public companies, such as Disney, Starbucks, Microsoft, Procter and Gamble, etc.

"Privately-held company" or "private company":

These terms refer to a business organization that is not a public company. All closely-held companies are considered privately-held companies, but some privately-held companies are not closely-held companies because they have too many shareholders.

Some companies have hundreds of shareholders even though their ownership interests are not publicly traded. The governance structure of these large private companies is similar to that of public companies – i.e., passive shareholders and professional managers.

Many private companies are somewhere between a closely-held company and a public company on the continuum of business organizations. They have several major shareholders active in the management of the firm, and a large number of passive shareholders who do not have any meaningful participation in management.

2-105 THE BASIC STRUCTURE OF BUSINESS ORGANIZATIONS:

It may be helpful to think of the business organization in terms of a simplified **bi-level structure**: There is **ownership** and **management**.

Ownership has the right to receive the profits of the business and to select the management.

Management has the right (and the duty) to manage the firm's business and affairs.

In the paradigm of the closely-held company, ownership and management will be in the hands of the same people. For example, in the case of Bob and Mary's bakery, Bob and Mary will decide how to divide ownership rights between them. They will also decide what management rights and authority each of them will have.

In a corporation, the default management structure includes a board of directors and executive officers. This management structure means that with the corporate form, there is normally a **corporate trio**:

The **shareholders**, the **board of directors**, and the **executive officers**.

In the corporation, the ownership body (i.e., the shareholders) elects the directors to the board, and the board appoints the executive officers (e.g., chief executive officer, president, general manager, etc.).

The **board of directors** is the decision-making body of the corporation. It *directs* the executive officers to carry out the board's decisions and it monitors the performance of the executive officers. Of course, in a closely-held corporation, the shareholders, directors, and executive officers will often be the same people.

Much of the study of corporate law focuses on the corporate governance of the corporation. **Corporate governance** refers to the legal rules and the private contractual arrangements addressing the internal governance of the firm, which usually means the relationship between the shareholders and whoever is in control of the corporation.

In the closely-held corporation, a **majority shareholder** or group of shareholders will often control the firm. Corporate governance in this context normally refers to the **relationship between the majority shareholders and the minority shareholders**.

In the large public corporation, where the shareholders are passive and the **board and executive officers are in control**, corporate governance refers to the **relationship between the corporate trio** – the shareholders, the board of directors, and the executive officers.

2-106 GOVERNING LAW:

The law of business organizations is largely a matter of state law. Each state has: (1) a corporate law statute; (2) an LLC statute; and (3) a partnership statute.

2-106(a) CORPORATE LAW STATUTES:

Each state has its own business corporation statute. The specific provisions of each statute will vary from state to state, but they will address the same issues. Many states have adopted some version of the American Bar Association's **Model Business Corporation Act**. Throughout the text, we will refer to the Model Business Corporation Act generally as the "**MBCA**." We will refer to the most recently revised version of the Model Business Corporation Act as the "**RMBCA**."

Even if your jurisdiction has not adopted the RMBCA, or an earlier version, it is still a good tool for learning corporate law. The corporate law statutes of many jurisdictions are poorly drafted and difficult to understand without an understanding of the fundamental concepts and issues of corporate law. Learning the RMBCA will provide you with this understanding.

Throughout the text, we will often compare the RMBCA to Delaware corporate law. Because a majority of U.S. public companies are incorporated in Delaware, Delaware corporate law plays an important role in our nation's capital markets. We refer to the **Delaware General Corporation Law** as the "**DGCL**."

2-106(b) LLC STATUTES:

Each state also has its own LLC statute. The National Conference of the Commissioners of Uniform State Laws created the **Uniform Limited Liability Company Act** and has revised it several times. We refer generally to the Uniform Limited Liability Company Act as "**ULLCA**," and to it most recent version as "**RULLCA**."

The ULLCA has not been adopted as widely as the MBCA. As a result, there is less consistency between the LLC statutes of the various states. Throughout the text, we will explore the various different approaches state statutes might take with respect to important LLC issues.

2-106(c) PARTNERSHIP STATUTES:

The National Conference of the Commissioners of State Laws created the **Uniform Partnership Act** in 1914. It was widely adopted by the states. In 1997, the Uniform Partnership Act was revised. States have been steadily adopting the revised version over the past several years. Throughout the text, we will refer to the Uniform Partnership Act of 1914 as "**UPA**" or "**UPA 1914**" and we will refer to the most recently revised version of the Uniform Partnership Act as "**RUPA**."

2-106(d) COMMON LAW:

The law of business organizations is also highly influenced by the common law. Judges interpret the various business organization statutes when their provisions are vague or unclear. In addition, common law rules still control on many important issues because statutes do not address the issues or have not expressly overruled the prior common law approach.

This text attempts to include a discussion of business-organization cases that are both influential and interesting.[2] You will discover that there are a disproportionate number of cases from Delaware. As stated earlier, a majority of public corporations are incorporated in Delaware. Because of the large number of public companies incorporated in Delaware, Delaware courts have developed great expertise in corporate law. Other jurisdictions respect this

---

[2] Please keep in mind that students and professors may disagree on the definition of "interesting."

expertise. Judicial opinions from the **Delaware Supreme Court** and the **Delaware chancery court** (the trial level court) are very influential on the courts of other jurisdictions.

2-106(e) FEDERAL LAW:

Federal law does not play a large role in the internal governance of a business organization until the company becomes a **public company**. Once a business organization becomes public, and throughout the process of becoming public, **federal securities law** requires the company to make **disclosures** to the investing public, mainly with respect to financial and accounting information.

After the Enron accounting scandal, and other public-company accounting scandals of the early 2000s, Congress passed the Sarbanes-Oxley Act (popularly known as "**SOX**"), which changed the traditional role federal law played in the governance of public companies. Before SOX, federal securities law did not impose substantive governance rules on public companies. Instead, it focused on requiring public companies to disclose financial and accounting information. The substantive corporate governance rules for public companies were a matter of state law.

However, with SOX, Congress created substantive corporate governance rules for public companies. For example, SOX requires public companies to have independent directors (i.e., directors who were not also executive officers) and directors with specific knowledge of financial matters. It also requires the auditors of public companies to be free from conflicts of interests that might adversely affect their ability to audit a public company's financial records impartially.

Even after SOX, state law is still the source of most of the substantive law regarding the governance of public corporations. However, please keep in mind that **the internal governance of a public corporation** is subject to **state corporate law, federal securities law,** and the **rules of the stock exchange** where its stock is listed for trading.

This text focuses on state corporate law and its general application to both private and public companies. However, throughout the text, we will discuss, in more general terms, the application of state corporate law, federal securities law, and stock exchange rules to public corporations.

2-106(f) FIRM GOVERNANCE AND THE INTERNAL AFFAIRS DOCTRINE:

When we say a business organization is subject to *state* business-organization law, which state do we mean? There is a common law rule called the "internal affairs doctrine." The **internal affairs doctrine** provides:

The internal governance of a business organization is governed by the law of the business organization's state of organization or incorporation.

17

For example, assume a corporation is incorporated in Kentucky, but its offices and principal place of business are in Ohio. Kentucky law will still apply to any issue regarding the internal governance of the corporation, even if it holds its board and shareholder meetings in Ohio.

If there is a dispute about whether the directors have conducted themselves in accordance with their fiduciary duties, Kentucky law will apply. Similarly, if there is a question regarding whether the shareholders have a right to vote on corporate action, Kentucky law will apply.

2-107 BASIC FINANCE:

Finance is an intimidating word to those of us who have not received a formal education in business. Of course, business organization finance can be quite complex, but the basic underlying concepts are fairly simple.

To finance its projects, a business organization needs **capital**. For example, if BM Bakery wants to build a larger bakery plant, it will need cash to finance the project. There are three basic sources of capital for a business organization:

(1) **The company's earnings** – If the company makes a profit, it could choose not to distribute the profits to the owners. Instead, it could re-invest the profits back into the business.

(2) **Debt** – The company could borrow money to finance its projects.

(3) **Equity** – The company could issue new ownership interests to current owners or to new investors. The term "equity" refers to the ownership interest in business organizations.

2-107(a) DEBT FINANCING:

The debts of a business are also called "**fixed claims**." The creditors are called "**fixed claimants**." The creditors are called *fixed* claimants because they are entitled only to what the corporation promised, no more and no less. Their claims are fixed.

For example, if I lend $100,000 to BM Bakery at 10% interest, I have a legal right to have BM Bakery to repay me $100,000, plus interest. If BM Bakery uses my $100,000 to produce $1 million in profit, I will only have a right to receive my $100,000, plus interest. If BM Bakery uses my $100,000 and loses it all, I am still entitled to repayment of my $100,000 plus interest, although I might have trouble recovering it if BM Bakery is insolvent.

A business organization might seek debt financing through traditional bank loans, or it might borrow money from one or more of its current owners. If the business needs a large amount of capital, it might access the **market for debt securities**, also called the bond market. We will discuss debt securities in greater detail in Chapter 4, but here is the basic idea:

> Instead of borrowing money from one or two lenders, the company could borrow money from thousands of lenders. It issues each of the lenders a promise to repay a pro rata portion of the principal, plus interest. The promise is commonly called a "bond," but some are called "notes" or "debentures."

The corporation has other creditors/fixed claimants besides traditional lenders and bondholders. For example, there are trade creditors and employees.

> *Trade creditors* are suppliers who provide goods or services to the business on credit.

> *Employees* provide labor and services to the business in exchange for the payment of wages and benefits.

2-107(b) EQUITY FINANCING:

The ownership interest in a business organization is often referred to as **"equity."** The term "owner" does not always fit well when describing the holder of an equity interest in a business organization. The term owner implies a level of control and possession that is not necessarily given to equity holders in business organizations.

> For example, imagine I own 100 shares of Microsoft. I am one of the "owners" of Microsoft, but only in the broadest sense of the term "owner." If I were to break into the Microsoft offices late at night, it would do no good for me to say to the police, "don't worry, I am one of the owners."

The equity holders in many business organizations might not have control rights that we expect to attach to ownership rights. Control rights of equity holders will differ in corporations, LLCs, and partnerships.

The real defining aspect of equity holders is the financial claim they have on the company. They have a right to the equity of the business or, in economic terms, they have the **residual claim**. What does it mean to have the residual claim? The equity holders are entitled to **whatever is left over after the fixed claimants (i.e., the creditors) have been paid**.

> **Example of the residual claim:** Imagine BM Bakery dissolves and goes into liquidation. It has $150,000 in assets. It owes $90,000 to banks, suppliers, and employees. The assets will be liquidated and the proceeds

will be used to pay off the fixed claimants. The remaining $60,000 will go to the equity holders.

Of course, even if BM Bakery continued as a going concern, and did not go into liquidation, the residual claim would still be $60,000. How much of that $60,000 BM Bakery could distribute to its owners while it is still a going concern depends on the jurisdiction's rules regarding dividends and distributions.[3]

If a corporation wanted to raise capital to finance a project, it could sell new ownership interests to its current equity owners, or to new investors. If the company offered equity interests to the public at large, the company would be making a **public offering**.[4] If this were the first time the company was making a public offering, it would be called an **initial public offering**, or **IPO**.

> *Illustration:* There was a time when Google Inc. was a private corporation with only a few shareholders. In 2004, Google conducted an IPO. It sold shares to the public and listed those shares on a stock exchange (Nasdaq, in this case). Google went public not only to raise capital for its expansion, but also to give its pre-IPO shareholders, and its employees with stock and stock options, a market to sell their Google shares. Now Google is a public company listed on Nasdaq.

2-108 CHARACTERISTICS OF BUSINESS ORGANIZATIONS:

Business organizations have certain legal characteristics. Later, in Chapter 3, we will discuss how the characteristics of corporations, LLCs and partnerships differ. For now, however, it is important for you to understand these four basic characteristics:

(1) Limited liability; (2) Legal personality; (3) Centralized management; and (4) Freely transferable ownership interests.

2-108(a) LIMITED LIABILITY:

We have already briefly touched upon the concept of limited liability. Limited liability means the owners of the business are not personally responsible for the debts of the business. They only risk the amount they have invested in the business.

> **Quick preview:** The "shareholders" of a corporation and the "members" of an LLC enjoy limited liability. In contrast, the partners of a general

---

[3] Distributions to shareholders in corporations are often called dividends.

[4] The company could also make a public offering of debt securities.

partnership are personally responsible for the debts of the partnership's business, as are sole proprietors.

Limited liability has certain economic benefits and consequences. If the business cannot pay its debts, and the owners are not personally responsible, the risk of liability for the business debts does not simply disappear; rather, the risk of non-payment shifts to the creditors.

Economists call this phenomenon **externalizing costs**. In this context, limited liability allows the owners of a business to externalize costs by shifting some of the costs of doing business to the creditors. However, creditors understand this aspect of limited liability and they will often take steps to protect themselves.

If the business is closely-held, **the creditor might require one or more owners to guaranty the obligations of the business**, effectively drafting around limited liability. If it is impractical to ask the owners to act as guarantors, the creditors will adjust their price to compensate themselves for their increased risk. For example, a bank might charge the business a higher interest rate for a loan, and the supplier might charge the business a higher price for goods or services sold to the business on credit. The bank and the supplier might even refuse to give credit to the business if its financial situation is too risky. The creditors use contracts and pricing to force the business to pay for its limited liability. Economists would say that the creditors are forcing the owners of the business to **internalize costs**.

The lenders and suppliers described above are often called **voluntary creditors**. They become creditors of the business of their own volition. In other words, they are **contractual creditors**. However, limited liability also affects the **involuntary creditors** or **tort creditors** of the business. Tort creditors are not usually in a position to protect themselves from the torts the business's employees may commit.

> For example, the average pedestrian in not in a position to ask the owners of LMN Trucking Inc. to sign personal guaranties if one of their trucks ever runs her down in the future.

However, where tort claims are more contractual in nature, such as products liability claims, potential tort victims would be able to use contracts to force the owners to internalize costs.

> For example, before buying a product, a consumer can make sure the product has a warranty that will compensate her if the product has a defect that causes her injury.

2-108(b) LEGAL PERSONALITY:

When we say a business organization has a legal personality, we mean it (1) has perpetual existence; and (2) is a **legal person**,[5] separate and distinct from its owners, with many of the same rights as a natural person.

With the perpetual existence, the life or death of one or more of the owners is legally irrelevant to the life or death of the business organization. If one or all of the owners die, the business organization survives. Of course, in closely-held businesses, the owners are the key to the success of the business and it is often unimportant whether the business organization survives after they are gone.

As a separate legal person, a business organization can enter into contracts in its own name. It can also sue and be sued. Of course, a business organization is a legal person, not a natural person. Although it has the *legal* capacity to do things, it has no real physical capacity to do anything on its own. It cannot drive a truck, sign a contract, draft a letter, or negotiate a deal. A business organization must act through its agents.

> **Quick preview:** A corporation has legal personality, as does an LLC. A sole proprietorship is not a legal person – it has no legal existence separate from its owner. The law sometimes treats a partnership as a legal person, and sometimes it treats it merely as an aggregate of several individual owners.

2-108(c) CENTRALIZED MANAGEMENT:

The concept of centralized management is best explained through an example. The default rule of state corporate law is that the corporation's board of directors manages the business and affairs of the corporation. In other words, management power and authority are vested in a centralized board. Shareholders only have the right to elect the directors and vote on a few extraordinary transactions; they do not have the right to manage the corporation. Any shareholder who wants to participate in management may try to win election to the board.

You can easily understand the benefit of centralized management to large public corporations with thousands of shareholders. Without centralized management, the existence of these public corporations would be virtually impossible.

However, in a closely-held business organization, centralized management may be unnecessary. In most closely-held businesses, because the founders anticipate that they will be the owners and managers of the business, there will be no need to centralize management.

---

[5] Similar terms include "legal entity" and "juridical person."

Quick preview: The default rule for the corporation is centralized management. Closely-held corporations often draft around this rule to put management in the hands of the shareholders.

The default rule for the LLC is that management is directly vested with the members. However, the members of the LLC can choose to centralize management authority in one or more managers.

The default rule for the partnership is that management is directly vested with the partners. As a partnership grows in size, the partners will often amend the partnership agreement to provide for some form of centralized management.

2-108(d) FREELY-TRANSFERABLE OWNERSHIP INTERESTS:

Investors in business organizations often want to transfer their ownership interests. If you own stock in Apple Inc., you expect that you can freely sell your shares. For you, your purchase of Apple stock is an investment and you would like to be able to **exit** that investment (i.e., get out of the investment and convert it into cash) as you desire.

The free transferability of shares is crucial to an efficient stock market. If you did not have the freedom to sell your shares, you would be less likely to buy stock in Apple. Even if you were willing to buy Apple stock, you would pay less for it because it is less valuable without the freedom to sell it.

However, the situation is different in closely-held businesses. The owners of closely-held businesses often work closely together. Moreover, each one may possess skills that contribute to the success of the business. Under such circumstances, the owners would prefer that their co-owners could not transfer ownership interests.

Quick preview: In corporations, ownership interests are freely transferable. In closely-held corporations, shareholders often limit the transferability of shares by agreement. In LLCs and partnerships, ownership interests are normally not freely transferable. An owner who wants to sell her interests must get permission from the other owners.

2-109 ECONOMIC INCENTIVES:

Business organizations have many constituents. There are shareholders, directors, officers, employees, lenders, suppliers, and even the local community. Each of these constituents has some stake in the decisions the business makes. The study of business-organization law is, to a large extent, the study of how the law addresses the relationships between these constituents.

2-109(a) **THE RELATIONSHIP BETWEEN OWNERS AND MANAGERS:**

One of the most important relationships in the public company is the relationship between the owners (i.e., the equity holders) and the management. The owners want the managers to work tirelessly and selflessly to create a large residual for them. In contrast, the managers would generally prefer to work as little as possible. They might even be tempted to steal from the corporation, if not by outright embezzlement, then at least by taking underserved perquisites.

This problem is called the **agency problem**. Specifically, the agency problem refers to the fact that the interests of the agents (the management) are not perfectly aligned with the interests of the principals (the equity owners).

2-109(b) **AGENCY COSTS:**

The agency problem leads to **agency costs**. When academics discuss agency costs, they are referring to the costs of (1) **monitoring**; (2) **bonding**; and (3) **residual losses**.

> **Monitoring costs:** To make sure agents are not shirking or stealing, the principal needs to monitor them. How could you monitor your employees to make sure they are not shirking or stealing? You could install cameras to watch the employees, you could hire someone to look over their shoulders all the time, you could perform regular audits to catch theft, etc.
>
> ### *Illustration:*
>
> I was a security guard from midnight to 8 a.m. at an orange juice distribution plant in New York City when I was 19 years old. As part of my duties, I was required to walk the grounds every hour. At those hours of the night, no one was around to make sure I performed my rounds. Instead, there were stations positioned at various locations around the plant grounds. At each station, I would insert a key into a device. The key would make an imprint on a tape within the device to record the time and the station. This device was a low-cost monitoring method to ensure I was making my rounds as scheduled.

Both the principal and the agent have incentives to reduce monitoring costs. The principal incurs the costs of monitoring initially, but she will share the costs with the agent by reducing the compensation she pays the agent for her services.

In a large public corporation, the shareholders need to monitor those in actual control of the corporation, the executive officers. The shareholders want to ensure the executives and all the other employees are working hard, making good business decisions, and not stealing from the corporation.

The shareholders elect a board of directors to monitor the executive officers. As you might have guessed, having a board of directors does not completely solve the monitoring problem. Who monitors the board members to make sure they are working hard, making good decisions, and not stealing from the corporation?

Bonding costs: These are the costs the agent incurs in providing a reliable warranty to the principal that she will work diligently and honestly for the principal. It is possible that the agent is the most honest and hard-working person in the history of agents. She would like to say to the principal, "there is no need for you to spend money on monitoring me – I am honest and diligent." Naturally, the principal will tend to require some proof of diligence and honesty.

The agent might be able to procure an **actual bond** – a promise from a third party, normally an insurance company, that if the agent steals from the principal, the third party will indemnify the principal. Another common bonding method is for the agent to take some sort of incentive compensation. In other words, the agent will be paid in accordance with the success of the venture. The **incentive compensation** structure more closely aligns the agent's interests with the interests of the principal. Finally, agents **invest in their reputation** to provide a reliable signal to principals that they will be professional, diligent, and honest.

Both the agent and principal have an interest in reducing bonding costs. The agent initially bears the cost of bonding, but will eventually share them with the principal by requiring higher compensation

Residual losses: These costs are the losses the principal incurs due the agent's shirking and dishonesty, despite the investment in monitoring.

2-109(c) FIDUCIARY DUTIES:

Business-organization law imposes **fiduciary duties** on executives and directors that require them to **perform their responsibilities diligently and honestly**. However, as you will learn in Chapter 6, the law only holds them liable for the most egregious breaches of their fiduciary duties.

2-109(d) NON-LEGAL FORCES:

We must not lose sight of the fact that agents often work diligently and honestly even when they are not monitored or even when they would not be liable if their shirking or stealing were discovered. Why?

Of course, we could attribute this conduct to their fear of being caught, but agents and employees often do the right thing even when there is no chance of discovery. There are other forces at work policing the behavior of agents.

Moral forces: There are internal forces within most of us that encourage us to work hard and be honest. Your parents and society have instilled in you the idea that you should always be honest and do your best.

Social forces: There are external forces other than the threat of legal sanctions that encourage us to work hard and be honest. You are concerned with how other people view you. If they consider you indolent and dishonest, you will lose social opportunities.

Market for reputation: Market forces encourage us to work hard and be honest. If there is a perception in the job market that you are lazy, incompetent, or dishonest, you will lose economic opportunities.

2-109(e) THE RELATIONSHIP BETWEEN THE VARIOUS OWNERS:

The relationship between owners is especially important in closely-held businesses. When the owners are actively involved in the company's business, they are in control. Naturally, they are less concerned with the shirking or theft of the agents because they themselves are in control of the company's business and affairs.

In circumstances where the business has employed people in addition to the owners, the owners' costs of monitoring these employees will often be low because monitoring will not require extra effort. Because the owners are active in the business, many of their monitoring tasks will be activities they engage in as part of their normal routine.

In closely-held businesses, the main agency problem occurs between the several owners, not between owners and agents. More specifically, the agency problem in a closely-held business is the potential the **controlling shareholder will engage in opportunism** – i.e., the owner with control might use this control to benefit herself at the expense of the minority owners.

2-109(f) THE RELATIONSHIP BETWEEN THE EQUITY HOLDERS AND DEBT HOLDERS:

At first blush, it may seem that the interests of the owners (i.e., the equity holders or residual claimants) and the creditors (i.e., the fixed claimants) would be aligned. Both groups want to see the business succeed so that they can collect on their claims. However, the interests of the equity claimants may give them incentives to cause the management to adopt strategies that are against the interests of the fixed claimants.

The following example provides the clearest illustration of the conflict:

> Imagine the residual claim of ABC Inc. is zero. If the company were to liquidate now, it would have just enough money to pay off its creditors, and the shareholders would be left with nothing.

> Now, imagine you are a **shareholder of ABC Inc**. Would you tend to prefer that the management of ABC Inc. adopt a riskier business strategy, or a more conservative one?

>> With greater risk comes the potential for greater reward. With lower risk, the potential for reward is much lower. Thus, with a conservative business strategy, it is more likely that the residual claim will stay close to zero, with a low chance that it will increase or decrease significantly.

>> With a conservative strategy, you as a shareholder, stand to gain little or nothing. You have little **upside risk** or **upside potential**. In addition, because you will lose your investment in the company if the residual stays at zero, with a conservative strategy your **downside risk** is high.

>> In contrast, with a riskier business strategy, it is more likely that the residual claim will depart significantly from zero, with a greater chance that it will increase or decrease significantly. With a risky strategy, your upside potential is far better than a conservative strategy. In addition, because of limited liability, your downside risk is the same with a riskier strategy or a conservative strategy. Limited liability makes your downside risk the same whether the residual claim is zero or negative one billion. In either case, you only stand to lose your investment.

>> Because your upside potential is better with a higher-risk strategy than a conservative strategy, and your downside potential does not change with either strategy, **you, as a shareholder, would prefer a higher-risk strategy**.

> In contrast, imagine you are a **creditor of ABC Inc**. Would you prefer the company adopt a riskier business strategy or a conservative one?

>> With the residual claim at zero, you are assured of being able to collect on your claim against the company. If the residual claim drops below zero, it is cutting into the fixed claim (your claim and the claims of your fellow creditors).

27

If the residual claim exceeds zero, it does not benefit you at all. The company owes you a fixed claim that does not increase with the success of the company. If you lent the company $100,000 at 10% interest, you are entitled to repayment of the $100,000 plus interest and no more, regardless of how well the company performs.

Your downside risk increases with a riskier strategy because there is greater risk that the amount remaining to satisfy the fixed claims will decrease. Moreover, as a fixed claimant, your upside potential does not increase with a riskier strategy. Thus, **you, as a creditor, would prefer a more conservative strategy**.

2-200 ECONOMIC AND FINANCIAL TERMS AND CONCEPTS:

There are certain economic and financial concepts that are very important to the study of corporate law. The nomenclature may seem foreign to you, but the concepts should not.

2-201 TRANSACTION COSTS:

Every transaction has costs. A simple example would be the cost of shipping goods in a transaction between a seller in California and a buyer in Kentucky.

One of the most important principles of transaction costs is that no matter which party bears the cost under the contract or the default legal rule, both parties will eventually share the cost.

If the contract, or the default legal rule, requires the seller to pay for shipping, the seller will simply charge the buyer a higher price for the product. Because the parties effectively share the shipping costs, regardless of who the contract actually requires to pay them, the parties will want to shift the cost to the party that can deal with the costs more efficiently.

If the California seller is in a better position to arrange shipping from California to Kentucky at a lower cost than the Kentucky buyer, the parties will make the seller responsible for shipping, and seller will charge buyer accordingly. Both parties are better off this way. Clearly the buyer is better off because she will pay less for shipping than if she had arranged it herself. The seller is also better off. If the buyer had higher shipping costs, she would have less money to spend on seller's products.

Shipping costs are a very simple example of transaction costs. A more sophisticated example would be the **costs associated with risk**. Take for example a transaction for the sale of a house. Assume the buyer and the seller are unsure about whether there is hidden termite damage in the house. This situation creates a risk of termite damage.

If the contract (or the law) requires the seller to reimburse the buyer for repairs due to hidden termite damage buyer discovers after consummation of the sale, the seller bears the risk of termite damage. Similarly, if the contract (or the law) provides that the property is sold "as-is," with buyer having no recourse against seller if she discovers termite damage after the consummation of the sale, the buyer bears the risk of any hidden termite damage.

Because there are costs associated with the risk (the potential costs of repairs), the party bearing the risk will adjust her price for the transaction. If the buyer bears the risk, she will reduce the price she is willing to pay for the house in order to compensate herself for the potential repairs she might have to make in the future. If the seller bears the risk, she will increase the price of the house in order to compensate herself for the potential repairs she might have to make in the future.

The parties would prefer to shift the risk to the party who can deal with it more efficiently. Assuming neither of the parties can arrange for cheaper repairs, the party who can assess the risk more accurately is the one who is able to address the risk more efficiently.

2-202 AGENCY COSTS:

We already discussed agency costs in §2-109(b), above.

As a summary, agency costs are transaction costs that are specific to a situation where one party, a **principal**, gives a certain amount of control over her affairs to another party, an **agent**. The control gives the agent an opportunity to benefit herself at the expense of the principal.

The risk that the agent will engage in this kind of opportunistic behavior, leads to agency costs. Agency costs are the costs of (1) the principal monitoring the agent; (2) the agent bonding herself for the principal; and (3) the residual losses the principal suffer because of the agent's opportunistic behavior.

2-203 INFORMATION COSTS:

Information costs are the transaction costs associated with the lack of information. Essentially, information costs are either (1) research costs, or (2) the cost of adjusting prices higher or lower to compensate for the risk of something unknown.

Virtually all transactions have information costs because we rarely operate in situations where there is perfect information for both parties.

2-204 INFORMATION ASYMMETRIES:

Information asymmetries refer to any situation where one party to a transaction knows more than the other party. For example, when you go to a used car dealership to buy a car, the dealer knows far more about that car than you do. Virtually all transactions involve information asymmetries.

2-205 FREE-RIDER PROBLEM:

The free-rider problem refers to a situation where one person bears all of the costs of her conduct, but others will share in any benefit that result.

For example, imagine a condominium building where there is a common entrance serving six households. Resident A believes there is a clear need for a heavy-duty entrance mat that will cost about $50. If Resident A buys the mat, she will bear the entire cost, but all the households will benefit equally. We say the other residents are free riders. Resident A is less likely to buy the mat under these circumstances, unless, of course, other residents contribute.

In the study of business organizations, the free-rider problem normally arises in the context of public companies with dispersed shareholders. When there are a large number of shareholders, each with a relatively small percentage of the total outstanding shares, each shareholder has a disincentive to monitor the company's management to prevent or discover shirking. If one shareholder bears the costs of monitoring, all the shareholders will benefit from her efforts. The other shareholders are free-riders.

2-206 COLLECTIVE-ACTION PROBLEM:

The collective-action problem is concept is closely related to the free-rider problem. If we could simply get all relevant parties to work together to share costs, we could solve the free-rider problem. However, it is often very costly, or even cost prohibitive, to get everyone to work together.

If I am a shareholder in a public corporation and I discover mismanagement, the free-rider problem provides a disincentive for me to take action on my own, and the collective-action problem makes it very costly for all the shareholders to take action together. How will I communicate with the 10,000 other shareholders? How will we get together to agree on something?

2-207 **DIVERSIFICATION OF INVESTMENT:**

Diversification is a fundamental investment strategy. The essence of the strategy is to avoid putting all of your eggs in one basket. The ramifications of diversification of investment are especially important in the governance of public corporations.

When an investor buys stock in public companies, she should try to create a diversified portfolio. She will invest in different companies (diversification across companies) and she will invest in companies in different industries (diversification across industries). She will also invest in different investment products – stocks, corporate bonds, municipal, bonds. A diversified portfolio reduces risk for the investor. The success or failure of any one investment does not unduly affect her overall health of her investment portfolio.

Because she has spread her money around, she does not have a significant investment in any one company. Without a significant investment in any company, she does not have the incentives to monitor the management of any company. When she votes at shareholder meetings, her vote is uninformed because she does not have the economic incentives to inform herself.

The investor with the diversified portfolio will perform little or no monitoring. She is apathetic, but any other choice would make no sense. Therefore, we say she suffers from **rational apathy**.

2-208 **DISPERSED OWNERSHIP:**

Dispersed ownership refers to a situation where a corporation has many shareholders and none of the shareholders has significant shareholdings. This situation occurs because (1) investors diversify their investments; and (2) very few investors can afford to acquire significant shareholdings in public corporations.

The U.S. stock market is generally considered to be a stock market of dispersed shareholders, although there are still quite a few companies with controlling shareholders.

2-209 **INSTITUTIONAL INVESTORS:**

The U.S. stock market has individual investors, like you and me, who buy and hold stock in public companies. However, most of the investment in the U.S. stock market comes from institutional investors, such as insurance companies, pension funds, mutual funds, and hedge funds. Because institutional investors have greater resources, greater expertise, and a better ability to act

31

collectively than individual investors, they are able to engage in more monitoring of the management of public companies than individual investors.

2-210 MUTUAL FUNDS:

Many individual investors do not invest directly in public companies. Instead, they invest indirectly through mutual funds. Individual investors buy shares in the fund, and the fund invests the money it receives in a diversified portfolio of public companies (or corporate bonds, municipal bonds, etc.).

By investing in a mutual fund, the individual investor receives two benefits: (1) the financial expertise of the fund manager, and (2) a diversified portfolio.

2-211 PRIVATE ORDERING:

Private ordering refers to the act of structuring transactions to reduce costs. Any kind of arrangement to address a problem or transaction cost is private ordering.

For example, if a homebuyer is afraid the house has hidden termite damage, the parties can adopt some sort of private-ordering mechanism, such as a warranty by the seller, an inspection certificate from an expert, or insurance from a third party. Parties will adopt solutions that are less costly than the original problem.

2-212 PRIVATE BENEFIT:

A private benefit refers to a benefit you do not share with other persons. Normally, you can cause yourself to receive a private benefit if you are in control of the asset that creates the benefit. You will often see the term **private benefits of control** to refer to this situation.

For example, the controlling shareholder of the corporation causes the corporation to buy a plot of land from her, overcharging the corporation by $50,000. The controlling shareholder has received a $50,000 benefit that is not shared by the other shareholders.

2-213 OPPORTUNISM:

Opportunism simply means taking advantage of others. Control is often is the key to opportunism. In a business organization with dispersed ownership, the management is in control. This control provides the managers the opportunity to benefit themselves, through shirking or stealing, at the expense of the shareholders.

In contrast, when a business organization has a controlling shareholder, management opportunism becomes less likely because the controlling shareholder has the financial incentive to monitor management. Management never achieves the level of control that it would without a controlling shareholder. Indeed, the controlling shareholder will control the management, or manage the business herself, which allows the controlling shareholder to engage in opportunism.

2-300 EVALUATING THE EFFICIENCY OF BUSINESS-ORGANIZATION LAW:

Throughout your law school career, you have been asked to evaluate whether a particular statute, common law rule, or judicial decision is good. Of course, there are many standards for evaluating whether a particular law is good, but in the context of business-organization law, because the parties are motivated by economic considerations, we normally ask whether the law is **efficient**.

To determine whether the law is efficient, we generally speculate about whether most parties would prefer the rule. However, we evaluate default rules and mandatory rules in a slightly different way.

2-301 DEFAULT RULES:

Default rules are rules that parties can change by contract. Default rules save the parties the cost of drafting long contracts to address every possible contingency. If the rule is one that a majority of parties would adopt, it is efficient. If for some reason, the parties have special needs and want to structure their transaction differently from the default rule, they may do so; the law will not prevent it.

Naturally, whether parties in a majority of transactions would adopt the default rule is a matter of some speculation. However, we can use our knowledge of transaction costs and private-ordering strategies to provide a fair estimation of whether a default rule is efficient.

Illustration:

The Business Corporation Act of the state of _____ provides that all shares issued by the corporation must have the same financial rights and voting rights, unless otherwise provided in the corporation's articles of incorporation.

This provision means that the parties can issue shares with different voting or economic rights as they wish, but unless they specifically do so in their articles of, the shares will have the same rights.

Is this the rule that would be adopted in a majority of transactions?

2-302 MANDATORY RULES:

Mandatory rules are rules that the parties cannot change by contract. We attempt to evaluate the efficiency of mandatory rules much in the same way we evaluate default rules – by asking whether it would be adopted in a majority of the transactions. However, when evaluating mandatory rules, we have to ask a second question: Why doesn't the law allow the parties to draft a different rule?

The answer is that we believe allowing the parties to deviate from the rule through private ordering would permit one party to take unfair advantage of the other party in a large number of transactions.

Should we take this paternalistic attitude? Wouldn't each of the contracting parties be in the best position to determine whether drafting out of the rule would be in her best interest? To justify a mandatory rule because of the potential for abuse, there must be some sort of transaction cost that would make one party's decision to agree to draft out of the rule ill-informed. For example, in public corporations, the collective action problem is often cited as a justification for mandatory rules. The shareholders in public corporations are not in a position to bargain for the terms they want because of the collective action problem.

Illustration:

Imagine that there is proposed legislation that would require every share a corporation issues to have the same voting rights – one vote per share. The new rule makes one vote per share mandatory. A corporation would not be allowed to issue shares with varying voting rights.

Situation 1: BM Inc. issues 100 shares to Bob and 100 shares to Mary. Under the proposed rule, each of them would have 100 votes when shareholders vote on matters. The proposed rule is mandatory, meaning that if the parties wanted to give Mary shares with enhanced voting rights, or no voting rights, they would not be allowed to do so.

34

Why shouldn't Bob and Mary be able to negotiate the terms of the transaction as they want it? Is this a case where we think one party could abuse the other? Let's run through a possible scenario:

Mary and Bob are negotiating the founding of BM Inc. Mary tells Bob she wants each of her shares to have twice the voting power of Bob's. Bob rejects this proposal. In response, Mary refuses to partner with Bob. She will start a business on her own. Bob then acquiesces.

There has been no abuse. Bob could have taken his money and made another investment, or found another partner. The fact that, in the end, he gave Mary the terms she wanted demonstrates he felt partnering with Mary was worth the cost of her enhanced voting rights.

Situation 2: The founders of BM Inc. are planning to take the company public through an IPO. As a result of the offering, the public will receive 90% of the outstanding shares of the company and the founders will only retain 10% of the shares. However, the 10% retained by the founders will give them 51% of the voting rights. Under the proposed rule, this transaction would not be permissible.

Is this situation more susceptible to abuse than the situation with Bob and Mary in the closely-held corporation? Couldn't the prospective public investors simply find another investment for their money? If they did indeed invest under the terms proposed, wouldn't that demonstrate that they found the costs of the voting arrangement to be worth the price of the shares? If so, is there a justification the proposed mandatory one-share, one vote rule?

2-303 DEFAULT RULES AND MANDATORY RULES IN BUSINESS-ORGANIZATION LAW:

Business-organization law is largely **enabling** – which means it consists mostly of default rules the parties may change by contract. Evaluating whether a corporate-law rule is efficient may appear to be merely an academic exercise, but it will help you develop a good sense of how parties structure their business organizations. It will also give you a good sense of which rules you can modify and to what extent. This knowledge is important for transactional lawyers.

Evaluating the efficiency of business-organization law can also help you become more familiar with the structure of business-organization law and its specific rules without resorting to rote memorization. Finally, the law does not always expressly state whether a rule is default or mandatory. An understanding of the policies that underlie mandatory rules and a familiarity with mandatory rules will help you predict whether a court will permit your clients to deviate from a particular rule.

CHAPTER 3
ENTITY SELECTION AND FORMATION

UNIT 3C

F<small>ORMATION</small> – T<small>HE</small> LLC:

UNIT 3D
<u>FORMATION – THE PARTNERSHIP:</u>

UNIT 3A

Entity Selection:

The formation of a corporation or an LLC requires approval. The formation of a sole proprietorship or a general partnership requires no formalities or state approval.

The procedures for forming business organizations are quite simple. So simple, in fact, you will wonder why clients ask attorneys to do it, instead of doing it themselves. An attorney can add value to the process by helping the client in the following ways:

(1) Selecting an appropriate entity;
(2) Structuring the entity to achieve her desired management structure;
(3) Structuring her relationships with the other owners, if any; and
(4) Helping her navigate the income tax issues (with a qualified tax advisor if the attorney is not a tax specialist)

3A-100 The Choices:

As we learned in Chapter 2, there are four basic forms for a business organization: a **sole proprietorship**, a **partnership**, an **LLC**, and a **corporation**.[6]

Clients will ask your advice about which form is appropriate for their specific needs. Your opinion will depend on whether the client wants the protection of **limited liability** and what type of **management structure** the client envisions for the company. In addition, because the treatment of income tax for these entities often differs, your client will be concerned with how the choice of business organization affects the **income tax** and **self-employment tax** the entity and the client will have to pay on any business profits and any salaries or dividends she receives.

3A-200 Limited Liability:

In Chapter 2, we discussed the concept of limited liability. Limited liability means the owners of the business will not be personally liable for the debts of the business.[7]

---

[6] See Chapter 2, §2-100.

The members of an LLC are protected by limited liability. The same is true for the shareholders of corporation.[8] In contrast, the partners of a partnership and the owner of a sole proprietorship are not protected with limited liability – they are personally liable for the debts of their businesses.

Limited liability is very attractive to businesspeople. If your client wants the protection of **limited liability**, you would **recommend forming a corporation or an LLC**, and you would recommend against running the business as a sole proprietorship or partnership.[9]

3A-300 MANAGEMENT STRUCTURE:

In Chapter 2, we introduced the concept of **centralized management**,[10] where the owners do not run their business. Management is in the hands of a few managers, who may or may not be owners. If a business organization has centralized management, the only way for an owner to have meaningful participation in the management is for her to get a seat on the board of directors. In contrast to centralized management, the client might prefer **direct management by the owners**.

The law creates default management structures for the partnership, the LLC, and the corporation. As our course progresses, you will see that the default ownership structures for each of these entities may differ. However, because they are default structures, parties can usually change them by contract if they so desire. Part of your task for this course is to learn the various ways the law allows you to structure an entity to suit your client's needs.

The **default rule for a corporation is centralized management**. This means the law requires a corporation to be managed by its board of directors, not the shareholders. In later chapters, you will be exposed to techniques to either (1) draft out of this default rule by giving direct management powers to the owners, or (2) ensure your client sits on the board or controls the majority of the board seats.[11]

The **default rule for an LLC** is usually **direct management by the owners**. This means that when you create an LLC for your client, there will be no board

---

[7] See Chapter 2, §§2-101(a) and 2-108(a).

[8] The owners of an LLC are called "members." The owners of a corporation are called "shareholders" or "stockholders"

[9] Certain partnerships have some limited liability protection. We will discuss this in greater detail in §§3D-300 and 3D-400, below.

[10] See Chapter 2, §2-108(c).

[11] See Chapter 5, §§5A-202, 5A-207(a), 5A-208, and 5A-209.

of directors or any other centralized management team unless you take steps to create it.

The **default rule for partnerships** is the same as for the LLC – **direct management by the owners**. If the partners want centralized management, you will have to help them include it in their partnership agreement.

There really is **no default rule for a sole proprietorship**, because it is not necessary. A sole proprietorship is simply a one-owner business that is not formally set up as a corporation or an LLC. The sole owner is the management.

It might seem that your client's desire to have centralized or direct management would be the decisive factor in choosing between the corporation and the LLC. Management structure is indeed important, but less important than it appears at first blush because the law allows the parties to **change the default structure.**

3A-400 INCOME TAX:

3A-401 BUSINESS ENTITY INCOME TAX – INTRODUCTION:

For those of you who do not plan to be specialists in tax law, it may be disappointing to learn that **income tax plays a large role in entity selection and formation**. Of course, it is possible for you to set up a business entity without any knowledge of tax law, but it would be malpractice for you not to **strongly advise your client to seek out professional counseling on taxation issues.**

If you want to be able to competently advise your clients on tax issues, you need to become specialized by taking courses on business entity taxation. It will be well worth the time and money you invest in such courses. If you plan to practice in the area of business organizations, you should seriously consider taking a course in business entity taxation. Even if you do not plan to become an expert in business entity taxation, you should at least understand the basic concepts. With a good understanding of the basic concepts you will be able to better communicate with your client's tax advisor.

Until you become specialized in business entity taxation, you can still advise your client on business entity formation, but you must tell your client it is **crucial for them to get separate tax advice from a qualified tax attorney or CPA**. However, you still need to be able to understand the tax landscape so that you can communicate and work with your client and her tax advisor.

3A-402 DOUBLE TAXATION & PASS-THROUGH TAXATION – THE BASICS:

Maybe the most basic concepts in business entity taxation are **double taxation** and **pass-through taxation** (also called flow-through taxation).

Double taxation: Remember, corporations and LLCs are separate legal "persons." In other words, they have legal identities separate and distinct from their owners. This separate identity means they have a duty, just like natural persons, to pay income taxes. The owners also have an obligation to pay income taxes. If both the entity and the owner are paying income taxes on the entity's profits, we have double taxation.

Illustration 1:

ABC Corp. has income of $100,000 for the year.

Its tax rate is 28%.[12]

Thus, its net income after income taxes is $72,000.

ABC Corp. distributes its entire $72,000 income to its shareholders through a dividend. The shareholders must pay tax on the dividends they receive. The tax rate on dividends is 15%.[13]

After taxes, the shareholders are left with only $61,200.

Pass-through taxation (flow-through taxation): Under this taxation regime, the business entity does not pay tax on any of its income. The income is only taxed at the owner level, not at the entity level. We say, the income is "passed through" to the owners for tax purposes.

Illustration 2:

ABC Corp. has income of $100,000 for the year.

It pays no income taxes, but the shareholders must pay tax on the $100,000.

Let's assume, for the sake of simplicity, that all shareholders are in the same tax bracket and their personal tax rate is 28%.[14]

After taxes, the shareholders are left with $72,000.

Pass through taxation also means **pass-through of entity losses** to the owners.

---

[12] For illustration purposes only.

[13] For illustration purposes only.

[14] For illustration purposes only.

Illustration 3:

Xavier is an associate attorney earning $100,000 per year from his job. A few years ago, he bought some shares in his friend's company, ABC Corp. Xavier owns 10% of the outstanding shares of ABC Corp.

This year, ABC Corp. had no profits. In fact, it suffered a loss of $50,000. Because Xavier owns 10% of ABC, he can deduct $5,000 from his $100,000 income. Thus, he will only have to pay taxes on $95,000 because of the pass-through of ABC losses to him.

3A-403 DOUBLE TAXATION & PASS-THROUGH TAXATION – WHICH IS BETTER?

It might seem that pass-through taxation is more favorable than double taxation because there is one less tax involved, but pass-through taxation is not the best in all situations. Consider how double taxation may be more favorable with respect to undistributed profits, different tax rates for individuals, corporations, and dividends, and a zero-out strategy, where the corporation makes no profits.

3A-403(a) UNDISTRIBUTED PROFITS:

With double taxation, the owners only pay taxes on the profits the entity actually distributes to them.

In contrast, with **pass-through taxation**, the **owners pay taxes** on the entity's profits **even if the entity does not distribute the profits** to the owners.

Illustration 4:

Xavier owns 10% of the outstanding shares of ABC Corp.

ABC Corp. makes $1,000,000 in profits, but the board decides not to distribute those profits.

Xavier's share of the corporation's profits is $100,000.

If ABC Corp. has pass-through taxation, Xavier must pay income tax on $100,000 even though the company did not distribute his share of the profits to him.

Practice tip: Lawyers often draft distribution or dividend policies into relevant organizational documents and agreements to address this issue.

3A-403(b) DIFFERENT TAX RATES:

Individual and entity tax rates will vary based on income. In addition, distributions (i.e., dividends) from non pass-though entities are taxed differently from ordinary income. **Actual distributions from non pass-through entities are taxed at the dividend tax rate (around 15%). In contrast, pass-through income is taxed at the individual's income tax rate.** Whether pass-through taxation is more favorable for a client depends on these rates.

Illustration 5:

Rowena wants to start a business. She is expecting the business to make a modest income of no more than $45,000 per year. The corporate tax rate is 15% for income under $50,000.[15]

Rowena expects the corporation to issue her a dividend each year equal to the corporation's net profit. The dividend tax rate is 15%.[16]

Rowena has income from other sources that put her in the highest income tax bracket – 35%.[17]

Is pass-through taxation better for Rowena?

Double taxation alternative for Rowena:

Corporate tax on $45,000 (45,000 x .15) = **$6,750**

Rowena's tax on the $38,250 dividend (38,250 x .15) = **$5,738**

Her net after all income taxes (45,000 – 6,750 – 5,738) = **32,512**

Pass-through taxation alternative for Rowena:

No corporate tax on $45,000.

Rowena's tax on the $45,000 (45,000 x .35) = **$15,750**

Her net after all income taxes (45,000 – 15,750) = **$29,250**

Based on these assumptions and these tax rates, **double taxation is better for Rowena.**

---

[15] For illustration purposes only.

[16] For illustration purposes only.

[17] For illustration purposes only.

3A-403(c) ZERO-OUT STRATEGY:

Double taxation might be better for the parties if they adopt a **zero-out** strategy. When a company zeros-out, **it intentionally makes little or no profit on paper for tax purposes**. If it makes no profit on paper, it will pay no taxes.

The goal is to distribute "profits" to the owners in a form that the company will be able to deduct as an expense.

Illustration 6:

Rowena is the owner and CEO of a company. The company has $800,000 in revenue. It has $460,000 in various expenses, including a salary of $50,000 for Rowena. As a result, the company made a profit of $340,000 before taxes. The company will distribute the entire profit after taxes to Rowena.

Under double taxation, the company would pay tax on the $340,000 profits, AND Rowena would also pay tax on the distribution of profits she receives from the company.

Let's assume, for the sake of illustration:
- The company's tax rate is 33%
- Rowena's tax on the distribution is 15%
- Tax on her salary will vary with her income, from a low rate of 20% with a modest salary of $50,000 or less, to a high of 33% with an income over $200,000.

Company's profits:	340,000
Tax (33%):	(112,000)
Net profit after taxes:	228,000
Distribution to Rowena:	228,000
Tax on distribution (15%):	(34,200)
Net distribution for Rowena:	193,800
Salary to Rowena:	50,000
Tax on salary (20%):	(10,000)
Net salary for Rowena:	40,000
Total net cash for Rowena:	**233,800** [193,800 + 40,000]

But, what if we **give Rowena a salary of $390,000, instead of $50,000**? The company would zero-out – it would not make a profit.

Rowena would net more money after taxes if the company adopted this strategy.

Company's profits:	0
Tax (33%):	0
Net profit after taxes:	0
Distribution to Rowena:	0
Tax on distribution (15%):	0
Net distribution for Rowena:	0
Salary to Rowena:	390,000
Tax on salary (33%):	(128,700)
Net salary for Rowena:	261,300
Total net cash for Rowena:	**261,300**

Of course, tax regulators understand how inflated salaries can reduce tax revenue in a double-taxation regime. Consequently, **federal tax law will not allow us to give Rowena an unreasonably high salary in a double-tax business entity**. Her salary must be reasonable in relation to her job, the size of her company, etc. In other words, her salary may not be unreasonably disproportionate with the salaries of people in positions similar to hers.

———————

3A-404 INCOME TAXATION & ENTITY SELECTION:

Which entities have pass-through taxation and which have double taxation?

The short answer:

LLC:

The default rule under the Internal Revenue Code is **pass-through taxation**, BUT the LLC may choose to be taxed with double taxation.

Corporation:

The default rule under the Internal Revenue Code is **double taxation**, BUT the corporation may qualify for pass-through taxation if it meets the requirements for Subchapter S status (see below).

Partnership:

The default rule under the Internal Revenue Code is **pass-through taxation**, BUT the partnership may choose to be taxed with double taxation.

Sole Proprietorship:

There is no entity, so there is no entity tax. The owner is taxed on all business income personally.

The long answer:

The Internal Revenue Code has several subchapters on business entity taxation. The three relevant subchapters are Subchapter K, Subchapter C, and Subchapter S.

Subchapter K:

Partnership taxation means pass-through taxation. Partnerships are not really "entities," so they receive pass-through taxation. **LLCs are taxed like partnerships as a default rule,**[18] but they may choose to be taxed under Subchapter C or Subchapter S.

Subchapter C:

Corporate taxation means double taxation. Corporations are subject to double taxation unless they choose Subchapter S tax treatment. Corporations cannot qualify for Subchapter K tax treatment.

You will hear the term **C-corp**. It means a corporation that has been formed under state law and that is taxed under Subchapter C. It is also possible for an LLC to elect to be subject to C-corp taxation.

Subchapter S:

A corporation (or an LLC) can qualify for Subchapter S pass-through taxation if:

- It is a **domestic corporation or LLC** (i.e., a corporation or LLC organized under the laws of the United States)
- It has **100 or fewer shareholders/members** (but there are special counting rules for family members)
- All of its **shareholders/members are natural persons** (but some non-profit entities and some trusts are allowed)

---

[18] Actually, single-member LLCs are not taxed under Subchapter K. Instead, they are taxed like sole proprietorships (called "Disregarded Entity"). It is still pass-through taxation, but there are some differences between Subchapter K pass-through and sole-proprietorship pass-through.

- All of its **shareholders/members are U.S. citizens or resident aliens**.
- All of its outstanding **shares/membership interests have the same economic rights** (but different voting rights are allowed).

There are some differences between pass-through taxation in Subchapter K and Subchapter S. Some of these differences are discussed below in section 3A-500.

You will often hear the term "**S-corp.**" It means a corporation or an LLC that has been formed under state law and that has elected Subchapter S treatment by filing the proper forms with the IRS. You may hear an owner of business formed as an LLC say, "I have an S-corp." They mean: "I have an LLC that has Subchapter S status."

You may ask why an LLC might try to qualify for Subchapter S pass-through taxation if it automatically receives pass-through taxation under Subchapter K. Good question. The answer has to do with the different ways self-employment tax is treated under Subchapter K and Subchapter S.

3A-500 SELF-EMPLOYMENT TAX:

3A-501 SELF-EMPLOYMENT TAX – INTRODUCTION:

In addition to income tax, the owner of a business will often also have to pay self-employment tax. What is self-employment tax? It is simply "**FICA tax**" – the federal tax to support Social Security and Medicare benefits.

When you look at your monthly paystub (and your W-2's at the end of the year), you will see that **7.65% has been deducted from your salary for FICA**. What you don't see is that your employer has also contributed the equivalent of 7.65% of your salary to FICA. This means that **a total of 15.3% of your salary is given to the government for FICA** – half by you, and half by your employer. If you are self-employed or an independent contractor, you must pay the entire 15.3%. We refer to this as the **self-employment tax**.

3A-502 SELF-EMPLOYMENT TAX – THE BASICS:

Let's see how self-employment tax affects Rowena from our earlier illustrations (Illustrations 5 and 6 in 3A-403(b) and (c), above):

Illustration 7:

Rowena's business entity receives pass-through tax treatment.

She is subject to an individual tax rate of 35%

The company has a profit of $45,000 for the year.

Without self-employment tax:

> 45,000 – 15,750 [income tax] = 29,250
>
> Total net after income tax = **$29,250**

With self-employment tax:

> 45,000 – 15,750 [income tax] – 6,885 [self-employment tax] = 22,365
>
> Total net after income tax and self-employment tax = **$22,365**

You can see why Rowena would prefer to avoid self-employment taxes, but how can she? Because self-employment tax only applies to wages and salaries, Rowena would argue that the $45,000 company income attributable to her as the owner was not her salary; it was her return on her investment in the company.

As an illustration, imagine I am employed by Microsoft as a software engineer and receive an annual salary of $100,000. In addition, I purchased Microsoft stock and receive a $5,000 dividend each year. My salary is clearly subject to self-employment tax (and income tax), but my $5,000 dividend is not because it is not wages or salary – it is a return on my investment in Microsoft stock.

Rowena would like the same tax treatment for her situation as I receive as an employee and shareholder of Microsoft. She wants to distinguish between the money she receives as a salary for the work she does for her company and the money she receives as a return on her investment in the company.

Will the IRS buy her argument? It depends on whether the entity is taxed under Subchapter K or Subchapter S:

Subchapter K entities:

If the owner does **any work** for the entity, the entire amount of the company's income attributable to her is subject to self-employment tax and income tax.   If the owner is **completely passive**, she can avoid the self-employment taxes, but must still pay income taxes on the company's income attributable to her.

Subchapter S entities:

If the owner does any work for the entity, she **may categorize some of the company's income attributable to her as return on her investment**. This amount categorized as investment return will not be subject to self-employment tax, but will be subject to income tax. The remainder will be subject to both the self-employment tax and income tax. The portion of the profits she categorizes as salary must not be unreasonably low, otherwise the owner would be avoiding her FICA taxes.

Because **LLCs are taxed under Subchapter K as a default**, they sometimes file for Subchapter S status to avoid **some self-employment taxes.** As mentioned earlier, you will often here owners of LLCs say they have formed an S-Corp. You should understand they mean they have formed an LLC and have elected taxation under Subchapter S of the Internal Revenue Code.

You might ask what justification is there for the law treating self-employment taxes differently in Subchapter K entities and Subchapter S entities. The short answer is that there probably is not a good justification.

3A-503 INCOME TAX AND SELF-EMPLOYMENT TAX - ILLUSTRATIONS:

How do the income taxes and self-employment taxes work together to create an overall tax burden for the owners of a business entity?

Some basic concepts are important:

1) A business's income (i.e., profits) equals its revenue minus its expenses.

2) Half of the 15.3% self-employment tax is deductible as a business expense, which means it will lower income for either the business entity or the owner, depending on whether it is a pass-through entity.

The chart on the following page provides three examples to show how self-employment taxes and income taxes work for each of the three types of tax regimes: Subchapter C; Subchapter K; and Subchapter S. They also illustrate how the treatment of self-employment tax is different for Subchapter K and Subchapter S entities.

The common assumptions are as follows:

The business has two owners, Alvin and Bette. Each owns half of the business.

Both Alvin and Bette are employees of the entity. Reasonable salaries for the work they perform are $50,000 each. They have no income other than what they receive from the business.

The business has $320,000 in revenue and $120,000 in expenses, not including expenses for Alvin and Bette's salaries or expenses for self-employment taxes on those salaries.

All the tax rates assumed below are not necessarily reflective of the actual tax rates, but they are close approximations.

You might be surprised to find that, based on our assumptions and the tax rates we used, Bette does better under Sub-C double taxation than she does under Sub-K pass-through taxation. From this example, you can see why it is important for you to advise your client to seek advice from a tax expert.

See illustrations on next page

SUBCHAPTER C:

COMPANY'S TAX LIABILITY:

Revenue:	320,000
Expenses:	(120,000)
Salary expenses:	(100,000)*
FICA expenses:	(7,650)
Income before taxes:	92,350
Corporate tax (21.5%):	(19,855)
Net income after taxes:	72,495
Dividend to owners:	72,495**
Retained earnings:	0

BETTE'S PERSONAL TAX LIABILITY:

Taxable salary:	50,000
Income taxes (17%):	(8,500)
FICA (7.65%):	(3,825)
Net salary:	**37,675**
Dividend:	36,248
Dividend tax (15%):	(5,437)
Net dividend:	**30,811**

Bette's net after taxes:
68,486 [50,000 + 36,248 – 8,500 – 3,825 – 5,437]

* $50,000 for Alvin plus $50,000 for Bette

** $36,247.5 to Alvin and $36,247.5 to Bette

SUBCHAPTER K:

COMPANY'S TAX LIABILITY:

Revenue:	320,000
Expenses:	(120,000)
Salary expenses:	0*
FICA expenses:	0
Income before taxes:	200,000
Entity tax (none):	0
Net income:	200,000
Dividend to owners:	not relevant
Retained earnings:	not relevant

BETTE'S PERSONAL TAX LIABILITY:

Salary:	100,000**
FICA Deduction (7.65%):	-7,650***
Taxable salary:	92,350
Income taxes (21%):	(19,394)
FICA (15.3%):	(15,300)****

Bette's net after taxes:
65,306 [100,000 – 19,394 – 15,300]

* Owners' salaries are not deductible business expenses for pass-through entities.

** Bette's 50% share of entity's net income. Salary & return both treated as salary

*** Bette's taxable income is reduced by half of her total FICA payment.

**** 15.3% of the entire $100,000 salary

SUBCHAPTER S:

COMPANY'S TAX LIABILITY:

Revenue:	320,000
Expenses:	(120,000)
Salary expenses:	0*
FICA expenses:	0
Income before taxes:	200,000
Entity tax (none):	0
Net income:	200,000
Dividend to owners:	not relevant
Retained earnings:	not relevant

BETTE'S PERSONAL TAX LIABILITY:

Salary:	50,000
FICA Deduction (7.65%):	-3,825**
Taxable salary:	46,175
Return on investment:	50,000
Total taxable income:	96,175
Income taxes (21%):	(20,197)
FICA (15.3%):	(7,650)***

Bette's net after taxes:
72,153 [100,000 – 20,197 – 7,650]

* Owners' salaries are not deductible business expenses for pass-through entities.

** Bette's taxable salary is reduced by half of her total FICA payment.

*** 15.3% of the $50,000 salary only

3A-600 **OTHER IMPORTANT TAX CONCEPTS:**

There is one more income tax issue that is especially important to the formation of closely-held businesses. **When an investor contributes cash** to a corporation in exchange for shares or to an LLC in exchange for a membership interest, there is **no taxable event**. The business entity does not need to pay tax for the cash it received, nor does the investor have to pay tax on the shares or membership interest she received.

In contrast, **when an investor contributes services, real property or personal property** in exchange for ownership interests in a corporation of an LLC, there is the potential for a taxable event. You and your client will need to work with her tax advisor to find a way to postpone paying the taxes.

3A-601 **CONTRIBUTIONS OF REAL OR PERSONAL PROPERTY:**

Property you have acquired might appreciate in value. If you eventually sell the property for a price greater than the price you paid to acquire it, you will **"realize" the gain** and pay **capital gains tax** on the difference. The tax rate for capital gains tax is usually somewhere **around 15%,** but can vary from year to year and can differ for short-term and long-term gains.

> ***Illustration 1:***
>
> Mary purchases Blackacre for $100,000.
>
> > Mary's tax basis in Blackacre is $100,000.
>
> Five years later, Mary sells Blackacre for $120,000
>
> Mary will pay capital gains tax on the $20,000 she received that exceeded her tax basis in Blackacre.

If we change the illustration just slightly to involve Mary's formation of a closely-held business, you can easily see how Mary might experience a tax event when she makes her investment.

> ***Illustration 2:***
>
> Mary purchases Blackacre for $100,000.
>
> > Mary's tax basis in Blackacre is $100,000.
>
> Five years later, Blackacre is worth $120,000, at which time Mary transfers title to Blackacre to ABC Inc. in exchange for 1,000 shares.

You can see that both illustrations involve the transfer of Blackacre in exchange for consideration – in once case the consideration was cash and in the other case the consideration was corporate stock. And both illustrations involve the transfer of an asset whose value has appreciated since its acquisition.

As far as the tax law is concerned Mary owes capital gains taxes under both circumstances. When she receives cash as consideration for her disposition of Blackacre, she will be able to put aside some of that cash to pay the capital gains tax. When she receives stock in exchange for her disposition of Blackacre, she will have to find another source of cash to pay the capital gains tax. When Mary receives stock in exchange for Blackacre, she would prefer to postpone paying any capital gains tax until she sells the stock she received.

3A-601(a) CORPORATIONS:

Internal Revenue Code Section 351 allows an investor to defer paying capital gains tax on her transfer of real or personal property to a corporation in exchange for stock until she sells the stock. There is one important qualification, however: none of the other investors in the corporation contributed services for more than 20% of the stock.

In other words, if all the investors who contribute cash, personal property, or real property in exchange for stock acquire 80% of the outstanding voting stock (and 80% of any other outstanding class of stock),[19] then they may defer any capital gains they in their contributed property until the time they dispose of their stock.

Illustration 3A:

Mary purchases Blackacre for $100,000.

Five years later, Blackacre is worth $120,000, at which time Mary transfers title to Blackacre to ABC Inc. in exchange for 1,000 shares.

Bob contributes $96,000 cash to ABC Inc. in exchange for 800 shares.

Carol contributes accounting services to ABC Inc. in exchange for 200 shares.

There are no other outstanding shares.

Mary will be able to defer capital gains, if any, until she sells her stock.

Once again, you might seek a justification for the 80% rule, but there does not seem to be one. In fact, when the business entity is an LLC the 80% does not apply, providing some evidence that this rule is somewhat arbitrary.

---

[19] Possibly one investment transaction or a series of related investment transactions.

The investor's **basis** in the shares is her original basis in the property. When she later disposes of her shares, she will pay capital gains tax based on her basis in the property.

Illustration 3B:

Mary purchases Blackacre for $100,000.

> Her tax basis in Blackacre is $100,000.

Five years later, Blackacre is worth $120,000, at which time Mary transfers title to Blackacre to ABC Inc. in exchange for 1,000 shares.

> Her tax basis in her shares is $100,000, the same as her tax basis in Blackacre.

Several years later, Mary transfers her 1,000 shares for their fair value of $130,000. Mary will pay capital gains tax on the $30,000 increase on her basis.

3A-601(b) **LLCs:**

The 80% rule does not apply to LLC investors. In other words, any capital gains tax is deferred until the member eventually disposes of her LLC membership interest, regardless of whether she and the other investors who transferred property in exchange for ownership interests controlled 80% of the membership interests after the transfer. An investor who contributes services in exchange for an LLC membership interest will not cause the others to forfeit their ability to defer any capital gains they may have otherwise realized on their transfer of property to the LLC.

3A-602 **CONTRIBUTIONS OF SERVICES:**

When you receive compensation for your services, you must pay income taxes. Most of us are more familiar with the more common paradigm of cash compensation for services. We know that we must pay income taxes on any cash compensation we receive, but we would also be required to pay income taxes on compensation that came in the form of a car, a plot of land, tickets to a baseball game or, more apropos for this chapter, an equity interest in a corporation or LLC. As we already discussed, paying income taxes on consideration that comes in the form of equity interests requires the investor to find an alternative source of cash flow.

Illustrations:

Mary contributes accounting services to XYZ Corp. in exchange for 1,500 shares.

Bob contributes his services as CEO to XYZ Corp. in exchange for 5,000 shares.

Under Internal Revenue Code Section 83 the investor who contributes services in exchange for equity interests does not immediately recognize the value of shares as compensation for income for tax purposes.

The major qualification for delayed recognition of the income is that the **investor must bear a substantial risk of forfeiture of her stock**. To qualify for the substantial risk of forfeiture, the investor usually receives what is often referred to as **restricted stock**. Under the terms of the restricted stock, she would lose the shares if some sort of **employment-related condition** (or service-related condition for independent contractors) is not met.

Illustration:

Bob contributes his services and CEO to XYZ Corp. in exchange for 5,000 shares of restricted stock. If Bob does not increase sales over the next 5 years by 20%, he will lose his stock.

The IRS had made it clear that in order for there to be a substantial risk of forfeiture, if when the corporation grants the restricted stock there is a meaningful probability that the condition will fail.

The investor may defer the taxes only for as long as the risk of forfeiture is in effect or when she is allowed to freely transfer the shares. When the restriction on the stock expires, she will have to pay taxes on the shares at their **fair value when the restriction expires**. In other words, she may eventually have the same problem she had at the outset – difficulty finding cash flow to pay income taxes. The problem may be even more acute when the restrictions eventually expire if the value of her shares has increased and her tax burden has increased proportionately.

In our discussion up to now, we have assumed that the recipient of the equity interests will be an investor, but businesses might give key employees equity interests in the company to reward them, incentive them, and align their interests with the investors. This type of grant of equity interests are subject to the tax rules discussed here. When an employee receives this type of equity grant, she often signs an agreement with the business entity and the owners that requires her to sell her shares to the other owners or the entity itself when she leaves her job.[20] Unfortunately, this arrangement will NOT cause the employee to bear substantial risk of forfeiture of her equity. The IRS has made it clear that they do not consider the possibility of involuntary termination to be a substantial risk of forfeiture.

The same rules govern LLC membership interests received in exchange for services.

---

[20] These agreements are commonly known as buy-sell agreements. We discuss buy-sell agreements in detail in Chapter 7, §7A-300 et seq.

UNIT 3B

FORMATION – THE CORPORATION:

3B-100 FORMATION PROCESS – IN GENERAL:

The actual process to incorporate is quite straightforward. You deliver the **"articles of incorporation,"** along with the proper fee, to the secretary of state in the state in which you wish to incorporate.

3B-101 ENGAGEMENT LETTER:

Representation of a client usually begins with informal discussions to understand the client's need for representation. During these discussions, the attorney and client will lay out the general parameters for their relationship. These discussions are usually followed by a formal engagement letter between the client and attorney.

3B-102 CHECKLIST:

Most attorneys will create a good checklist to help them interview clients and draft the articles, bylaws, and agreements between the shareholders. The checklist should have all the major issues the attorney needs to consider to determine the client's needs and how to draft the documents to meet them.

3B-103 REPRESENTING MORE THAN ONE CLIENT:

It is quite common for two or more "business partners"[21] to ask an attorney to set up a corporation for them. They view corporation formation as a bureaucratic formality that does not involve traditional courtroom-advocacy representation. However, the attorney should recognize that the business partners will often have divergent interests and conflicts with respect to internal governance of the corporation, their relationship as shareholders, their economic and financial goals, etc. In addition, once the corporation comes into existence, their personal interests might conflict with those of the corporation. When the attorney sets up the corporation and drafts the relevant documents,

---

[21] I am using "business partners" here in the more generic sense to refer to the co-promoters who will also be shareholders in the corporation once it is formed.

who does she represent? Whose interests does she seek to promote and protect? Does she represent one of the business partners, both of them, or does she represent the soon-to-exist business entity?

A preliminary question that attorney needs to consider is whether she is allowed to accept representation of both business partners. The ABA Model Rules of Professional Conduct, Rule 1.7 provides:

> (a) Except as provided in paragraph (b), a lawyer shall not represent a client if the representation involves a concurrent conflict of interest. A concurrent conflict of interest exists if:
>
> > (1) the representation of one client will be directly adverse to another client; or
> >
> > (2) there is a significant risk that the representation of one or more clients will be materially limited by the lawyer's responsibilities to another client, a former client or a third person or by a personal interest of the lawyer.
>
> (b) Notwithstanding the existence of a concurrent conflict of interest under paragraph (a), a lawyer may represent a client if:
>
> > (1) the lawyer reasonably believes that the lawyer will be able to provide competent and diligent representation to each affected client;
> >
> > (2) the representation is not prohibited by law;
> >
> > (3) the representation does not involve the assertion of a claim by one client against another client represented by the lawyer in the same litigation or other proceeding before a tribunal; and
> >
> > (4) each affected client gives informed consent, confirmed in writing.

In the end, under the ABA Model Rules, even though the interests of the business partners may be different, the attorney may represent both if she reasonably believes she can provide competent representation to each of the business partners AND each of them gives informed consent. In these situations, the attorney should carefully draft the engagement letter to address the different interests the clients might have and the potential conflicts they might face in the future and explain the parties.

The clients often do not understand the scope of the attorney's representation forming a corporation. Nor do they understand the potential conflicts they now face or might face in the future. They often look upon the attorney's job of forming the corporation as one of a scrivener. In addition, they often view the state as the other party to the deal, since it is the approval of the secretary of state that is required. They see each other on the same side of the deal.

In addition, in their optimism, exuberance, and spirit of friendship, they often are unable to critically examine how their interests are not perfectly aligned. They cannot imagine that they will not be able to resolve amicably any problem that arises. Rest assured, they will run into problems that will nearly destroy their relationship. It almost always happens, no matter how strong the personal relationship is between the two business partners.

In addition to determining whether rules of professional ethics allow her to represent both business partners when forming a business entity, the attorney must consider whether it makes good business sense for her legal practice. In the future, when the parties have a disagreement, each business partner will finally realize she needs an attorney who will seek to protect her interests. She will want an attorney who is unequivocally on her side. However, she will likely see the attorney as the representative of the parties' common goals, as will her partner. The attorney risks losing her clients.

I am not sure if there is a very good solution to this problem. I have seen engagement letters that expressly state that the law firm's client is the corporation-to-be-formed, not the business partners. I also know of attorneys that will only represent one of the business partners; they instruct the other party to seek counsel elsewhere. I suspect that many firms will choose to represent the wealthy business partner, which is indeed the better business strategy.

3B-200 ARTICLES OF INCORPORATION:

Think of the articles of incorporation as the corporation's constitution. The articles have the most basic provisions regarding the nature and governance of the corporation. In some states, the articles of incorporation are called the **certificate of incorporation**. In some circles, the articles or the certificate might also be referred to as the **charter**.

There is another corporate document that also has provisions regarding the nature and governance of the corporation – the **bylaws**. How do the articles and bylaws differ?

> First, the **articles are filed with the secretary of state**. In contrast, the bylaws are an internal document. The secretary of state does not want them.

> Second, any **amendments to the articles of incorporation require the approval of the shareholders**. It is one of the few times the

shareholders get to vote on corporate matters. In contrast, an amendment to the bylaws does not necessarily require shareholder approval (more on this in Chapter 5).

Third, any **amendments to the articles of incorporation must be filed with the secretary of state**. Amendment to the bylaws requires no filing.

Fourth, anything you put in the bylaws you can put in the articles. In contrast, there are some things that must be in the articles, and putting them in the bylaws would be inappropriate.

Finally, and most importantly, the bylaws may not contradict the articles. **If there is a conflict between the articles and the bylaws, the articles control**. Similarly, if there is anything in an agreement between the shareholders that contradicts the articles, the articles control. Once again, think of the articles as the corporation's constitution.

What items and information must be in the articles?

The articles can be very simple. RMBCA 2.02 requires only four items in the articles of incorporation:

1) The name of the corporation
2) The number of authorized shares
3) The street address of the corporation's initial registered office and the name of its initial registered agent
4) The name and address of each incorporator

3B-201 **THE NAME OF THE CORPORATION:**

RMBCA §4.01 requires that the corporation's name must contain "corporation," "company," "limited," "corp.," "inc.," "co.," "ltd." or something similar. The justification for such a requirement is that it provides those dealing with the corporation fair warning that the owners are protected by limited liability.

In addition, the name must not be confusingly similar to an existing company organized in that state. The secretary of state's website should have a search function that allows you to search names to see if they are available.

> ***Practice tip:*** Even though a company name might be available in your state, the name might violate trademark rights. For example, "Microsoft" might be available in your state of incorporation, but if your client uses this name, Microsoft will send a cease and desist letter to protect its trademark. Even if your client might be able to win any lawsuit related to its company name, the battle will have large costs. It is best to avoid this potential problem at the beginning.

There are companies that will perform a thorough search for your client to provide some comfort that the company name will not infringe on existing intellectual property rights. The fees for this type of service can be significant. You can save your client some money by doing the search yourself. You can use the U.S. Patent and Trademark Office website to search trademarks registered with the federal government. Each state should have a similar on-line registry for state-registered IP rights. You should also do a general internet search.

Your search will not be as thorough as the professional search but it will save your client money upfront. Later, however, your client may run into a dispute because your search failed to uncover something that a professional search would have. **Make sure you discuss the risks and benefits with your client and draft the scope of your search, if any, in the engagement letter.**

3B-202 THE NUMBER OF AUTHORIZED SHARES:

A corporation will issue shares or stock to its equity investors. Regular stock is called **common** or **common stock**. The corporation might also issue stock that has superior dividend rights or special voting rights. This type of stock is normally called **preferred stock**.

If your corporation is simple, you may only need to issue common stock. If you are only issuing common stock, then all you need to write in the articles of incorporation is the number of shares the corporation is authorized to issue and sell. There is a difference between "**authorized shares**" and "**issued and outstanding**."

Illustration:

In its articles of incorporation, XYZ Inc. has 1,000 authorized shares. The board of directors approves the issuance and sale of 300 shares to Mary and 250 shares to Betty. After consummation of the transactions, XYZ has **1,000 authorized** shares and **550 shares issued and outstanding**.

This means that XYZ can still issue and sell 450 shares of stock without amending the articles of incorporation. If it wants to issue more than 450 shares, it will need to amend the articles of incorporation to increase the number of authorized shares. This requires the approval of the shareholders (who are now Mary and Betty).

If the corporation wants to authorize and issue preferred stock, the authorized preferred stock and the terms of the preferred stock must also be in the articles of incorporation. We will discuss preferred stock in Chapter 4.[22]

> ***Practice tip 1:*** Before you choose to create a large number of authorized shares, check to see what the rules are in your state. In some states there is an additional fee for having more than a certain number of authorized shares.

> ***Practice tip 2:*** The secretary of state only cares how many shares are authorized. She does not care how many shares you have issued, nor does she care who your shareholders are. You only need to file the articles, not a shareholder list, with the secretary of state. If you amend the articles to increase the number of authorized shares (or for any other reason), you must file an "articles of amendment" with the secretary of state.

3B-203 THE STREET ADDRESS OF THE INITIAL REGISTERED OFFICE:

The street address of the corporation's registered office could be your client's home address. You do not need to have a special or separate "office" for your corporation. However, the address must be **within the state of incorporation**. Also, it must be a street address – a post office box will not suffice.

3B-204 THE NAME OF THE INITIAL REGISTERED AGENT:

You also need to provide the name of the **initial registered agent** in the articles of incorporation. The registered agent is not an agent who can bind the corporation in contract. The registered agent is there **to accept service of process on behalf of the corporation** if someone sues the corporation. If you serve the registered agent with process, you have served the corporation.

The registered agent can be any individual, but she must be a resident of the state and have the same office address as the corporation's registered office.[23] The registered agent can also be a corporation that has the same business office as the corporation you are incorporating.[24]

> ***Practice tip 1:*** The registered agent will probably be your client or one of the other promoters of the corporation (note: a **"promoter"** is one of

---

[22] See Chapter 4, §4A-204(b) for a discussion of preferred stock.

[23] RMBCA §5.01.

[24] Id.

the people behind the creation of the corporation and the business). Indeed, you, the attorney, could serve as the registered agent as long as the corporation's registered office is your office. This may sound a bit confusing, but remember that sometimes a business will incorporate in a state where it does not do business. This is especially true for Delaware. Many companies that incorporate in Delaware do not have any real presence in Delaware. However, they must have a registered office and agent. In Delaware, there is a cottage industry of companies that provide registered agent and registered office service.

Practice tip 2: The registered agent must consent to act as the registered agent and sign a consent form. You must include the consent with the articles when you file them. In many states, the form for the articles of incorporation and the consent of the registered agent are the same form. If the corporation ever changes its registered agent, it needs to file the change with the secretary of state. However, a change of the registered agent will not require an amendment to the articles of incorporation. The articles list the "initial" registered agent. Any later registered agent is not the initial registered agent. Ditto for the initial registered office (notify the secretary of state of the change, but no need to amend the articles).

3B-205 **THE NAME AND ADDRESS OF EACH INCORPORATOR:**

The incorporator is the person who files the articles of incorporation with the secretary of state. Often, it is you, the attorney. If the promoter sends in the articles to the secretary of state, the promoter is the incorporator. Being the incorporator does not make you a shareholder, a director, a promoter, or an agent. It simply means that you filed the articles with the secretary of state. An incorporator does have a certain amount of limited power before the board is appointed, but once the board of directors is in place, the incorporator is automatically relieved of all power.

3B-206 **CORPORATE PURPOSE:**

Many corporate law statutes in the past required the articles of incorporation to state a purpose for the corporation. The purpose created governance problems. If the corporation undertook some course of action or engaged in some act or transaction that could not fit squarely within the corporate purpose, it was **ultra vires** – beyond the corporation's legal authority. Shareholders could sue the board of directors for authorizing ultra vires activities.

Nowadays, very few corporate law statutes require the articles of incorporation to state a corporate purpose. Even when they do, it can be a broad purpose that allows the corporation to do anything that is legal. Delaware law even suggests the following:

> It shall be sufficient to state, either alone or with other businesses or purposes, that the purpose of the corporation is to engage in any lawful act or activity for which corporations may be organized under the General Corporation Law of Delaware, and by such statement all lawful acts and activities shall be within the purposes of the corporation, except for express limitations, if any.[25]

3B-207 **OTHER PROVISIONS IN THE ARTICLES:**

The articles of incorporation may have other provisions regarding the governance of the company. As you progress through the course and this text, you will become familiar with the other possible governance provisions. At this point, just keep in mind that there are two corporate governance documents – the articles and bylaws. There are a few governance provisions that must be in the articles. The reasoning behind this is that these provisions are so important, they need to be within the corporations "constitution." Other provisions can be written into either the articles or the bylaws.

> ***Practice tip:*** When the statute permits a governance provision to be the articles or the bylaws, you will have to determine if it is so important for your client that it deserves the extra reverence and protection it will receive from being in the articles. Remember – it is generally much more difficult to amend the articles than the bylaws.

---

[25] DGCL §102(a)(3).

3B-208 <u>CONTENT THAT IS TYPICALLY NOT INCLUDED IN THE ARTICLES:</u>

3B-208(a) <u>A LIST OF SHAREHOLDERS:</u>

Laypersons and inexperienced lawyers often feel the need to list the shareholders and how many shares they have in the articles of incorporation. Not only is this unnecessary, it is a deviation from standard practice. The corporation's officers (usually, the corporate secretary) will maintain a shareholder ledger that keeps track of who the shareholders are and how many shares they each hold.

Shares are freely transferable. We should not have to amend the articles every time a shareholder transfers shares. If the shareholders would like to place limitations on the transfer of shares, they can do so through contract.[26]

3B-208(b) <u>A LIST OF THE DIRECTORS:</u>

The articles may list the *initial* directors – i.e., the persons who will serve as the first directors once the secretary of state has filed the articles of incorporation. The initial directors will only serve until the next annual shareholders meeting, where the shareholders will elect a new board. The articles should not list permanent directors. The shareholders have a right to elect directors and the articles cannot dictate who the directors will be.

———————

3B-300 <u>POST INCORPORATION FORMALITIES:</u>

3B-301 <u>ORGANIZATION ACTIVITIES</u>

Once the secretary of state has filed your articles of incorporation, you will receive a notice. The corporation exists as soon as the secretary of state has filed the articles, but there are other organization activities that must be completed.

Who is responsible for the organization activities?

If the articles of incorporation filed with the secretary of state listed the initial directors,[27] then those directors will form the board and complete the organization of the corporation.

———————

[26] See Chapter 7, §7A-301.

[27] We could have listed the initial directors in the articles, but it was not required.

If the articles did not list the initial directors, the incorporator will either: (1) appoint the directors and let them complete the organization; or (2) complete the organization and then appoint the directors.

Typical organization activities:

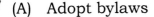

- (A) Adopt bylaws

- (B) Appoint officers and establish their compensation

- (C) Create stock certificates (if necessary)

- (D) Adopt an accounting period

- (E) Adopt a principal office

- (F) Approve the opening of a bank account

- (G) Adopt promoter transactions (see later in this Chapter)

- (H) Issuance of stock to shareholders

- (I) Federal S Corp resolution (if desired)

- (J) Adopting shareholders' agreement (the corporation will often be a party to the shareholders' agreement)

3B-302 SHAREHOLDERS' AGREEMENT(S):

If the corporation has more than one shareholder, you should strongly advise your client to have a shareholders' agreement.

The shareholders' agreement will generally deal with three major topics:

1) The incorporation of the firm, including each shareholder's promise to purchase a specific number of shares for a specific price (these agreements may be in separate contracts, often called a **Pre-Incorporation Agreement** and a **Subscription Agreement**);

2) The governance of the firm (may be in a stand-alone agreement);

3) The shareholders' transfer of their stock to third parties and each other (may be in a stand-alone agreement often called a **Buy-Sell Agreement**).

3B-303 **ANNUAL FILINGS:**

Once a corporation's formation is completed, the law usually requires it to file annual statements with the secretary of state each year – with a filing fee, of course. These annual statements are very simple. The forms are available on your state's secretary of state website. Usually, the annual report requires no more than a list of the current directors and officers of the corporation and a reconfirmation of the corporation's registered agent and principal office.

3B-304 **REGISTERING AS A FOREIGN CORPORATION:**

You will need to advise your client whether her corporation must qualify as foreign corporation in another state. As far as one state is concerned, a corporation incorporated in any other state or country is a foreign corporation. For example, the State of Iowa considers any non-Iowa corporation to be a foreign corporation.

In order to be able to **transact business** in a state other than the state of incorporation, a corporation must register and qualify as a foreign corporation. The filing is usually quite simple, but there will be a filing fee and a fee each year to maintain the qualification.

Some states try to define what constitutes transacting business within the state. The RMBCA simply provides a non-exhaustive list of activities that do not constitute transacting business within a state.[28] It may help you to think of a continuum of activities:

> At one end of the continuum are the transactions that generally constitute transacting business within a state. For example, if a foreign corporation establishes an office, a store, or other place of business in the state, it is transacting business within the state.

> At the other end of the continuum are the transactions that generally do NOT constitute transacting business within the state. For example, soliciting orders from potential customers within the state is NOT transacting business within the the state.

Between these two extremes are all the other activities that might require your client to qualify as a foreign corporation in any particular state. You will have to do research to determine what activities in the target state constitute transacting business that requires qualifying as a foreign entity in that state.

---

[28] RMBCA §15.01(b).

3B-305   DOING BUSINESS UNDER AN ASSUMED NAME (d/b/a):

Corporations often have very generic names, or names unrelated to their business. Although a corporation's name can be related to its general branding strategy, it is not necessary to have a corporate name that is the same as the business name or brand name.

Illustration:

Mary's corporation, M Ventures II, Inc., opens a store in a mall to sell smart phones. The name of the store is "Smart Phone Sally's."

When a corporation, an LLC, a partnership, or even a sole proprietor does business under a different name, it must make a filing with the secretary of state. In some states, the filing is for an **assumed name**, in other states it is for a **fictitious name**.

3B-306   DISSOLUTION:

The state breathes life into legal persons, such as corporations and LLCs. Only the state can terminate the existence of these legal persons. There is a formal process for dissolution of business entities that requires **filing articles of dissolution with the secretary of state.** We will discuss the dissolution process in more detail in Chapter 9.

3B-400   PROMOTER LIABILITY:

3B-401   PROMOTER LIABILITY – THE SET-UP:

A corporation exists when the secretary of state files the articles, not when the incorporator delivers the articles to the secretary of state. Normally, the secretary of state will send a notice to the incorporator that she has filed the articles. The process can take some time. The process is a bit easier in our modern digital age. An incorporator can easily do a search on the secretary of state's website to determine whether the articles have been filed.

What happens if a great opportunity comes along before the secretary of state has filed the articles? The promoters of a corporation might want to cause the corporation to enter into the contract before the corporation has legally come into existence. If they do so, they risk personal liability under the contract.

It is helpful to conceptualize the promoter-liability fact patterns into two broad categories:

Before incorporation, promoter signs a contract on behalf of the corporation, as if the corporation already existed, or signs a contract on behalf of the corporation, but somehow indicates she is signing on behalf of a corporation to-be-formed.

After taking steps to form the corporation, but before the secretary of state has actually filed the articles, the promoter signs a contract on behalf of the corporation.

We discuss these fact patterns in more detail immediately below.

3B-402 CATEGORY 1 – PRE-INCORPORATION CONTRACTS:

Before incorporation, a promoter might sign a contract on behalf of the corporation, as if the corporation already existed.

It some instances, the signature might not indicate the corporation has not yet been formed

Illustration:

Polly Promoter

This type of signature is particularly problematic because it appears that Polly Promoter is signing the contract on her own behalf, not on behalf of the corporation. Because courts take an objective approach to contract interpretation, the other party might try to hold Polly personally liable on the contract because he reasonably believed Polly was signing on her own behalf. Polly might be able to present other evidence that the other party was not reasonable in such a belief, but she runs the risk that the judge will not admit the evidence because of the parole evidence rule or the plain meaning rule. There is also the risk that the fact finder will simply not believe her.

It some instances, the signature will indicate that the promoter is signing on behalf of the corporation.

Illustrations:

Polly Promoter, agent for XYZ Corp.

Or

XYZ Corp.
By: *Polly Promoter,* Promoter

Or

72

XYZ Corp.

By: *Polly Promoter, CEO*

These types of signatures are still problematic. A basic rule of agency law is that an agent acting on behalf of a non-existent principal is personally liable. Here, the promoter is acting as the agent of a principal, the corporation, which does not exist yet. Once again, Polly could argue that the other party understood that the corporation, not Polly, would be liable under the contract, but she has an uphill battle in court.

In other cases, a promoter signs a contract on behalf of the corporation, but somehow indicates she is signing on behalf of a corporation that is not yet formed.

Illustrations:

XYZ Corp. *Polly Promoter, Promoter*

Or

Polly Promoter, Promoter of XYZ Inc., a corporation to be formed

Or

XYZ Corp., a corporation to be formed:

By: *Polly Promoter, Promoter*

These signatures give Polly a better argument that the other party understood (or should have reasonably understood) she as the promoter would not be liable under the contract, but it is not clear that she would prevail.

Because contract interpretation is based on the intent of the parties, taking an objective approach, the intent of the parties becomes a question for the court. Because the analysis is very fact-specific and may include facts of the conversations between the parties, past dealing between the parties, and other circumstances, it is hard to say how a court will decide on a matter based on any one particular signature format. However; we would expect courts to take one the following approaches, depending on the facts of the case:

(1) The promoter is personally liable; an agent is personally liable for contract she enters on behalf of a non-existent principal.
(2) The promoter is personally liable, and if the corporation is later formed and adopts the contract, both promoter and corporation will be liable.

(3) The promoter is relieved of liability if the corporation is later formed and adopts the contract.

No one, not even the other contracting party, is liable until the corporation is formed and adopts the contract (i.e., the third party has made a revocable offer to the corporation to-be-formed).

Promoter has merely made an implied promise to use her best efforts to cause the corporation to be formed.

Advice to client:

The conservative advice you might give the promoter is to suggest for her to wait until she has received confirmation of incorporation from the secretary of state. However, your job as a transactional lawyer is not to say, "Don't do it." Your job is to say, "Here are some possible ways to accomplish your goal."

If the promoter needs to enter into a transaction before incorporation, you can suggest these possible alternatives:

(1) She can try to **negotiate an assignable option** with the other party. In other words, the other party grants the promoter an option to rent the space, buy the goods, receive the services, provide the services, sell the goods, etc. When the corporation is formed, the promoter will transfer the option to the corporation and the corporation will exercise the option.

(2) You can draft the terms of the contract very clearly. It should **expressly state that promoter is not liable under the contract** and that she will make a good faith effort to incorporate and cause the corporation to adopt the contract.

Either of the alternatives above would work well for your client, but is the third party likely to agree to them? Neither of these arrangements provides the third party with a high level of certainty.

Maybe the following contractual provisions would be acceptable to the third party:

The promoter is liable under the contract until the corporation adopts the contract, at which point the corporation becomes liable and the promoter is relieved of liability.

The risk to your client is under this arrangement arises only if **the corporation is never formed or the never adopts the contract**. The risk will be nil if your client is the sole promoter, sole shareholder, and will completely control the corporation, because corporate adoption of the contract will be within her power. However, if there are other promoters and other shareholders, she might need their cooperation to cause the corporation to adopt the contract. Ideally, a shareholders agreement would address the adoption of this promoter contract and others like it.

Finally, you can suggest the promoter sign the contract on her own behalf and then cause the corporation to adopt the contract when the articles have been filed. This option has **additional risk – the risk of corporate breach/non-performance**. When the promoter signs on her own behalf, she bears liability even if the corporation adopts the contract as its own. The corporate adoption binds the corporation, but does not relieve the promoter of her liability. If the corporation fails to perform, the promoter will be liable for the breach.

You need to consider the following things as you advise your client: (1) will the promoter be in control of the corporation; (2) and will the corporation have the capability to perform the contract?

3B-403 **CATEGORY 2 – DEFECTIVE INCORPORATION:**

After taking steps to form the corporation, but before the secretary of state has actually filed the articles, the promoter signs a contract on behalf of the corporation. These cases often involve situations where the articles have been lost in the mail or where the secretary of state has rejected the articles for some sort of deficiency (e.g., an indistinguishable name). These fact patterns are often called **defective incorporation**.

Cases involving defective incorporation can arise when the contracting party sues the promoter personally for breach of the contract or when the "corporation" sues the contracting party for breach of the contract:

(1) The contracting party sues the promoter personally when the "corporation" breaches the contract.

Courts may apply the following doctrine to protect the promoter, depending on the jurisdiction:

> **De facto corporation** – A promoter will not be personally liable for contracts entered into on behalf of a nonexistent corporation if: (1) the jurisdiction has a valid incorporation statute; (2) **there was a good faith or colorable attempt to incorporate in compliance with the statute**; and (3) there was actual use of corporate privilege.

Note that some courts apply a similar doctrine under the moniker "Corporation by estoppel."

In situations where the other contracting party knows the articles had not yet been filed, but insists on execution of the contract in the name of the corporation, some courts might protect the promoter through corporation by estoppel.

> **Corporation by estoppel** – The contracting party is estopped from denying the existence of the corporation if it relied only on the credit of the "corporation," not the promoter.

(2) When the "corporation" sues the other party under the contract, that party may claim the contract is void because she signed a contract with a non-existing person. Possibilities include situations where the corporation is later formed or where the corporation is never formed.

Courts may apply **corporation by estoppel** to prevent the contracting party from escaping her obligations under the contract.

UNIT 3C

FORMATION – THE LLC:

3C-100 FORMATION MECHANICS FOR THE LLC - INTRODUCTION:

The legal process for organizing an LLC is virtually the same as the process for incorporating a corporation, with some conceptual differences and a few substantive differences. Instead of delivering articles of incorporation to the secretary of state, you deliver **articles of organization**.

3C-200 ARTICLES OF ORGANIZATION:

The articles of organization contain the most basic provisions regarding the governance and capital structure of the LLC. In addition, most LLC statutes envision, but do not require, the members of the LLC will enter into an **operating agreement**.

LLC statutes generally do not require or envision bylaws, but there is nothing preventing an LLC from creating bylaws. Most LLCs have simple articles of organization and an operating agreement with more details about form governance, rather than bylaws. In a single-member LLC, you will typical see either a very simple, bare-bones operating agreement or no operating agreement at all. Think of the operating agreement as a combination of corporation's bylaws and the shareholders agreement.

Although the LLC's articles of organization and operating agreement are the virtual equivalents of the corporation's articles of incorporation, bylaws and shareholders agreement, there is one significant substantive difference: between the members of the LLC, **the operating agreement takes precedence over the articles of organization**. If there is a conflict between the articles and the operating agreement about the relationship, rights and responsibilities of the members, the operating agreement controls.

> #### Illustration:
>
> Bob and Mary are the only two members of an LLC. The articles of organization state that the members will share profits equally, but the operating agreement states that 60% of the profits will go to Mary and 40% will go to Bob.
>
> The provisions of the operating agreement control: Mary gets 60% of the profits and Bob gets only 40%.

In contrast, when the dispute is between a third party and the LLC (or one of its members), **the articles will control when the third party has relied on the articles**.

> **Illustration:**
>
> Supplier is contemplating signing a long-term supply agreement with an LLC. Bob and Mary are members of the LLC. Supplier finds the LLC's articles of organization on file with the secretary of state. The articles state that all members of the LLC have the authority to bind the LLC to a contract. Supplier does not know that the LLC's operating agreement gives exclusive power to Bob to sign contracts on behalf of the LLC. Supplier enters into a contract with the LLC. Mary signs the contract on behalf of the LLC without Bob's knowledge. Bob claims the LLC is not bound by the contract.
>
> The provisions of the articles of organization control. The contract is binding on the LLC. However, with respect to the relationship between Bob and Mary; Mary has breached her contract with Bob.

What items of information must be in the articles of organization?

Similar to a corporation's articles of incorporation, an LLC's articles of organization can be very simple. ULLCA §203 only requires four items to be in the articles of organization:

1) The name of the company
2) The address of the company's initial designated office
3) The name and street address of the initial agent for service of process
4) The name and address of each organizer

You will notice that the above four items are virtually the same requirements for a corporation's articles of incorporation, except that the corporation's articles must have the number of authorized stock (more on that below).

In addition, there are several items that must be in the articles of organization, **but only if** they apply to the LLC in question

5) The **duration or term** of the company *if* it has a limited duration or term.
6) A provision stating that the LLC is **manager-managed** *if* it is to be managed by one or more managers, not by the members.
7) The names and addresses of the LLC's **initial managers** *if* it is to be managed by one or more managers, not by the members.

8) A provision providing that one or more **members of the LLC will be liable for the company's debts and obligations** _if_ one or more of the members do indeed agree to give up their limited liability.

The name of the company:

Under ULLCA §105, the name of the LLC must contain "limited liability company," "limited company," "LLC," "LC" or another abbreviated version. This name provides notice to those dealing with the company that the owners are protected by limited liability. Some jurisdictions may allow an LLC to simply use "company," "co.," or "ltd." Instead of the longer LLC monikers. Please note an LLC cannot use "inc.," "corp." or anything similar in its name because the LLC is not a corporation.

In addition, as we saw with the corporation, the name of the LLC must be distinguishable from any existing company which is organized in that state.[29]

The address of the company's initial designated office:

This requirement is the same requirement that the RMBCA has for providing the street address of the corporation's registered office. [30]

The name and street address of the initial agent for service of process:

This requirement is the same requirement that the RMBCA has for a corporation's articles – namely, the name of the initial registered agent at the corporation's registered office – except that the ULLCA has no express requirement that the agent's address coincide with the address of the LLC's designated office.[31]

The name and address of each organizer:

This requirement is the same requirement that the RMBCA has for a corporation's articles listing the incorporators.[32]

The duration or term of the company _if_ it has a limited duration or term:

The default rule for the LLC (as it is for the corporation) is perpetual existence. In other words, it will continue to exist until it is dissolved voluntarily by the members or by a court order. However, if one so desires, the LLC may have a specified duration, after which it will automatically dissolve. This duration must be in the articles.

---

[29] See §3B-201, above.

[30] See §3B-203, above.

[31] See §3B-204, above.

[32] See §3B-205, above.

Practice tip: Most LLC's are perpetual. It is rare that the parties will want their LLC to have a limited duration, but it is possible. There are certain ventures that may only take a limited amount of time to realize the full return on the investment. If the LLC is formed solely for that venture and we know the far end of the time line for realizing a full return on investment, we may choose to set up and LLC with a limited duration.

A provision stating that the LLC is manager-managed _if_ it is to be managed by one or more managers, not by the members:

As we discussed earlier in this chapter, the default rule for the LLC is that there is no centralized management – the members themselves directly manage the LLC's business and affairs. We also said that an LLC could draft out of the default rule and choose to have centralized management similar to that of the corporation. An LLC with centralized management is a **manager-managed LLC**. If the LLC elects to have centralized management through one or more managers, it must do so through a provision in its articles.

The names and addresses of the LLC's initial managers _if_ it is to be managed by one or more managers, not by the members:

If the LLC chooses to be a manager-managed LLC, it must list the name and addresses of the **initial** managers. In contrast, it is not mandatory for the corporation to list its initial directors in the articles of incorporation.

> *Practice tip:* Although the ULLCA never requires the LLCs articles of incorporation to be amended when the initial managers are replaced, it might be a good idea to do so to at least remove the name of the replaced manager. To a third party, the name of the former manager in the articles might create an incorrect, but reasonable, assumption that the former manager was a current manager, with the authority to bind the LLC. We will discuss the authority of managers to bind the LLC in Chapter 5.

A provision providing that one or more members of the LLC will be liable for the company's debts and obligations _if_ one or more of the members agree to give up their limited liability:

Members of the LLC enjoy limited liability, but they can elect to give it up. Often, members will give up their limited liability for specific transactions through agreement. For example, they might co-sign or guarantee a loan to the LLC. The members could also give up their limited liability wholesale through a provision in the articles.

Other provisions in the articles:

The articles of organization may have other provisions regarding the governance of the company that are inconsistent with the relevant LLC statute.

Provisions that are typically omitted from the articles of organization:

The authorized capital: You will remember that the articles of incorporation for a corporation must provide the authorized capital of the corporation. So for example, if the authorized capital of a corporation is 10,000 shares, the board of director could issue up to 10,000 shares to one or more investors without having to amend the articles. If the board wanted to issue more than 10,000 shares, the shareholders would have to approve an amendment to the articles to increase the number of authorized shares.

In contrast, LLCs do not usually have authorized capital. LLCs do not have shares or stock. Instead they have membership interests. Membership interests are usually expressed in terms of a percentage (e.g., 20% ownership interest) rather than in units (e.g., 55 ownership units). In addition, it is not as necessary for LLCs to have authorized capital. In a corporation, the authorized capital is a check on board discretion to issue stock. The shareholders give the board the discretion to issue stock only up to the limit stated in the articles. In the LLC, because the default rule is that the members directly manage the affairs of the company, including the issuance of new membership interests, there is no need for a check on a board of directors. In addition, the default rule for LLCs is that **no new members can be admitted without the unanimous consent of all the current members**. In other words, any member can prevent the LLC from issuing new membership interests. Under these default rules, authorized capital would be superfluous. We will discuss the transfer of membership interests in more detail in Chapter 7.[33]

Of course, the LLC is a very flexible entity: you can make it closely resemble a corporation if that is your client's wishes. The more it resembles a corporation – with centralized management and freely transferable ownership interests – the more you may want to consider having ownership interests expressed in units and a maximum authorized capital. In a manager-managed LLC, you may want to draft authorized capital into the articles of organization and the operating agreement to allow the managers to raise capital from new members without the need to receive the approval of the current members.

The names of the members are and their relative ownership percentages: There is really no purpose for listing the names of the

---

[33] See Chapter 7, §7C-300 et seq.

members or their ownership percentages in the articles of organization. LLC membership interests are not freely transferable without the consent of each of the other members, so listing the names of members in the articles would be a superfluous attempt to restrict the transfer of shares.[34] The articles are a public document. Unless there is some reason your client wants to make it publicly available that she is a member of the LLC, you should consider not listing her name in the articles. On the other hand, listing the members' names in the articles might make it easier for third parties to determine whether the person they are dealing with actually has the power to bind the LLC. In Chapter 5, we will discuss the authority of members to bind an LLC. [35]

The LLC's purpose: The law does not usually require the LLC to have a specific purpose in its articles. You should only state a purpose if the parties want to limit the activities of the LLC.[36]

3C-300 ANNUAL FILINGS FOR THE LLC:

See Annual Filings for the Corporation at §3B-303, above.

3C-400 REGISTERING AS A FOREIGN LLC:

See Registering as a Foreign Corporation at §3B-304, above.

3C-500 DOING BUSINESS UNDER AN ASSUMED NAME (D/B/A):

See Doing Business under an Assumed name at §3B-305, above.

3C-600 OPERATING AGREEMENT:

If the LLC has more than one member, you should strongly advise your client to have an **operating agreement**. The operating agreement is roughly analogous to the bylaws and the shareholders' agreement in the corporation.[37]

---

[34] We will discuss the transferability of membership interests in greater detail in Chapter 7, §7C-300 et seq.

[35] See Chapter 5, §5C-104 et seq.

[36] See §3B-205, above

[37] See §3B-400, above.

However, because the default rules for internal governance of the LLC are much more flexible, **an operating agreement is essential for an LLC with more than one member** to outline the voting rights of the members and how decisions will be made.[38]

The operating agreement will address three major issues:

1) The organization of the firm including each member's promise to purchase a certain percentage of the company's membership interests for a certain price.

2) The governance of the firm (e.g., voting, meetings, responsibilities/offices of each member, etc.)

3) The transfer of membership interest to third parties and other members.

Under RULLCA, an operating agreement is valid even if it is not in writing, but you should advise your client to reduce the agreement to writing to minimize the potential for disputes.

3C-700 **LLC PROMOTER LIABILITY:**

See Promoter Liability at §3B-400 et seq., above.

---

[38] For a detailed discussion of these issues, see Chapter 5, Unit 5C, LLCs – The Decision-Making Processes.

UNIT 3D

FORMATION – THE PARTNERSHIP:

3D-100 THE DIFFERENT TYPES OF PARTNERSHIPS:

There are actually several different forms of partnerships. We will focus on three of them:

(1) The general partnership (GP)
(2) The limited partnership (LP)
(3) The limited liability partnership (LLP)

3D-200 THE GENERAL PARTNERSHIP:

3D-201 THE GENERAL PARTNERSHIP – FORMATION:

The general partnership is the traditional partnership. It has two very important characteristics:

(1) Its partners **are not protected by limited liability**.
(2) Its formation requires **no governmental filings or fees**.

Two or more persons may create a partnership simply by saying "let's be partners." However, the parties do not have to use any magic words such as "partner" or "partnership" to form a partnership. In fact, a business with two or more owners is a partnership even if the parties have not gone through the process of forming a business entity, such as a corporation or an LLC.

The legal definition of general partnership is **two or more persons carrying on as co-owners of a business for profit**. An enterprise that fits this definition is a general partnership even if the parties had no intent to form a partnership.

Courts often **consider the following factors** to help them determine whether a person was acting as a **co-owner**:

Did she **contribute cash or property** to the enterprise?

Did she **share profits**?

Did she **share losses**?

84

Did she have **control** over the business?

Whether a person was a partner in a business is important for two reasons:

> If she is a partner, she will be personally liable for the business's debts. In fact, most of these cases arise because a plaintiff cannot recover from a business. She sues the defendant, claiming she should be allowed to recover from defendant's personal assets because defendant was a partner in the business.

> If she is a partner, she will have to share profits with her co-partners.

3D-202 THE GENERAL PARTNERSHIP – LEGAL CONSEQUENCES:

As you proceed through this text and your course, you will understand the full legal consequences of being a partner in a general partnership. However, the most important consequences for you to grasp right now are:

(1) A partner is **personally liable for debts of the partnership**: This means that partners do not enjoy limited liability.[39] However, RUPA requires the **partnership's creditors to first seek satisfaction of their claims out of the partnership's assets** before trying to recover from the personal assets the partners.[40] After the partnership's assets have been exhausted, the creditors may recover from the personal assets of the partners. In that sense, **the partners are the guarantors of the partnership's debts**.

(2) Each partner is **jointly and severally liable** for the debts of the partnership.[41] This means that if you are a partner, you alone might have to pay off all of the partnership's debts. You can sue the other partners for **contribution** to recover their share of the partnership's debts that you have paid on their behalf.

(3) A partner is **not personally liable for debts the partnership incurs before she became a partner**.[42] A partner is **not personally liable for debts the partnership incurs after she dissociates from the partnership** (i.e., exits, withdraws, or leaves the partnership).[43]

---

[39] RUPA §306(a).

[40] RUPA §307(d).

[41] RUPA §306(a).

[42] RUPA §306(b).

[43] RUPA §703(a).

(4) Each partner has **equal rights to participate in the partnership's business**[44] and the **authority to bind the partnership to contracts** with third parties.[45] The partners can change this rule by agreement.

3D-203 THE GENERAL PARTNERSHIP VERSUS THE JOINT VENTURE:

A joint venture is simply a business venture for a specific purpose. A joint venture is just a partnership by another name. When people make a distinction between a partnership and a joint venture, they are really simply trying to determine the scope of the business.

Illustration 1:

We decide to go into business together to develop condominium communities whenever we find a good opportunity. Generally, we would call this a partnership.

Illustration 2:

We decide to go into business together to develop a condominium community on a specific plot of land. We might call this a joint venture, which is really just a partnership with a limited scope. We could also call it a partnership.

In any case, calling a business enterprise a partnership or a joint venture is just a start to determining the scope of the business venture.

3D-300 THE LIMITED PARTNERSHIP (LP):

3D-301 THE LIMITED PARTNERSHIP (LP) – INTRODUCTION:

The limited partnership is a partnership with two classes of partners: general partners and limited partners.

General partners are not protected with limited liability

Limited partners enjoy limited liability

---

[44] RUPA §401(f).

[45] See Chapter 5, §5B-203 et seq.

3D-302 THE LIMITED PARTNERSHIP (LP) – FORMATION:

Formation of a limited partnership **requires governmental filings** similar to those required for corporations and LLCs. The limited partnership must have "LP," "limited partnership" or some variation in its name.

3D-303 THE LIMITED PARTNERSHIP (LP) – LEGAL CONSEQUENCES:

A **general partner** is **personally liable** for debts of the limited partnership and has the **right to participate in the partnership's business** and the **authority to bind the partnership to contracts** with third parties.[46]

A **limited partner** enjoys **limited liability** but has **no management rights** and has **no authority** to bind the partnership. The limited partner is analogous to the passive shareholder in the corporation.

3D-400 THE LIMITED LIABILITY PARTNERSHIP (LLP):

3D-401 THE LIMITED LIABILITY PARTNERSHIP (LLP) – INTRODUCTION:

The LLP is a general partnership where the partners enjoy some aspects of limited liability, but not full limited liability.

3D-402 THE LIMITED LIABILITY PARTNERSHIP (LLP) – FORMATION:

Formation of a limited liability partnership **requires governmental filings** similar to those required for corporations and LLCs. The limited liability partnership must have "LLP," "limited liability partnership" or some variation in its name.

---

[46] See §3D-202, above

3D-403 THE LIMITED LIABILITY PARTNERSHIP (LLP) – LEGAL CONSEQUENCES:

The partners of the LLP are **general partners**,[47] each with the **right to participate in the partnership's business** and the **authority to bind the partnership to contracts** with third parties.[48]

The partners receive some limited liability protection, but do not enjoy complete limited liability. Jurisdictions vary on what level of limited liability protection partners receive in LLPs. When reading the relevant statute, you need to ask yourself whether the partner is personally liable for: [49]

1) Torts committed by another partner in the course of the business (usually malpractice)

2) Torts committed by the partnerships employees

3) Partnership contractual obligations.

---

[47] In some jurisdictions, the LLP may also have limited partners. These types of partnerships are called "limited liability limited partnerships – LLLPs".

[48] See §3D-202, above

[49] RUPA §306(c) is the relevant RUPA provision.

CHAPTER 4
RAISING CAPITAL

UNIT 4A
RAISING CAPITAL – THE CORPORATION:

4A-100 **RAISING CAPITAL – INTRODUCTION:**

4A-200 **EQUITY FINANCING – STOCK:**

    4A-201   EQUITY FINANCING – THE FOUR STAGES:
        4A-201(a)   FIRST-STAGE EQUITY FINANCING – FOUNDERS, FRIENDS, AND FAMILY:
        4A-201(b)   SECOND-STAGE EQUITY FINANCING – ANGEL INVESTORS:
        4A-201(c)   THIRD-STAGE EQUITY FINANCING – VENTURE CAPITAL INVESTORS:
        4A-201(d)   FOURTH-STAGE EQUITY FINANCING – IPO OR ACQUISITION:
    4A-202   CONTROL RIGHTS OF STOCKHOLDERS:
    4A-203   ECONOMIC RIGHTS OF STOCKHOLDERS:
    4A-204   CLASSES OF STOCK – COMMON AND PREFERRED:
        4A-204(a)   COMMON STOCK:
        4A-204(b)   PREFERRED STOCK:
        4A-204(c)   OTHER CLASSES OF STOCK:
        4A-204(d)   SERIES OF STOCK:
        4A-204(e)   S-CORP STATUS AND CLASSES OR SERIES OF STOCK:
    4A-205   ISSUING STOCK – THE PROCESS:
        4A-205(a)   AUTHORIZED CAPITAL:
        4A-205(b)   CONSIDERATION FOR STOCK:
        4A-205(c)   PAR VALUE AND STATED VALUE:

4A-300 **DEBT FINANCING AND THE CORPORATION:**

    4A-301   TRADITIONAL LENDING:
    4A-302   DEBT SECURITIES:

4A-400 **SECURITIES LAW:**

    4A-401   WHAT ARE SECURITIES REGULATIONS?
    4A-402   WHAT IS A SECURITY?
        4A-402(a)   CORPORATIONS:
        4A-402(b)   LLCS AND PARTNERSHIPS:

UNIT 4D
<u>Business Valuation – The Basics:</u>

UNIT 4A

RAISING CAPITAL – THE CORPORATION:

4A-100 RAISING CAPITAL – INTRODUCTION:

As we briefly discussed in Chapter 2, a corporation can raise capital to finance its various projects by issuing equity securities (i.e., "stock") to investors or by borrowing money.[50] We also said that there are two ways a corporation can borrow money to finance its projects: (1) it could borrow from traditional lenders, such as banks or a group of banks working together; or (2) it could issue debt securities to a large number of investors.

In this section, we will explore the most common types of equity and debt securities that corporations issue.

4A-200 EQUITY FINANCING – STOCK:

A corporation will issue stock to its initial stockholders soon after its incorporation. Later in its existence, the corporation might issue stock to existing stockholders or new stockholders to raise capital for various projects. The corporation's stockholders have certain control rights and economic rights.

4A-201 EQUITY FINANCING – THE FOUR STAGES:

This section provides a stylized and simplified model of the equity financing stages of a company. Although it is not accurate for all companies, it will help you gain a basic understanding of the stages of equity financing for a corporation.

4A-201(a) FIRST-STAGE EQUITY FINANCING – FOUNDERS, FRIENDS, AND FAMILY:

At this stage, the founders provide the capital the corporation will need for its initial planning and set-up. The founders often ask their friends and family members to invest.

---

[50] See Chapter 2, §2-107 et seq.

4A-201(b) SECOND-STAGE EQUITY FINANCING – ANGEL INVESTORS:

At this stage, the corporation needs some more substantial investment to finance its operations and implement its business plan. It might seek investment from angel investors. Although there is no set definition for "angel investor," the paradigm is the wealthy entrepreneur who has already lead her own company to success. She is now interested in being involved in a new venture. In addition to providing capital, the angel investor will often provide advice, guidance, and leverage her business connections for the company.

Not all companies seek angel investment. Some are able to attract venture capital investment at early stages (see next stage).

4A-201(c) THIRD-STAGE EQUITY FINANCING – VENTURE CAPITAL INVESTORS:

When the company needs a major capital influx to realize its business plan, it will often seek out venture capital funding. In the venture capital market, there are venture capital funds seeking investment opportunities. Most of the famous technology companies you are familiar with received venture capital funding at various stages in their development before becoming the large public companies that they are today. For example, venture capital investment played a large role in helping Google and Facebook develop their businesses and eventual become major players in the global internet market.

The basic strategy for a venture capital fund is to take an equity stake (i.e., become a shareholder) in a company that has great potential for growth. Naturally, there is great risk in investing in these companies, so venture capital funds expect high returns. In addition, venture capital funds invest in many companies to diversify their investment risks. Most of the venture capital funds investments will fail, but as long as there are one or two successful companies in its portfolio, the venture capital fund will generate a return for its investors.

Success for the venture capital fund usually takes the form of one of the following two possible scenarios: (1) the company the fund has invested in makes an **initial public offering (IPO)** and lists its stock on a public securities exchange, or (2) a larger, more established company acquires the company the fund has invested in.

4A-201(d) FOURTH-STAGE EQUITY FINANCING – IPO OR ACQUISITION:

After one or more successful rounds of venture capital financing, the company will often reach a stage where it needs more capital to implement its long-term business strategy. An IPO or an acquisition will provide the company with the additional resources it needs. In addition, the venture capital funds hope to eventually exit their investments in the company, which can be achieved through an IPO or an acquisition.

In either the **IPO scenario** or **acquisition scenario**, the venture capital fund is able to **exit its investment** (i.e., sell its shareholdings), hopefully for a profit. In the IPO scenario, the venture capital fund sells its shareholdings to the public. In the acquisition scenario, the acquirer will normally buy out the venture capital fund's shareholdings.

4A-202 CONTROL RIGHTS OF STOCKHOLDERS:

Stockholders, as a group, have a bundle of **limited control rights**. They do not have the right to directly control the corporation's ordinary business matters. Their control rights are limited to electing the board of directors and approving certain fundamental changes to the corporation. We will discuss shareholder voting rights in greater detail in Chapters 5 and 9.

4A-203 ECONOMIC RIGHTS OF STOCKHOLDERS:

The stockholders' **economic claim** on the corporation's assets is the claim to the **residual**. The residual is the value of the assets that remain after the corporation pays its creditors. In practical terms, the shareholders' residual claim is a right to the **residual in liquidation** and the right to the **residual of the going concern**:

> **Residual in liquidation:** Liquidation normally occurs after the company formally dissolves. We will discuss dissolution in more detail in Chapter 9, but for now you should consider it the formal end of a corporation's legal existence. When a company dissolves, it goes through a process of liquidation, which simply means it turns its assets into cash by selling the assets or collecting from its debtors. The company uses the liquidation proceeds to pay its creditors. Any remaining assets are distributed to the shareholders.

> **Residual of the going concern:** When a business is still operating, we say it is a going concern. The shareholders' residual claim in a going concern is effectively the **right to the corporation's profits** ("earnings"). Sometimes a corporation will distribute some or all of the profits to the shareholders in the form of a cash **dividend**. However, the shareholders do not have an absolute right to receive dividends. Generally, the board of directors has complete discretion over the issuance of dividends to the shareholders. Even when the board decides not to distribute the profits to the shareholders, the profits are still considered part of the shareholders' residual claim. If the corporation does not distribute all or part of its profits to shareholders, it credits the shareholders' account with the profits. This account is called **retained earnings**. Similarly, if

the company suffers a loss, the company will reduce the shareholders' claim by reducing the retained earnings account. You can find this account on the balance sheet under owners' equity (or shareholders' equity). Here's an example how it works:

Company makes a net profit of $100,000.

Company distributes $20,000 to shareholders in the form of a cash dividend.

The company increases the shareholders' retained earnings account by $80,000.

Please note: The retained earnings account is not an actual bank account containing cash set aside for shareholders. The company is allowed to spend any cash that represents the retained earnings. Think of **retained earnings** as an *accounting* reserve, not an actual *cash reserve*. The idea is that the number in the retained earnings account is backed by actual assets – cash, real property, equipment, intangible property, or money owed to the company. If the number in the retained earnings is not backed by sufficient assets, the retained earnings account will naturally be reduced through the accounting and bookkeeping processes.

4A-204 CLASSES OF STOCK – COMMON AND PREFERRED:

The stockholders, as a group, have the residual claim, but a corporation can divide that claim among different classes of stock. For example, one class of stock might have a right to a greater dividend than another class of stock.

Theoretically, there are an unlimited number of possible different classes and variations of stock, but there are two major categories we see most often – **common stock** and **preferred stock**.

4A-204(a) COMMON STOCK:

The first type of equity interest in a corporation is called "common" or "common stock." When people think of stock ownership, they are usually thinking of common stock. If your friend suggests you buy 100 shares of Citigroup stock, she is almost certainly referring to Citigroup's common stock, not its preferred stock. When you hear on the financial news that PG&E stock has risen, it is PG&E's common stock they are referring to. Both Citigroup and PG&E have outstanding preferred stock, but that is not the stock people usually mean when they refer to "stockholders."

Common stock is the **default stock interest**. For example, if the articles of incorporation have 1,000 authorized shares, and they do not specify different

96

classes of stock, all 1,000 shares are common stock. If common stock is a corporation's only class of stock, then the common stockholders have the entire residual claim and the whole package of shareholder control rights. However, if there are other classes of stock, the common will share the residual claim and/or voting rights with the other classes.

A stockholder shares in the residual claim in proportion to her stockholdings.

> **Illustration:**
>
> LMN Corp. has 5,000 authorized shares, of which 1,000 shares issued and outstanding. The board of directors decides to distribute a cash dividend of $10,000 to the common shareholders. Mary owns 50 shares of LMN Corp.'s common stock. Her share of the dividend is $500 [50/1,000 x $10,000 = $500]

4A-204(b) PREFERRED STOCK:

Preferred stock is a class of stock that has some sort of **preference or priority over the common stock**. The terms of the preferred must be in the articles of incorporation. Usually, the preference addresses economic rights, but sometimes the preference will address voting rights. The typical economic preferences are **dividend and liquidation preferences**.

Dividend preference: .Before the common stock receives their dividends, the preferred stock must receive their dividend. A dividend preference does not give the preferred stockholders an absolute right to receive dividends. It simply gives them a priority over the common stock to any dividends the corporation's board of directors decides to issue.

> **Illustration:**
>
> "$10.00 preferred stock" would receive a $10 dividend per share before the common stock could receive any dividend. If the company does not pay a dividend to the preferred stockholders, the common stockholders will not receive any dividend. Similarly, if the corporation only pays a $5.00 dividend per share to the preferred stockholders, the common stockholders will not receive any dividend.

A dividend preference may be **cumulative** or **non-cumulative**, **participating** or **non-participating**.

> **Cumulative dividend preference:** If the corporation fails to pay the preferred shareholders a dividend one year, or pays less than the full amount, the amount of the dividend shortfall is added to next year. In other words, the **unpaid dividends accumulate from year to year**.

Illustration:

The corporation does not distribute any dividend to the holders of the "$10.00 cumulative preferred." Next year, the preferred stockholders would be entitled to receive a $20 dividend per share before the common stock could receive any dividend.

Non-cumulative dividend preference: The unpaid dividends in any year are lost forever for the preferred stockholders. The **unpaid dividends do not accumulate from year to year**.

Illustration:

The corporation does not distribute any dividend to the holders of the "$10.00 non-cumulative preferred." Next year, the preferred stockholders would only be entitled to receive a $10 dividend per share before the common stock could receive a dividend.

> *Practice tip:* When drafting the terms of preferred stock, you should expressly state whether the dividend preference is cumulative or non-cumulative. You can find cases that support the proposition that if the articles are silent as to whether the dividend preference is cumulative, a court will assume it is cumulative. Nonetheless, you should draft terms of the preferred clearly to avoid disputes and litigation.

Participating dividend preference: If the holders of preferred stock have a participating dividend preference, it means they double dip on the dividend. The holders of participating preferred stockholders not only receive a dividend before the common, they **also share in any dividend distributed to the common**. They may be **fully participating**, which means they would share equally any dividend the common stockholders receive. They may be **partially participating**, in which case they would receive some ratio of the dividend issued to the common stockholders (e.g., 2:1, 1:3, etc.) or a fixed amount.

Non-participating dividend preference: If preferred stock does not share in the dividend the common receives, it is non-participating preferred.

Liquidation preference: If the company dissolves, liquidates it assets, and pays off its creditors, the holders of preferred stock with a liquidation preference will receive their share of the remainder before the common stock receives any. A liquidation preference might be expressed in specific amount – e.g., $75 per share – or it may be expressed in a ratio compared to the common – e.g. 2:1.

Other economic terms of preferred stock: The above preferences are the preferred terms we see most often, but you may draft any type of terms you want. For example, the terms of preferred might give the preferred shareholders a right to a party, with ice-cream cake, a clown, and a pony. It is a silly example, but it demonstrates the flexibility that corporate law permits in creating the terms of preferred stock. There are some other common terms we often see in preferred stock.

> **Convertible preferred:** Preferred stock can be drafted to give the preferred shareholders an option to convert their preferred shares into common stock at a set ratio. Preferred shareholders will want this option if they think there is potential that the common stock of the company will become more valuable in the future.

> Venture capital investors often get convertible preferred. They will convert to common when the company is about to go public and list its shares on a stock exchange or when the company is about to be merged into another corporation.

> **Callable, redeemable:** If preferred stock is redeemable or callable at the option of the corporation, the corporation has the option to repurchase the preferred shares at a set price. If preferred stock is redeemable or callable at the option of the preferred shareholders, the preferred shareholders have the option to force the corporation to repurchase the preferred shares at a set price.

Voting rights of preferred stock Error! Bookmark not defined.**:** It is possible to draft preferred stock with a voting preference. For example, we could draft a class of stock that has two votes per share, while the common only has one vote per share.

> **Right to elect directors**: When we see preferred stock in a public company, the terms of the preferred stock do not usually give preferred shareholders any right to vote to elect directors unless the corporation has failed to pay dividends to the preferred stockholders for several dividend periods.

> In contrast, when venture capitalist funds purchase preferred stock in a private company, the terms of the preferred will normally give the venture capital funds a right to elect a certain percentage of the board of directors.

> **Right to vote on fundamental matters:** Often, the terms of the preferred will give preferred shareholders a right to vote on fundamental transactions, such as an amendment to the articles, a merger, dissolution, etc. When the terms of the preferred are silent regarding the right to vote on fundamental matters, or even when the terms specifically provide that the preferred stock is **non-voting**, corporate law statutes

normally give preferred shareholders the right to vote on fundamental transactions that affect the preferred. For example, the common shareholders could not amend the articles of incorporation to reduce the dividend preference of the preferred without the approval of the preferred stockholders, even if preferred is non-voting preferred. We will explore in greater detail the legal rights of non-voting stock in Chapter 5.

4A-204(c) OTHER CLASSES OF STOCK:

Although common stock and preferred stock are the most widely-used classes of stock, parties are free to create whatever classes of stock they want.

Illustration:

If Agnes, Betty, and Cecil want to create a corporation where they will each serve on the board of directors, we could create three classes of stock: Class A, Class B, and Class C. We could draft the terms in the articles so that the board of directors is comprised of three directors and each class has the right to elect one director. When the corporation issues and sells the stock, Agnes gets all the Class A stock and can elect herself to the board, and so on.

4A-204(d) SERIES OF STOCK:

Normally, we say that common stock and preferred stock are different "classes" of stock. If your company issues different types of preferred stock, these are usually called "series" of preferred stock. Typically, a company would have two "classes" of stock, common and preferred, and two or more "series" of preferred stock.

There is no rule dictating how a corporation must name the different series of preferred stock, but you would not be surprised to find that the first series issued is often called Series A, and the next series is called Series B, and so on. The different rights of each series of a particular class of stock will be spelled out in the articles of incorporation.

Illustration:

Company XYZ is seeking venture capital investment, and it expects that it might go through several rounds.

In the **first round** of venture capital investment, the VCs invest $2 million dollars in the company and receive **Series A** cumulative preferred stock, with a preference over the common stock.

After the first round of VC financing, the company struggles with its business. Its prospects for long-term success are more doubtful. The company needs more capital, but it is now a **riskier investment**.

In the **second round** of venture capital investment, the new VCs invest $1 million dollars in the company and receive **Series B** cumulative preferred stock, with a preference over the common stockholders and the Series A stockholders.

After the second round of VC financing, the company's business develops very favorably. Its long-term prospects improve dramatically. It is now a much **less risky investment**.

In the **third round** of venture capital investment, the new VCs invest $2 million dollars in the company and receive **Series C** cumulative preferred stock, with a preference over the common stock, but subordinated to the Series A and Series B preferred stockholders.

4A-204(e) S-CORP STATUS AND CLASSES OR SERIES OF STOCK:

Different classes of stock may be incompatible with a corporation's pass-through taxation status under Subchapter S. One of the requirements of Subchapter S is that the corporation (or LLC) can only have one class of stock with respect to economic rights.[51] A Subchapter S corporation (or LLC) may have different classes of stock if the only difference between the classes is voting rights.

Illustration 1:

A corporation has two classes of stock: Class A and Class B. The holders of each class have the same dividend rights and liquidation rights in proportion to their shareholdings. The Class A shareholders have the right to elect twice as many directors as Class B shareholders, regardless of the number of shares issued and outstanding for each class.

The different classes of stock do not disqualify the corporation from Subchapter S pass-through taxation because they only have different voting rights.

Illustration 2:

A corporation has two classes of stock: Class A and Class B. Class A shares have a $2.00 dividend preference over Class B shares.

The different classes of stock disqualify the corporation from Subchapter S pass-through taxation because they have different economic rights.

Sometimes students misunderstand this Subchapter S requirement to mean that all *shareholders* must have the same economic rights. In fact, all

---

[51] See Chapter 3, §3A-404.

shares must have the same economic rights, but the shareholders may have different economic rights in proportion to their shareholdings.

> ### Illustration:
>
> A corporation has one class of stock and two shareholders. Bob owns 30 shares and Mary owns 70 shares. Bob is only entitled to 30% of the residual because he only owns 30% of the outstanding stock. Mary is entitled to 70% of the residual because she owns 70% of the outstanding stock.
>
> The difference between the two shareholders does not disqualify the corporation from Subchapter S pass-through taxation because each share of stock has the same economic rights.

4A-205 ISSUING STOCK – THE PROCESS:

4A-205(a) AUTHORIZED CAPITAL:

Raising capital through the issue of stock is a business decision for the board of directors. However, the board can only issue new shares if the corporation has a **sufficient number of authorized shares** remaining.

> ### Illustration:
>
> A corporation's articles have 1,000 common shares authorized, of which 800 shares are issued and outstanding. The board cannot issue more than 200 additional shares unless the shareholders approve an amendment to the articles of incorporation increasing the number of authorized shares.

If the articles do not specify otherwise, authorized stock is all common stock. If there is not enough authorized stock in the articles, the company must first amend the articles to increase the number of authorized stock. Amendment of the articles requires shareholder approval.

Preferred stock and its terms must also be specified in the articles in order for the corporation to issue any preferred stock, which creates some practical problems. A corporation may need a certain amount of flexibility to issue preferred stock that meet current market demands. By the time the shareholders meet to approve the amendment of the articles of incorporation, the market may have changed. To avoid this problem, and to give corporations the flexibility they need to tailor their preferred stock to current market demands, many state corporate law statutes allow what is commonly called **blank check preferred**.

Blank check preferred simply means that the articles of incorporation give the board the discretion to determine the terms of preferred stock and amend the articles of incorporation without shareholder approval.

The RMBCA allows a corporation to authorize blank check preferred. RMBCA §6.02 provides:

> If the articles of incorporation so provide, the board of directors is authorized, without shareholder approval, to:
>
> > (1) classify any unissued shares into one or more classes or into one or more series within a class,
> >
> > (2) reclassify any unissued shares of any class into one or more classes or into one or more series within one or more classes, or
> >
> > (3) reclassify any unissued shares of any series of any class into one or more classes or into one or more series within a series

Example of blank check preferred:

The Walt Disney Company has the following two provisions in its certificate of incorporation:

> . . . The total number of shares of stock which the Corporation shall have authority to issue is 4,700,000,000, of which 4,600,000,000 shares shall be shares of common stock having a par value of $.01 per share ("Common Stock") and 100,000,000 shares shall be shares of preferred stock having a par value of $.01 per share ("Preferred Stock") and issuable in one or more classes or series as hereinafter provided. . . .

> Shares of the Preferred Stock of the Corporation may be issued from time to time in one or more classes or series, each of which class or series shall have such distinctive designation, number of shares, or title as shall be fixed by the Board of Directors prior to the issuance of any shares thereof. Each such class or series of Preferred Stock shall consist of such number of shares, and have such voting powers, full or limited, or no voting powers, and such preferences and relative, participating, optional or other special rights and such qualifications, limitations or restrictions thereof, as shall be stated in such resolution or resolutions providing for the issue of such series of Preferred Stock as may be adopted from time to time by the Board of Directors prior to the issuance of any shares thereof pursuant to the authority hereby expressly vested in it, all in accordance with the laws of the State of Delaware. By Certificate of Designations dated November 17, 1999, the

Corporation authorized the issuance of Series A Voting Preferred Stock, a copy of which Certificate of Designations is attached hereto as Exhibit A. . . .

With respect to Disney's preferred stock, these provisions tell us:

(1) Disney's certificate of incorporation authorizes the board to issue and sell up to 100 million shares of preferred stock;

(2) Disney's board has the discretion to determine the terms of the preferred stock and amend the articles accordingly; and

(3) Disney issued a series of preferred stock in November of 1999, the board determined the terms of that preferred stock series, and the board amended the certificate to include the terms of the newly issued preferred (amended by an exhibit called a Certificate of Designations).

How does a company determine the terms of the preferred? The terms of the preferred are a product of market forces. Let's look at how market forces operate in two different scenarios:

Scenario #1 – The private placement: When a company wants to sell preferred stock to a specific investor or group of investors, it will actually negotiate the terms of the preferred and the price per share with the investors. The parties will come to an agreement about the preferences, voting rights, convertibility and other terms.

Scenario #2 – The public offering: When a company wants to sell preferred stock to the public at large, it will have to gauge the market's appetite for price and terms. Normally, when a company makes a public offering of its securities, it engages an investment bank to advise on market conditions and help sell the securities. The investment bank is familiar with the current securities market and has connections with the large institutional investors that routinely purchase securities in public offerings.

4A-205(b) **CONSIDERATION FOR STOCK:**

A corporation may issue stock in exchange for **cash**, of course. In addition, the corporation may accept other **property** and **services** in exchange for stock, which is more common in the context of the small, closely-held corporation. A **promissory note** is also permitted consideration.

Property: Property includes personal property, real property and intellectual property, and other tangible and intangible property.

Services: Generally, corporate law statutes permit a corporation to issue stock in exchange for past services or a promise for future services. As an example, the New York Business Corporation act allows a corporation to issue its stock for "services rendered" or "a binding obligation to perform services having an agreed value."[52] When a corporation receives services in exchange for shares, lawyers tend to address the issue in a shareholders agreement, with an attached employment agreement.

Illustration:

Entrepreneur with an innovative business idea is seeking investment from venture capitalists. The venture capitalists will invest $1,000,000 for 60% of the stock of the company. They want the entrepreneur to have significant shareholdings in the company, to give her the proper incentives make the company successful. They agree that in exchange for 40% of the company's stock, the entrepreneur will act as the company's CEO. The company and the CEO enter into an employment agreement.

Promissory note: It is common for corporate law statutes to permit the issuance of stock to an investor in exchange for the investor's binding promise to pay cash. This binding promise usually takes the form of a promissory note.

When the corporation receives consideration other than money for its shares, the incorporators, the directors, or the shareholder must make a determination of the fair value of the consideration. There are also tax issues that the parties must consider.[53]

4A-205(c) PAR VALUE AND STATED VALUE:

Some state corporate law statutes require each share of a corporation's stock to have a par value. This par value must be provided in the company's articles of incorporation. The law generally gives the corporation great latitude to determine the par value of its stock. For example, the corporation may assign a par value of one cent (or less) to each share of common stock.

Par value is confusing because it is largely arbitrary. One of the most important things for you to remember is that **par value does not represent the market value of the shares, nor does it represent the actual amount of consideration the company received for the shares**. Par value is merely a minimum amount of consideration the company may accept when it issues stock.

---

[52] New York Business Corporation Law §504

[53] See Chapter 3, §3A-600 et seq.

Illustration:

XYZ Company has 10,000 authorized shares of common stock, par value $1 per shares, which means the company cannot accept anything less than $1 per share for its common stock. The company issues 5,000 shares to investors, and the investors pay $20 per share.

Par value has two purposes:

(1) It assures the shareholder that other shareholders have paid a minimum amount for each share; and

(2) It is a factor in calculating the size of the dividend a corporation may distribute to its shareholders, which we will discuss in Chapter 10.[54]

When a corporation issues stock for less than par value it is called **watered stock**. The directors may be personally liable for the difference between the par value and the actual capital received for the stock.

Stated value (or legal value) is a similar concept to par value, except the board has the discretion to determine the minimum value of each share of stock each time they issue the stock. In a par value jurisdiction, the par value for any class of stock is in the articles of incorporation and may only be changed by amending the articles. In contrast, the stated value will not be in the articles of corporation; it comes about by board resolution each time the board issues stock.

Illustration:

XYZ Company has 10,000 authorized shares of common stock.

In 2015, the company issues 1,000 shares to investors, and the investors pay $20 per share. The board determines the legal value to be $1 per share.

In 2016, the company issues 4,000 shares to investors, and the investors pay $22 per share. The board determines the legal value to be $0.50 per share.

Usually, when a corporation has a par value or stated value for its stock, it is far below any estimated market value of the stock.

The RMBCA does not require a corporation to have a par value or stated value for its shares. However, a corporation in an RMBCA jurisdiction may assign a par value to its shares in its articles of incorporation if it chooses to do so.[55]

---

[54] See Chapter 10, §10A-202 et seq.

[55] RMBC §2.02(b)(2)(iv).

4A-300 DEBT FINANCING AND THE CORPORATION:

A corporation may borrow money from a bank or other traditional lender. Current shareholders can also be a source of credit. Finally, instead of borrowing from one lender or a small group of lenders, a corporation can borrow from the market by issuing debt securities.

The corporation's board decides whether to issue debt securities, just as the board would decide whether to borrow money from a bank. Unless the articles of incorporation provide otherwise, **the shareholders have no say** in the decision to borrow money.

4A-301 TRADITIONAL LENDING:

Traditional lending institutions, like commercial banks and credit unions, have loan programs for businesses. Large businesses can borrow large amounts of capital from individual banks or groups of banks. Lending institutions also lend to small businesses, but might require the shareholders to **co-sign** or **guaranty** the loan, at least until the business has an established history of credit. Requiring a shareholder to co-sign or act as guarantor for a loan to the corporation defeats the limited-liability default rules that would otherwise protect the shareholder from personal liability. If the corporation has sufficient collateral or adequate credit, the lender may not require the shareholder to co-sign or guaranty the loan.

The terms of these loans typically require the borrower to pay **interest** and **principal** each month, although they can be structured with repayment of the principal in several large payments during the term of the loan or one large payment at the end of the loan term.

Loans can be secured or unsecured. With a **secured loan**, the company or its guarantors provide collateral for the loan. The lender has lien on the specific collateral, and can foreclose and force the sale of the collateral if the company defaults on the loan. With an **unsecured loan**, the company puts up no collateral. Unsecured loans involve greater risk for the lender, so the interest rate will be higher.

In addition, it is common in closely-held corporations for **one of more of the shareholders to lend money to the corporation**. A shareholder that has lent money to the company is both an equity holder and a fixed claimant. The corporation usually executes a promissory note in favor of the lending shareholder.

107

4A-302 DEBT SECURITIES:

The sale of debt securities is similar, in some ways, to the sale of stock. The investor receives a portion of a claim against the company. In the case of stock, the claim is a portion of the residual claim. In the case of debt securities, the claim is a portion of a fixed claim.

The terms of debt securities will not be in the articles of incorporation. The terms of debt securities are contractual provisions between the corporation and the **debtholders**. The terms are effectively a loan agreement; The debtholders are creditors to the corporation and the terms of the debt securities are the terms of the loan.

Debt securities are generally referred to as **corporate bonds**, although we can divide them into several categories. There are an unlimited number of ways to draft debt securities, but the market normally lumps them into four broad categories:

Debentures:

Debentures are **long-term** obligations (10 to 30 years, or more) that are **not secured** by the borrower's assets.

Bonds:

Bonds are **long-term** obligations (10 to 30 years, or more) that are **secured** by the borrower's assets.

Notes (or Unsecured Notes):

Notes are **short-term** obligations (less than 10 years) that are **not secured** by assets.

Secured Notes:

Secured Notes are **short-term** obligations (less than 10 years) that are **secured** by the assets of the borrower or its guarantors.

Normally, the issuer of debt securities pays interest to the debtholders at regular intervals – quarterly or semiannually. At the end of the term of the securities, the issuer repays the entire principal.

The "loan agreement" between the company and the numerous debtholders is called an **indenture**. Because the debtholders suffer from a collective action problem, they are not in a good position to enforce their rights under the indenture, so there is usually a **trustee** who acts on behalf of all the debtholders.

———————

4A-400 SECURITIES LAW:

The sale of securities is **highly regulated** by federal and state law. Similar to business-entity taxation, securities law is a specialized area of law that requires you to acquire the relevant expertise or to work with someone with the relevant expertise.

Law schools have a separate course on securities regulation that you should take if you intend to practice in the area of business organizations. Until you take that course, or have otherwise acquired the relevant knowledge, you should at least understand the major issues.

4A-401 WHAT ARE SECURITIES REGULATIONS?

In short, securities laws have **registration and information requirements**:

> They prohibit any **sale** of securities or any **offer** to sell securities unless the securities are first **registered** with the proper state or federal government authorities.

> They also usually require that the seller **provide the prospective investor with specific information** about the company and the securities. The information must be in a specific format, called a **prospectus**.

Before your client sells a security or offers to sell a security, you must jump through many state and federal hoops. Because it can be very expensive to comply with all the rules, lawyers try to help their clients find exemptions from the securities laws.

4A-402 WHAT IS A SECURITY?

The definition of a security is very technical and can differ between federal law and state law and even from state to state. However, for the purposes of our course, there are a few things you need to remember:

4A-402(a) CORPORATIONS:

Any type of **stock is a security**. In addition, the **debt securities we listed above are all securities**.[56]

---

[56] See §4A-302, above.

4A-402(b) **LLCs AND PARTNERSHIPS:**

LLC membership interests and partnership interests may or may or may not be securities.[57]

4A-403 **HOW CAN MY CLIENT AVOID SECURITIES REGULATIONS?**

Federal and state securities laws generally provide that **any sale or offer to sell securities** must be **registered** with the relevant securities authorities and the potential investors must receive **specific information** about the company and the securities. To avoid the expense of these registration and information requirements, you will help your client **find an exemption** under the law.

4A-403(a) **FEDERAL SECURITIES LAW EXEMPTIONS:**

Theoretically, the registration and information requirements under federal law only apply to public offerings of securities. The paradigm of a **public offering** is the **IPO** (initial public offering). In an IPO, a private company decides it wants to "go public" and list its shares for trading on a stock exchange. It hires investment bankers, lawyers, accountants, and other advisors to help it navigate the market and the regulatory environment. In the end, it publicly advertises its offering to the world, sells it shares to interested investors, raises a large amount of cash, and lists its shares on a stock exchange (Nasdaq or NYSE, for example).

The federal Securities Act provides that a **non-public offering** (aka **private placement** is **exempt from federal registration and information requirements**. Unfortunately, it does not explain what qualifies as a non-public offering. Clearly, an IPO to thousands of potential investors would not qualify as a non-public offering, but would a sale of stock to 200 investors qualify as a non-public offering? How about a sale to 5 investors after the corporation had made offers to 200 investors? The answer for either is unclear under the Securities Act, although my best advice to my client, without any more facts, would be that neither would qualify for as a non-public offering.

To make matters even more complicated, the U.S. Supreme Court has interpreted "non-public offering" to mean: (1) there are only a few number of offerees; (2) the offerees are sophisticated enough to understand the investment; and (3) the offerees have sufficient information to evaluate the investment.[58]

The Securities and Exchange Commission (SEC) has created **safe-harbors and exemptions** from the registration and information requirements of federal

---

[57] See §§4B-400 and 4C-400, below.

[58] *Securities and Exchange Commission v. Ralston Purina Co.*, 346 U.S. 119 (1953),

securities law. If your client complies with any of these safe harbors or exemptions, it will not run afoul of federal securities laws. The safe harbors themselves are complicated and not susceptible to summary treatment here.

4A-403(b) STATE SECURITIES LAW EXEMPTIONS:

Once you have helped you client navigate federal securities law to find an exemption for its sale of securities, you must now do the same for state securities laws. Your client might have to comply with the securities laws of several states, depending on (1) where it is located, (2) to whom it is selling, and (3) where it negotiated the transaction, signed the purchase contract, or delivered the securities.

4A-404 WORDS OF ADVICE REGARDING THE SALE OF SECURITIES:

Never advertise your offering: Your client should never advertise its sale of securities or use any other method of **general solicitation**. Use of general solicitation is a **public offering**.

> *Illustration:*
>
> Your client is a corporation that sells smart-phone cases. It has a website. It plans to put the following note on its website:
>
> > "We are looking for investors. If you are interested in being a part of our exciting company, please contact us."
>
> Your advice should be a loud and emphatic **"Don't do it!!"** Work with a securities lawyer to help your client create a plan to raise capital. There are exceptions under federal securities law when your client will be allowed to engage in general solicitation of investors, but you first need to know whether your client's securities offering qualifies for these exceptions.

Don't say anything to investors that may be false or misleading: Even if your client qualifies for exemptions under state and federal securities laws, it is still subject to the anti-fraud provisions these laws. Any intentionally, knowingly, or recklessly false or misleading statement will expose the company, and the individual making the statement, to civil liabilities and possible criminal sanctions.

Issuing shares to founders? It's okay . . . probably: Attorneys rarely look for a safe harbor or an exemption for the issuance of stock from the newly formed corporation to the promoters and founders of the company. This type of issuance of shares is probably the only true non-public offering. However, if the purchaser of the shares is merely labeled "promoter" or "founder," without actually being a moving force behind the creation of the corporation, the company and those who control it are running a significant risk of violating the securities laws.

UNIT 4B

RAISING CAPITAL – THE LLC:

4B-100 RAISING CAPITAL – INTRODUCTION:

An LLC can raise capital through selling equity interests, borrowing from traditional lenders, or selling debt securities. An LLC is no different from a corporation in this respect.

4B-200 EQUITY FINANCING – MEMBERSHIP INTERESTS:

Equity interests in LLCs are called membership interests. Membership interests in LLCs have both economic rights and control rights.

4B-201 CONTROL RIGHTS OF MEMBERS:

Unlike the shareholders in a corporation, each member of an LLC has a right to participate directly in the management of the LLC, as a default rule. The parties may change this rule by agreeing that only certain members have a right to participate in management. Alternatively, the parties can adopt a manager-managed LLC model, with a centralized management structure. We will discuss management and control rights in LLCs in Chapter 5.

4B-202 ECONOMIC RIGHTS OF MEMBERS:

The members, as equity holders, have the right to the company's residual, just like the shareholders in a corporation. As we have already discussed, the residual claim is a right to the **residual in liquidation** and the right to the **residual when the company is a going concern**. More simply, the residual claimants have the right to the profits of the company.[59] The law gives the members of an LLC a tremendous amount of flexibility to allocate profits and losses among themselves as they see fit.

---

[59] See §4A-202, above.

4B-202(a) SHARING PROFITS:

The allocation of economic rights in an LLC is one area where you have to keep alert to protect your client's interests. The default rule under RULLCA is that **each member receives an equal share of the profits** without regard to ownership proportions or relative capital contributions.[60] This default rule could provide an unexpected result for your client. It differs from the default rules under corporate law statutes, which provide for allocation of profits based on number of shares owned.[61]

RULLCA §404(a) provides:

> Any distributions made by a limited liability company before its dissolution and winding up must be in *equal shares among members* . . .

In contrast, some jurisdictions, like Delaware have, as a default rule, that members are entitled to share in the profits **based on their relative investments**. The Delaware Limited Liability Company Act §18-503 provides:

> The profits and losses of a limited liability company shall be allocated among the members, and among classes or groups of members, in the manner provided in a limited liability company agreement. If the limited liability company agreement does not so provide, profits and losses shall be allocated on the **basis of the agreed value** (as stated in the records of the limited liability company) **of the contributions made by each member** . . .

The two different approaches have radically different consequences for the members of an LLC.

Illustration:

Bob and Mary formed an LLC together. Bob invested $8,000 and Mary invested $2,000 in exchange for their membership interests.

The company had a good first year and will make a distribution of $50,000 to its members.

> Under the RULLCA default rule, Mary and Bob are each entitled to $25,000 – they are entitled to equal shares despite their different capital contributions.

> Under the Delaware default rule, Bob is entitled to $40,000 and Mary is entitled to $10,000.

---

[60] RULLCA §404(a)

[61] See §4A-203(a), above.

114

It is important that you know the default rule in your jurisdiction so that you can draft the operating agreement to protect your client's interests. Please also keep in mind that you may create **preferred membership interests** analogous to preferred stock if such an arrangement suits your client's needs.

4B-202(b) SHARING LOSSES:

When we refer to the allocation of the LLC's losses, please keep in mind that the allocation of losses for tax and accounting purposes does not change the rule that the members are not be personally liable for the LLC's obligations.

You may recall that LLCs enjoy default pass-through taxation under Subchapter K. Pass-through taxation means that the entity's profits and losses pass through to the members for tax purposes.[62] The law gives the members of an LLC a tremendous amount of flexibility to allocate losses among themselves as they see fit. Parties may allocate losses to members that are not proportionate to their membership interests or to their share in the profits.

Illustration 1A:

The only two members of an LLC have made capital contributions to the LLC in the following amounts:

> Abel: $20,000
> Carol: $20,000

They have agreed to share profits, in proportion to their capital contributions. They have agreed to share losses, in the following proportions:

> Abel: 10%
> Carol: 90%

You might be curious why Carol would assume 80% of the losses when she only receives 30% of the profits. Generally, parties structure the losses in such a manner because one party can make better use of the losses to offset other income and, thereby, reduce her overall tax burden.

For example, we might imagine that Carol makes significant income outside of the LLC that places her in a high income tax bracket, let's say 35%. The LLC's losses will reduce her income tax burden more than it would for Abel, who we might imagine is in a 15% income tax bracket.

---

[62] See Chapter 3, §3A-402.

Illustration 1B:

The LLC suffers a **$10,000 loss**.

Pass-through losses according to capital contributions:

Abel is in a 15% tax bracket. If the losses pass through to him in proportion to his capital contribution, he would reduce his taxable income by $5,000 and, thus, **pay $750 less in taxes** (i.e., saves 15% of $5,000).

Carol is in a 35% tax bracket. If the losses pass through to her in proportion to her capital contribution, she would reduce her taxable income by $5,000 and, thus, **pay $1,750 less in taxes** (i.e., saves 35% of $5,000).

Total income tax saved for Abel and Carol together: $2,500

Pass-through losses according to agreement – Abel, 10%; Carol, 90%:

Abel is in a 20% tax bracket. If the parties agree to allocate 10% of the losses to him, he would reduce his taxable income by $1,000 and, thus, **pay $200 less in taxes** (i.e., saves 20% of $1,000).

Carol is in a 35% tax bracket. If the parties agree to allocate 90% of the losses to her, she would reduce her taxable income by $9,000 and, thus, **pay $3,150 less in taxes** (i.e., saves 35% of $9,000).

Total income tax saved for Abel and Carol together: $3,350

Abel and Carol, collectively, would save more in income taxes if they allocated most of the losses to Carol.

These types of arrangements are permissible under the tax code, but only if they are not a pretense. Tax regulations require that the allocation of losses must have **substantial economic effect.** The test the IRS uses to determine if there is a substantial economic effect is too detailed for an introductory course in business organizations, but the main import is that the losses cannot be allocated merely for tax purposes; **the members must actually suffer the economic impact of the loss**. Effectively, this means that as an accounting matter, Carol must actually bear the losses in her **capital account** (see immediately below).

———————

4B-203 CAPITAL ACCOUNTS – ACCOUNTING FOR PROFITS AND LOSSES:

To better understand how an LLC's profits and losses are passed on to the members for accounting and tax purposes, it is helpful to look at the **capital accounts** of the members.

Each member will have a capital account. The capital account includes the amounts the member contributed as her investment plus her share of the accumulated profits and losses.

Illustration:

Imagine Betty contributes $10,000 in exchange for 25% of the membership interests in an LLC. The operating agreement provides that members will share in profits and losses on the basis of relative contributions to the LLC.

When **Betty invests $10,000 in the LLC**, her capital account will look like this:

Betty's capital: 10,000

Let's imagine that the **company makes a profit of $4,000** in the first year. Betty's share of the profits is 25%, or $1,000. Her capital account would increase by $1,000:

Betty's capital: 11,000

Now, let's say Betty and the other members each **take a distribution[63] of $500**. Her capital account would decrease by $500:

Betty's capital: 10,500

The next year the **company suffers a loss of $8,000**. Betty's share of the loss is 25%, or $2,000. Her capital account would decrease by $2,000:

Betty's capital: 8,500

Finally, imagine that over the next several years **the company loses $40,000**. Betty's share of the losses is 25%, or $10,000. Her capital account would decrease by $10,000:

Betty's capital: (2,500)*

*Betty's account is at negative 2,500.

If we assume that all of the members' capital accounts are at a deficit, like Betty's, it means the company does not have enough money to pay off its

---

63 Often called a "draw"

creditors. However, because Betty is protected by limited liability, she is under no obligation to make up the deficit or repay the creditors with her personal assets. In addition, Betty is under no obligation to make up the deficit by making another contribution to the LLC, unless she agreed to do so in the operating agreement.

> ***Note:*** Betty would not be able to pass-through any losses for tax purposes once her capital account is in the negative. In other words, as soon as her capital account is down to zero, she can no longer use the company's losses to reduce her individual tax burden. This is an oversimplification of the tax law, but it serves our purpose here.

4B-204 **PASS-THROUGH TAXATION STATUS:**

As a default, LLCs are taxed under **Subchapter K,** which means they enjoy pass-through taxation regardless of how their economic interests are structured. However, if an LLC hopes to qualify under Subchapter S to avoid some self-employment taxes[64] or for other reasons, it must meet all of the Subchapter S requirements.[65] The most relevant requirement for our discussion here is that all outstanding **membership interests must have the same economic rights**. This rule would effectively require the members of an LLC with S-corp status to **allocate profits and losses in proportion to capital contributions**.

4B-300 **DEBT FINANCING AND THE LLC:**

An LLC can borrow from lenders and issue debt securities the same way a corporation can.[66] In addition, as with the closely-held corporation, it is common for one of more of the members to lend money to the business and receive a promissory note evidencing the debt.[67]

---

[64] See Chapter 3, §3A-500 et seq.

[65] See Chapter 3, §3A-404

[66] See §4A-300 et seq., above.

[67] See §4A-301, above.

4B-400 <u>SECURITIES LAW AND THE LLC:</u>

Under federal securities law, an LLC membership interest is not automatically considered a security. If it is not a security, the issuance and sale of the membership interests would not need to comply with the extensive federal regulations on the sale of securities.[68] If it is a security, you will need to help your client comply with the securities laws or find some sort of exemption.

To determine whether an LLC interest is a security, courts use the Howey test.[69] We will save the details of the Howey test for a course on securities regulation, but under the test, **an LLC membership interest is NOT a security if the investor purchasing the membership interest will be active in the management of the company**. In contrast, if the investor will be a passive member of the LLC, her membership interest is a security, and the offer and sale of that membership interest is subject to federal securities laws.

You may ask yourself, how passive does the investor need to be under the Howey test? What if she has voting rights and veto rights, but does not exercise them – does this make her an active member or a passive member? Indeed, courts have also struggled with these issues. Suffice it to say, that the analysis and the outcome are very fact-specific.

Further confusing the issue is the fact that state securities laws do not have a consistent approach to LLC membership interests. Under some state securities laws, an LLC membership interest is always a security. Other states, however, may use a fact-specific approach similar to the Howey test.

------

[68] See §4A-401, above

[69] *Securities and Exchange Commission v. W. J. Howey Co.*, 328 U.S. 293 (1946).

UNIT 4C

Raising Capital – The Partnership:

4C-100 Raising Capital – Introduction:

Raising capital in the partnership is very similar to raising capital in the LLC or corporation.

4C-200 Equity Financing – Partnership Interests:

Equity interests in partnerships are simply called partnership interests. Partnership interests have both economic rights and control rights.

4C-201 Control Rights of Partners:

Similar to the members of an LLC, each partner has a right to participate directly in the management of the partnership's business. The parties may change this rule by vesting management rights in a smaller subset of partners. Alternatively, the parties can adopt a limited partnership (LP) model, where the general partners have management rights and the limited partners are passive. We will discuss management and control rights in Chapter 5.

4C-202 Economic Rights of Partners:

The partners have the right to the partnership's residual, just like the shareholders in a corporation or the members of an LLC. The law gives parties a tremendous amount of flexibility to draft how they allocate profits and losses among individual partners.

4C-202(a) Sharing profits:

The default rule under RUPA is that partners share equally in profits without regard to their relative contributions of capital or the proportion of their partnership interests.

RUPA §401(b) provides:

> Each partner is entitled to an equal share of the partnership profits and is chargeable with a share of the partnership losses in proportion to the partner's share of the profits.

This approach is identical to the RULLCA approach to allocation of profits in LLCs.[70] Please keep in mind that you should ascertain whether your client would prefer another arrangement and draft the partnership agreement accordingly.

4C-202(b) SHARING LOSSES:

The default rule under RUPA is that partners share equally in losses without regard to their relative contributions of capital.

RUPA §401(b) provides:

> Each partner is entitled to an equal share of the partnership profits and is chargeable with a share of the partnership losses in proportion to the partner's share of the profits.

It important to remember that allocation of losses in the context of a partnership affects more than accounting losses. A general partner bears the risk of personal liability for all of the partnership's debts, not just for her agreed share of the losses. However, with respect to the other partners, a partner is only responsible for her agreed share of the losses. In other words, if a partner pays more to the partnership's creditors that her agreed share of the losses, the other partners must repay her for their share. This is called **contribution**.

4C-300 DEBT FINANCING AND THE PARTNERSHIP:

Loans from banks and other lending institutions are available for partnerships, just as they are available for corporations and LLCs. The same is true with respect to the issuance of debt securities.

4C-400 SECURITIES LAW AND THE PARTNERSHIP:

Similar to an LLC interest, under federal law a partnership interest is not necessarily a security unless it meets the requirements of the **Howey test**.[71]

---

[70] See §4B-202(a), above.

[71] See §4B-400, above.

Once again, the main element of the Howey test revolves around whether the partner is a passive owner, or an active one.[72]   It is a fact specific analysis of the specific partnership arrangement.

In general, however, limited partnership interests are securities because the law does not allow them any direct control over the partnership's business and affairs. In this sense, limited partners are not distinguishable from shareholders in a corporation. There may be instances where the parties draft specific provisions into the partnership agreement that give limited partners enough control and participation so that their interests will not be considered securities.

---

[72] See §4B-400, above.

UNIT 4D

BUSINESS VALUATION – THE BASICS:

4D-100 INTRODUCTION TO VALUATION:

In the practice of business organization law, the valuation of a business often becomes an important issue. Attorneys and students sometimes incorrectly assume that the company's assets minus its liabilities equal the market value of the company. It does not. The market value of the company lies not in the net value of its assets, but in its ability to use the assets to make profits.

Imagine you are the sole shareholder of ABC Inc. ABC Inc. has assets of $300,000 and liabilities of $100,000. If a buyer offered you $200,000 for your entire shareholdings, would you sell? You might be tempted to think that the buyer has offered you a fair price, but you should think again. Before you sell, you need to consider one more crucial piece of information: What are the **future profits** of the company?

If you projected ABC Inc. to make $100,000 per year for the next 10 years, you would never sell your shareholdings in the company for $200,000.

Here is a helpful analogy for those of us who prefer to live in a fantasy world:

> Imagine you have a magic pen that spews forth $1,000 per week when you wave it over your piggy bank. You would like to sell the pen. How would you determine its value? You would NOT examine the pen and say:
>
> > "There is about ten cents worth of plastic in the pen, about five cents worth of ink, and about twenty cents of labor and resources, so I will sell the pen for thirty-five cents."
>
> The value of the pen lies in the money it produces, not the in the value of its parts. The same is true for the value of a company.

4D-200 PRESENT VALUE:

The value of a company is based on the **present value of the company's future profits**. To understand what this means, we first need a basic understanding present value.

Consider the following:

I promise to pay you **$1,100** in one year if you give me money today. How much money would you give me today?

The answer to that question depends on how much money you want to make from the transaction. How much money you want to make from the transaction depends on two main factors:

(1) the risk you face because of the possibility I will not repay you; and
(2) how much money you could make on an equally risky transaction.

Let's say I have a credit rating that is reasonably good, but not stellar. You calculate that an equally risky transaction would give you a 10% return. You would like to make a **10% return** on the transaction with me, otherwise it would not be worth your while.

So now, you ask yourself: How much money should I pay today so that I will make a 10% return when I receive $1,100 in one year?

The answer is $1,000

If you give me $1,000 now, and I pay you back $1,100 in a year, you will make a 10% return.

We would say that the **present value** of the transaction is $1,000. **Or the present value of $1,100 received to be received one year from now is $1,000.**

You might have been able to do the calculation for the above example in your head, but you will need a formula for more complicated fact patterns. Here is the formula for calculating present value:

Future Cash ÷ (1+ rate) = Present Value

Here is the application of the formula to the fact pattern:

1,100 ÷ (1.10) = 1,000

The "rate" in this fact pattern was .10 (i.e., 10%)

What if I promised to pay you $1,100 **in 2 years**? How much money would you lend me now so that you would make a 10% return?

The formula is almost the same, except we add a "**2**" as an exponent for the **two-year** time period:

Future Cash ÷ (1+ rate)^2 = Present Value

1,100 ÷ (1.10)^2 = 909

If you give me $909 now, and I pay you back $1,100 in two years, you will make a 10% return per year.[73]

What if I promised to pay you $1,100 **in 3 years**? How much money would you lend me now?

We add a "**3**" as an exponent for the **three-year** time period:

Future Cash ÷ (1+ rate)^3 = Present Value

$$1,100 \div (1.10)^3 = 826$$

If you give me $826 now, and I pay you back $1,100 in three years, you will make a 10% return per year.[74]

4D-300 PRESENT VALUE OF THE FUTURE PROFITS OF A COMPANY:

A company is simply an asset (or an accumulation of assets) that produces a return. Now that you understand the basics of present value, you can use those principles to determine the market value of a company.

To determine the value of a company, you must:

1) Estimate the future profits of the company over a number of years; and
2) Come up with the rate of return you desire.

Once you have done those two things, you can calculate the present value of the future profits to determine the present value of a company. This process is called **discounted cash flow**.

Illustration:

Imagine you are negotiating to buy ABC Inc. You and your financial advisors have examined the financial data of the company, the economic forecasts for its industry, and the economic forecasts for the economy.

Step 1: Based on all this information, you **estimate the profits** of ABC Corp. for a certain number of years in the future. Let's say we choose to use a ten-year time period:

See chart on following page

---

[73] Compounded annually: which means you not only make 10% on the principal each year, but you also make 10% on interest that is due each year.

[74] Id.

125

Year 1	200,000
Year 2	200,000
Year 3	200,000
Year 4	220,000
Year 5	220,000
Year 6	220,000
Year 7	240,000
Year 8	240,000
Year 9	240,000
Year 10	240,000

Step 2: Next, you have to estimate the **terminal value of the company**. At year 10, how much will the company be worth if we sold it. Let's assume that based on the information we have, you expect the company to produce profits for the next 10 years and, at the end of year ten, you would be able to liquidate the assets of the company and receive a net of **$400,000** after paying the company's creditors.

Step 3: Once you have estimated the future profits and the terminal value, you need to **determine the rate of return** you want. Running a small business is a relatively risky proposition. Let's assume that after much consideration and analysis (and the help of a financial professional), you determine you want a **20% return**.

Step 4: Using the 20% rate, you calculate the **present value of the estimated future profits and the estimated terminal value**:

	Estimated Future Cash Flow	Formula	Application of the Formula	Present Value of Cash Flow
Year 1	200,000	Future Cash $\div$ (1+ rate)	200K $\div$ (1.20)	166,667
Year 2	200,000	Future Cash $\div$ (1+ rate)^2	200K $\div$ (1.20)^2	138,889
Year 3	200,000	Future Cash $\div$ (1+ rate)^3	200K $\div$ (1.20)^3	115,741
Year 4	220,000	Future Cash $\div$ (1+ rate)^4	220K $\div$ (1.20)^4	106,096
Year 5	220,000	Future Cash $\div$ (1+ rate)^5	220K $\div$ (1.20)^5	88,413
Year 6	220,000	Future Cash $\div$ (1+ rate)^6	220K $\div$ (1.20)^6	73,678
Year 7	240,000	Future Cash $\div$ (1+ rate)^7	240K $\div$ (1.20)^7	66,980
Year 8	240,000	Future Cash $\div$ (1+ rate)^8	240K $\div$ (1.20)^8	55,816
Year 9	240,000	Future Cash $\div$ (1+ rate)^9	240K $\div$ (1.20)^9	46,514
Year 10	240,000	Future Cash $\div$ (1+ rate)^{10}	240K $\div$ (1.20)^{10}	38,761
Year 10 Terminal Value	400,000	Future Cash $\div$ (1+ rate)^{10}	400K $\div$ (1.20)^{10}	64,603
			TOTAL:	962,158

The market value of ABC Inc. is somewhere around $960,000.

4D-400 MORE DETAILS ABOUT VALUATION:

Determining the value of the company by finding the present value of its future profits is called **discounted cash flow**. The word "discount" here does not mean some sort of bargain or reduced price. It means we take a future cash flow (which we called "profit") and use the formula to discount it back to its present value.

When parties use discounted cash flow, they need to project future profits. They will use the company's past performance as a basis for projecting profits. However, they will not necessarily look at the "net profit" number from the company's income statement. In fact they will probably adjust the income statement's net profit number to come up with a number that better represents the company's cash profits.

4D-500 COMPARING BOOK VALUE, ADJUSTED BOOK VALUE, LIQUIDATION VALUE, AND FAIR MARKET VALUE:

There are different methods of valuing of businesses, each of which generally falls within one of four approaches: book value, adjusted book value, and fair market value.

4D-501 DEFINITIONS:

"Book value" generally refers to the balance sheet value of a company: assets minus liabilities. It is effectively the owners' equity on the balance sheet.

"Adjusted book value" generally refers to the balance sheet value of the company, but adjusted to account for the actual fair market value of the company's assets.

"Liquidation value" generally refers to the value of the company after selling the assets and paying off the company's liabilities and other obligations. Liquidation value differs from book value in that liquidation value considers the actual market value of the assets, where the book value of the assets is determined by the cost of acquisition less depreciation. Book value will not always be an accurate reflection of the actual market value of the asset. Liquidation value will also take into account certain obligations that will not appear as liabilities on the company's balance sheet, e.g., a contractual commitment to lease office space from landlord under a long-term lease.

127

"**Fair market value**" or "**going-concern value**" generally means the price a willing buyer and willing seller would agree upon based on the assumption the business will continue producing profits. Of course, buyers and sellers need to use some sort of valuation method to determine the fair market value. They usually retain financial professionals, who use **discounted cash flow**, among other methods, to determine the value of the company. Financial professionals also look at "comparables" – i.e., the prices other similar businesses have sold for – to help them determine the fair market value of the company.

4D-502 **THE BALANCE SHEET:**

To understand the valuation methods and their differences, you must have a basic understanding of a company's balance sheet. A balance sheet shows the company's assets, liabilities, and owners' equity. Look at the following simple balance sheet and refer back to it as we discuss book value, adjusted book value, and liquidation value:

ASSETS:

Cash	50,000
Accounts receivable	16,000
Inventory	5,000
Land	35,000
Building	90,000
depreciation	(25,000)
Company car	22,000
depreciation	(4,000)
TOTAL ASSETS:	189,000

LIABILITIES:

Accounts payable	12,000
Salaries payable	7,000
Utilities payable	6,000
Bank loan	80,000
TOTAL LIABILITIES:	105,000

OWNERS' EQUITY:

Capital	20,000
Retained earnings	64,000
TOTAL EQUITY:	84,000

Book value: The book value of this company is **$84,000**. This number simply comes from subtracting the total liabilities on the company's balance sheet from the total assets on the balance sheet.

Here, the company has $189,000 in total assets and $105,000 in total liabilities, leaving a net book value of $84,000.

You will note that $84,000 is also the number for total owners' equity. This is not a coincidence. Book value will be equal to total owners' equity.

Adjusted book value: We cannot calculate the adjusted book value of the company based on the numbers we have in the balance sheet. We need more information.

To calculate adjusted book value, we would **need to know the actual fair market value of the company's assets**. We are mainly interested in adjusting the value of the company's fixed assets, such as land, buildings, and equipment. Accounting conventions require that the value of the fixed assets on the balance sheet should be the **cost of acquisition**.

Here, we know the company acquired the **land** for $35,000, the **building** for $90,000, and the **car** for $22,000.

In addition, accounting conventions require that fixed assets, except for land, must be **depreciated on the balance sheet**. Depreciation is merely a rough estimate of the use, wear, and tear of the asset over time. It does not represent the actual reduction in the fair market value of the asset.

Here, we know that the **building** has depreciated $25,000 on the company's books. We could say that the building has a **book value** (i.e., balance sheet value) of $65,000 – cost of acquisition of $90,000 minus accumulated depreciation of $25,000.   However, the actual fair market value of the building may be greater than or less than $65,000.

We also know that the **car** has depreciated $4,000 on the company's balance sheet. We could say that the car has a **book value** (i.e., balance sheet value) of $18,000 – cost of acquisition of $22,000 minus accumulated depreciation of $4,000.   However, the actual fair market value of the car may be greater than or less than $18,000.

When we calculate the adjusted book value of a company, we use the fair market value of the assets, not the book value of the assets. Let's assume that based on careful research, we make the following estimates of the fair market value of the company's assets:

Asset	Book value	Fair market value
Land	35,000	75,000
Building	65,000	69,000
Car	18,000	15,000

With those assumptions, we can now calculate the adjusted book value of the company:

The **fair market value of the assets is $230,000** [50,000 + 16,000 + 5,000 + 75,000 + 69,000 + 15,000]. After subtracting the total liabilities of 105,000, **the adjusted book value of the company is $125,000**.

Liquidation value: Liquidation value is the value of company after it liquidates all of its assets and pays off all of its debts. The remaining cash is the liquidation value of the company.

To estimate the liquidation value of the company, without actually liquidating the assets and paying off all debts, we need to know: (1) the fair market value of the assets on the balance sheet, and (2) other rights or obligations not reflected on the balance sheet.

There are obligations that will not appear on the company's balance sheet. The balance sheet only reflects the company's accrued liabilities. Accrued liabilities only include transactions where the company has already received goods or services, but has not yet paid for them.

Illustration 1:

The company enters a contract to buy 500 items from a supplier for $10,000. This transaction is NOT reflected on the balance sheet as a liability.

Illustration 2:

The supplier delivers 500 items to the company and allows the company 30 days to pay the $10,000 price. This transaction IS reflected on the balance sheet as a liability.

Illustration 3:

The company enters into a three year employment contract with a new IT director for $150,000 per year.

As a practical matter, we would look at this contract as a $450,000 obligation of the company. However, as discussed above, for accounting purposes, this contract does NOT appear as a liability on the company's balance sheet. For this reason, it would not be calculated into book value or adjusted book value.

If the company decided to dissolve and liquidate, it would have to satisfy all of its contractual obligations, including the contract with the IT manager.

If we wanted to determine the liquidation value of the company, we would have to estimate how much the company would have to pay to satisfy the employment contract.

Let's assume that our company has entered into a five-year lease for $1,500 per month, with three years remaining on the lease. Let's also assume that the lease agreement provides that if the company breaches the lease, it will have to pay liquidated damages of $200 for each month remaining on the lease – $7,200 for the three years that are left.

Based on the assumptions we made calculating the adjusted book value, the **fair market value of the assets is $230,000** [50,000 + 16,000 + 5,000 + 75,000 + 69,000 + 15,000].

The company's obligations in liquidation would be $112,200, which equals the liabilities that are on the balance sheet plus the lease obligation that is not on the balance sheet [105,000 + 7,200].

Based on these simplified assumptions, the **estimated liquidation value of the company would be $117,800** [230,000 – 112,200]

4D-503 **ILLUSTRATIONS:**

Consider the following illustrations, which are designed to help you better understand the difference between book value, liquidation value, and market value. We will refer back to these illustrations in later chapters.[75]

Illustration 1:

Imagine I put a loaded gun to you head and I said, "Transfer your shares of the company to me, or else." Under the threat, you transfer your shares to me.

Clearly, I have unjustly taken something from you. I have taken the value of the company from you.

---

[75] See Chapter 6, §§6A-211(d), 6B-202(d); and Chapter 7, §7A-203(a).

Illustration 2:

Imagine I put a loaded gun to you head and I said, "Transfer your shares of the company to me, or else. In exchange, I will pay you the **book value** [or liquidation value] of the company."

I lay the cash equivalent of the book value [or liquidation value] on the table and walk away with your shares.

Clearly, I have unjustly taken something from you, but I claim that you suffered no harm. I gave you cash for the shares, so you are no worse off than before. Before you had the shares, now you have the cash value of those shares. Your shares are really just economic interests. They are not like a family heirloom or an antique car you treasure. You only have the shares because of the economic value they represent.

Am I correct? No, I am not correct. The book value [or liquidation value] of the firm **does not take into account the potential future profits** of the company. **When I paid you the book value or liquidation value of your shares, I effectively stole the company's future profits from you**.

Illustration 3:

Imagine I put a loaded gun to you head and I said, "Transfer your shares of the company to me, or else. In exchange, I will pay you the **market value** of the company."

I lay the cash equivalent of the fair market value on the table and walk away with your shares.

In this situation, I have a very good argument that you are no worse off than before. Before you had the shares, now you have the cash value of those shares, which **includes the future profits of the company**. The fair market value, by definition, includes the present value of the future profits of the company.

CHAPTER 5

GOVERNANCE MECHANICS: DECISION-MAKING IN BUSINESS ORGANIZATIONS

UNIT 5A
CORPORATIONS – DECISION-MAKING:

5A-100 SHAREHOLDER VOTING – GENERAL INTRODUCTION:

5A-200 SHAREHOLDER VOTING – THE DETAILS:

UNIT 5B
PARTNERSHIPS – DECISION-MAKING:

UNIT 5C
LLCs – The Decision-Making Processes:

5C-100 **LLC Voting and Authority – General Introduction:**

    5C-101 Patterns to look for in your LLC statute:

    5C-102 Sources of LLC law:

    5C-103 Voting rights in LLCs:

        5C-103(a) Member-managed:

        5C-103(b) Manager-managed:

    5C-104 Authority in LLCs:

        5C-104(a) Authority in member-managed LLCs:

        5C-104(b) Authority in manager-managed LLCs:

    5C-105 The role of the operating agreement in LLC decision-making:

    5C-106 Summary of the general introduction to LLC voting and authority:

5C-200 **LLC Voting and Authority – The Details:**

    5C-201 Voting rights in LLCs:

        5C-201(a) Relative voting rights of members:

        5C-201(b) Voting on ordinary matters:

        5C-201(c) Voting on extraordinary matters:

        5C-201(d) Electing managers, removing managers, filling vacancies:

        5C-201(e) Meetings, proxies, and consents:

        5C-201(f) Classes of members and classes of managers:

        5C-201(g) Appraisal rights:

    5C-202 Authority in LLCs:

        5C-202(a) Authority in the member-managed LLC:

        5C-202(b) Authority in the manager-managed LLC:

    5C-203 LLC member information rights:

UNIT 5A

CORPORATIONS – DECISION-MAKING:

Businesses need to make decisions. These decisions run the gamut from the mundane to the significant. Who makes these decisions in business organizations: the owners, the employees, a management board or committee? There are academics who study how and why organizations make the decisions they make. Our focus of study will be narrower. We will focus on **how the law allocates decision-making power** among owners, management boards, and employee-agents.

As you go through the materials in this chapter, keep this simplified hypothetical in mind:

> **Who would make the following decisions in a business organization:**
>
> The owners? The employees? The management board?
>
>> A decision to buy a ream of paper.
>>
>> A decision to borrow a significant amount of money to finance the construction of a large retail outlet.
>>
>> A decision to merge the business organization into another business organization.

Shareholders are the "owners" of the corporation, but only in the broadest sense of the word. Shareholders do not have the true control that we expect of people we call "owners." Shareholders' rights to control and participate in corporate decision-making are very limited.

The board of directors is the true decision-making body of the corporation. Shareholders who desire control rights will want to sit on the board of directors. A shareholder will be able to get herself elected to the board if she owns enough shares or by agreement with other shareholders.

The executive officers and the other employees of the corporation carry out the board's decisions and the corporate policies established by the board. They also make the day-to-day decisions of the corporation. It would be impractical to call a board meeting to decide whether the corporation should buy a stapler, for example.

139

SHAREHOLDER VOTING:

5A-100 SHAREHOLDER VOTING – GENERAL INTRODUCTION:

Students of corporate law should be familiar with this section, which discusses the most basic aspects of shareholder voting.

5A-101 PATTERNS TO LOOK FOR IN YOUR CORPORATE LAW STATUTE:

The corporate law statutes of each state may vary. Nonetheless, there are certain patterns to look for or expect when reading your jurisdiction's approach to shareholder voting.

Shareholders' votes are counted **by shares, not per capita**. For example, if a shareholder owns 90% of the shares, that shareholder will have sufficient voting control to pass any shareholder resolution, even if there are 1,000 shareholders who all vote against the resolution.

Shareholder voting rights are **usually passive/reactive voting rights**. This means that shareholders generally cannot propose to initiate a transaction. Their rights to vote on a transaction come **in response to a proposal initiated by the board of directors**.

State corporate law statutes all have similar provisions regarding the **mechanics of the shareholder voting process** with respect to: shareholder meetings; quorum requirements; approval requirements.

Shareholders have the **right to vote on a very limited number of matters**:

Shareholders have the **right to elect and remove directors**. This is arguably their most important voting right. Please note, however, shareholders do NOT have a right to appoint the executive officers or any other employee.

Other than the election of directors, the shareholders only have a **right to vote on certain fundamental transactions**.

Under most corporate law statutes, shareholders will only have a right to vote on:

Dissolution of the corporation

Mergers with other corporations

Sale of substantially all of the corporation's assets

Amendment of the articles of incorporation

Amendment of the bylaws*

> *****Note:*** *The shareholders usually share the right to amend the bylaws with the board of directors. In other words, the board or the shareholders may amend the bylaws without the other's approval. The shareholders will not have a right to vote on the board's amendment of the bylaws, but the shareholders will normally be able to undo whatever amendment the board has made.*

In this chapter we will discuss amending the corporate articles of incorporation and bylaws in detail. We will discuss dissolution, mergers, and assets sales until Chapter 9, but you should already have a basic sense of what they involve.

What do all these transactions have in common? Of course, they are all major transactions, but the **shareholders do NOT get to vote on a transaction simply because it is a major business decision of the corporation**.

The matters shareholders have a right to vote on are transactions that:

> **change the fundamental nature of the corporation** (dissolution, merger, sale of substantially all the assets);
>
> **change the rights of shareholders** (amendment of the articles, and, in some cases, mergers); or
>
> **change the internal governance of the corporation** (amendment of the bylaws or the articles).

Illustration:

A corporation's decision to invest significant capital into the construction of a large production facility is indeed a major transaction for the corporation, but shareholders would NOT have a right to vote on that decision.

Although this transaction would have a major impact on the business of the corporation, it does not change the **fundamental nature** of the corporation itself, nor does it change the **rights of the shareholders** or the **internal governance** of the corporation.

5A-102 SHAREHOLDERS MEETINGS:

5A-102(a) ANNUAL SHAREHOLDERS MEETINGS:

When shareholders have a right to decide on a matter, they do so by voting at a shareholders meeting. Most corporate law statutes require the corporation to hold **at least one meeting per year**. Not surprisingly, this meeting is called the **annual shareholders meeting.** At the annual meeting, shareholders **elect directors** and vote on **other matters that properly come up** for a shareholder vote.

5A-102(b) SPECIAL SHAREHOLDERS MEETINGS:

Corporate law statutes also anticipate **special shareholders meetings**. Corporations will call these special meetings to have shareholders vote on matters when it is not practical to wait until the annual shareholders meeting.

> ### Illustration:
>
> If the board of directors has completed its negotiations and approval of a sale of all of the corporation's assets by late July, it would probably not make good business sense to wait until the corporation's next annual shareholder meeting next March for a shareholder vote on the matter.

Special shareholders meetings can also be used by shareholders **to remove directors from the board or to fill sudden vacancies on the board** (because a director resigned, died, or was removed).

5A-102(c) PROXIES AND CONSENTS:

Shareholders do not need to physically attend the annual or special shareholders meetings. A shareholder **may attend a meeting by proxy** - which means she may **appoint an agent to attend the meeting on her behalf and cast her votes.**

We could conceivably run into a situation where we have a shareholders meeting without the physical attendance of a single shareholder because they all appointed the board of directors as their proxies. Nonetheless, there would still be a shareholders meeting with the shareholders attending by proxy.

Corporate law statutes in most jurisdictions authorize shareholders to **decide on matters without holding an actual shareholders meeting**. To do so, the corporation will need to obtain **written consents** (not proxies) from the shareholders to approve an action without meeting. Many jurisdictions will allow shareholders to take action without meeting only if there is **unanimous consent by the shareholders**. Other jurisdictions might be more lenient, but will still require significant shareholder support for action in lieu of meeting through the consent process.

5A-103 ELECTING DIRECTORS:

As stated earlier, the right to elect directors is quite possibly the most important shareholder voting right. The directors are responsible for directing the corporation's business. Shareholders elect directors at the annual shareholders meeting. The election of directors is different from most voting processes you are familiar with. The most important thing to remember is that, normally, the **election of directors is NOT based on the principle of majority voting.**

Directors are elected by **plurality**. Election by plurality means that you do not need a majority of votes to win, you just need **more votes than the other candidates**. You could theoretically win election to the board with only one vote, for example, if no other candidate received as many votes as you received.

Most corporate law statutes provide for two possible voting processes for the election of directors – **straight voting** and **cumulative voting.** Straight and cumulative voting are explained in detail below,[76] but in either case, the voting standard for election to the board is a plurality, not a majority.

> *Quick note:* In recent years, some public corporations have adopted a majority voting scheme. Under a majority voting system, a plurality is not enough to elect a director to the board. The nominee will not be elected unless she receives a majority of the votes.

Shareholders have the right to nominate candidates for election to the board of directors. This is one of the few times where a shareholder has a right to make a proposal that will be binding on the corporation if approved by the shareholders. Comparing these two different scenarios will help you understand the shareholder right to nominate a person for election to the board, as opposed to other voting rights, where a shareholder has no right to propose a transaction.

> *Illustration:*
>
> Shareholder X can propose that the shareholders should elect her to the board of directors (i.e., she nominates herself for election to the board). If the shareholders elect her, the corporation is bound to give Shareholder X a board seat.
>
> In contrast, Shareholder X could *not* propose that the shareholders vote to cause the corporation enter into a merger transaction. Although shareholders will have a right to vote on the merger, only the board can initiate a proposal regarding a merger.

---

[76] See §5A-202 et seq., below.

The board of directors will also have the right to nominate candidates for election to the board. In other words, the shareholders' right to nominate is coextensive with the board's right to nominate candidates for directorships, although the ultimate right to elect directors lies solely with the shareholders.

5A-104 REMOVING DIRECTORS:

Shareholders also have the right to remove directors. The removal of directors is **another instance where a shareholder has a right to initiate a proposal for shareholder approval**. This means that shareholders not only have a right to vote to remove a director, they may also propose to remove a director without waiting for a proposal from the board.

5A-105 SHAREHOLDER VOTING ON OTHER MATTERS:

As we have already mentioned, shareholders only have a right to vote on a limited number of matters: (1) dissolution, (2) mergers, (3) sale of substantially all of the corporation's assets, (4) amendment to the articles of incorporation, and (5) amendments to the bylaws (except where the board may amend the bylaws without shareholder approval).

The corporate law statute of your particular jurisdiction will have specific provisions detailing the **quorum and approval requirements** necessary for the above transactions.

5A-105(a) QUORUM REQUIREMENTS:

Before shareholders may vote on any matter at a shareholders meeting, a certain number of shares must be present. A share is present if the owner of the share or her proxy is present. The number of shares required to be present is called a **quorum**. It is important to remember that we count a quorum by **the number of _shares_ present, not by the number of _shareholders_ present at a meeting**.

In most jurisdictions, the quorum requirement is the **attendance of a majority of shares entitled to vote on a matter**. Although some statutes may be drafted using language indicating "shareholders" in attendance, the **attendance of shares counts, not shareholders**.

For example, you might see a state corporate law provision or even a bylaw provision that states the quorum requirement like this:

> The attendance of shareholders, in person or by proxy, representing at least a majority of shares entitled to vote on the matter shall constitute a quorum.

144

You should be able to spot that this provision requires the attendance of the majority of _shares_ entitled to vote, even though it may seem to the untrained eye to focus on _shareholder_ attendance.

The law might require a **higher quorum requirement to provide greater protection for shareholders**. In addition, the law may allow the corporation to change the quorum requirement, usually within certain limits, through its articles of incorporation or its bylaws.

> ### _Illustration:_
>
> If our corporation has four shareholders with 25 shares each (100 shares total issued), we might draft our quorum requirement to be 80% to ensure that we could not take action without all shareholders in attendance. We should also recognize that such a provision allows one shareholder to veto any transaction simply by not attending the shareholders meeting.

_5A-105(b)_ APPROVAL REQUIREMENTS:

Of course, once there is a quorum, the shareholders (or their proxies) may vote their shares to approve or reject the proposal before them.

The voting standard is **one vote per share** unless the articles of incorporation provide otherwise.

To **approve the proposal**, a certain number of shares must be cast in favor of the proposal. The exact number, usually expressed in terms of a proportion, depends on the matter being voted upon and the jurisdiction.

In your jurisdiction's corporate law statute, you should expect to see one or more of the following approval requirements:

> **Simple majority:** Approval of the majority of the shares present at the meeting. Abstentions effectively count as votes against.
>
> _Example of simple majority:_
>
> **10,000** shares are **entitled to vote** on the matter.
>
> If **6,000** of those shares **are present** at the meeting,
>
> and only **5,000** actually **vote** on the matter (with 1,000 shares abstaining),
>
> approval requires **3,001** shares **cast in favor** of the proposal (i.e., 3001 = majority of 6,000 present).

145

Votes-cast majority:[77] Approval of the majority of the shares that actually vote at the meeting. Abstentions do not count as votes against.

Example of "votes-cast majority":

10,000 shares are **entitled to vote** on the matter.

If **6,000** of those shares **are present** at the meeting,

and only **5,000** actually **vote** on the matter (with 1,000 shares abstaining),

approval requires **2,501** shares **cast in favor** of the proposal (i.e., 2,501 = majority of 5,000 that actually voted).

Absolute majority: Approval of majority of shares, whether or not they attend the meeting. Non-attendance and abstentions effectively count as votes against.

Example of absolute majority:

10,000 shares are **entitled to vote** on the matter.

If **6,000** of those shares **are present** at the meeting,

and only **5,000** actually **vote** on the matter (with 1,000 shares abstaining),

approval requires **5,001** shares **cast in favor** of the proposal (i.e., 5,001 = majority of 10,000 shares entitled to vote).

Supermajority: Approval of some percentage of shares greater than a majority (*e.g.*, 2/3, 3/4, 60%, 80%, etc.). Supermajority voting may take any of the above forms - i.e., simple supermajority, votes-cast supermajority, or absolute supermajority.

---

[77] I created the term "votes-cast majority." No one, to my knowledge calls this a "votes-cast majority." The standard is a "plurality standard" because it does not require a majority of votes in attendance – it just requires more votes in favor than opposed. However, I find it easier to think of the standard as a majority of the votes actually cast, to contrast with either a majority of all shares present (simple majority) and a majority of all shares outstanding (absolute majority).

5A-105(c) YOUR JURISDICTION'S APPROACH TO QUORUM AND APPROVAL REQUIREMENTS:

Which quorum and approval standards will you see in your jurisdiction's corporate law statute?

Your task as a corporate attorney is to **familiarize yourself with the shareholder meeting quorum and approval requirements of your jurisdiction.** If you really want to impress your clients and supervisors, memorize the provisions and recite them off the top of your head. Personally, I have chosen not to memorize them because I need room in my brain's hard drive to store baseball statistics.

If you remember to look for the following patterns, it will be easier for you to understand and internalize the rules of your jurisdiction, rather than committing them to rote memorization:

> **Quorum:** Usually a majority of shares entitled to vote, BUT for more major transactions, like mergers, the percentage may be higher.

> **Approval:** Usually a simple majority or a votes-cast majority, BUT for more major transactions, the approval requirement may be an absolute majority or some sort of supermajority standard.

5A-105(d) NON-VOTING SHARES:

If a corporation has issued non-voting shares (remember, the shares will only be non-voting if the articles of incorporation expressly say so), you may be surprised to discover that **corporate law statues usually give these non-voting shares voting rights to approve amendments to the articles when the amendments affect their rights**.

> *Example 1:* An amendment to the articles to increase the number of authorized shares of *regular* common stock.

>> ***Non-voting shares would, most likely, NOT have rights to vote on this amendment.***

> *Example 2:* An amendment to the articles to increase the number of authorized shares on *non-voting* common stock.

>> ***The non-voting common may or may not have rights to vote on this amendment, depending on the jurisdiction.***

> *Example 3:* An amendment to the articles to require cumulative voting for the election of directors.

>> ***Non-voting shares would, most likely, NOT have rights to vote on this amendment.***

Example 4: An amendment to the articles to provide that the non-voting shares would receive only half the dividend of the regular common stock.

Non-voting shares would, most likely, have the right to vote on this amendment.

With respect to each of these examples, your jurisdiction's corporate law statute might take a different approach. It is important for you to be able to read your statute to determine the voting rights of non-voting shares, if any.

5A-105(e) PREFERRED SHARES:

The terms of the preferred stock in the articles of incorporation will generally specify when preferred shareholders will have a right to vote. Often, but not always, preferred stock will be non-voting stock.[78] When the preferred stock is non-voting stock pursuant to the terms in the articles, the preferred stock is treated the same as non-voting stock above - i.e., preferred shareholders will only have a statutory right to vote on amendments to the articles when the amendments affect their rights.

5A-106 SHAREHOLDER VOTE-POOLING AGREEMENTS AND VOTING TRUSTS:

Shareholders may want to enter into binding agreements with other shareholders on how to vote their shares.

Illustration:

I might agree to vote for your nominee for director if you promise to vote for my nominee. Similarly, we might agree to vote our shares as a bloc against (or for) a proposed sale of all of the corporation's assets.

Alternatively, our agreement could be less specific. We might agree to vote our shares together as a bloc, with our agreement providing a process for how we will agree to vote our shares when a matter comes before the shareholders for their approval.

These agreements usually take two forms:

1) **The vote-pooling agreement:** A simple contract where **two or more shareholders agree how to vote their shares**.

   Under relevant law, shareholders usually have an **unfettered right to enter into vote pooling agreements**. Some jurisdictions require the shareholders to file the agreement with the corporation and limit the duration of the agreement to ten years.

---

[78] See Chapter 4, §4A-203(b).

2) **The voting trust:** Two or more shareholders **transfer their shares to a trustee who votes the shares in accordance with the instructions in the trust agreement**.

Corporate law statutes usually limit the duration of voting trusts to **no more than ten years** and require the parties to **file the agreement with the corporation**.

_____

5A-107 SHAREHOLDERS ARE NOT AGENTS:

We should quickly emphasize that shareholders' control rights are limited to voting. They are not agents of the corporation. In other words, a shareholder cannot bind the corporation to a contract simply because she is a "shareholder."

It is possible for a shareholder to be an agent of the corporation if the board gives her authority, but that would apply equally to any person to whom the board gives authority to act on behalf of the corporation.[79] **The fact that a person is a shareholder gives her no special legal status to act on the corporation's behalf**. The officers and employees act on the corporation's behalf when dealing with third parties.

_____

5A-108 SUMMARY OF THE GENERAL INTRODUCTION TO SHAREHOLDER VOTING:

Before you move on to the detailed explanations of shareholder voting, make sure you can clearly explain the following concepts:

Shareholders' limited voting rights

Passive/reactive shareholder voting _vs._ right to initiate

Annual shareholders meeting

Special shareholders meeting

Proxy

Shareholder action without meeting and consents

Quorum

Electing directors by plurality

---

[79] We discuss authority of agents in greater depth in 5A-700 et seq., below

Removal of directors

Other matters shareholders have a right to vote on

Simple majority

Votes-cast majority (plurality)

Absolute majority

Supermajority

Vote pooling agreement

Voting trust

Voting by non-voting shares and preferred shares

5A-200 SHAREHOLDER VOTING – THE DETAILS:

The following sections explore shareholder voting in greater detail. To help you digest this information, you should first make sure you have a good grasp on the basic concepts introduced in the general introduction.

5A-201 NOTICE OF SHAREHOLDERS MEETINGS:

5A-201(a) RECORD OWNERS:

Shareholders are entitled to notice of shareholder meetings a sufficient time in advance of the meeting. However, not all shareholders are entitled to notice. Only the **record owners** of shares (or "shareholders of record") are entitled to notice. A record owner is the **person listed in the corporation's stockholder ledger** as the owner of the shares.

Sometimes the **beneficial owner** of the shares, the person who we consider to be the true "owner," is not the record owner. When would a beneficial owner not be the record shareholder? There are several possible scenarios:

Voting trust: The owner of the shares might have been party to a voting trust agreement. In such a case, she would transfer the shares to the trustee, who would then become the shareholder of record. The original shareholder would be the beneficial owner.

Other trusts: The shares might be the subject matter of some other trust. As such, the trustee is the record owner of the shares and the beneficiary of the trust would be a beneficial owner.

Nominees: Most shareholders in public corporations today are not the shareholders of record. They hold their shares through a nominee, who is the shareholder of record.

> *Explanation:*
>
> When you buy stock in a company in the public markets, you place an order with your broker and your broker credits your account with the stock.
>
> The broker does not get the share certificates for you. Instead, your broker is a member of a large clearinghouse called the DTC (Depository Trust Company). Other brokers are also members of the DTC.
>
> Your broker informs the DTC that one of its clients has purchased 100 shares of Disney, for example.
>
> The DTC will credit your broker's account with 100 shares. (Of course, there will be some other broker somewhere who will report

to the DTC that one of its clients sold 100 shares of Disney, so that the universe is in balance.)

The DTC similarly never receives the actual share certificate. The DTC's nominee, Cede & Co., is the shareholder of record and has one or more stock certificates for a large number of shares of Disney stock.

When you look at the shareholder record of Disney, you will never see your name. You will however see DTC's nominee, Cede & Co., as one of Disney's shareholders of record.

Federal securities law requires all notices of shareholders meetings and proxy solicitations to go to you, the beneficial shareholder, through the various participants in the system.

5A-201(b) RECORD DATE:

In addition, only record owners as of the **record date** will be entitled to vote at the upcoming shareholders meeting and to receive notice of the meetings. The corporation must set a **cut-off date for shareholders entitled to notice and voting rights**, especially corporations whose shares are actively traded. This cut-off date is called the "record date" and it is set before each meeting.

If you purchase shares after the record date, you are indeed a record shareholder, BUT you will not be entitled to vote at the upcoming shareholders meeting.

In fact, the person who sold the shares to you will be entitled to vote the shares, even though she is not longer a shareholder of record at the time of the meeting.

If you want to be able to vote the shares you purchased after the record date, you must get a proxy from the seller of those shares.

5A-201(c) WAIVER OF NOTICE:

A record shareholder entitled to notice may be able challenge any shareholder action taken at a meeting for which she did not receive proper notice. The shareholder may **implicitly waive notice by attending without objection** or she may **expressly waive notice** (usually must be in writing).

In fact, express, written waivers of notice for shareholders meetings are commonplace in closely-held corporations. The shareholders, who are often also the board members and key employees, are often so busy running the business that they either forget to cause the corporation to send notice of shareholder meetings or they cannot send notice because they will hold an impromptu meeting when time allows. In these instances, the shareholders will sign waivers of notice at these meetings to prevent challenges to the shareholders meeting based on lack of notice.

5A-202 ELECTING DIRECTORS:

As we briefly mentioned earlier, shareholders do not elect directors using a majority voting standard. Directors are elected by a **plurality** vote using either a **straight voting** or **cumulative voting** process.

5A-202(a) STRAIGHT VOTING FOR DIRECTORS:

Under **straight voting**, each shareholder votes for the nominee or nominees she wants to see elected to the board. She gets **one vote for each share she owns. She has no "against" votes**. In other words, a shareholder may vote "yes" for the nominees she supports, but she does NOT have the power to vote against any other nominee. The nominees who receive the most votes win.

An example of straight voting:

The shareholders of Goo Corp. are electing the directors at the annual meeting. Let's say that Goo Corp. has only two shareholders, Bob and Mary. Here are the remaining pertinent facts:

> Goo Corp. has 100 shares issued and outstanding.
>
> Mary owns 51 of those shares and Bob owns the remaining 49 shares.
>
> **Three directors seats** need to be filled at this year's annual meeting.
>
> There are **six nominees** for those three positions.
>
> Mary supports nominees A, B, and C.
>
> Bob supports nominees X, Y, and Z.

You might think that because Bob owns nearly half of the shares, 49% to be exact, he will at least be able to elect one of his nominees. **Unfortunately for Bob, he will not be able to elect any of his nominees under straight voting.** Here is why:

> Mary will vote her 51 shares in favor of A. Mary will also vote her 51 shares in favor of B. Mary will also vote her 51 shares in favor of and C. Thus, A, B, and C each have 51 votes.

Bob will vote his 49 shares in favor of X. Bob will also vote his 49 shares in favor of Y. Bob will also vote his 49 shares in favor of and Z. Thus, X, Y, and Z each have 49 votes.

With three open positions, only the top three vote-getters will be elected. As you can see, the top 3 vote-getters are all Mary's candidates.

For those of you who process information in graphic form, here is how the straight voting process would occur:

	A	B	C	X	Y	Z
Mary (51 shares)	51 yes	51 yes	51 yes	0 yes	0 yes	0 yes
Bob (49 shares)	0 yes	0 yes	0 yes	49 yes	49 yes	49 yes
Vote total for each nominee	51*	51*	51*	49	49	49

*One of the top three vote-getters.

There are three things you should note about straight voting:

First, in my example, the three nominees that won actually received a majority of the votes, but that was not necessary for them to win. They **simply needed a plurality** – i.e., more votes than the other nominees. To understand this, let's change the facts a bit. Assume the six nominees for the three directorships each received the following number of votes:

A = 51;   B = 48;   C = 43;   X = 27;   Y = 45; Z = 37

A, B, and Y are elected to the board, even though neither B nor Y obtained a majority. These three nominees were the top vote-getters.

Second, shareholders are restricted to voting for a limited number of nominees. A shareholder may only vote for a number of nominees equal to the number of seats open.

Bob or Mary could only vote "yes" for three nominees because there are only three director seats being filled.

Third, a shareholder who holds a majority of the outstanding shares will ALWAYS be able to elect all of her nominees under straight voting system. The minority shareholder (or shareholders) will not be able to elect even one board member while there is a shareholder who owns a majority of the shares and elections are held under a straight voting regime.

154

5A-202(b) __Cumulative voting for directors:__

As we saw above, under straight voting, not only will a majority shareholder be able to control the board, she will be able to monopolize the board.

Cumulative voting, however, makes it possible for minority shareholders with a sufficient number of shares to elect at least one board member, and possibly more, depending on the number of shares the minority shareholders own.

How exactly does cumulative voting differ from straight voting? Let's look once again at Goo Corp., with shareholders **Mary (51 shares) and Bob (49 shares)**.

Mary, with her majority control will be able to elect all of her nominees to the board under straight voting – and Bob does not stand a chance. Why? Mary has 51 votes to Bob's 49.

However, **under cumulative voting, votes are counted differently**. Under cumulative voting votes are counted as follows:

(number of shares owned) x (number of board seats up for election)

Thus, under cumulative voting,

Mary will have 153 votes (51 shares x 3 board seats up for election)

and **Bob will have 147 votes** (49 shares x 3 board seats up for election.

Now, here is how this all works so that Bob has a chance to elect one of his nominees:

Remember that under straight voting, Mary could vote "yes" 51 times for each of her nominees and Bob could vote "yes" 49 times for his nominees?

Well, under cumulative voting, **Mary only has 153 votes in total that she must distribute among her nominees**. She may cast all her votes for one nominee, spread them among two nominees, or spread them among three.

Similarly, **Bob only has 147 votes,** and he must come up with a strategy to distribute his shares among his nominees to get the greatest representation on the board. **His ability to cumulate his votes for one single candidate (which he could not do under straight voting), gives him a better chance of electing one of his nominees.**

Now that you understand the concept of cumulative voting, it will be easier for you to understand a corporate law cumulative-voting statute.

Read the following provision from Delaware law and make sure it is consistent with how you understand the process:

> "The certificate of incorporation of any corporation may provide that at all elections of directors of the corporation, or at elections held under specified circumstances, each holder of stock or of any class or classes or of a series or series thereof shall be entitled to as many votes as shall equal the number of votes which (except for such provision as to cumulative voting) such holder would be entitled to cast for the election of directors with respect to such holder's shares of stock multiplied by the number of directors to be elected by such holder, and that such holder may cast all of such votes for a single director or may distribute them among the number to be voted for, or for any 2 or more of them as such holder may see fit."   (Delaware General Corporation Law §214).

Let's run through some possible scenarios:

Scenario #1: Foolish Mary *vs.* Smart Bob:

Let's imagine that Mary is greedy and wants all three board seats, so she distributes her 153 votes equally among her nominees, A, B, and C. Let's assume Bob knows that Mary plans to vote this way, so he comes up with a strategy to maximize his representation on the board by spreading his 147 votes between his two nominees:

	A	B	C	X	Y
Mary: 153 votes (51 shares x 3 open board seats = 153)	51 yes	51 yes	51 yes	0 yes	0 yes
Bob: 147 votes (49 shares x 3 open board seats = 147)	0 yes	0 yes	0 yes	74 yes	73 yes
Vote total for each nominee	**51**	**51**	**51***	**74***	**73***

*One of the top three vote-getters.

Mary has shot herself in the foot. Her misunderstanding of cumulative voting has lost her control of the board. Bob's understanding of cumulative voting has allowed him to gain control of the board.

156

Scenario #2: Smart Mary *vs.* Smart Bob:

Let's assume that both Mary and Bob understand the cumulative voting system. Both have applied the cumulative voting formula (introduced below) and have concluded that Bob will be able to get one board seat (if he plays his cards right), but no more than one board seat (if Mary plays her cards right). The results of the election will look like this:

	A	B	X[80]
Mary: 153 votes (51 shares x 3 open board seats = 153)	77 yes	76 yes	0 yes
Bob: 147 votes (49 shares x 3 open board seats = 147)	0 yes	0 yes	147 yes
Vote total for each nominee	77*	76*	147*

*One of the top three vote-getters.

The following **cumulative voting formula** tells us **how many shares a shareholder needs to ensure one seat on the board**. It assumes that all other shares will vote collectively against her.

Here is the formula to determine how many shares a shareholder needs to **ensure one seat** on the board:

$$\frac{total\ number\ of\ shares\ entitled\ to\ vote}{number\ of\ board\ seats\ up\ for\ election\ +\ 1} + 1\ (or\ a\ fraction)$$

Here is the formula to determine how many shares a shareholder needs to **ensure more than one seat on the board** (*x* number of seats):[81]

---

[80] C and Y drop out because neither Bob nor Mary would vote for or nominate them when Bob is voting smart.

[81] I like to think that the person who came up with this formula was a Nobel Prize-winning mathematician, but it was probably just someone who actually understood junior high school algebra (not me).

$$\frac{total\ number\ of\ shares\ entitled\ to\ vote\ (x)}{number\ of\ board\ seats\ up\ for\ election + 1} + 1\ (or\ a\ fraction)$$

Application of the formula to Goo Corp., with **100** shares[82] issued to Bob and Mary, and **3** board seats up for election.[83]

$$\frac{100}{3+1} + 1 = 26$$

Thus, in Goo Corp., a minority shareholder needs 26 shares to ensure herself one seat on the board.

If we wanted to determine how many shares would be required to elect a **majority of the Goo Corp. board**, which in this case is **2** directors:

$$\frac{100\ (2)}{3+1} + 1 = 51$$

Applying the formula to another hypothetical corporation:

Assume that GU Inc. has:

10,000 shares of common stock **authorized,**

5,000 shares of which are **issued** and outstanding.

550 shares of the issued and outstanding common stock are **non-voting** common.

The board of directors of GU Inc. consists of **5 director seats**, all of which are up for election this year.

How many shares do I need to ensure that I can **elect one director**?

I know many of you chose to go to law school because someone told you there would be no math. Sorry.

[82] Although the shareholders will actually cast 300 votes (100 shares x 3 board seats open) at the shareholders meeting, **the formula uses the original number of shares (100), not the number of votes they will actually have (300)**.

[83] Do not forget **Please Excuse My Dear Aunt Sally**. The order of operations is: (1) Parenthesis, (2) Exponents, (3) Multiplication, (4) Division, (5) Addition, (5) Subtraction.

Formula:

$$\frac{total\ number\ of\ shares\ entitled\ to\ vote}{number\ of\ board\ seats\ up\ for\ election\ +1} + 1\ (or\ a\ fraction)$$

Plug in the numbers:

$$\frac{4,450}{5+1} + fraction\ (to\ round\ up\ to\ next\ whole\ number)\ = 742$$

Answer:

I need 742 shares to ensure that I can elect at least one board seat in this election (but I may be able to elect more with 742 shares if the other voting shares are not voting as a group).

Comments:

The numerator is 4,450 because only 4,450 shares are entitled to vote (10,000 are authorized, not issued. Of the 5,000 issued, only 4,450 may vote because 550 are non-voting common).

In this case, $\frac{4,450}{5+1} = \frac{4,450}{6} = 741.667$. When you have a fraction like this, you do NOT add one to it to bring it to 742.667; instead, you simply add enough to bring it to the next whole number, which is 742 shares.

How many shares do I need to ensure that I can **elect a majority of the board**?

Formula:

$$\frac{total\ number\ of\ shares\ entitled\ to\ vote\ (x)}{number\ of\ board\ seats\ up\ for\ election\ +1} + 1\ (or\ a\ fraction)$$

Plug in the numbers:

$$\frac{4,450(3)}{5+1} + 1\ = 2,226$$

Answer:

I need 2,226 shares to ensure that I can elect at least 3 directors in this election (but I may be able to elect more with 2,226 shares if the other voting shares are not voting as a group).

Comments:

In this case $x=3$ because I want a majority of the 5 person board, which is 3. Thus, $\frac{4,450(3)}{5+1} = \frac{13,350}{6} = 2,225$. When you have a whole number like this, you add one share, which, in this case, means that 2,226 shares are needed.

5A-202(c) MAJORITY VOTING FOR DIRECTORS:

As we mentioned in the general introduction, some public companies have moved to a majority voting standard for the election of directors. In these companies, a nominee cannot be elected to the board unless she receives a majority of affirmative votes of the shares attending the meeting. A plurality (i.e., more votes than the next nominee) is not sufficient.

5A-203 STAGGERED/CLASSIFIED BOARD:

To this point, we have been assuming that every board seat comes up for election each year. Indeed, this format for electing directors is generally the default rule under state corporate law statutes. For example, if the board comprises 9 directors, each director seat will come up for election every year.

However, corporate law statutes generally allow corporations to change the default rule and **stagger** (or "classify") their boards into **two** or **three** groups. Here is the typical language of a corporate law statute allowing a staggered board:

> "The directors of any corporation organized under this chapter may, by the certificate of incorporation or by an initial bylaw, or by a bylaw adopted by a vote of the stockholders, be divided into 1, 2 or 3 classes; the term of office of those of the first class to expire at the first annual meeting held after such classification becomes effective; of the second class 1 year thereafter; of the third class 2 years thereafter; and at each annual election held after such classification becomes effective, directors shall be chosen for a full term, as the case may be, to succeed those whose terms expire. . . ."[84]

So, according to this statute, if a nine person board is staggered into two groups (or "classes"), it would look like this:

---

[84] Delaware General Corporation Law §141(d).

Group 1 (made up of 4 or 5 board seats):

> **Year 1** (*i.e.,* the first year of classification): Elected to the board for a one-year term.

> **Year 2:** Elected to the board for a one-year term

Group 2 (made of the remaining 4 or 5 board seats):

> **Year 1** (*i.e.,* the first year of classification): Elected to the board for a two-year term.

> **Year 2:** Not up for election this year.

> **Year 3:** Elected to the board for a two-year term

In principle, each class of board seats will be up for election every other year, but the first term for one of the classes can only be a one-year term, otherwise the classes would not be staggered (*i.e.,* both classes would come up for election every other year, but on the same year).

What is the purpose and significance of having a staggered/classified board? Staggering a board provides **continuity** for the board and for the corporation's business. The entire board will not turn over every year. However, a staggered board **makes it more difficult for a minority shareholder to gain a seat on the board using cumulative voting**.

Let's look at how a staggered board would affect the minority shareholder of GU Inc.

> We concluded that a minority shareholder in GU Inc. would need 742 shares to ensure she would be able to elect one director to the 5-person board.

$$\frac{4,450}{5+1} + fraction \ (to \ round \ up \ to \ next \ whole \ number) \ = 742$$

But, if the board is staggered and only 3 directors are up for election this year, she would **need more shares to ensure she could elect one director** – 1,113 shares, to be precise. Here is the application of the formula:

$$\frac{4,450}{3+1} + fraction \ (to \ round \ up \ to \ next \ whole \ number) \ = 1,113$$

A staggered board also has implications for a majority shareholder under a straight voting process. Imagine a situation where I acquire a majority of the shares of a corporation and I want to gain control of the 9-person board. If the entire board comes up for election, I will easily be able to elect all of my 9 nominees to the board at the next annual meeting. However, if the board is staggered and only 3 seats are up for election this year, it will take me two consecutive annual shareholders meetings to gain control of the board with six seats. Of course, I might be able remove the directors and then replace them with my candidates, but that requires a bit more maneuvering.

A **staggered board** provides the corporation with more continuity in leadership, but it can also **help the incumbent directors entrench themselves on the board**.

5A-204 **REMOVING DIRECTORS:**

As we discussed in the general introduction, **shareholders actually have the right to propose the removal of directors**. The proposal will then go before the shareholders who are entitled to vote.

The process for shareholder voting to remove a director is different from the election process – there is no straight voting or cumulative voting, per se.

Instead, the process is like shareholder voting on any other matter: the proposal to remove directors will pass if the shareholders support it, which could be a simple majority vote, an absolute majority vote, or a votes-cast majority vote, depending on the jurisdiction, or the company's articles or bylaws.

There are three general points to consider when learning your jurisdiction's statute on removal of directors:

1) ***Does it require calling a special shareholders meeting?*** Depending on the jurisdiction, shareholders may not be able to remove a director at an annual shareholders meeting, but may do so at a special shareholders meeting.

2) ***Can the shareholders remove a director without cause?*** Generally shareholders can remove a director without cause because they have the ultimate and unfettered right to determine who runs the corporation on their behalf. The articles or bylaws might be able to limit removal of directors to situations where there is cause.

3) ***Can the board also remove directors?*** In some jurisdictions, the board may also have a right to remove a director, but their rights are normally limited to remove for cause or a limited number of other specific circumstances.

4) ***Are there special protections for directors elected by minority shareholders?*** If minority shareholders have been able to elect a representative on the board, either through voting as a class or through

cumulative voting, it would undermine their efforts if the majority shareholders could simply remove these directors by majority vote.

Special protections for a director elected by a class of shares:
Imagine the articles of incorporation grant the owners of Class A shares the right to elect one of the corporation's three directors.

The law of most jurisdictions provides that only the Class A shareholders could remove this director (but this limitation is something that you might want to clearly draft in the articles in any case).

Special protections for a director elected by cumulative voting:
Imagine that I am a minority shareholder who owns just enough shares to elect one director using cumulative voting.

If the process of removal of directors simply requires a majority vote, I will not be able to prevent the removal of the director I elected through cumulative voting.

Most corporate law statutes provide that a director who was elected by cumulative voting cannot be removed if the number of shares voting against her removal would have been sufficient to elect her to the board.

> *Illustration*:
>
> Assume Director X was elected by cumulative voting, but now there is a proposal to remove her. Further assume that under the cumulative voting formula, she needed 742 shares voted for her to be elected. If shareholders voted 742 shares **against** her removal, she could not be removed, even if all of the 3,708 remaining shares are voted in favor of her removal.

5A-205 VOTING ON OTHER MATTERS:

We have said it before, but it bears repeating: Corporate law statutes envision shareholder voting on a limited number of fundamental matters, other than the election of directors. These matters usually include:

(1) Dissolution of the corporation;

(2) Merger of the corporation;

(3) Sale of substantially all of the corporation's assets;

(4) Amendment of the articles of incorporation; or

(5) Amendment of the bylaws (but the board has a coextensive right to amend the bylaws without shareholder approval).

Corporate statutes generally provide **greater approval requirements**, a **higher quorum**, or **both** for more "revolutionary" transactions.

Here are some **rules of thumb** to serve as guidelines for you as you become familiar with the corporate law of your jurisdiction:

>*Bylaw amendments:* Regular quorum and approval requirements.

>*Article amendments:* Regular quorum and approval requirements

>*Merger:* Heightened quorum and/or approval requirements

>*Sale of substantially all the assets:* Heightened quorum and/or approval requirements

>*Dissolution:* Heightened quorum and/or approval requirements

BUT, these are simply guidelines. **Your jurisdiction's corporate law statute may vary**.

For shareholder voting on fundamental matters, the law provides default rules for quorum and approval. You may be wondering if there is a **default standard for shareholder voting for matters other than the matters listed above**.

Corporate law statutes do not always envision shareholder voting on matters other than the fundamental matters mentioned above and the election of directors.

Indeed, **shareholders will not be voting on other matters unless**:

(1) the bylaws or articles specifically give shareholders the right to vote (e.g., shareholder approval of executive compensation);

(2) the vote is precatory (i.e., a suggestion from the shareholder body to the board of directors); or

(3) the board of directors require a shareholder vote on a matter through a board resolution.

In any of these three situations where shareholders are voting, you should first check the bylaws or articles for quorum and voting requirements. If the bylaws or articles are not specific, you should search your corporate law statute for a default provision.

We address the dissolutions, mergers, and sale of substantially all of the corporation's assets in later chapters. In the following sections, we will go through the process of **amending the bylaws** and **amending the articles**.

———————

5A-206 **AMENDING THE BYLAWS:**

Amending the bylaws is not a "fundamental transaction" in the strictest sense. It may be helpful to think of amendment of the bylaws as a separate category of transaction entitled to shareholder voting.

The board of directors can amend the bylaws without shareholder approval and the shareholders can amend the bylaws without board approval. This pattern differs from the pattern in dissolution, mergers and sale of substantially all the assets, which usually require both board approval *and* shareholder approval.

What types of provisions are in the bylaws? Usually, **the bylaws contain procedures and rules regarding the governance of the corporation,** such as rules addressing quorum, approval, number of directors, proxy voting, etc.

Most any bylaw provision, however, may be placed in the articles of incorporation. As we discussed in earlier chapters, the articles are akin to the "constitution" of the corporation. Provisions within the articles are entitled to special deference and protection. **When a corporation makes a choice to include a specific provision in its articles, rather than its bylaws, the choice implies that such provision is fundamental to the corporation and changing it requires overcoming a greater hurdle.**

In fact, some provisions are so important that the law requires them to be in the articles and not the bylaws. For example, if the corporation chooses to have different classes of shares, the designation of these classes, as well as their relative rights, must be in the articles of incorporation, not the bylaws.

The law establishes a hierarchy of importance between the articles and the bylaws. **Provisions in the articles merit greater protection. Provisions in the bylaws merit less protection.** When familiarizing yourself with your jurisdiction's approach to amending the bylaws, you should expect quorum and approval requirements at the more lenient end of the spectrum - i.e., requirements that do not create a great hurdle for approval of the amendment.

5A-206(a) **SHAREHOLDER PROPOSALS TO AMEND BYLAWS:**

The right of the shareholders to propose and pass bylaw amendments may not appear interesting or unique, but you must look at it in the greater context of the general approach to corporate law and shareholder control rights.

Shareholders' control rights are very limited. Even when they have a right to vote on a matter, it is generally a "reactive right" - in other words, the board makes a proposal and the shareholders vote "yea" or "nay" to such proposal.

However, **under most corporate law statutes, the shareholders actually have the right to propose and approve a bylaw amendment and completely bypass the board.** The amendment of bylaws can become an interesting battleground for the balance of power between shareholders and the board of directors, but it is subject to one VERY important proviso:

Most jurisdictions forbid the use of bylaw provisions to interfere with the board's discretion to conduct the business and affairs of the corporation.

Here is the general logic underlying this rule: Corporate law statutes generally charge the directors with the obligation and the right to manage the business and affairs of the corporation. As an example, Delaware's corporate law statute famously states:

> The business and affairs of every corporation organized under this chapter *shall* be managed by or under the direction of a board of directors, except as may be otherwise provided in this chapter or in its *certificate of incorporation*. . . . (Delaware General Corporation Law §141(a)).

Note the mandatory language "shall." Note also that the statute allows corporations to change this rule, but only through the articles of incorporation (known as the "certificate of incorporation" in Delaware), not through the bylaws. **Thus, it is improper for a bylaw provision to interfere with the board's obligation and right to manage the business and affairs of the corporation.**

The shareholders could propose and approve amendments to the bylaws that address **procedural issues** (unless the statute expressly limits the procedural issue to the articles of incorporation).

Illustration:

The shareholders could propose and approve the following amendments/additions to the corporation's bylaws:

> "The annual meeting shall take place on the last Friday of March each year. If the date falls on a legal holiday, the meeting will be held on the following business day that is not a holiday."

> "Prior to the shareholders meeting, the secretary of the corporation shall prepare a list of shareholders, in alphabetical order according to shareholder last names. The list shall show the address of each shareholder and the number of shares entitled to vote by each shareholder."

> "The board of directors shall not take any action without meeting, regardless of whether all directors have consented to the action in writing."

On the other hand, the shareholders **could NOT** amend or create a bylaw provision that **interferes with the board's management** of the business of the corporation.

For example, a bylaw provision could NOT provide:

> "The board shall not outsource product assembly to workers outside of the United States."

> "The board shall adopt green technology for all of the company's manufacturing plants."

> "The board shall not allow the corporation to advertise in publications that contain pornographic images."

5A-206(b) THE BOARD'S RIGHT TO AMEND THE BYLAWS:

Under most state corporate law statutes, the board of directors has a right to amend the bylaws that is coextensive with the shareholders right to do the same. The **coextensive right** of these two groups, who may have divergent interests, raises the need for the law to provide for a **"tiebreaker."**

Illustration:

> The shareholders might pass an amendment to the bylaws requiring the board to have 7 directors, only to have the board amend the bylaws the next day to restore the number of directors to 13.

Generally, corporate law statutes have a tiebreaker provision that favors the shareholders. It allows the shareholder to take some measures to prevent the board from amending a specific bylaw or amending the bylaws altogether. For example, under the RMBCA, the shareholders can either expressly state that the board cannot amend a particular bylaw provision (by noting it in the bylaw provision itself) or completely forbid the board from amending the bylaws, through a provision in the corporation's articles.[85]

5A-207 AMENDING THE ARTICLES OF INCORPORATION:

The shareholders have a right to vote on nearly every amendment to the articles of incorporation. There may be a few ministerial amendments that simply require board action, and do not require shareholder approval.

Aside from those few provisions, amendments to the articles will require a **proposal by the board of directors and approval by the shareholders**. In most jurisdictions, shareholders do not have a right to initiate or propose an

---

[85] RMBCA §10.20(b).

amendment to the articles. They merely have a right to vote on a proposed amendment brought before them by the board of directors.

When we say the "shareholders" have a right to vote on amending the articles, **which shareholders** have a right to vote on amendment to the articles? Our corporation might have **several different classes of shares**.

For example, we may have:

common stock,

non-voting common stock,

or several series of **preferred stock**.

Do they all get to vote on amendment? If they do, do they all vote together as one shareholder body or does each class get to vote as a group separately?

5A-207(a) CLASS VOTING:

If your corporation only has one class of stock (*i.e.*, common stock), this is a moot point because, in fact, all shareholders will get to vote as one class (because there is only one class). In contrast, however, if you have a variety of classes (such as common stock, preferred stock, non-voting common, etc.), you must consider whether the shareholders of all classes will vote together as one body, or whether any class will have the right to vote separately as a class.

The right to vote as a class is very important because it gives that class the right to veto the transaction no matter how small the class and no matter how much support the proposal receives from other classes.

Here is a simple example to illustrate how class voting creates a veto right for a class of stock:

Imagine **LMN Inc**. has three classes of shares, **class A, B, and C, each with 100 shares issued and outstanding** (i.e., 300 shares altogether, divided evenly among the three classes).

At the annual shareholders meeting, the shareholders vote on the following amendment to the articles of incorporation:

Class C shares will no longer have a right to receive a dividend.

Class A and Class B shareholders unanimously vote in favor of the amendment (200 votes in favor).

Class C shareholders naturally vote unanimously against the amendment (100 votes against).

If the shareholders of all classes vote together as one body, the amendment passes with overwhelming support:

200 in favor *vs.* 100 opposed

If, however, Class C shareholders vote separately as a class, they can veto the amendment, regardless of how the other classes vote. Even if Class A and B shareholders unanimously approve the amendment, Class C shareholders could veto the amendment if it failed to win their favor.

From this example, you probably have been able to discern that **corporate law statutes usually require a class vote on amendments to the articles when such amendments affect the rights of a particular class**. The class or classes that are affected by the amendment will each vote as a class and the voting shares that are not affected will vote as a body, even if they are of different classes.

Before we delve into the details of how the shareholders of various different classes and series of shares will vote (or not) on a proposed amendment to the articles, we should develop the context:

What types of amendment to the articles will we see? The articles can be very simple or very detailed, depending on the corporation and the circumstances. There are provision in the articles that we can think of as **article provisions of general applicability**. In other words, they do not affect any one class of shares (or series of shares) in any unique or individual way. For example:

"The name of the corporation is XYZ Corp."

"The board of directors shall consist of 5 directors."

"The corporation shall hold all shareholders meetings within the state of ___."

"The corporation's principal place of business is _____."

The articles might also have **provisions that are specific to one or more of the various classes of shares**. You may remember from Chapter 4[86] that the terms of any class of stock with preferred rights or rights different from common stock must be in the articles of incorporation. There may be proposed amendments to the articles that directly affect a class or series of shares. Examples include proposals to:

Reclassify the Series A Preferred to Series B Preferred.

Increase the authorized shares of common stock.

---

[86] See Chapter 4, §4A-205(a).

Change every one share of common stock into two shares (a **stock split**).

Change every two shares of common stock into one share (a **reverse stock split**).

Change the dividend or liquidation preferences of Series A Preferred.

Change the voting rights of Series A Preferred.

Here are some **rules of thumb** to keep in mind as you read your jurisdiction's relevant corporate law statute. Your jurisdiction's approach may vary somewhat from these rules of thumb, but they provide a base point from which you can read and understand your jurisdiction's specific approach:

Amending **generally applicable article provisions**

Illustration:

Changing the name of the corporation in the articles:

The common stock will vote (unless the articles expressly say otherwise) [Common stock gets to vote on everything that shareholders vote on].

Non-voting common stock will NOT vote (unless the articles say otherwise) [We designated it "non-voting" for a reason].

Preferred stock normally gets to vote only if the articles of incorporation provide for voting rights [Preferred stock can be drafted in many ways, so it really depends on what the articles say, but preferred stock is generally drafted to have lesser voting rights than common stock. If the preferred stock has no voting rights, it is treated like non-voting common].

> **There will be no class voting** [We only get class voting when the amendment directly or indirectly affects the rights of a specific class].

Amending article provisions that **directly or indirectly affect a particular class's rights**:

The common stockholders will vote (unless the articles expressly say otherwise). The common stock will vote as a class only when the amendment directly or indirectly affects the rights of the common stock (or unless the articles specifically say so).

The preferred stockholders will not vote unless they have the right to vote as a class (unless the articles give them the right to vote). They will vote as a class if the amendment directly or indirectly affects the preferred stockholders' rights.

Non-voting common stockholders will not vote unless they have the right to vote as a class (unless the articles give them the right to vote). They will vote as a class if the amendment directly or indirectly affects the rights of the non-common stock.

Here is an illustration that brings all these concepts together:

Illustration:

Abel Inc. has two classes of shares:

Common stock: 200 shares authorized; 100 shares issued and outstanding; and

Preferred stock: 100 shares authorized; 100 shares issued and outstanding;

Terms of the preferred: $4.00 dividend preference over the common; preferred shareholders only have voting rights when the corporation has missed 8 consecutive quarterly dividends, but the corporation has never missed a dividend.

The following amendments to the articles are submitted to the shareholders for approval:

"Increase authorized common stock to 300 shares."

Analysis of common stock:

Common stockholders have a right to vote.

Analysis of preferred stock:

Preferred stockholders have no right to vote.

"Increase the authorized preferred stock to 200 shares."

Analysis of common stock:

Common stockholders have a right to vote. Common stock will generally always have a right to vote on any amendment to the articles, even when the amendment is with respect to another class.

Common stock will most likely get to vote as a class because the increase in the authorized shares of the preferred stock has an indirect affect on the common. The preferred stockholders have economic rights that are superior to the common. By increasing the authorized shares of the preferred, the economic rights of the common will be diluted (BUT, make sure you check your jurisdiction's law).

171

Analysis of preferred stock:

Preferred stockholders would likely have a right to vote and a right to vote as a class. Even though the articles do not grant the preferred shareholders a right to vote, the increase in authorized preferred directly affects the preferred class, entitling them to a vote. (Of course, **you need to check the specific provisions of your state's statute**. The most recent changes to the RMBCA, for example, would not give the preferred a right to vote at all, although earlier versions of the RMBCA would.)

> *Drafting note:* When drafting the terms of the preferred stock in the articles of incorporation, do not rely on the statute to provide for voting rights; draft them clearly into the terms of the preferred stock in the articles.

"Create a new class called "Preferred A" with a $2.00 dividend preference over the Preferred and Common"

Analysis of common stock:

Common stockholders have a right to vote. Common stock will generally always have a right to vote on amendment to the articles.

Common stock will most likely get to vote as a class because the creation of a new preferred class has an indirect affect on the common. The new preferred stockholders will have economic rights that are superior to the common. The economic rights of the common are weakened by the creation of a new preferred class.

Analysis of preferred stock:

Preferred stockholders would likely have a right to vote and a right to vote as a class. Although the articles do not grant the preferred shareholders a right to vote, the creation of a new Preferred Class A with rights superior to the current preferred stock weakens the value of the current preferred shareholders' economic rights.

5A-207(b) ADDITIONAL PROTECTIONS:

Your jurisdiction's corporate law statute *might* give protections in addition to class voting to shareholders of a class of shares when the articles are amended.

These additional protections normally arise when the amendments alter the rights of that class to:

dividends,

liquidation,

voting, or

redemption.

The additional protections may take the form of one of more of the following:

Heightened quorum requirements;

Heightened approval requirements; or

Appraisal/dissenter's rights

> We will address appraisal rights (also referred to as "dissenter's rights") in more detail in Chapter 9, but for now, a brief introduction will suffice.

> If a shareholder is not in favor of the amendment to the articles, she can **require the corporation to buy her shares from her** if the amendment receives the approval of other shareholders. The corporation must pay her the **fair market value** of her shares.

> *Note:* not all jurisdictions give appraisal rights for amendment of the articles of incorporation.

––––––––––

5A-208 SHAREHOLDER VOTE-POOLING AGREEMENTS AND VOTING TRUSTS:

5A-208(a) VOTE-POOLING AGREEMENTS:

The concept of a vote-pooling agreement is not difficult to grasp: **Two or more shareholders agree on how they will vote their shares**.

Vote pooling agreements are most often associated with the election of directors, but shareholders may agree to pool their votes on any matter that shareholders have a right to vote on.

A vote-pooling agreement may be a stand-alone contract, or it **might be part of a larger shareholders agreement** containing other agreements between the shareholders, such as:

A **pre-incorporation agreement**,[87]

A **buy-sell agreement**,[88] or

An **agreement providing other policies** of the corporation.[89]

––––––––––

[87] See Chapter 3, §3B-302.

[88] See Chapter 7, §7-300 et seq.

To illustrate the use of a vote-pooling agreement, consider the following example:

> Imagine that **A**lice, **B**etty, and **C**arol form a closely-held corporation. The articles provide for a three-member board of directors.
>
> Alice, Betty, and Carol recognize that the locus of power and authority in the corporation is in the board of directors and they each want one of the board seats. Because board members are elected by the shareholders, they have to devise a way to be elected to the board. They have three options:
>
>> (1) Provide for **cumulative voting** in the articles;
>>
>> (2) Provide for **three separate classes of shares** for each of the shareholders in the articles:
>>
>>> Alice receives A Shares, Betty receives B Shares, and Carol receives C shares.
>>>
>>> The three classes of shares have the same economic rights, but they each have the right to elect one of the three directors. (**Note:** because the shares all have the same economic rights, the corporation will not undermine their S-Corp status).[90]
>>
>> (3) Sign a **vote-pooling agreement** whereby Alice, Betty, and Carol agree to elect each other to the board of directors.

Legally speaking, vote-pooling agreements are uncontroversial. The law permits shareholders to enter these types of agreements. It is not necessary for all the shareholders to enter the agreement. There are usually **no duration limitations** for these agreements (but, check your statute), and there is usually **no requirement that these types of agreements be disclosed to the corporation** or other non-signing shareholders (but, check your statute).

Many state corporate law statutes explicitly allow vote-pooling agreements among shareholders. Others may not have a specific provision, but as a matter of common law, vote-pooling agreements are generally considered legal, enforceable, and subject to no significant restrictions or limitations (as long as they address voting on matters that are within the purview of shareholder voting and not matters that are normally within the province of the board of directors). Some jurisdictions may limit the duration of vote-pooling

---

[89] See §5A-213(b), below.

[90] See Chapter 3, §3B-404.

174

agreements to ten years or may require the parties to notify the corporation of the agreement.

5A-208(b) VOTING TRUSTS:

The voting trust accomplishes the same purpose of the vote-pooling agreement but through a slightly different mechanism. **The shareholders who are parties to a voting trust will relinquish ownership of their shares to a trustee.** The trustee will usually become the shareholder of record and the original shareholders become the beneficiaries of the trust.

The trustee may issue trust certificates to these beneficiaries. **The trust agreement will provide the trustee with instructions on voting the shares that are subject to the trust.** Most corporate law statutes require the voting trust to be filed with the corporation and limit the duration of the voting trust to ten years, but it is usually renewable.

5A-208(c) VOTE-POOLING AGREEMENTS VS. VOTING TRUSTS:

The possible advantage of a voting trust over a vote-pooling agreement is that the voting trust is **self-enforcing**, which means that we would not need the court to enforce the agreement in the event that one of the parties no longer wants to abide by it.

Illustration:

Alice, Betty, and Carol enter into a voting trust that instructs the trustee to vote their shares to elect each of them to the board.

Assume that Alice is no longer happy with the trust agreement and would like to vote her shares in another way.

What action could she take to breach the voting trust? None. Because she is no longer the record owner of her shares, she has no right to vote them in a meeting. The trustee will vote them in accordance with the trust agreement.

In contrast, although vote-pooling agreements are specifically enforceable by a court, Alice could show up at the shareholders meeting and vote her shares in breach of the vote-pooling agreement.

Neither Betty, Carol, nor the chair of the shareholders meeting could stop her from voting her shares in violation of the vote-pooling agreement at the shareholders meeting, unless they received a court injunction prior to the meeting.

The costs of taking the matter to the court to specifically enforce the agreement would fall on Betty and Carol. Accordingly, a transactional attorney tries to think beyond whether a contract is legally enforceable or not; she also tries to draft it in a way that minimizes enforcement costs for her client in the event of breach.

Transactional attorneys are very clever. They have devised **a way to use irrevocable proxies to make vote-pooling agreements self-enforcing** and, thereby, reduce transaction costs for their clients. The use of irrevocable proxies with vote-pooling agreements will be discussed immediately below in the section on proxies.

Here is a chart comparing vote-pooling agreements and voting trusts:

Vote-pooling Agreement	Voting Trust
Usually no limitation on duration	Usually a maximum duration of 10 years, but often renewable
Usually no need to disclose to corporation of other shareholders	Usually must be filed with the corporation
Not self-enforcing (except when coupled with an irrevocable proxy)	Self-enforcing

5A-208(d) LEGENDS ON SHARE CERTIFICATES:

When shareholders enter into **vote-pooling agreements**, they may be concerned that the other shareholders to the agreement may transfer their shares. They would like to make sure the agreement will bind subsequent transferees of the shares. Generally speaking, as a matter of contract law, transferees will be bound only if they agree to be bound, expressly or implicitly.

The shareholders who are parties to the agreement will often require agree to place **legends** (i.e., notations) **on their share certificates.** The legends state the shares are subject to a vote-pooling agreement and subsequent transferees will be bound by it. By accepting transfer of the shares that have legends, the transferee implicitly assents to be bound to the vote-pooling agreement. A legend may look something like the following:

> The shares represented by this certificate are subject to the terms and provisions of a Voting Agreement dated May 5, 2015. The Voting Agreement is automatically binding on anyone who acquires shares by assignment, transfer, pledge or other disposition. A copy of the agreement is available for inspection at the corporation's offices.

There is less need for legends on share certificates indicating a **voting trust** since the shareholders are not in a position to transfer the shares (the trustee is the owner of the shares). However, legends might still play a role in voting trusts in the following ways:

1) You might see legends on **share certificates** that are subject to a voting trust that puts potential transferees on notice that the shares are subject to a voting trust and cannot be transferred by the trustee without the consent of the trust beneficiaries.

2) You might see legends on the ***trust certificates*** the trustee issues to the beneficiaries, stating that the trust certificate is subject to a trust agreement that is binding on all transferees.

5A-209 PROXIES:

5A-209(a) THE FUNCTIONS AND USES OF PROXIES:

As discussed in the general introduction to shareholder voting, a "proxy" is simply a **power of attorney (i.e., appointment of an agent)**.

With a proxy, **the shareholder gives the agent authority to vote her shares on her behalf** at the shareholders meeting (or to sign consents on her behalf when action is taken without meeting).

The proxy mechanism itself is unremarkable, but the uses of proxies is fascinating and important ("fascinating" to the law professor; "important" to the law student who will eventually be tested by the law professor).

The word "**proxy**," when used in connection with shareholder voting, generally has **several different meanings**. It may be used to mean:

> **The agent voting on behalf of the shareholder** (*e.g., "I cannot attend the meeting, but Jim James will act as my proxy."*);

> **The authority the shareholder grants to the agent to vote on her behalf** (*e.g., "I gave Jim James my proxy"*); or

> **The actual written form appointing a proxy** (*e.g., "Let's assign the task of drafting the proxy to the most junior associate."*).

Proxies serve the following **functions**:

> **To allow a shareholder to vote at a meeting she cannot attend**. In a sense, the proxy is analogous to an absentee ballot, except that the shareholder is not voting her shares herself; she is asking someone else to cast her ballot on her behalf at the meeting.

> **To enable a corporation with a large number of shareholders to obtain a quorum**. The more shareholders a corporation has, the smaller the stake of each shareholder. The smaller the stake of the shareholder, the less incentive she has to attend shareholders meetings. In addition,

the more shareholders a corporation has, the more difficult it will be to find a venue that can accommodate all of them. The proxy mechanism allows the corporation to solicit proxies for shareholders' meetings, which ensures the shareholder meeting will meet quorum requirements (attendance by proxy functions as attendance for quorum purposes).

To get your nominees (or yourself) elected to the board of directors. In a perfect world – a world where all of a corporation's shareholders would attend the shareholders meeting in person – you could attempt to get your nominee elected to the board by nominating your candidate at the meeting and convincing the other shareholders to vote for her. However, in the real world, where most shareholders in large corporations will not attend the shareholders meeting, the only way for you to garner votes for your nominee is to solicit proxies before the meeting. Proxies are the method by which the shareholders "attend" and vote at shareholder meetings. To get support for your nominee, you would send out a proxy form to each of the corporation's shareholders (or maybe just the largest shareholders) asking them to appoint you as their proxy. You might draft the proxy like this:

Form A:

Appointment of Proxy

The undersigned shareholder (the "Shareholder") of XYZ Inc. (the "Company") hereby appoints <u>Ms. Polly Proxy</u> as proxy, with full power of substitution, for and in the name of the Shareholder to attend all shareholder meetings of the Company and to act, vote, and execute consents with respect to any or all shares of the Company belonging to Shareholder.

This appointment may be revoked by the Shareholder at any time, but if not revoked will continue in effect until December 31, 2015.

Sign and date here: _____

Print your name here: _____

Or, it may look like this:

see next page

Form B:

Appointment of Proxy

The undersigned shareholder (the "Shareholder") of XYZ Inc. (the "Company") hereby appoints <u>Ms. Polly Proxy</u> as proxy, with full power of substitution, for and in the name of the Shareholder to attend the annual shareholders meeting of the Company to be held on March 12, 2015 and to act or vote at such meeting and any adjournment thereof with respect to any or all shares of the Company belonging to Shareholder as directed below and in her discretion as to other business matters that may properly come before the meeting or any adjournment thereof:

> **To vote FOR the following nominee to be a director of the Company:**
>
> Ms. Polly Proxy

Sign and date here: _____

Print your name here: _____

Can you spot the main differences between these two appointments of proxy? Either form could be used by the person soliciting the proxy to secure votes for her nominee to the board.

> **Form A** is more general and might be used to ensure a quorum or to provide a convenient method of voting for shareholders who are unable to attend. Of course, it could also be used for the purpose of soliciting votes for the proxy holder's nominee.

> **Form B** seems to be drafted for no other purpose than securing votes for the proxy holder's nominee - which is the proxy herself, in this case.

In a corporation where there are many shareholders who will not attend shareholders meetings, the corporation itself – i.e., **the board of directors – will solicit proxies**. The board of directors will generally have two motivations for soliciting proxies:

> (1) To **ensure a quorum** at the shareholders meeting; and
> (2) To ensure that the **nominees favored by management** and the board are elected.

In the large public corporation, the board of directors will solicit proxies to ensure there is a quorum of shares at the shareholder meeting and to make sure the nominees that it supports will have the best chance of getting elected to the board of directors. The nominees for director seats on public companies are normally selected by a board committee called the **nominating committee**. The slate of nominees selected by the nominating committee is often called the **management's slate.**

5A-209(b) REVOCABLE AND IRREVOCABLE PROXIES:

Proxies are normally revocable. The shareholder can revoke the agent's authority to vote on her behalf at any time before the vote. The shareholder may revoke this authority either **expressly or implicitly**.

> The shareholder can **implicitly revoke** a proxy by executing a **subsequent proxy** – a later proxy implicitly revokes all earlier proxies.

> Similarly, if the **shareholder attends the shareholders meeting and asserts her right to vote**, she is implicitly revoking any proxy she previously executed for that meeting.

However, the shareholder and the agent might want to create a situation where **the proxy authority is irrevocable**, i.e., the shareholder cannot revoke the agent's right to vote on the shareholder's behalf. Usually, the agent will only want the proxy authority to be irrevocable when the shareholder has given the agent authority to vote on her behalf as part of another transaction.

In most jurisdictions **a proxy is only irrevocable only when**:

> (1) it **expressly states it is irrevocable**; and

> (2) it is **coupled with an interest**.

The phrase "**coupled with an interest**" simply refers to the proxy authority being part of a larger transaction. It may help to think of "coupled with an interest" as a close relative of the consideration doctrine you learned in contracts. In other words, **the shareholder's promise to not revoke the proxy is only legally enforceable if the promise is supported by a specific type of consideration**, which corporate law calls "coupled with an interest."

A proxy will usually be **coupled with an interest** if it is given under one of these circumstances:

<u>Given to a **pledgee** in connection with the **pledge of shares**:</u>

> Sharon Shareholder borrows money from Lenny Lender. Sharon shareholder uses her shares in XYZ Corp. as collateral for the loan; she gives Lenny lender a secured interest in shares, which is called a "pledge."

> Sharon is the pledgor and Lenny is the pledgee.

Lenny might prefer to have a right to vote the shares to protect the value of the collateral, the shares. Because he does not own the shares, the only way he can receive the right to vote them is to receive proxy authority from Sharon. To protect his interests in the collateral when he makes his loan to Sharon, he will ask her to give him an irrevocable proxy. Sharon will not be able to revoke the proxy because it is coupled with an interest.

Given to a **purchaser** in connection with the **purchase of shares or the promise to purchase shares:**

Sharon Shareholder enters into a stock purchase agreement with Penelope Purchaser. Sharon agrees to sell her shares in XYZ Corp. to Penelope and Penelope agrees to purchase the same.

The parties have entered into a binding agreement, but the transaction might not take place for period of time (for various reasons, such as, Penelope might need to get financing or the parties might need to get consents from the other shareholders, etc.).

Between the signing of the contract and the closing of the transaction, Penelope might prefer to have a right to vote the shares to protect their value. Indeed, if Sharon has already entered into a binding agreement to sell the shares, she has little interest in investing the time and effort required to make informed voting decisions.

Penelope will ask Sharon to give her an irrevocable proxy to vote the shares between the contract signing and the closing. Sharon will not be able to revoke the proxy because it is coupled with an interest.

or

Sharon Shareholder sells her shares to Penelope Purchaser, but because the shares were **transferred after the record date** Penelope will not have a right to vote at the next annual shareholders meeting (even though Penelope is now a shareholder).

If Penelope's lawyer was careful when she structured the purchase, she would have required Sharon to give Penelope an irrevocable proxy. Sharon would not be able to revoke the proxy because it is coupled with an interest.

Given to a **creditor** in connection to **credit extended to the corporation:**

This time, Lenny Lender lends money directly to the corporation. Because he is a creditor (a fixed claimant) of the company, he bears some risk of the company's decisions.

181

To protect himself against that risk, he might contractually prohibit the corporation from taking certain risky actions or he might want some ongoing voice in corporate decisions.

One of the large shareholders, Sharon Shareholder, might give Lenny an irrevocable proxy to vote some or all of her shares in order to induce Lenny to make the loan to the corporation. Sharon would not be able to revoke the proxy because it is coupled with an interest.

> **Note:** If Sharon used her shares as collateral for the loan to the corporation and gave Lenny an irrevocable proxy in connection, it would also be a coupled with an interest, a pledge.

Given to an **employee** in connection with an **employment agreement:**

Suppose the corporation wants to hire Ellen Executive, a superstar CEO. Ellen will only take the job if she has some assurances that things will be done her way. In other words, she wants control.

One of the large shareholders, Sharon Shareholder, might give Ellen an irrevocable proxy to vote some or all of Sharon's shares in order to induce Ellen to take the CEO job. Sharon would not be able to revoke the proxy because it is coupled with an interest.

Ellen is more likely to ask for this type of control when she has accepted a compensation package that is based heavily on incentive compensation. Ellen will be more willing to accept such an arrangement if she can ensure that business will be conducted her way.

Given to a **party to a vote-pooling agreement** in connection with a **vote-pooling agreement:**

Sharon Shareholder enters into a vote-pooling agreement with another shareholder, Sal Stockholder. Sharon might give Sal an irrevocable proxy to vote her shares, or Sal might give Sharon an irrevocable proxy to vote his shares.

If each party is concerned that the other party will vote in contravention of the agreement at the shareholders meeting, they may each appoint a third party as their proxy, such as an arbitrator or the corporation itself. This way, when the shareholder meeting comes around, neither Sharon nor Sal will be able to vote their shares in breach of the agreement because they will not have the right to vote their shares. They have given that right away through an irrevocable proxy that is coupled with an interest – the vote-pooling agreement.

> ***Drafting note:*** The RMBCA says an irrevocable proxy is coupled with an interest if it is given to a "party" to a vote-pooling agreement.[91] To increase the likelihood that a court will find the proxy given to the arbitrator or corporation is "coupled with an interest," the arbitrator or corporation should be a party to the vote-pooling agreement.

Finally, when any of the interests in the above situations no longer exists, the proxy is no longer irrevocable.

5A-210 CONSENTS:

As already mentioned in the general introduction, **written consents** may allow shareholders to take action without meeting. **Consents are not proxies**. With a written consent, a shareholder is not authorizing anyone to vote on her behalf. The written consent **serves as both her consent to action without meeting** and her direct vote on the proposed action.

Written consents are quite common in closely-held corporations. Often, the corporate action requires a shareholder vote, but there is no dissent or controversy that justifies the time and expense of actually holding a shareholders meeting. Generally, corporate law still requires the corporation to hold an annual shareholders meeting, although some statutes might allow consents in lieu of the annual meeting.

The **rule of thumb** for action without meeting through written consents is that the action is only valid if **all shareholders consent**. In various jurisdictions, the corporation may be able to diverge from this unanimity requirement through amendment of the articles or bylaws.

Read this provision from Kentucky's Business Corporation Act. Kentucky has a rule permitting shareholder action without meeting only upon unanimous written consent of the shareholders entitled to vote. However, it allows corporations to change the unanimous-consent rule as follows:

> **If the articles of incorporation so provide**, any action except the election of directors by cumulative voting . . . required or permitted by this chapter to be taken at a shareholders' meeting may be taken without a meeting and without prior notice, . . . if the action is taken by shareholders entitled to vote on the action representing not less than eighty percent (80%), or such higher

----

[91] RMBCA §7.22(c)(5).

percentage required by this chapter or the articles of incorporation, of the votes entitled to be cast.[92]

5A-211 SHAREHOLDER INFORMATION RIGHTS:

In order to fully exercise their voting rights, shareholders need **access to information about the company and its management**.

Although the shareholders have no right to order the board to adopt a specific course of action with respect to the corporations business, they can indirectly affect the direction of the corporation by electing new directors. In order to make intelligent choices about the election of directors and in order to monitor the performance of the current directors, shareholders need access to information.

State corporate law statutes generally provide shareholders with access to the company's books and records. In a later chapter, we will discuss how federal law further regulates how, when, and what information must be disclosed by public companies to the market. In this chapter, however, **we will limit ourselves to state corporate law shareholder information rights, applicable to both public and private companies.**

First, let us conceptualize what types of information shareholders might want. Arguably, the most important information is the financial condition of the company. The main function of the board of directors is to maximize the company's profits. Shareholders want to see the **company's financial statements** to help them assess whether the current board is serving that function well.

Many jurisdictions, especially those following the RMBCA approach, **require a corporation to provide a shareholder with annual financial statements**.[93] An attorney should consider whether more specific provisions regarding the frequency and format of the corporation's financial reports and their distribution to shareholders should be drafted into the articles, bylaws, or shareholders agreement.

Most jurisdictions require corporations to file some sort of **annual report** with the secretary of state in the state of incorporation.[94] However, **these annual reports should not be confused with the detailed annual reports that public corporations** (and many private corporations) provide to their shareholders. The annual reports that corporations file with the secretary of

---

[92] Kentucky Business Corporation Act §7-040(2).

[93] RMBCA §16.20(a).

[94] See Chapter 3, §3B-303.

state of their respective states of incorporation **usually only have some very basic information**, such as the name of the corporation, the names of the current directors and officers, the current address of the company's registered office, the number of issued shares, etc. Although this information may be useful to the shareholder, it does not provide her with the necessary financial information about the company that she needs to assess management's performance.

Besides information regarding the financial condition of the company, **what other information might the shareholders want?** If a shareholder is planning to nominate herself or another candidate for election to the board, she will usually want access to the **list of shareholders** in order to solicit proxies.

In a closely-held corporation with only two or three shareholders, a shareholder might not need to solicit proxies in order to garner votes (and even if she did, she might not need access to the list of shareholders). Assuming the shareholders all attend the annual meeting, she could simply nominate herself at the annual meeting and persuade her fellow shareholders to vote for her.

However, the more shareholders a corporation has, the more likely that shareholders will not attend the meetings. The need to use the shareholder list and the proxy mechanism to secure votes for one's nominees becomes increasingly important as shareholder physical attendance at meetings declines.

Besides the shareholder list, there are **other corporate books and records** that shareholders might want to see to keep them abreast of corporate activities and to monitor the board for possible mismanagement. Under Delaware law and the RMBCA approach, the shareholder wishing to inspect the shareholder list, stock ledger, or other books and records must make a formal demand to the corporations **stating a proper purpose** for her access to corporate books and records. If the corporation refuses to allow the shareholder access to the records she requested, she may bring an action in court to compel the corporation to provide her with the records.

Under Delaware law, the corporation will have the burden of proof to show that the shareholder had an improper purpose when she requested access to the list of stockholders. With respect to other books and records, the shareholder will have the burden of proof to show she had a proper purpose.

Delaware's corporate law statute divides corporate books and records into two categories - the first is the stock ledger/list of stockholders and the second is a broad category of "other books and records."

The Delaware corporate law statute does not expressly limit the scope of "other books and records." Conceivably a shareholder could ask for very sensitive information, trade secrets or other information that the corporation would prefer not to disclose in a competitive market. In addition, a shareholder could request minute details of transactions, e-mail correspondences, or broad swaths of bookkeeping records that would take the corporation a significant amount of time to compile.

The only express provision in the Delaware corporate law statute that limits shareholder abuse of the broad right to inspect "other books and records" is the grant of discretion to the court to limit inspection or award other relief to the shareholder that the court deems "just and proper." In Delaware, the scope of the "other books and records" a shareholder may inspect is largely a matter of common law.

The RMBCA expressly limits the books and records a shareholder may inspect and divides them into two categories:

(1) Records shareholders may inspect as a matter of right; and

(2) Records that a shareholder may inspect if: (a) she makes a demand in good faith and with a proper purpose; (b) the demand describes, with reasonable particularity, the purpose and the records; and (c) the records are directly connected to the proper purpose.

The **records that shareholders are allowed to inspect as a matter of right** include the most basic records that we would consider **necessary for a shareholder to understand her rights as a shareholder and stay updated on corporate activities**.

To understand her most **basic rights**, a shareholder should have access to:

The **articles of incorporation;** and

The **bylaws.**

To keep herself **updated on corporate activities**, a shareholder should have access to:

Minutes of recent shareholder meetings; and

Correspondence from the corporation to the shareholders.

Finally, as a most basic right, a shareholder should be able to easily find out who is in charge of the corporation. Therefore, she should have access to:

A **list of current directors and officers**.

Other records available to a shareholder under the RMBCA **require demand and a proper purpose**. Such records are necessary for the shareholder to monitor the performance of the board of directors.

In order to monitor the board's performance, a shareholder making a demand and showing a proper purpose, may have access to:

Excerpts from **the minutes of board meetings,**

Accounting records (other than the most recent financial statements, which the shareholder has an absolute right to receive upon request), and

The **shareholder list** or stockholder ledger.

"Proper purpose" may be defined in a state's corporate law statute or by case law. The Delaware statute defines the "proper purpose" of a shareholder requesting access to corporate books and records as "**a purpose reasonably related to such person's interest as a stockholder**."[95]   Other jurisdictions have similar standards. The basic idea is that I cannot use my right to access corporate records for social causes or personal benefit not common to other shareholders.

However, shareholders will be able to articulate proper purposes for many social causes. For example: "I would like access to certain records regarding the corporation's disposal of toxic waste because I am concerned with the company's image, which, if damaged, would reduce the value of my shares."

Courts generally interpret "proper purpose" broadly, but one could imagine a situation where a shareholder had an improper purpose: For example: to use the shareholder list for direct marketing purposes; to get access to sensitive information for competitors, etc. The court might not allow a shareholder access when she had an improper purpose, even if she could articulate a proper purpose.

5A-212 SHAREHOLDER PROPOSALS AT SHAREHOLDER MEETINGS:

Could a shareholder stand up at a shareholders meeting, make a proposal that requires the board to take a specific course of action, then put the matter to a vote before the shareholder body? No, she could not (at least in the vast majority of circumstances).

As we have previously emphasized, shareholders have very little in the way of control rights. Their only avenue to exercise control over the decisions of the corporation is through their limited voting rights. Most shareholder voting rights are "reactive" in the sense the board makes a proposal and asks the shareholders to approve (or reject) it. **Shareholders rarely have the right to initiate corporate action**.

As discussed previously, there are generally **three instances where shareholders can initiate action** at a shareholders meeting:

---

[95] DGCL §220(b).

187

Nominating candidates for election to the board.

Proposing to remove a director.

Proposing to amend the bylaws.

Other fundamental transactions (e.g., mergers, sale of substantially all of the corporations assets, amendment of the articles, and dissolution) are ultimately put to a shareholder vote only after a proposal by the board of directors. Granted, there may be some state corporate law statutes that allow shareholders to propose amendments to the articles or even propose dissolution. However, I am not aware of any jurisdiction that allows shareholders to initiate merger proposals or proposals to sell substantially all of the company's assets.

Importantly, ordinary business matters are for the board to decide. Shareholders do not have any formal say in ordinary business matters, such as the decision to move the company's principal place of business to a new state, to lay off a large number of workers, or to take out a large loan to pay for a new project. Corporate law generally prohibits shareholders from interfering with the board, except through the election and removal process.

For example, it would most likely be **improper** for a shareholder to stand up at a meeting and ask the shareholders to vote on her proposal **demanding the board adopt a more comprehensive recycling policy**. This matter is an ordinary business decision within the exclusive purview of the board.

However, it would most likely be **proper** for a shareholder to raise the corporation's recycling policies as a **discussion item** at a shareholders' meeting and to even propose voting on a *non-binding* **shareholder resolution** *suggesting* the board take action, i.e., a precatory shareholders resolution.

Of course, to maintain order at shareholders' meetings and to prevent them from turning into multi-day retreats, the bylaws might place restrictions on these types of shareholder proposals, such as requiring shareholders to give advance notice or limiting the number of proposals a shareholder may make. These are called **advance notice bylaws**, which may become controversial in public corporations when they are abused by management.

5A-213 TAKING AWAY POWER FROM THE BOARD OF DIRECTORS IN THE CLOSELY-HELD CORPORATION:

Can the shareholders take away the board's exclusive authority to manage the business of the corporation? In other words, may the shareholders have more power to run the corporation than corporate law traditionally provides them?

The answer is generally "yes," but to understand the question and the answer you must first fully understand the context underlying this question. Although allocating the real decision-making authority of the corporation to the board of directors may indeed be an efficient default for businesses with a large number of owners, it is not necessarily an efficient default for closely-held businesses with only a few owners. These owners might prefer to vest decision-making authority with the owners directly, not indirectly through a board of directors.

Illustration:

Imagine Alice, Betty and Carol want to set up a corporation. With the corporate form, comes a centralized management body – the board of directors.

For Alice, Betty, and Carol to have true say in the corporation's business and affairs, they must each have a seat on the board.

To ensure they have a seat on the board, they must enter into a voting arrangement and elect each other to the board.

Establishing the board of directors was simply an extra obstacle for Alice, Betty, and Carol to overcome.

5A-213(a) DISPENSING ENTIRELY WITH THE BOARD OF DIRECTORS:

Most corporate law statutes allow shareholders to either completely do away with the board of directors or to otherwise "encroach" on the board's traditionally exclusive authority to manage the business and affairs of the corporation.

Both Delaware law and the RMBCA specifically and expressly allow a corporation to do away with a board of directors and allow shareholders to directly manage the business and affairs of the corporation.

For example, Delaware law provides:

> The business and affairs of every corporation organized under this chapter shall be managed by or under the direction of a board of directors, except as may be otherwise provided in this chapter or in its certificate of incorporation. If any such provision is made in the certificate of incorporation, the powers and duties conferred or imposed upon the board of directors by this chapter shall be exercised or performed to such extent and by such person or persons as shall be provided in the certificate of incorporation.[96]

---

[96] DGCL §141(a).

Of course, such a radical departure from the traditional corporate governance model of centralized governance in a board of directors requires some paperwork. In Delaware, it simply requires a provision in the certificate of incorporation (i.e., articles of incorporation).

The corporate law statute in a jurisdiction following the RMBCA approach would require a provision in the articles (or bylaws) approved by all shareholders at the time. Alternatively, the parties could memorialize the provision in a written shareholders agreement, signed by all shareholders at the time, and notify the corporation of the existence of the agreement.[97]

The ability of shareholders in closely-held businesses to completely do away with a board of directors is much less significant now than it was years ago. This is because parties that want this much flexibility will now likely choose the LLC over the corporation. Unit 5C discusses the flexibility of the LLC form with respect to management structure.[98]

5A-213(b) SHAREHOLDERS AGREEMENTS LIMITING THE DISCRETION OF DIRECTORS:

Even when the shareholders of a closely-held corporation have not completely dispensed with the board of directors, they still might enter into agreements that address matters that are traditionally within the purview of board discretion.

When we discussed shareholder vote-pooling agreements, we discussed promises between shareholders regarding how they would vote their shares on matters such as electing directors, amending the bylaws, and fundamental transactions.

It is not uncommon for shareholders to use the same written agreement to stipulate **other corporate policies that are NOT normally a matter for shareholders to decide**.

Typically, one often sees provisions in these shareholder agreements:

Setting dividend policies (a matter for the board to decide),

Determining officers of the corporation (a matter for the board to decide),

Determining the salary of the officers (a matter for the board to decide); or

Making policies with respect to other business matters

---

[97] RMBCA §7.32(a)(1) & 7.32(b).

[98] See §5C-103 et seq., below.

190

Early on, courts were reluctant to enforce these agreements because directors have **fiduciary duties to make decisions in the best interest of the corporation.** Courts were concerned that such agreements would encourage directors to make decisions regardless of the effect on the corporation.

However, courts recognized that closely-held corporations were corporations in form only, but partnerships in spirit. The parties chose a corporation for the purposes of obtaining limited liability, not because centralized management through an independent board was the most efficient structure for their relationship.

These parties needed some leeway within the corporate form to order their relationships to best suit their financial needs and realities. **Courts began to permit such agreements but only when all of the corporation's shareholders were parties to the agreement.** The implicit reasoning was that by requiring all shareholders agree, the possibility that such agreements would cause harm to the corporation was minimized.

Other courts have gone even farther by **enforcing these agreements even when all shareholders were not parties to the agreement as long as such agreements were fair to the shareholders who were not parties to the agreements.**

Some state corporate law statutes specifically address shareholder agreements on matters within the purview of the board of directors. **The RMBCA** approach resembles the common law approach by requiring **all shareholders to be parties to the agreement.** More specifically, the RMBCA specifically allows these types of agreement if they are:

> memorialized in a provision in the articles (or bylaws) that was approved by **all shareholders** at the time; or

> they are memorialized in a **written shareholders agreement made known to the corporation** and signed by **all shareholders** at the time.[99]

5A-213(c) LEGENDS ON SHARE CERTIFICATES:

When shareholders enter into a legally enforceable agreement that restricts the discretion of the board of directors, they will often want to **bind transferees** of the shares that were subject to the agreement. Many corporate law statutes expressly address the effect of a transfer of such shares **to a third party who has no notice** of the restriction.

There are **several possible approaches** a statute might take when the transferee of shares had no notice that the shares were subject to the shareholders agreement:

---

[99] RMBCA §7.32(a)(1)-(8) & 7.32(b).

(1) the agreement is no longer valid;

(2) the third party purchaser can rescind the purchase and get her money back from the seller; or

(3) the third party can force the corporation to buy her out. The consequences depend on the particular statute.

In order to protect themselves and their agreement, the shareholders who are parties to the agreement will often require each other to place **legends** (i.e., notations) on their **share certificates** that state the shares are subject to a shareholders agreement and that subsequent transferees will be bound by it. Effectively, the legend either forecloses the argument by the transferee that she bought the shares without notice, or makes the argument very unconvincing.

5A-213(d) APPROACHING THESE AGREEMENTS:

Here is a suggested approach for training yourself to spot and deal with **shareholder agreements that restrict the discretion of directors**:

(1) Look for provisions that are not normally matters for shareholder voting.

(2) Check to see if your jurisdiction has a statute that addresses these agreements. If so, try to draft the agreement to comply with the statute.

(3) If you cannot meet the needs of your client by complying with the statute, look for common law precedent that would better suit your client's needs and determine whether the statute has preempted common law in this area.

(4) Inform your client of the risks that the agreement will be unenforceable, depending on what your research reveals.

(5) Make sure that the agreement requires legends on the share certificates.

5A-214 SHAREHOLDER VOTING – INTERESTING FACTS:

Drafting **minutes of shareholders' meetings** is usually a job for the corporate secretary, but it is common for the company's lawyer (either in-house or outside counsel) to help prepare these minutes. Minutes are not supposed to be verbatim accounts or transcripts of everything that was said in a shareholders meeting. The minutes, at a minimum, should reflect what resolutions were put before the shareholders and whether the shareholders passed these resolutions. You can find sample minutes and guides to drafting minutes in commercial treatises and other commercial formbooks aimed at corporate law practitioners.

Corporate law does not always provide answers for all of the **procedural issues at shareholders meetings**. It would be a good idea for you to help your clients formulate rules for their shareholders meetings, such as when and for how long shareholders may speak, etc. Robert's Rules of Order may be helpful, but the official comments to RMBCA §7.08(b) warn that "[c]omplicated parliamentary rules (such as Robert's Rules of Order) ordinarily are not appropriate for shareholder meetings." Further, the RMBCA provides "any rules adopted for, and the conduct of, the meeting shall be fair to shareholders."[100]

There are rules about how shareholders should sign proxies and ballots and when a corporation can accept or reject **potentially defective proxies or ballots**. If you are interested in a sample of these types of rules, read RMBCA §7.24.

Many shareholders meetings rely on very **detailed scripts** that were carefully drafted and rehearsed beforehand. These scripts help to prevent misstatements, breaches of etiquette, angry exchanges, and procedural faux pas. The use of a script contributes to a professionally run meeting, which helps the management win the confidence of their shareholders.

The executives of any company generally want to **boast and possibly exaggerate** about past and predicted performance of the company. Lawyers tend to rein them in because any material misstatements may create liability for the executive and the company under SEC Rule 10b-5 and state law anti-fraud rules. The attorney has to help the management find a balance of providing the information that the shareholders need without allowing management to cross the line into misleading hyperbole and optimism.

When attorneys **draft the various shareholder agreements** we have discussed in this unit, they do not start from scratch. They will have a good form agreement available (either a commercial form or something the law firm has prepared) and also some similar agreements drafted in the past to work from. These past agreements are often called "precedents". In addition, because the same issues tend to come up for every case, the lawyer will often interview a client using a checklist of issues and questions. She then refers to the client's answers to draft the agreement. Good forms and good checklists are essential to good drafting.

---

[100] RMBCA §7.08(c).

DECISION-MAKING BY THE BOARD OF DIRECTORS:

5A-400 BOARD VOTING – GENERAL INTRODUCTION:

This section discusses the most basic aspects of board voting that any student of corporate law should understand.

5A-401 PATTERNS TO LOOK FOR IN YOUR CORPORATE LAW STATUTE:

To a large extent, the processes of board decision-making is much more straight forward than shareholder decision-making. There are certain things you should look for when learning your jurisdiction's corporate law statute:

First, the board has the power and the **right to make all corporate decisions _unless_** corporate law or the company's articles of incorporation reserve the ultimate decision-making authority to the shareholders. The board is the corporate "decider."

Second, each member of the board of directors gets **one vote** – a director's shareholdings in the corporation, or lack thereof, does not determine her voting power on the board.

Third, there are certain common patterns among corporate law statutes with respect to:

Board meetings

Quorum requirements

Approval requirements

5A-402 BOARD POWERS:

The board of directors has the power to manage the business and affairs of the corporation, except where the law, the bylaws, or the articles of incorporation require approval by shareholders.

For example, the board may:

Sell or purchase assets in the ordinary course of business – e.g., it may sell the products the corporation manufactures and purchase the raw materials the corporation needs to manufacture the products.

194

Sell or purchase assets not in the ordinary course of business – e.g., it may sell the factory and the equipment the corporation uses to make its products (unless it sells substantially all the corporation's assets, in which case it will need shareholder approval) or it may purchase a factory and equipment the corporation needs to manufacture its products.

Appoint officers – e.g., a principal executive officer ("CEO," "President"); a principal financial officer ("CFO," "Treasurer"), a corporate secretary, etc.

Declare dividends – i.e., distributing the company's profits to the shareholders.

Borrow money –e.g., from banks, from trade creditors, or through an issue of debt securities, etc.

Issue and sell shares to investors – to raise money to finance the corporation's operations and growth (BUT, the board may only issue shares if there are enough remaining within the corporation's authorized shares as stated in the articles).

Set the rights and preferences of "blank check preferred" – if the articles authorize the board to set the rights and preferences of the preferred stock without shareholder consent, the board may do so in its discretion.

The above is **not an exhaustive list**. Essentially, the board has all the powers to run the business of the corporation, unless the law or the articles limit those powers.

You will often see articles of incorporation that expressly list the board powers. For example, you might see any or all of these board powers expressly stated the articles or bylaws:

Authorize the issuance of corporate bonds, notes, and other obligations;

Authorize the pledge or mortgage of corporate property as security for corporate obligations;

Declare dividends;

Establish employee pension and profit sharing plans;

Appoint permanent and special board committees.

Such an enumeration of board powers would usually be followed by "**and any and all powers necessary or reasonable to carry on the business and**

affairs of the corporation" to indicate that the list is not exclusive of any other powers.

You may find it curious that the articles of incorporation would enumerate these powers when the board would have the default power to do these things under most state corporate law statutes. The attorney lists the board's authority in the articles of incorporation is likely using the articles to instruct the clients on board powers. As we mentioned in our discussion of shareholder voting, articles and bylaws are often repetitive of the default rules in the state corporate law statute.

This method of drafting articles and bylaws provides the board and shareholders with an efficient means of accessing the law without having to research the statute themselves or contact an attorney for every little issue. Indeed many corporate law statutes follow the same pattern of enumerating a long list of board powers while clearly indicating the list is not exclusive.[101]

5A-403 SHAREHOLDER APPROVAL OF CERTAIN BOARD DECISIONS:

As we said in our discussion of **shareholder voting**, certain corporate decisions require the approval of the shareholders. We have seen that most state corporate law statutes require shareholder approval only in the following situations (most will be discussed in further detail in later chapters):

Amendment of the articles of incorporation

Merger

Sale of substantially all of the corporation's assets

Dissolution

The articles of incorporation or a shareholders' agreement might also require shareholder approval of other corporate actions. You are far more likely to see these types of shareholder approval requirements in a closely-held corporation than in the public corporation. Some typical article provisions might require shareholder approval for:

Any dividend or distribution to the shareholders

Executive salaries

Any disposition of real property owned by the corporation

Any transaction exceeding a specific dollar amount

---

[101] See, for example, RMBCA §3.02.

Any corporate loans to the directors or employees

5A-404 POWERS OFTEN SHARED BY THE BOARD AND SHAREHOLDERS:

There are certain actions that either the board or the shareholders can take without the approval of the other:

Amending the bylaws

Filling vacancies on the board

Removing directors (maybe the board will have this power, depending on the jurisdiction)

We will discuss each of these transactions in more detail later in this unit.

5A-405 DIRECTORS ARE NOT AGENTS OF THE CORPORATION:

Directors are not agents of the corporation. Directors cannot bind the corporation to a contract or represent the corporation to third parties unless the board gives the directors the authority to do so.

The board of directors appoints the officers of the corporation. These officers are responsible for the day-to-day management of the corporation under the supervision and direction of the board of directors and in accordance with board policies and are generally considered the agents of the corporation. It is the officers and employees of the corporation who generally have the authority to act as the corporation's agent and bind the corporation in contract.

Of course, it is possible and conceivable for the board to expressly appoint one of its directors to act as an agent for the corporation. Indeed, the board could give Jim James's Aunt Tilly the authority to represent and bind the company. This express appointment of an agent is formally called a "Power of Attorney." Without this express power of attorney, however, you would not expect that a director (or Aunt Tilly for that matter) could act as an agent to represent or bind the corporation.

The power to bind the corporation is discussed in more detail later in this unit.

5A-406 BOARD MEETINGS:

The board of directors will have **regular board meetings** and **special board meetings**. Because corporate law statutes do not require the board to meet at certain times or for a specific number of times in a year, the difference between regular and special meetings simply depends on how the corporation schedules its board meetings.

Many closely-held corporations only schedule one regular board meeting each year, which usually occurs after the annual shareholders meeting adjourns.

5A-406(a) REGULAR BOARD MEETINGS:

The corporation may schedule regular meetings in its articles or bylaws, but it is usually done by board resolution. Of course, the bylaws or articles might require a certain number of meetings in a year, but leave the specific dates of the meetings to a board resolution.

5A-406(b) SPECIAL BOARD MEETINGS:

In addition to the regularly scheduled meetings, the board may meet as needed throughout the year. Most corporate law statutes do not specify who has the power to call special board meetings. It is generally assumed that the corporation's president (chief executive officer) or the chairman of the board will have the right to call special board meetings.

5A-406(c) PROXIES AND CONSENTS:

Most state corporate law statutes do not allow directors to attend board meetings by proxy. However, they generally allow directors to participate in meeting through some form of **remote communication device that allows the directors to hear each other instantaneously,** such as telephone or video conference calls.

In addition, corporate law generally authorizes the board to take action without a meeting as long as all directors consent in writing. This pattern is very similar to the pattern we saw when we discussed shareholder consents in lieu of meeting. In this instance, the consent forms will look very much like the consent forms used for shareholders.[102]

5A-407 BOARD VOTING:

Most state corporate law statutes contemplate that all the **board of directors will decide all matters as a group,** at a meeting or through written consents in lieu of meetings. The board of directors in a closely-held corporation, where the shareholders, directors, and officers are all the same people, may be less apt to have formal board meetings. Because all the principals are involved in day-to-day management, they are consulting and conferring with each other on

---

[102] See §5A-210, above.

a regular basis. As stated above, in these types of closely-held corporations, you might only see one formal board meeting each year.

For this reason, it is not uncommon for the board to ratify all acts of the officers during the past year at their one board meeting. Indeed, you will often also see the following action item for the annual shareholders' meeting in closely-held corporations:

> Ratification of all acts by the directors and officers during the past year.

5A-407(a) QUORUM REQUIREMENTS:

Generally, a quorum of the directors must be present, either in person or by some sort of remote communication device, but not by proxy, for any action by the board to be valid. Under most state corporate law statutes, a **majority of the board of directors constitutes a quorum**. Note, however:

> The corporation may **fix the number of directors in its articles or bylaws**, in which case the quorum is a majority of the fixed number.

> If the corporation does not have a fixed number of directors, it will usually have a **range in its bylaws or articles (e.g., 9 to 13 directors)** and a method for setting the number within the range (e.g., board resolution, shareholder resolution, etc.). When the range has been properly set by the method prescribed, a quorum consists of a majority of the set number of directors. When the range has not been set, a quorum will be the majority of directors in office immediately before the board meeting.

Corporations may generally change the quorum requirements through their bylaws or articles, but the relevant statutory provision might not allow them to decrease the quorum below a certain percentage.

There are also several instances where the state corporate law statute may expressly provide a **lower quorum** than normal.

For example, in a situation where **directors are conflicted** in the transaction under consideration, the conflicted directors normally do not participate in the vote. When a significant number of directors are conflicted and do not participate, leaving less than a regular quorum of directors, corporate law statutes generally provide that the **quorum is a majority of the non-conflicted directors**.[103]

Similarly, one can also imagine a situation where a **large number of director vacancies** has resulted because of a dispute or a tragic accident. When there are a large number of empty board seats, corporate statutes usually allow the

---

[103] See Chapter 6, §§6A-103(b) and 6A-202.

remaining directors to fill the vacancies even though they do not constitute a regular quorum. Under such circumstances, **the quorum is a majority of the remaining directors** (but usually only for the purposes of filling the vacancies).

5A-407(b) APPROVAL REQUIREMENTS:

Approval usually requires a **simple majority**, which means a majority of the directors present must vote in favor of the proposal. Abstentions effectively count as votes against. State statutes generally allow a corporation, through its articles or bylaws, to require a greater approval standard of directors (e.g., supermajority or absolute majority) for any or all transactions, but these statutes do not generally allow a lower approval requirement.

5A-500 BOARD VOTING – THE DETAILS:

5A-501 SIZE AND COMPOSITION OF THE BOARD:

5A-501(a) SIZE:

Many jurisdictions only require one board member. Some jurisdictions require at least three members on the board, but may allow fewer members if there are fewer than three shareholders.

In addition, state statutes usually permit corporations to either **fix the number** of directors in the articles or bylaws or establish a **variable range** of directors on the board and a method of setting the number of directors within that range. The method will either be a board resolution or a shareholder resolution or both.

In many jurisdictions, the corporate law statute does not have an express edict requiring the corporation to put the number of directors in the articles or bylaws. However, because the statutes generally contemplate that articles or the bylaws will state the fixed number of directors or the range and method of determining the number, you should make sure to draft for this in the bylaws or the articles.

5A-501(b) QUALIFICATIONS:

State corporate law statutes rarely, if ever, impose qualifications on the board of directors, such as shareholding or residency requirements. Generally, the only qualifications are that a director must be a **natural person** and at least **eighteen years old**. The age requirement is usually not expressly stated in state statutes. However, because eighteen is the age of majority in most states, it would be problematic if decisions by the board are unenforceable because one or more of the directors are minors.

A corporation may create qualifications for its directors in its articles or bylaws. In closely-held corporations, you might see a requirement that directors be shareholders or have experience or expertise that is relevant to the corporation's business. In public corporations, directors might have to meet qualifications set by stock exchanges or relevant federal securities laws.

———————

5A-502 POWERS OFTEN SHARED BY THE BOARD AND SHAREHOLDERS:

As we have already mentioned, it is often the case that the relevant state corporate law statute gives the power to **amend the bylaws** or fill **board vacancies** to the board or to the shareholders.

In addition, although the shareholders will have the power to remove directors, some statutes might also grant the board certain limited powers to remove directors. Of course, any time two separate groups each have the right to act, the question arises regarding which group's rights take precedence. When learning the approach of your state's statute you should keep the following in mind.

5A-502(a) AMENDING THE BYLAWS:

Many state corporate law statutes allow either the board or the shareholders to amend the bylaws, but generally **allow the shareholders to prevent the board from undoing a shareholder-approved bylaw provision**. The reverse is not usually the case: the articles or bylaws may not prohibit the shareholders from undoing any board-approved bylaw provision (see §5A-206(b) for a more detailed discussion).

5A-502(b) FILLING BOARD VACANCIES:

A vacancy on the board may occur when a director resigns, a director dies, a director is removed, or the size of the board increases. Many state corporate law statutes give the power to fill board vacancies to either the board or the shareholders.

As a practical matter the board will fill the vacancy in most instances. The directors will see no need to call a shareholders meeting to fill a vacancy on the board when the directors can vote to fill the vacancy themselves.

When will the shareholders actually get to fill a vacancy on the board? Here are the most likely scenarios that will result in shareholders filling a board vacancy:

> When the board decides it is politically imprudent for them to fill the vacancy without shareholder approval.

> If the articles (or possibly bylaws) expressly give the right to the shareholders to fill vacancies.

> When the vacancy occurs because of a proposal from a shareholder to remove a director at a special shareholders meeting and the notice also proposes filling the vacancy by a shareholder vote.

Of course, there are some other issues you should consider when reading your corporate law statute:

It may be possible for the articles (or bylaws) to give the board the exclusive right to fill vacancies.

If the director who vacated the seat was elected by a specific class of shares (e.g., the articles provide that the shareholders of Class A Common get to elect three of the nine directors), you should check whether your jurisdiction's law expressly gives the exclusive right to fill the vacancy to the shareholders of that class or the other directors elected by that class (in any case, you might want to draft that right into the terms of that class of shares in the articles).

5A-502(c) REMOVING DIRECTORS:

As we discussed in greater detail in the readings on shareholder voting earlier in this chapter, **shareholders are often permitted to remove directors either without cause**, or with certain conditions designed to protect minority shareholders.[104] In some jurisdictions, the **directors also _may_ be allowed to remove directors**. In jurisdictions where the board has this right, the board may usually only remove directors **for cause** or **under certain conditions**.

In Ohio, for example:

The directors may remove any director and thereby create a vacancy in the board:

(1) If by order of court the director has been found to be of unsound mind, or if the director is adjudicated a bankrupt;

(2) If within sixty days, or within any other period of time as is prescribed in the articles or the regulations, from the date of the director's election the director does not qualify by accepting in writing the director's election to that office or by acting at a meeting of the directors, and by acquiring the qualifications specified in the articles or the regulations; or if, for such period as is prescribed in the articles or the regulations, the director ceases to hold the required qualifications.[105]

In other jurisdictions, the board may not have a right to directly remove a director, but it will have a right to seek a court order to remove a director if the director has engaged in fraudulent conduct or some other abuse of trust with regard to the corporation or its shareholders.

In any case, if the directors feel that they need to remove one of their own and the law does not allow them to do so, **they can pass a board resolution and submit it to the shareholders for their approval**.

---

[104] See §5A-204, above.

[105] Ohio General Corporation Law §1701.58(B).

5A-503 NOTICE OF BOARD MEETINGS:

Generally, there is no need to provide directors with notice of *regular* board meetings, although it is probably a wise practice to do so. Special board meetings, on the other hand, require notice, but the notice generally does not need to state the purpose of the special meeting unless the articles of incorporation or bylaws so require. Regardless of the statutory requirements for notice, it is **good practice to provide directors notice** of a meeting and its purpose so that the directors can prepare for the meeting.

5A-504 THE RELATIONSHIP BETWEEN THE BOARD AND THE EXECUTIVE OFFICERS:

The board of directors appoints the officers. It is inevitable that the board will delegate a significant number of their responsibilities to the officers of the corporation, but all major decisions concerning the enterprise must be approved by the directors. The board will also monitor the executive officers to ensure the officers are faithfully fulfilling their duties.

5A-504(a) THE CLOSELY-HELD CORPORATION:

In a closely-held corporation, the shareholder, directors, and officers will often be the same people. The distinction between the shareholder, director and officer loses its significance. However, the continuum of the closely-held corporation includes corporations that may rely on professional managers rather than owner-managers. In these types of closely-held corporations, the shareholders themselves may still be on the board of directors, but they have hired non-owners to key executive positions. The more a closely-held corporation relies on professional managers, the more the relationship between the board and the officers resembles the dynamic we see in the public corporation.

5A-504(b) THE PUBLIC CORPORATION:

In a public corporation, the shareholders rely on the directors to monitor the activities of the executive officers. However, the **executive officers may have a large amount of influence over the board of directors**.

The most senior executive officers of the corporation will often also be directors. Directors who are also executive officers are often called "**inside directors**." The directors who are not executive officers are called "**outside directors**."

For the outside directors, serving on the board is essentially a part-time position. The board only meets several times a year. This situation means that the outside directors are not as well informed about the company as the executive officers.

The outside directors must rely on the inside directors and the other officers to provide the information they need to make corporate decisions and to monitor the officers. Although we expect the board to create policies and monitor the executive officers, it is often the executive officers who create the policies for the public corporation, with the board simply approving them and hopefully not acting as a mere rubber stamp. Moreover, the board's ability to monitor the executives is hampered by the informational disadvantage it has vis-à-vis the executive officers.

5A-505 THE DOCTRINE OF ULTRA VIRES:

Ultra vires is a doctrine used to invalidate corporate action outside of its scope of powers or hold directors liable for causing the corporation to act outside of its scope of powers.

The doctrine of ultra vires was much more important in the bygone days of corporate law when a corporation was granted a charter from the state legislature to engage in a specific undertaking. Under these charters, corporations could not engage in any business other that what was specifically stated in their charters. Any corporate act outside of the charter's scope was ultra vires.

Even later, when anyone could incorporate under a state general incorporation statute, these statutes normally required corporations to state a specific purpose in their articles of incorporation. Any corporate act that did not serve the specific purpose in the articles was ultra vires.

The ultra vires doctrine is far less important today because all states' statutes allow corporations to engage in **any lawful business**. Many corporations have the following statement, or something similar, in their articles of incorporation under the title "Purpose," "Powers," or "Business":

> This corporation may engage in or transact any and all lawful activities or business permitted under the laws of the United States, the state of incorporation, or any other state, county, territory or nation.

In fact, under most statutes there is no need to put such a statement in the articles of incorporation. It is the default rule and the parties may use the articles of incorporation to limit the corporation's purpose if they so choose.

In modern corporations, the doctrine of ultra vires raises its head only under a few circumstances. You should probably look for ultra vires issues in the following circumstances:

When the **articles of incorporation expressly limit the power** of the corporation to engage in a lawful activity.

Where **shareholders have a right to vote on a transaction** and the board did not submit the matter for shareholder approval.

Where the corporation **indemnifies a director** or officer with respect to a lawsuit against the director or officer and the law does not allow such indemnification. In Chapter 8, we will discuss when the law prohibits a corporation from indemnifying a director or officer when she is a defendant to a lawsuit.[106] If the corporation indemnifies the director or officer when the law prohibits it, the action is ultra vires.

When the corporation makes a **charitable donation**.

Many modern state corporate law statutes expressly allow corporations to make donations to charitable organizations.

You should check to see whether your statute requires a donation to serve some sort of corporate purpose or somehow benefit the corporation. Many statutes do not require the charitable donation to benefit the corporation, but if they do, here are some arguments that the donation benefits the company:

Benefiting the community creates goodwill/good publicity for the corporation.

Benefiting the community improves the economic situation of our customer base.

Benefiting the community makes it a better place and helps us attract better employees.

5A-506 THE CHAIRMAN OF THE BOARD:

In general, the board selects the chairman from among its ranks. In some jurisdictions, the chairman is considered an officer of the corporation. In others, the chairman is simply a director who presides at board meetings. Indeed, some state statutes do not mention the chairman of the board at all.

---

[106] See Chapter 8, §8A-200 et seq.

The actual role of the chairman in the corporation depends on the company's needs. Corporations often explicitly define the role of the chairman in their bylaws.

In many companies, the chairman position might be equivalent to the chief executive officer ("CEO"). In other companies, although the chairman and CEO are separate positions, the title of CEO and chairman may be held by the same person. Here is a relevant provision from the bylaws of General Electric Company:

> As determined by the Board of Directors, the officers of this Company shall include . . . [a] Chairman of the Board, who shall be chosen by the Directors from their own number. The Chairman of the Board shall be the Chief Executive Officer of the Company and in that capacity shall have general management, subject to the control of the Board of Directors, of the business of the Company, . . .

In some public corporations where the CEO is also the chairman of the board, the board may also elect one of the "outside" or "independent" directors to act as the **lead director** to reduce the risk the CEO and executive team will have too much influence over the board of directors.

5A-507 BOARD COMMITTEES:

Most state corporate law statutes expressly allow the board to delegate some authority to board committees. As you learn the relevant corporate law statute of your jurisdiction, you should first look for an express statutory provision that authorizes the creation of board committees. If your jurisdiction does not have such a provision, you should research common law precedent: the authorization for the board to delegate decision-making power to committees was generally recognized under common law.

5A-507(a) WHAT PURPOSE DO BOARD COMMITTEES SERVE?

The board may establish a committee to research a matter and report to the board with either information or a recommendation. In certain cases, the board may delegate authority to a committee to actually decide a matter. In other words, the committee will make the decision and will not ask the entire board to review or approve the committee's decision.

The use of board committees can help the board operate more efficiently. It allows directors to develop expertise in specific areas and reduces the burden on all the directors. It can also empower independent directors by providing them with an opportunity to learn more about the company through committee work or by making them the majority in an important committee.

Board committees may be **standing** or **ad hoc**. Standing committees are permanent committees established either in the bylaws, the articles or by board resolution. Typical standing committees one might see in a public corporation are:

> **Executive committee:** Has the power to act for the board in between regular board meetings.
>
> **Audit committee**: Reviews the corporation's finances with an outside auditor.
>
> **Nominating committee:** Determines who the board will nominate for the upcoming shareholder election of directors.
>
> **Compensation committee:** Reviews and establishes the compensation packages and compensation policy for the corporation's executive officers.

Ad hoc committees are established by board resolution to deal with certain matters as they arise.

For example, when the board is contemplating a transaction where a number of directors have a conflict of interest, the board might establish a committee composed of the directors who are not conflicted. This **committee of non-conflicted (or "disinterested") directors** will review the proposed transaction and either make a recommendation to the board or pass a resolution itself, depending on the charge it receives from the board. The process of disinterested director review and approval of conflict-of-interest transactions is discussed in detail in Chapter 6.[107]

Another common ad hoc committee is the **special litigation committee**. A board will often establish this committee to deal with shareholder derivative suits. The role of the special litigation committee in shareholder derivative lawsuits is discussed in detail in Chapter 8.[108]

Many state corporate law statutes protect directors who rely on information in reports prepared by board committees.

---

[107] See Chapter 6, §§6A-202(d) and 6A-202(k).

[108] See Chapter 8, §8A-104 et seq.

5A-507(b) __THE FORMALITIES OF ESTABLISHING COMMITTEES:__

When you examine your jurisdiction's approach to establishing board committees, you should look for the following possibilities:

The board can create committees ***unless*** the articles or bylaws restrict or prohibit the board's authority to do so.

The board can create committees ***only if*** the articles or bylaws grant the board the authority to do so.

In addition, your jurisdiction's relevant statutory provision may require that a board committee be made up of at least two directors, although some jurisdictions allow for single-director committees.

5A-507(c) __THE EXECUTIVE COMMITTEE:__

Many public companies have an executive committee of directors. In large public corporations, the board of directors only meets several times a year. An executive committee allows the board of directors to exercise its authority between regular board meetings, without the hassle of calling special board meetings.

The executive committee's scope of authority depends on two things:

How its scope is defined in the corporation's bylaws or articles; and

Any limits the state corporate law statute has on the delegation of authority to board committees.

Here is an excerpt from bylaws of Citigroup Inc. establishing an executive committee and defining its scope of authority:

SECTION 1. The Executive Committee shall be composed of the Chairman and such additional Directors not less than three, appointed by the Board, who shall serve until the next annual organization meeting of the Board and until their successors are appointed. A majority of the members of the Executive Committee shall constitute a quorum. The vote of the majority of members of the Executive Committee present at a meeting at which a quorum is present shall be the act of the Executive Committee. Any vacancy on the Executive Committee shall be filled by the Board of Directors.

SECTION 2. The Executive Committee may exercise all powers of the Board of Directors between the meetings of the Board except as otherwise provided in the General Corporation Law of the State of Delaware and for this purpose references in these By-laws to the

Board of Directors shall be deemed to include references to the Executive Committee.

5A-507(d) LIMITS ON COMMITTEE AUTHORITY:

The corporate law statute of your state may carve out certain board functions that the board may not delegate to committees. It is perhaps not surprising that statutes limiting committee authority focus on the **most important functions of the board**. For example, Delaware limits the authority of board committees as follows:

> . . . but no such committee shall have the power or authority in reference to the following matter: (i) approving or adopting, or recommending to the stockholders, any action or matter (other than the election or removal of directors) expressly required by this chapter to be submitted to stockholders for approval or (ii) adopting, amending or repealing any bylaw of the corporation.[109]

Thus, in Delaware a board committee alone could not approve a fundamental transaction that required shareholder approval.

In comparison, the New York Business Corporation Law goes somewhat farther than Delaware in limiting the authority of board committees. The relevant New York provision states:

> . . . no such committee shall have authority as to the following matters:
>
> (1) The submission to shareholders of any action that needs shareholders' approval under this chapter.
>
> (2) The filling of vacancies in the board of directors or in any committee.
>
> (3) The fixing of compensation of the directors for serving on the board or on any committee.
>
> (4) The amendment or repeal of the by-laws, or the adoption of new by-laws.
>
> (5) The amendment or repeal of any resolution of the board which by its terms shall not be so amendable or repealable.[110]

---

[109] DGCL §141(c)(2).

[110] New York Business Corporation Law §712.

5A-507(e) PUBLIC COMPANIES AND COMMITTEES:

A public company is not only subject to the corporate law statute of its state of incorporation, it is also subject to federal securities laws and the rules of the stock exchange on which its shares are listed (e.g., New York Stock Exchange, NASDAQ).

Pursuant to federal securities laws and stock exchange rules, public companies might be required (or expected) to have certain committees. For example, it is generally expected that public corporations will have an audit committee. Stock exchange rules require the members of the audit committee, or those directors serving in a similar capacity, to meet certain qualifications.

5A-508 COMPENSATION OF THE BOARD OF DIRECTORS:

Not all directors receive compensation for their service on the board. In a large public corporation, director compensation may be quite lucrative. In a closely-held corporation, the directors might receive no compensation for serving on the board because they receive salaries as officers and dividends as shareholders.

Some state corporate law statutes expressly authorize directors to set their own compensation. In some corporations, the articles or bylaws give the board the authority to set their own compensation. Of course, the directors are obviously conflicted in this decision and may seek approval of the shareholders even though the statute or bylaw provision does not expressly require shareholder ratification.

Directors who are not also officers or high-level employees of the corporation are often referred to as outside directors. Outside directors are generally compensated separately for any services they perform for the corporation, other than participating in board meetings (such as legal services performed for a company by an outside director who is an attorney).

Here is a sample bylaw provision that demonstrates one possible way a corporation may compensate its directors:

> The directors who are not full-time officers and employees of the corporation will receive a retainer for their services as directors. The retainer is to be fixed by the Board of Directors, but shall not exceed Ten Thousand Dollars ($10,000) per director per year. In addition to the retainer, directors will each receive a sum for attendance at regular or special meetings of the board and other committee meetings. Such sum will be fixed by resolution of the Board of Directors, but shall not exceed One Thousand Dollars ($1,000) per meeting. In addition, the corporation shall reimburse

each director for reasonable travel and lodging expenses incurred for the purposes of attending board and committee meetings.

5A-509 TAKING AWAY POWER FROM THE BOARD:

As discussed in the sections on shareholder voting, the shareholders of a closely-held corporation may agree to completely do away with the board of directors or limit the discretion of the directors with respect to certain decisions – e.g., dividends policy, the appointment of certain persons as officers, etc.[111]

5A-510 BOARD VOTING – INTERESTING FACTS:

The board's meetings should be reflected in **formal board minutes**, which the corporation should keep on file. Like the minutes of shareholders meetings, the minutes of board meetings are not intended to be transcripts or verbatim accounts. The minutes of routine board meetings will be very simple – normally stating the proposal and noting whether or not the proposal passed, with very little specificity. However, the level of specificity of the minutes may increase depending on the nature of the transaction. In order to discourage shareholder lawsuits, the board might use the minutes to demonstrate the great care they took and the substantial discussion they had about an important or controversial matter. Similarly, if the transaction involves a conflict of interest for one or more board members, the minutes will often be more detailed.

The secretary is responsible for **drafting the minutes of board meetings**, but it is common for the company's lawyer (either in-house counsel or outside counsel) to help prepare these minutes. You can find sample minutes and guides to drafting minutes in commercial treatises and other commercial formbooks aimed at corporate law practitioners.

A board meeting in **executive session** is not the same as a meeting of the executive committee. When a board meets in executive session, it expels from the room any person who is not a board member. It may also ask the inside directors to leave, with only the outside directors remaining in the room.

---

[111] See §5A-213 et seq., above.

THE ROLE OF EXECUTIVE OFFICERS AND EMPLOYEES IN CORPORATE DECISION-MAKING:

5A-700 THE AUTHORITY OF OFFICERS AND EMPLOYEES – GENERAL INTRODUCTION:

5A-701 THE POWER TO BIND THE CORPORATION – THE LAW:

In the preceding sections discussing the roles of shareholders and directors in corporate decision-making, we briefly mentioned that neither shareholders nor directors are **agents** of the corporation. That is to say, directors and shareholders do not represent the corporation and cannot bind the corporation to a contract with a third party simply by virtue of the fact they are directors or shareholders.

We now admit that this analysis is a bit simplified and incomplete. It is a good rule of thumb to remember, but it is, as we said, incomplete. The better analysis is as follows:

Anyone can represent and bind the corporation (or any **principal** for that matter) as long as she has the **authority** to do so.

The putative agent has authority to bind the corporation under the following circumstances.

> **Express authority:** The board of directors expressly grants the agent the authority to bind the corporation through a board resolution.

> **Implied authority:** The agent has a reasonable belief, based on some sort of conduct by the corporation, that she has the authority to bind the corporation.

> **Apparent authority:** The third party has a reasonable belief, based on some sort of conduct by the corporation, that the agent has the authority to bind the corporation.

———

5A-702 **THE POWER TO BIND THE CORPORATION – AN ANALYSIS:**

Let's do a very simple analysis of the authority of three possible agents.

The putative agents:

Agent #1: **Olive the Office Manager** – Olive's works for GU Inc. Her official title in the company is "Office Manager" and the company has provided her business cards with all the typical business card information including, without limitation, her name, her title, and the company's name and address.

Agent #2: **Iris the Intern** – Iris is a part-time intern employed at GU Inc. She gets coffee, runs errands, and fills in where she can. She has no business cards.

Agent #3: **Serge the Street Mime** – Serge performs daily in front of the building in which GU Inc. has its offices. The employees of GU Inc. are on good terms with Serge. They often watch his performances, put money in his hat, and have very one-sided conversations with him. Otherwise, Serge has no connection to GU Inc.

The transaction: The "agent" walks to Third Party Paper Supply and fills out an order for 300 reams of paper on behalf of GU Inc. (clearly written on the order form) for delivery to GU Inc.'s offices. The clerk at Third Party accepts the order and provides a receipt stating that the paper will be delivered before 5pm on the same day, with payment due upon delivery.

Question: Which of our three putative "agents" would have the authority to bind GU Inc.?

5A-702(a) EXPRESS AUTHORITY OF AGENTS:

Any (or all) of the three persons would have the express authority to bind GU Inc. *if* the board of directors passed a resolution expressly giving authority to that person to buy 300 reams of office paper from Third Party for a specified price or price range. Of course, it is unlikely that the board would actually meet to consider the matter of purchasing 300 reams of paper for the office.

5A-702(b) IMPLIED AUTHORITY OF AGENTS:

Based on the simple facts provided, Third Party has the most convincing argument that, among the three persons, Olive was reasonable in believing she has the authority to bind GU Inc. to a purchase of 300 reams of paper. The corporation gave her the title of "office manager" and it seems that purchasing paper is inherent to her job.

If **Olive the Office Manager** was reasonable in believing that she had the authority to purchase the paper on behalf of GU Inc., Third Party can hold GU Inc. liable for the purchase. We could add facts that make Olive's belief even more reasonable:

She had purchased paper in the past and none of her superiors in the company indicated she did not have the authority to do so; or

She had a job description, approved by the board of directors, giving her the authority to buy office supplies, including paper.

> **Note:** you might argue that this job description gave her express authority to buy paper since paper is expressly noted. There is a fine line between express authority and implied authority. Usually an express authority analysis is reserved for situations where the principal gives very specific authority to enter into a discrete transaction;

> or

She had a job description, approved by the company's president, giving her the authority to buy office supplies, including paper. In addition to asking whether she was reasonable in believing her job description gave her the authority to buy the 300 reams of paper from Third Party, we also must ask whether she was reasonable in believing the president had the authority, based on the actions of the board of directors, to approve her job description. The president approved the job description, not the board, and the board is the corporate "decider."

We could add other facts that make Olive's belief less reasonable:

> The president told her never to buy paper from Third Party; or

> GU Inc. was a small company that never used more than 5 reams of paper in a month.

Iris the Intern would NOT have a very solid argument that she reasonably believed she had the authority to bind the company simply because of her title and position: part-time intern. On the other hand, we could imagine plausible circumstances that would support an argument her belief was reasonable:

> She had purchased paper on behalf of the company in the past and none of her supervisors had protested; or

> Olive instructed Iris to go place the order for 300 reams of paper with Third Party. In this case, her reasonable belief depends on whether she reasonably believed Olive has the authority to give her authority to purchase 300 reams of paper from Third Party.

Of course, it is difficult to argue that **Serge the Street Mime** would have a reasonable belief he could bind GU Inc. to a purchase of paper from Third Party unless we add more facts, such as:

> Olive asks Serge to place the order for her because she is busy and her intern is out sick. Serge's reasonable belief depends on whether he could reasonably believe Olive had the authority to ask him to get paper on behalf of GU Inc. Did he know she was GU Inc.'s office manager? Did he at least have reason to believe she held some position of authority in the company?

5A-702(c) APPARENT AUTHORITY OF AGENTS:

Remember, the focus of apparent authority in on Third Party's reasonable belief, based on the conduct of GU Inc., the principal, that any of the three putative agents had the authority to bind GU Inc. to make this purchase.

It is not hard to imagine that Third Party would be reasonable in believing **Olive the Office Manager** had the authority if we add a few facts:

> Olive presented the business cards (which GU Inc. furnished her) to Third Party; or

> Olive had made similar purchases in the past and GU Inc. had never refused to pay.

Similarly, there are plausible facts we might add to bolster Third Party's argument that it was reasonable in believing **Iris the Intern** had authority to bind GU Inc. in this situation:

> They knew she was GU Inc.'s intern. Of course, they might be reasonable in believing GU Inc. would send an intern to take care of such an errand; or

> Iris had made similar purchases in the past and GU Inc. had never refused to pay.

With respect to **Serge the Street Mime**, however, it is more difficult to imagine plausible fact patterns that would give Third Party a reasonable belief that GU Inc. authorized Serge to purchase 300 reams of paper.

5A-702(d) AGENT AUTHORITY AND ITS IMPACT ON THIRD PARTIES:

What is Third Party's strategy for protecting itself ex ante? Third Party will be able to hold GU Inc. liable for the purchase if there was express authority, implied authority, or apparent authority.

Of course, Third Party does not want the expense of having to litigate this matter in court. Third Party's strategy is to **minimize its risk that GU Inc.**

will refuse to pay for the paper because the putative agent was not authorized.

> **Strategy A:** One method for Third Party is to **require immediate payment** by the putative agent. In this way, Third Party has completely removed the risk that GU Inc. will refuse to pay upon delivery. There is the possibility that GU Inc. will go to court to try to get the transaction rescinded based on the agents lack of authority, but the burden is on GU Inc. to bring a lawsuit, not on Third Party.
>
> The downside of this strategy is Third Party may lose a sale. If Third Party was not willing to extend credit to GU Inc. under normal circumstances, it will not lose the sale because of the risk of agency authority. If, however, Third Party would be willing to extend credit to GU Inc. otherwise, it might lose the sale if it refused credit simply because of the risk the agent did not have authority.
>
> **Strategy B:** Third Party could simply **call someone from GU Inc. to confirm the "agent" has authority**. Of course, this raises an issue about whether the person answering the phone has the authority to confirm the authority. Third Party could make things perfectly clear by asking for a copy of the board resolution giving the agent the authority. However, because we have already established that it is highly improbable that the GU Inc. board would meet to decide on such a matter, Third Party would likely lose the sale.

Thus, Third Party must weigh the **benefits and risks of making the sale to the putative agent**.

What factors play into this analysis?:

> Does Third Party have the paper in stock, or would it have to go to costly lengths to procure the paper?
>
> What are the costs of delivering 300 reams of paper to GU Inc.? Is GU Inc. in the same building, next door, across town?
>
> Would delivering the paper to GU Inc. prevent Third Party from making another sale?
>
> What is the risk that the agent does not have authority?
>
> Assuming the agent does not have authority, what is the risk that GU Inc. would refuse to pay?
>
> What is the risk that by refusing to accept the order, Third Party would damage its relationship with GU Inc.?

What is the risk that by accepting the order, Third Party would damage its relationship with GU Inc.?

As the stakes of the transaction increase, and as the risk that the agent has no authority increases, the third party will be better off adopting a more conservative approach to the transaction

If you were Third Party's lawyer and you advised your client to take the safest route (no sale on credit or requiring a copy of a board resolution) without considering the above factors, you did not serve your client's interests well.

———————

5A-800 THE AUTHORITY OF OFFICERS AND EMPLOYEES –

THE DETAILS:

5A-801 WHO ARE THE OFFICERS AND WHAT DO THEY DO?

Certain state corporate law statutes require the corporation to have a **president**, a **treasurer**, and a **secretary**. Generally, one person is permitted to serve all three positions. Even though many corporate law statutes do not prescribe the officers a corporation must have, a corporation will generally have officers who will serve the functions of a president, treasurer, and secretary.

Corporations are effectively given free rein to determine their internal hierarchy and job descriptions according to their needs. Even in jurisdictions that require specific officers – namely, a president, a treasurer and, secretary – the people who serve those functions may also have other titles and duties. For example, a corporation's "general counsel" may serve as the secretary and its "comptroller" or "chief financial officer" may serve as its treasurer.

The traditional officers and their functions are:

The president is the principal executive officer of the company. Her specific responsibilities will be provided for in the bylaws or her job description, but she is generally responsible for overseeing and directing the corporation's business and developing corporate policies and strategies for board approval. Essentially, it is her job to make the company successful. Some corporations call this person the chief executive officer ("CEO") or the general manager. In some corporations, the Chairman of the Board functions as the principal executive officer and the CEO or President functions more like a chief operating officer. In some corporations, the positions of Chairman of the Board and the CEO must be held by the same person according to the company's own bylaws.

The treasurer is the officer who signs checks on behalf of the corporation and is responsible for the corporation's bank accounts and other financial matters.

The secretary is responsible for corporate record keeping. She is responsible for keeping minutes of shareholder and board meetings and maintaining the shareholder ledger and other corporate books and records.

The chairman of the board in some jurisdictions is considered an officer of the corporation, not simply one of the directors. Her actual functions and how she works with the corporation's CEO or president depends on the circumstances of the particular corporation.

Other common corporate officers:

As mentioned above, the corporation might call its principal executive officer the "chief executive officer" or "general manager." Some corporations may have a CEO and a **chief operating officer (COO)**. In such a case, the CEO usually serves the function of supervisor and figurehead, focusing on the big-picture, while the COO actually implements the policies on a day-to-day basis.

Many corporations also have a **chief financial officer (CFO)**, who is, naturally, responsible for the corporation's financial matters. More specifically, the CFO is responsible for determining the most inexpensive way for the corporation to finance a project (e.g., issue new shares, issue debt securities, traditional bank lending, selling assets, retaining earnings, etc.). The CFO is also responsible for determining which project provides the best rate of return among the several projects the corporation may be considering. The CFO might also serve as the corporate treasurer. In a larger corporation, the treasurer might serve under the CFO. A corporation might also have a **comptroller** or other principal accounting/auditing officer of some kind, who might also serve under the CFO.

Of course, a large corporation might have several persons with the title of "president" and a whole bevy of people with the title of "vice president." What are the meanings of these titles? It all depends on the corporation's internal designations.

5A-802 WHAT AUTHORITY DO THE OFFICERS HAVE:

5A-802(a) EXPRESS, IMPLIED, AND APPARENT AUTHORITY:

The express authority and implied authority of the above-mentioned officers depends on specific board resolutions, bylaw provisions, article provisions, job descriptions, and customary practices within the company.

The apparent authority of these officers depends on what the third party reasonably believes, which, in turn, depends largely on the facts of the specific transaction in question.

5A-802(b) SECRETARY'S CERTIFICATES:

The secretary is the corporate officer responsible for record keeping. As such, she usually has the implied and apparent authority to authenticate specific corporate documents.

In transactions where the third party wants greater assurance that the person signing the contract on behalf of the corporation has authority to do so, she might request a certificate from the secretary.

The certificate the secretary issues depends on the transaction and how much assurance the third party needs. The certificate might be a simple "Certificate of Incumbency" that states who the officers of the corporation are or it might specifically state that a particular officer has the authority to bind the corporation to a specific transaction.

In major transactions, the third party will often require a copy of the board resolution, certified by the secretary, authorizing the agent to sign the contract on the corporation's behalf.

The following shows a form secretary's certificate with a board resolution excerpted from the minutes of a board meeting:

SECRETARY'S CERTIFICATE

The undersigned, [Susan Secrest], does hereby certify:

(1) She is the Secretary of [____ , Inc.] (the "Company") and has the authority to execute this certificate on behalf of the Company;

(2) The attached resolution is a true and accurate copy of the resolution adopted by the Company's board of directors on [May 25, 2014] at a duly held meeting at which a quorum of directors was present; and

(3) The resolution has not been rescinded or modified as of the date of this certificate.

Susan Secrest

Susan Secrest, Corporate Secretary, [____ Company, Inc.]
Date: June 8, 2014

RESOLUTION OF THE BOARD OF DIRECTORS OF ___ , INC.

"RESOLVED, that the board approves [*description of transaction*] (the "Transaction") and authorizes the president of the corporation to execute all instruments on behalf of the corporation necessary to effectuate the Transaction."

221

Does this secretary's certificate irrefutably establish the agent's express authority? No. It is possible the corporate secretary completely fabricated the board resolution.

However, this certificate should still provide the third party with the security she needs because:

1. It is unlikely that the secretary fabricated the resolution; and

2. Even if the secretary fabricated the resolution, the certificate still creates a VERY strong case for **apparent authority** – i.e., the agent mentioned in the certificate has apparent authority because the third party was reasonable in believing the statements on the certificate because the secretary has the express, implied, or apparent authority to issue such certificates.

———————

5A-803 OTHER AUTHORITY ISSUES:

In addition to express authority, implied authority and apparent authority, a principal may be bound by her agent's actions if there is **ratification, agency by estoppel**, or **inherent authority**.

5A-803(a) RATIFICATION:

When the agent enters into a contract on behalf of the principal, but the agent has no authority, the principal will still be bound if she ratifies the contract after the fact.

She may **expressly ratify** the contract (e.g., "My agent had no authority, but I want to be bound anyway because this is a good deal for me."); or

She may **implicitly ratify** the contract (by knowingly accepting the benefits of the contract).

5A-803(b) AGENCY BY ESTOPPEL:

If a principal is aware that a non-agent is representing to third parties that she has the authority to bind the principal, the principal might be responsible for the contracts of this non-agent unless she takes some affirmative action to notify potential third parties that the non-agent does not have authority. Normally, the principal's liability under agency by estoppel also requires some sort of act of reliance or change of position by the third party.

5A-803(c) **INHERENT AUTHORITY:**

Inherent authority as a separate basis for authority is really **a doctrine that gives the court the power to find authority when the third party was in particularly sympathetic circumstances and the agent did not have express, implied, or apparent authority**.

Do not confuse this basis of liability with the implied or apparent authority argument that the agent or the third party was reasonable in believing the agent had authority because it was "inherent" to her position. When you argue that the authority was inherent to a person's position, you are arguing for apparent authority or implied authority.

UNIT 5B

PARTNERSHIPS – DECISION-MAKING:

5B-100 PARTNERSHIP VOTING AND PARTNER AUTHORITY – GENERAL INTRODUCTION:

The partnership model of decision-making and agency authority stands in sharp contrast to the corporate model.

In corporate law, there is a clear distinction between residual claimants (shareholders), central decision-makers (board of directors), and agents (executive officers and employees).

In partnership law, however, we do not have these distinctions as the default. The residual claimants are also the decision-makers and the agents. If you are a partner, you have a residual claim, a right to vote on partnership decisions, and the authority to bind the partnership.

5B-101 PATTERNS TO LOOK FOR IN YOUR PARTNERSHIP STATUTE:

Most states have adopted the Uniform Partnership Act (UPA) or the Revised Uniform Partnership Act (RUPA). In addition, state partnership law is influenced by the common law.

When learning how your jurisdiction's partnership law specifically handles matters of partnership voting and authority, you should look for the following patterns:

Partners normally have a **right to vote on all partnership decisions**.

Each partner has **equal voting rights**, regardless of the proportion of her investment in the partnership.

Each partner is an **agent of the corporation**, with the apparent authority to bind the partnership because of her status as partner.

The law **does not require formal meetings** of partners for partnership decisions.

The partnership has great leeway to **change any of the above rules by contract** so that:

Partners may have no voting rights or limited voting rights, voting rights in proportion to their investments, etc.

Partners may have no authority to bind the corporation (but note the partnership agreement would not be able to eliminate a partner's apparent authority to bind the corporation because apparent authority is based on what third parties reasonably believe).

5B-102 SOURCES OF PARTNERSHIP LAW:

Your jurisdiction's partnership law is most likely a version of the Uniform Partnership Act. The Uniform Partnership Act was created in 1914 by the Uniform Law Commission ("ULC").[112] In our discussion below, the 1914 version of the Uniform Partnership Act will be referred to as the "**Uniform Partnership Act**," or "**UPA**."

ULC revised UPA in 1994 and further amended it in 1997. In our discussions below, the 1997 revised and amended versions of UPA are referred to as the "**Revised Uniform Partnership Act**," or "**RUPA**."

According to the ULC website, 36 states have adopted RUPA, or some partnership law substantially similar to RUPA. The remaining states, except Louisiana, still use UPA for their partnership statutes.

5B-103 PARTNERSHIP VOTING:

As mentioned previously, the default rule for **voting** in a partnership is **per capita voting**, not voting power in proportion to investment. Thus, each partner has one vote regardless of how much or how little capital she has invested.

Illustration:

Ann, Barbara, and Carol enter into a partnership together. Ann invests $50,000, Barbara invests $10,000, and Carol invests $500.

Unless the parties agree otherwise, each of them will receive one vote.

This allocation of voting power, without regard to investments, may seem strange and unfair at first blush. However, you must keep in mind that each of the partners is potentially personally liable for the partnership obligations. If the partners vote to approve transactions that cause the partnership to become

---

[112] Formerly known as the National Conference on the Commissioners on Uniform State Laws.

insolvent, any of the partners could be held personally liable for all of the partnership's debts. Because of this potential personally liability, each the partners might want an equal say in whether the partnership should enter into any particular transaction.

Of course, a partner who invests a large percentage of the partnership's total capital has more at risk, at least initially. Because the partnership assets must be exhausted before any of the partners can be held personally liable,[113] she has more at stake while the corporation is still solvent. Indeed, when partners' capital contributions are not equal, they might draft for voting rights in proportion to investment. Partnership law allows them to decide on any voting scheme they may choose. They may even deny voting rights to a partner in their partnership agreement.

Even though partners have an equal vote as a default rule, they do not necessarily get to veto transactions.

> Partnership voting with respect to **ordinary matters** requires **approval of a majority of partners**.

> Partnership voting with respect to **extraordinary transactions** requires **unanimous approval of the partners**.

> Any **changes to the partnership agreement** require **unanimous approval of the partners**.

5B-104 PARTNER AUTHORITY:

A partner's authority to bind the partnership is based on the principles of agency authority we have already discussed.[114] Simply stated, the partner will be able to bind the partnership if the partner has authority to do so. As a quick review of agency authority, **Partner X** (the putative agent) will have the authority to bind the partnership (the principal) to a contract with a third party if:

> **Partner X has express authority**: The partners voted to grant Partner X the authority to enter into the transaction with the third party on behalf of the partnership;

> **Partner X has implied authority**: Partner X reasonably believed that the other partners had given her the authority to enter into the transaction with the third party on behalf of the partnership;

---

[113] See §5A-702 et seq., above.

[114] See §§5A-700 et seq. and 5A-803, above.

226

or

Partner X has <u>apparent authority</u>: The third party reasonably believed Partner X had authority to bind the partnership based on conduct by the partnership.

One instance where partnership law expressly supplements the standard common law authority rules is with respect to apparent authority. Partnership law provides that **a partner has apparent authority to bind the partnership simply by virtue of being a partner**.

5B-105 SUMMARY OF THE GENERAL INTRODUCTION TO PARTNERSHIP VOTING AND PARTNER AUTHORITY:

Before you move on to the detailed explanations of partnership voting and authority, make sure you understand and can clearly explain the following concepts:

Default voting rights of partners

Voting on ordinary matters

Partners' authority to bind the partnership

Express authority

Implied authority

Apparent authority

How partnership law specifically deals with the apparent authority of partners

---

5B-200 PARTNERSHIP VOTING AND PARTNER AUTHORITY –

THE DETAILS:

5B-201 PARTNERSHIP VOTING:

As mentioned, the default rule under RUPA is that each partner has one vote on any matter that requires a vote of the partners. Approval standards differ for ordinary matters and extraordinary matters.

5B-201(a) VOTING ON ORDINARY MATTERS:

As already mentioned in the general introduction, partnership voting on **ordinary matters** requires **approval of a majority of the partners**. Both RUPA and UPA are in accord on this matter.

As one might expect, neither UPA nor RUPA provides a specific enumeration of matters that qualify as ordinary business matters. Such a list could never be complete and it would differ from partnership to partnership based upon the specific circumstances and business model of each partnership.

It might be a simple truism to say that ordinary matters are those matters that are not extraordinary, but it may be useful to think in such terms to help you determine the scope of ordinary matters. **Any act outside of the partnership's ordinary business is not an ordinary matter**. Once again, the determination is fact-specific, based on the particular circumstances of each partnership.

UPA and RUPA do not envision that the partners will vote on every ordinary transaction. Instead, **if a matter is an ordinary transaction, the partners will only vote on it if there is a "difference" among the partners regarding the matter.** Once a partner has expressed dissent with respect to an ordinary business matter (or, I suppose, once a partner has recognized the possibility that there will be differing opinions among the partners) each partner will have a right to vote upon the matter. **No formal meeting or voting mechanism is required by law.**

Once it is determined that the partners will indeed vote on an ordinary matter, the question becomes whether the law requires a majority vote in favor of the matter or a majority vote against the matter. In other words, who has the burden: those in favor of the transaction or those opposed?

Generally, courts require **a majority vote to change the status quo**. If the transaction in question was consistent with past practices, those opposed to the transaction would need a majority of the partners to vote against it. Of course, there may be a certain amount of disagreement about how to characterize the status quo of the partnership's business or whether the current transaction is consistent with the past practices of the partnership.

With respect to **extraordinary matters**, UPA is silent on the voting requirement, but courts have generally held that extraordinary matters require **unanimity**. UPA lists some transactions that require the unanimous consent of all partners, but these transactions are not an exhaustive list of extraordinary matters.

RUPA, in contrast, clearly states that extraordinary matters require the unanimous consent of all partners, but does not provide a any list of extraordinary transactions as UPA does. Neither UPA nor RUPA provides any express standard to determine what constitutes an extraordinary matter. However, there are several areas where the law expressly requires unanimous approval of the partners in both UPA and RUPA:

> **Admission of a new partner** requires consent of all partners.

> **Any act in contravention of the partnership agreement** requires the consent of all partners.

> **Amendment of the partnership agreement** requires the consent all partners.

The above transactions are easy to understand. Moreover, the reasons for requiring unanimous approval of these matters are fairly obvious.

> Each partner would normally want a right to veto the ***admission of a new partner***. A partner may be held personally liable for the debts of the partnership depending on the financial condition of the partnership and the other partners (partners are normally jointly and severally liable when the partnership is unable to meet its debts). Moreover, the new partner will be able to bind the partnership. The reputation, credit, and financial circumstances of the new partner, as well as her business acumen, are all relevant to the level of risk each partner bears for the of the debts of the partnership.

> We would also expect, as a default rule, that each partner would have a right to veto ***changes to the partnership agreement*** or ***acts in contravention of the partnership agreement*** because the modification of any contract requires the consent of all the parties to the contract.

In addition to those matters listed above, **UPA lists** the following actions that require unanimous approval of the partners:

> **Assignment of the partnership property in trust for creditors** (akin to a state law alternative to bankruptcy proceedings)

> **Assignment of the partnership property on assignee's promise to pay the debts of the partnership** (essentially getting a third

party to pay the debts of the partnership and assigning the partnership's property to the third party. Maybe this was more common in 1914 when UPA was drafted.

Disposal of the goodwill of the business. It helps to think of the "goodwill" of the business as the value of the business over and above the net value of its assets.

> If a business has $200,000 in assets and $100,000 in liabilities, we might say it has a net value of $100,000. However, if the business is able to generate $75,000 in profits per year using the $100,000 net value, the business is probably worth somewhere between $200,000 and $400,000 on the market - let's say $300,000 for argument's sake. The difference between the $100,000 net value and the $300,000 market value is called the goodwill.

If the partnership sells an asset, it is not selling any "goodwill." But if the partnership sells a group of assets (e.g., contracts, equipment, intellectual property, etc.) that make up a specific part of the partnership's business, and they sell these assets for a price greater than the net value of the assets, the partnership is selling its goodwill. If the partnership is selling all or part of is "business," in contrast to simply selling its assets, it is disposing of its goodwill.

Any act that would make it impossible to carry on the partnership's ordinary business (fairly self-explanatory, but the possibilities are numerous)

Confession a judgment (admitting liability in court)

Submitting a partnership claim or liability to arbitration or reference. In 1914, when UPA was drafted, arbitration was not as common as it is today. Nowadays, arbitration clauses in contracts are commonplace. However, if UPA applies in your jurisdiction, an arbitration clause in a contract with a partnership would require the unanimous consent of the partners, unless the partnership agreement provided otherwise.

> In an RUPA jurisdiction, submitting a partnership claim or liability to arbitration most likely does NOT require the unanimous consent of the partners.

RUPA has no similar list. Even though RUPA does not expressly list extraordinary transactions, it is likely that most courts will still consider the items in the UPA list to be extraordinary transactions under RUPA (except for the provision on arbitration clauses).

There are a few additional transactions for which RUPA **requires unanimous consent** of the partners:[115]

Merger of the partnership with another entity (you will better understand the details of mergers when you read Chapter 9).

Conversion of the partnership into a limited partnership.

Essentially, these transactions are all fundamental to the partnership and its business. Except for confessing a judgment and agreeing to arbitration, these actions are very analogous to the fundamental transactions we discussed in the context of the corporation.

It is important for you to remember that the transactions expressly listed in UPA and RUPA requiring unanimous approval of the partners are **not an exhaustive list of extraordinary transactions**. You still need to evaluate each transaction individually to determine whether it is "extraordinary."

When considering whether a proposed transaction is extraordinary in the partnership context, however, do not forget that partners bear the risk of personal liability for partnership obligations. **A transaction that would not be considered fundamental or extraordinary for a corporation, might indeed be considered extraordinary for a partnership**.

For example, a decision to expand the business of the partnership or embark on a new, risky transaction exposes the partners to greater **potential personal liability** and, thus, might be considered an extraordinary transaction. In contrast, a decision by a corporation to expand the business or take on more risk would not create greater potential personal liability for the shareholders because they are protected by limited liability.

5B-201(c) CHANGING DEFAULT RULES THROUGH A PARTNERSHIP AGREEMENT:

The default voting rights of partners can be changed through the partnership agreement. The partners can make their partnership very traditional, with each partner having equal voting and management rights. Similarly, they can structure their partnership to make it look and operate more like a corporation, with management and voting power for ordinary matters restricted to a few partners (i.e., a management committee) or a CEO type partner (i.e., a managing partner).

Are there any limits on how far parties can go in taking away the management and voting rights of partners through their partnership agreement? If any partner agrees to give up or limit her management or voting rights, she must have an economic reason for doing so. She must believe that it will benefit her

---

[115] Although UPA does not specifically list these two transactions, we can probably assume that they are extraordinary transactions in UPA jurisdictions.

to give up or limit these rights and allow others to exercise them. Courts generally allow partners to relinquish or limit their management or voting rights.

However, because of the risk of personal liability, these voting and management rights are generally so important to partners, **courts will construe any such provisions in the partnership agreement very narrowly**. If there is any ambiguity, vagueness, or room for doubt, the court will assume the partner did not relinquish her rights, or only relinquished the smallest portion of her rights that a reasonable interpretation of the contract allows.

5B-202 ACCESS TO PARTNERSHIP BOOKS AND RECORDS:

The law generally provides partners with broad access to partnership books and records. It is very important for a partner to have this broad access to information about the partnership. A partner needs to closely monitor her investment because she bears potential personal liability for partnership debts. She also needs access to information to exercise her management rights in an informed manner.

A partner's right to information is not limited to receiving information from the partnership. The partner also has a right to receive information from other partners as well.

5B-202(a) THE RIGHT TO RECEIVE INFORMATION FROM THE PARTNERSHIP:

Under RUPA, a partner has a right to review and copy books and records kept by the partnership.[116] The partner is entitled to this information as a matter of course, subject to the following limitations:

The partner or her agents must inspect during ordinary business hours;

The partnership may impose reasonable fees for providing copies of documents; and

The partnership might not actually keep the records the partner seeks.

> *Drafting note:* the partnership agreement should specify what records the partnership should keep.

The partnership must also provide other information that a partner may demand regarding the partnership's business and affairs (i.e., information that is not normally in the books and records kept by the partnership). The partnership may only refuse the partner's demand for this type of information if the demand is unreasonable or improper.

---

[116] RUPA §403.

232

Finally, the partnership is obligated to provide the partner with "any information concerning the partnership's business and affairs reasonably required for the proper exercise of the partner's rights and duties."[117] The partner need not demand this information – she has a right to receive it without having to request it.

5B-202(b) THE RIGHT TO RECEIVE INFORMATION FROM OTHER PARTNERS:

A partner is also entitled to receive information regarding the partnership's business and affairs from other partners. This right might seem strange compared to what we see in the corporation – after all, shareholders have no right to receive information from other shareholders. However, partners are also managers. Furthermore, partnerships often have less formal structures, so there may not be a centralized information repository. In the corporation, the board serves this function.

A partner may demand another partner provide her information. A partner may only refuse the demand if the demand is unreasonable or improper. In addition, a partner is obligated to provide her partners with "any information concerning the partnership's business and affairs reasonably required for the proper exercise of the partner's rights and duties."[118] She must provide this information even if there has been no request for it.

5B-203 PARTNER AUTHORITY:

As we discussed in the introduction, a partner is an agent of the partnership who can bind the partnership when she has **express authority, implied authority, or apparent authority**. Her status as partner gives her apparent authority to bind the partnership.

5B-203(a) APPARENT AUTHORITY BASED ON PARTNERSHIP STATUS:

A partner is an agent of the partnership, having the apparent authority to bind the partnership simply by virtue of the fact she is a partner. However, the apparent authority of a partner based on her status as a partner is not unfettered.

> According to UPA, a partner only has apparent authority to bind the partnership based on her status as partner . . .
>
> > for *apparently* carrying on in the *usual way of the business* of the partnership.

---

[117] RUPA §403(c).

[118] Id.

RUPA states the same concept in a slightly different way, by providing that a partner only has apparent authority because of her status as partner . . .

> for **apparently** carrying on in *the **ordinary course of the partnership business or business of the kind*** carried on by the partnership.

The general theme of both provisions is that **a third party is reasonable in believing a partner, simply because she is a partner, has the authority to bind the partnership to transactions that reasonably appear to be within the ordinary scope of the partnership's business** (unless, of course, she knows the partner does not have the actual authority to do so).

More specifically, for a partner to have apparent authority based solely on her status as partner, the third party must:

(1) know of the partnership;
(2) know the party with whom she is dealing is a partner in the parntership; and
(3) reasonably believe the partner's actions were for "carrying on in the ordinary course of the partnership business or business of the kind" (or for "carrying on in the usual way of the business of the partnership" for jurisdictions still under UPA).

Furthermore, the law makes it clear that a **third party who knows the partner had no actual authority to bind the partnership cannot rely on apparent authority based on partner status**. This is an obvious corollary of apparent authority – i.e., you are not reasonable in believing a partner has authority if you know she does not.

RUPA takes this one step further by providing that a third party cannot rely on apparent authority based on partnership status if she either knows of the partner's lack of actual authority or she has **received notification** to that effect.[119] She will have "received notification" if the partnership delivered notice to her "place of business or at any other place held out by [her] as a place for receiving communications."[120]

Although the partnership agreement or a vote by the partners could expressly take away the authority of a partner to bind the partnership, either for a particular transaction or for any transaction, she would still have apparent authority with respect to ordinary partnership transactions if the third party was not aware of the contractual limitation or partnership vote.

---

[119] RUPA §301(1).

[120] RUPA §102(d).

234

There are certain circumstances where a partner will not have apparent authority to bind the partnership simply because she is the partner. The following transactions were mentioned above when we discussed actions that require the consent of all partners. With respect to these actions, a partner will not have apparent authority to bind the partnership simply by virtue of her status as partner:

Assignment of the partnership property in trust for creditors

Assignment of the partnership property on assignee's promise to pay the debts of the partnership

Disposal of the goodwill of the business

Any other act that would make it impossible to carry on the partnership's ordinary business

Confession of a judgment

Submitting a partnership claim or liability to arbitration or reference

The partner may bind the partnership to any of the above transactions only if she has been authorized by all the other partners.

5B-203(b) APPARENT AUTHORITY NOT BASED ON PARTNERSHIP STATUS:

There are situations where a partner might have apparent authority for some reason other than her status as partner. General principles of apparent authority still apply to partners. A partner will have apparent authority if the third party is reasonable in believing the partner had authority to bind the partnership based on past transactions or other conduct attributable to the partnership.

5B-203(c) ACTUAL AUTHORITY:

Of course, a partner can always bind the partnership if she has actual authority in the form of:

Express authority from the other partners; or

Implied authority from the other partners.

Thus, even in situations where a third party could not reasonably believe the partner's actions were for carrying on the business of the partnership in the usual way, the partner could still bind the partnership as long as the partner has express authority or implied authority to do so.

5B-203(d) AUTHORITY AND THE CONVEYANCE OF REAL PROPERTY OF THE PARTNERSHIP:

The conveyance of a partnership's real property can be a legal quagmire because of the various ways title to partnership property is held and recorded. Title to partnership property may be held in the name of:

> The partnership;

> A single partner; or

> Several partners.

In any of the above situations, who will have the authority to sign the deed conveying the property to the transferee? Should the partner sign in her own name or in the name of the partnership?

Both UPA and RUPA have specific rules regarding who has the authority to execute a conveyance of partnership real property held in the name of the partnership or in the name of one or more partners. RUPA provides an additional measure of legal certainty in transactions involving the transfer of real property held in the name of the partnership. RUPA allows a partnership to file **a statement of authority with the relevant state agencies.**

This statement of authority must provide the names of the partners who are authorized to execute an instrument transferring real property held in the name of the partnership. The filed statement will protect a third party transferee of real property from the partnership as long a she gave value and was not aware that the partner did not have the authority to transfer the property. The statement of authority is discussed in detail immediately below.

5B-203(e) THE STATEMENT OF AUTHORITY:

As mentioned above, under RUPA, the partnership may file a statement of authority designating the partner or partners who are authorized to sign a deed of transfer for real property held in the name of the partnership.[121] In addition, the same statement of may state limits on partner authority with respect to matters other than the transfer of real property.

Here are the differences between the two different kinds of statements a partnership may make on a statement of authority:

---

[121] RUPA §303.

	Statement of authority to transfer real property in the name of the partnership	**Statement of authority with respect to other transactions**
Effect on partnership	Conclusive against the partnership if: (1) the third party gave value; (2) the third party did not have knowledge the partner was acting without actual authority; (3) there was no limitation on the partner's authority in another filed statement of authority; and (4) the statement of authority is also **recorded in the office for recording transfers of real property.**	Conclusive against the partnership if: (1) the third party gave value; (2) the third party did not have knowledge the partner was acting without actual authority; and (3) there was no limitation on the partner's authority in another filed statement of authority.
Effect on third party	A third party is deemed to know of a recorded limitation on the authority of a partner in a statement of authority properly filed.	A third party is **NOT** deemed to know of a limitation on the authority of a partner in a statement of authority properly filed.

5B-203(f) THE AUTHORITY OF OTHER PARTNERSHIP EMPLOYEES:

A partnership may have employees that are not partners. The authority of these employees to bind the partnership depends on the general principles of agency law.[122]

---

[122] See §5A-702 et seq., above.

UNIT 5C

<u>LLCs – The Decision-Making Processes:</u>

5C-100 <u>LLC Voting and Authority – General Introduction:</u>

The law governing LLCs borrows both from partnership law and from corporate law. It generally allows parties a great deal of flexibility to structure the governance of their LLC to look more like a partnership or more like a corporation.

5C-101 <u>Patterns to Look for in Your LLC Statute:</u>

There is much less uniformity among the various state LLC statutes than we see in state partnership statutes. It is important for you to understand the various provisions one might see in a state LLC statute.

When learning how the law of your jurisdiction handles matters of voting and authority in LLCs, you should look for the following patterns:

> The LLC owners are called **"members,"** as opposed to "shareholders" or "partners."

> The members of the LLC may choose for their LLC to be ***member-managed*** or ***manager*-managed.**

> In ***member*-managed** LLCs, each ***member* has voting rights** on ordinary and extraordinary matters and the right to act as an agent of the LLC.

> In ***manager*-managed** LLCs, each ***manager* has voting rights** on ordinary matters and the right to act as agent of the LLC. Members who are not managers have the right to vote on extraordinary matters and are generally NOT agents of the LLC.

> In some jurisdictions, **each member has one vote**, regardless of her capital investment in the LLC, much like the default rules of partnership law.[123] In **other jurisdictions, a member's voting power is in proportion to her investment** in the company or in proportion to her share in the profits, much like the default rules of corporate law.[124]

---

[123] See §5B-103, above.

[124] See §5A-101, above.

The law **does not usually require formal meetings** of the managers or members of the LLC.

LLC statutes are shorter, simpler, and have **fewer default rules** and fewer decision-making and voting formalities. Therefore, drafting the LLC operating agreement becomes very important.

It may help to think of an LLC in the following terms:

For one or two persons who want to start a business and enjoy limited liability, the LLC is a wonderful fit. LLC statutes generally have sufficient default terms to enable the parties to make decisions, solve routine differences, and manage internal governance without a detailed agreement. Moreover, the formalities of most LLC statutes are sufficiently lenient to avoid getting the parties bogged down with formal meetings, meeting notices, proxies, quorum requirements, etc.

However, as an LLC increases in size and scope and involves more than just a few members, decision-making and voting formalities become more important. LLC statutes generally do not provide detailed default rules for these formalities, but they do provide the parties a wide berth to draft such formalities into their operating agreements.

5C-102 SOURCES OF LLC LAW:

As stated above, we see much less uniformity in state LLC statutes than we see in partnership statutes.

In 1995, the Uniform Law Commission ("**ULC**")[125] created the **Uniform Limited Liability Company Act** ("ULLCA"). ULC amended ULLCA in 1996 and then completely revised it in 2006. We will refer to the 2006 revised version as the **Revised Uniform Limited Liability Company Act** ("**RULLCA**" or "**RULLCA 2006**").

According to the ULC website, only 9 states have adopted the original 1995/96 version of ULLCA. Even fewer states have adopted RULLCA of 2006 – only four. When we refer to ULLCA in our discussion below, we refer to the 1996 amended version of the original.

We will compare RULLCA, ULLCA and the **Delaware Limited Liability Company Act** ("DLLCA") because their approaches are different in some interesting and important ways. This comparison should provide you with a fair representation of the issues you can expect to encounter in the LLC statute of the jurisdiction of your choice.

---

[125] Formerly known as the National Conference on the Commissioners on Uniform State Laws.

5C-103 VOTING RIGHTS IN LLCs:

The voting rights in LLCs differ depending upon whether the LLC is member-managed or manager-managed. Under most LLC statutes, the LLC will be member-managed unless its articles of organization expressly state that it is manager-managed.

5C-103(a) MEMBER-MANAGED:

The decision-making processes of member-managed LLCs are very much like those of a partnership. **Members have direct management rights** like the partners in a partnership. In contrast, shareholders in a corporation do not have these direct management rights.

Generally, most state LLC statutes provide, as a default rule, that members **vote in proportion to their investment in the LLC** (similar to the shareholder voting in corporations, based on shareholdings) rather than on a per capita basis (as we see in the partnership model, based on equal voting rights for each partner). However, you should be aware that **in some jurisdictions, as a default rule, members have equal voting rights regardless of their respective investments**.

Of course, virtually all LLC statutes allow the parties to draft around the default provisions and allocate voting rights to members as they see fit.

There are normally **no formal meeting requirements** or required decision-making processes. If an LLC elects to have formal meetings, proxies and consents are usually allowed under the relevant state LLC statute.

Voting on **ordinary LLC matters** requires approval of a **majority of membership interest** (or majority of members in a per capita jurisdiction).

Extraordinary matters, however, require **consent of all the members**.

5C-103(b) MANAGER-MANAGED:

The manager-managed LLC looks and feels more like the closely-held corporation. There is a manager, or a management board, responsible for the ordinary business of the company (much like the corporation's board of directors. There is a body of residual claimants, the members, that has a right to vote on extraordinary matters (much like the corporation's shareholders).

In manager-managed LLCs, the **managers will make the ordinary business decisions** for the LLC, without the need for members' consent, approval, or vote in any way, unless the operating agreement provides otherwise. The **members have the right to select, replace, and remove managers**. Of course, the managers will most often be selected from among the members, in

240

which case all or some of the members will still be participating in ordinary business decisions in their positions as managers.

If there is only **one manager**, she will **make the ordinary business decisions** for the LLC. If there is **more than one manager**, the various managers will have equal rights in the management of the company and ordinary business decisions – **one vote per manager on ordinary business decisions**.

The several managers might operate very much like a board of directors, except that under most LLC statutes, there are usually no formal meeting requirements for managers. If the law or the operating agreement requires formal meetings for the managers, proxies are often allowed (which contrasts with the meetings of directors in corporations, where the law does not usually allow voting by proxy).

In manager-managed LLCs, the **members will have a right to vote on extraordinary transactions**, which often require the consent of all the members.

5C-104 AUTHORITY IN LLCs:

Naturally, any person who has the express, implied, or apparent authority to bind the LLC will, in fact, be able to legally bind the LLC to a contract with a third party. The more pressing question in the LLC context is: When will a member or a manager have the **apparent authority to bind the LLC simply by virtue of her status as member or manager**?

5C-104(a) AUTHORITY IN MEMBER-MANAGED LLCs:

In a member-managed LLC, **members have the apparent authority** to bind the LLC simply by virtue of being a member for acts that reasonably appear to be in the ordinary course of the LLC's business.

5C-104(b) AUTHORITY IN MANAGER-MANAGED LLCs:

In a manager-managed LLC, **managers have the apparent authority to bind** the LLC simply by virtue of being a manager for acts that reasonably appear to be in the ordinary course of the LLC's business.

Members in manager-managed LLCs generally do not have the apparent authority to bind the LLC simply by virtue of being a member. The member of a manager-managed LLC will not have the authority to bind the LLC to a contract with a third party unless she has actual authority (i.e., express or implied authority) or apparent authority based on something other than her status as member.

5C-105 THE ROLE OF THE OPERATING AGREEMENT IN LLC DECISION-MAKING:

As we discussed in earlier chapters on LLC formation, the operating agreement is roughly equivalent to a combination of the corporation's articles, bylaws, and shareholders agreement.[126]

Because state LLC laws are usually very light on decision-making formalities (such as meetings, quorum requirements, proxies, consents, etc.) it is up to the lawyer to draft these formalities into the operating agreement if she feels they are appropriate for the circumstances of the particular LLC. She will generally **borrow the formalities of corporate law and adapt them to the LLC**.

Once the members of an LLC have signed an operating agreement, they can later amend it. **State LLC statutes usually provide that amendment of the operating agreement requires consent of all the members**. In a manager-managed LLC, the members may amend the operating agreement without consent, approval, or initiation of the managers.

5C-106 SUMMARY OF THE GENERAL INTRODUCTION TO LLC VOTING AND AUTHORITY:

Before you move on to the detailed explanations of LLC voting and authority, make sure you can clearly explain the following concepts to your dear old mom and dad:

Member-managed LLC

Manager-managed LLC

Voting rights of members in member-managed LLCs

Voting rights of managers in manager-managed LLCs

Voting rights of members in manager-managed LLCs

The authority of members in member-managed LLCs

The authority of managers in manager-managed LLCs

The authority of members in manager-managed LLCs

---

[126] See Chapter 3, §3C-600.

5C-200 LLC VOTING AND AUTHORITY – THE DETAILS:

5C-201 VOTING RIGHTS IN LLCs:

5C-201(a) RELATIVE VOTING RIGHTS OF MEMBERS:

First, a quick review: In our discussion on shareholder voting in corporations, we said a shareholder's relative voting power was determined by the number of shares she owned in proportion to the number of shares eligible to vote. Because shares are generally issued and sold to investors in proportion to their relative investments in the corporation, the relative voting power of shareholders is usually based on the relative size of their investments.

In contrast, in our discussion on partner voting in partnerships, we said that the default rule is per capita voting – that is to say, each partner has one vote regardless of her relative proportion of investment in the partnership.

Of course, we must ask which approach LLC statutes take for **member voting**: Does the law provide as a default per-capita voting or proportionate voting?

Take a look at these provisions from three different LLC statutes. Which of these adopts **per capita voting** and which adopts **voting in proportion to investment**?

> **Iowa:** A difference arising among members as to a matter in the ordinary course of the activities of the company may be decided by a majority of the members.[127]

> **Ohio:** Unless otherwise provided in writing in the operating agreement, the management of a limited liability company shall be vested in its members in proportion to their contributions to the capital of the company, as adjusted from time to time to properly reflect any additional contributions or withdrawals by the members.[128]

> **Delaware:** Unless otherwise provided in a limited liability company agreement, the management of a limited liability company shall be vested in its members in proportion to the then current percentage or other interest of members in the profits of the limited liability company owned by all of the members . . .[129]

---

[127] Iowa Code §489.407(2)(c).

[128] Ohio Revised Code, Title 17 §17.05.

[129] DLLCA §18-402.

The profits and losses of a limited liability company shall be allocated among the members, and among classes or groups of members, in the manner provided in a limited liability company agreement. If the limited liability company agreement does not so provide, profits and losses shall be allocated on the basis of the agreed value (as stated in the records of the limited liability company) of the contributions made by each member to the extent they have been received by the limited liability company and have not been returned.[130]

As you were probably able to discern from reading the above provisions, under Iowa law, members vote per capita. In contrast, under Ohio law and Delaware law, members will have relative voting rights in proportion to their investments in the LLC. As you can see, however, there are apparently different standards in Ohio and Delaware for determining each member's "investment" in the LLC for the purpose of allocating voting rights.

In Ohio, the standard is *"in proportion to their **contributions to the capital** of the company."*

In Delaware, the standard is *"in proportion to the then current percentage or other **interest of members in the profits.**"*

However, the Delaware standard is not substantively different from Ohio. Although the Delaware statute focuses on the members' relative interests in the profits, such interest in the profits is determined based on the relative value of contributions the members have made to the LLC, which is effectively the same standard in Ohio for determining relative voting power among members.

Virtually all LLC statutes allow the operating agreement to deviate from default provisions and allocate voting rights to members as they wish. If you are drafting an operating agreement for a member-managed LLC, you must determine the following:

(1) Whether the parties want member voting per capita or member voting based on the relative proportion of investment by the members;

(2) If the parties want member voting based on relative proportion of members' investments, you must determine what their relative investments are. Parties will often invest different forms of capital in the LLC (such as services, cash, personal property, real property, and intellectual property), which requires the parties and their lawyers to put some thought into the relative value of each of these contributions.

---

[130] DLLCA §18-503.

LLC statutes may not specifically use the term **ordinary matter**. We use the term simply to signify **matters that require the approval of a majority of members (or managers, as the case may be).** We distinguish ordinary matters from matters that require some sort of higher voting requirement, usually consent of all the members, which we refer to as "extraordinary matters."

When we discussed partnership voting, we had some trouble nailing down a bright line separating ordinary matters and extraordinary matters.[131] Partnership law does not provide an exhaustive list of extraordinary matters. **Many LLC statutes, however, make our lives easier by providing an exhaustive list of extraordinary transactions.** Matters outside of that list are ordinary matters, unless the parties make such matters extraordinary by contract.

Member-managed LLCs: In member-managed LLCs, although all members have a right to vote on ordinary matters, **LLC statutes do not envision that members will actually vote on all ordinary matters**. Business would grind to a halt if we required member approval for every ordinary business decision. As a practical matter, decisions are made regularly by each member of the LLC, in her capacity as agent of the LLC, without formal meetings or consultations between all of the members.

This situation is very similar to that of the partnership. For partnerships, the law does not envision the partners voting on an ordinary matter until there is an actual dispute among the partners.[132] Comments to ULLCA indicate the same is contemplated for LLCs. The relevant comment states, "***disputes*** as to any matter related to the company's business may be resolved by a majority of the members."[133] Although other LLC statutes may not expressly provide, **the expectation is that members will not vote on ordinary business matters unless there is a dispute regarding the matter**.

If a member knows that at least one other member disagrees with the transaction, she has an obligation to let all the members vote on the matter. In addition, although it is not clear the law would require it, it would be advisable for a member to present an ordinary business matter to the other members for approval if she has reason to know it might cause some sort of dispute among the members.

---

[131] See §5B-201(b), above

[132] See §5B-201(a), above.

[133] ULLCA, comments to §104.

Drafting note: In the operating agreement, the parties might set a standard for transactions that do not require approval of the members unless there is a known dispute among the members. Such a clause would require pre-approval by the members of any transaction above a certain dollar amount, for example.

The approval requirement for ordinary business matters is normally an **absolute majority** – i.e., a majority of all the members in per-capita voting regimes or a majority of the voting interests in a voting regime based on proportionate investment. The parties may deviate from the default rule in their operating agreement to require supermajority voting or simple majority voting.

Manager-managed LLCs: For manager-managed LLCs, the default rule takes the ordinary business decisions away from the members and puts it in the hands of the manager or managers.

RULLCA is very clear on this matter. Under ULLCA, in a manager-managed LLC, the **managers have the "exclusive" right to decide the LLC's business.**[134] The default allocation of decision-making rights between managers and members in an ULLCA manager-managed LLC is virtually identical to the traditional allocation of power between the board of directors and shareholders in a corporation. The corporation's board of directors and the LLC's managers have the exclusive rights to decide ordinary matters. The corporation's shareholders and the LLC's members only have the right to vote on a few extraordinary matters. The LLC operating agreement can freely give members more power than the default rule if the parties so choose.

In contrast, the **Delaware LLC statute is far less specific** on the default powers of managers. In Delaware, if the LLC is manager-managed, the managers have the power to manage the company "to the extent so provided" in the agreement.[135] The effect of this provision is that Delaware does not have a default rule with respect to the rights and powers of managers in a manager-managed LLC. Attorneys must take care to draft the operating agreement appropriately.

In many jurisdictions, including those that have adopted ULLCA, if there is **more than one manager**, each manager generally has an **equal voice** in management. In other words, **voting on matters by the managers is per capita** as a default, much like the directors in a corporation. However, the law usually provides sufficient flexibility for the allocation of voting rights among managers as the parties see fit.

---

[134] RULLCA (2006) §407(c)(1).

[135] DLLCA §18-402.

Delaware, once again, is less specific regarding the default relative voting rights of managers. The relevant Delaware provision states:

> Voting by managers may be on a per capita, number, financial interest, class, group, or any other basis.[136]

Delaware gives free rein to parties to draft the relative voting rights of managers, but it does not provide a default rule if they do not address the issue in their agreement. A lawyer assisting a client in setting up a Delaware manager-managed LLC must draft for the relative voting rights of managers (if there is more than one manager) because the law is otherwise silent on the matter.

In contrast, under ULLCA, if there is more than one manager the following default rule applies:

> . . any matter relating to the business of the company may be exclusively decided . . . by a *majority of the managers*.[137]

As you can see, the default rule under ULLCA is clear: per capita voting by managers. Under ULLCA, if the operating agreement were silent on voting rights of managers, the default rule would control. In contrast, in Delaware there is no default rule. ULLCA allows the parties the same flexibility as Delaware to allocate relative voting rights among managers in any way through the operating agreement, but provides a default if they are silent on the matter.

5C-201(c) VOTING ON EXTRAORDINARY MATTERS:

As discussed above, the members in member-managed LLCs and the managers in manager-managed LLCs decide ordinary matters by majority approval when there is a dispute. The law treats extraordinary matters in a different manner.

We might define "extraordinary matter" as follows:

(1) In a **manager-managed LLC**, any matter for which default rules require member voting.

(2) In a **member-managed LLC**, any matter which requires more than majority approval.

Under many LLC statutes, any extraordinary transaction requires the **unanimous consent of all the members** as a default. Other statutes might require a majority or supermajority.

Some of the transactions that LLC statutes treat as extraordinary transactions are **identical or similar to the fundamental transactions we discussed in**

---

[136] DLLCA §18-404.

[137] ULLCA §404(b)(2).

the context of the corporation.[138] Thus, it should not surprise you that many LLC statutes treat the following transactions as extraordinary transactions:

> Amendment of the articles of organization
>
> Amendment of the operating agreement
>
> Merger of the LLC into another entity
>
> Sale of substantially all the LLC's assets
>
> Dissolution of the LLC

There are other matters LLC statutes often treat as extraordinary matters that differ from the fundamental matters under corporate law statutes. These matters are either similar to extraordinary transactions in partnership law or unique to LLC law. For example, an LLC statute might require unanimous member approval of the following transactions:

> Admission of new members
>
> Distributions
>
> Modification of an obligation to make a contribution to the LLC
>
> Actions with respect to the ratification of self-dealing transactions.

Once again, the various LLC statutes might address the above transactions in different ways. For example:

See chart on following page

---

[138] See §5A-205, above.

	ULLCA approach	**Delaware approach**
Distributions to members	**Consent of all members** in both member-managed and manager-managed LLCs[139]	In member-managed LLCs, approval of **majority of membership interests**. In manager-managed LLCs, approval of **majority of managers** (members do not vote).
Merger of the LLC into another entity	**Consent of all members** in both member-managed and manager-managed LLCs[140]	In member-managed LLCs, approval of **majority of membership interests**.[141] In manager-managed LLCs, approval of **majority of membership interests**.[142]

I do not suggest rote memorization of the RULLCA and Delaware approaches to member voting on extraordinary transactions. I present the information to provide you context for what to expect when learning your jurisdiction's LLC statute and its approach to extraordinary transactions. As a general approach, you should look for how **your jurisdiction's LLC statute addresses extraordinary transactions** by asking yourself three questions:

(1) Do these transactions require member approval in a manager-managed LLC?

(2) Do these transactions require something more than majority approval in member-managed LLCs?

(3) What approval standard is required? Majority? Supermajority? Unanimity?

The law will generally allow an LLC operating agreement to deviate from the default rules. Knowing how your jurisdiction approaches certain important matters will give you a starting point for drafting the operating agreement to best protect your client's interest.

---

[139] ULLCA §404(c)(6). RUPA does not require consent of all members to authorize a distribution.

[140] ULLCA §904(c)(1).

[141] DLLCA §18-209(b).

[142] DLLCA §18-209(b).

For example, if your client will invest the majority of the capital in the LLC, she might prefer for extraordinary transactions to be decided by the approval of a majority of membership interests in proportion to investment, not by unanimous consent, nor by per capita voting. This voting scheme would give her complete control over extraordinary transactions. Of course, the minority members might prefer per capita voting and/or unanimous consent. Indeed, they might not sign an operating agreement that did not provide more protection for the minority interests. Members voting rights for extraordinary transactions protect minority members against transactions that might harm their interests.

5C-201(d) ELECTING MANAGERS, REMOVING MANAGERS, FILLING VACANCIES:

As you may remember, corporate law provides a myriad of default rules regarding the election and removal of directors.[143] In contrast, LLC statutes are generally very unspecific about how managers are elected, how long they serve, and how they can be removed.

RULLCA provides basic approval requirements:

> A manager may be chosen at any time by the consent of the *majority of the members* . . . [144]

RULLCA treats the **selection and removal of managers in a manager-managed LLC** like it would treat any ordinary matter in a member-managed LLC: it requires **approval of a majority of the members**. It is effectively a straight voting system with an LLC twist – voting for managers is per capita based on majority voting, not based on proportional ownership interests and plurality, as we would see under a corporate law statute.[145]

As a default rule, election and removal of managers by a majority of the members under per-capita voting may be less than ideal. In many cases, you will want to draft around it.

> When there is straight-voting under a per-capita-voting regime, each member is equally insecure about whether she will be able to elect her nominee to be the manager or one of the managers. This is true even for a member who has contributed a majority of the LLC's capital (because she only gets one vote in a per capita voting system).

> Moreover, the ability of a majority of the members to remove managers without cause provides little security for any manager, even a manager

---

[143] See §5A-200 et seq., above.

[144] RULLCA (2006) §407(c)(5).

[145] See §5A-202(a), above.

supported by a member who invested a majority of the capital (because, once again, she only gets one vote in a per capita voting system).

Finally, in a two-member LLC, election and removal of managers by a vote of a majority of the members will result in deadlock.

Delaware law is even less specific about selection and removal of managers than ULLCA. Delaware law provides that a manager:

> . . . shall be chosen in the manner provided in the limited liability company agreement [and shall] cease to be a manager as provided in the limited liability company agreement.[146]

As you can see, Delaware provides no default rules specifically directed at the election and removal of managers. In the absence of a specific default rule, the default rule for ordinary transactions would apply – i.e., a majority based on each members share in profits.[147] This standard is virtually identical to straight voting in the corporation, which means the member who owns a majority of the ownership interests in a Delaware LLC will be able to select all the managers, just as the shareholder who owns a majority of the shares in a corporation will be able to elect the entire board of directors.[148]

Neither RULLCA nor Delaware are specific about **how long a manager will serve**.

> RULLCA provides that "a manager . . . remains a manager until a successor has been chosen, unless the manager sooner resigns, is removed, or dies . . . ."[149]

> Delaware law states a manager "shall cease to be the manager by or in the manner provided in a limited liability company agreement."[150]

Thus, **both RULLCA and Delaware expect the operating agreement to specifically address the duration of service for managers** if the parties desire to limit the time a manager will serve in her position.

Often, the members will expect to elect themselves managers and will not want to go through the formality of electing themselves as managers every year. These parties are less concerned with formal annual election processes and are more concerned with simply drafting provisions in the operating agreement

---

[146] DLLCA §18-402.

[147] See §5C-201(b), above.

[148] See §5A-202(a), above.

[149] RULLCA (2006) §407(c)(5).

[150] DLLCA §18-402.

that ensure they are initially appointed as managers and cannot be removed from those positions without cause.

5C-201(e) MEETINGS, PROXIES, AND CONSENTS:

Member meetings: LLC statutes do not usually require formal meetings or even the formal consents we see in corporate law. In fact, some of them are so unspecific about member meetings that it can be quite frustrating.

For example, Ohio's LLC statute does not even hint whether members decide matters with or without meeting. The only mention of meetings in Ohio's LLC statute is the provision on bylaws, which allows an LLC to adopt bylaws that provide for meetings, notice of meetings, etc. When you read your jurisdiction's LLC statute, do not be surprised if you cannot find any specific provision on whether formal meetings are required for member approval.

Not all LLC statutes are as nebulous about member meetings. RULLCA, for example, is a bit more certain. It clearly states:

> . . . action requiring the consent of members . . . may be taken without a meeting . . . [151]

Theoretically, a verbal comment or a nod of the head from a member indicating agreement to the action would suffice in jurisdictions that do not require meetings or formal consent processes. Of course, you would advise the parties to document these decisions to avoid disagreements later on.

Delaware law, on the other hand, envisions formal member meetings when the members need to take action on a matter, but it allows the parties to liberally use teleconferencing, proxies, and consents to substitute for actual physical meetings. In fact, the default rule allowing liberal use of consents in Delaware LLCs makes member meetings unnecessary.

Delaware law provides:

> Unless otherwise provided in a limited liability company agreement, on any matter that is to be voted on, consented to or approved by members, the members may take such action without a meeting, without prior notice and without a vote if consented to, in writing or by electronic transmission, by members having not less than the minimum number of votes that would be necessary to authorize or take such action at a meeting at which all members entitled to vote thereon were present and voted.[152]

---

[151] RULLCA (2006) §407(d).

[152] DLLCA §18-302(d).

Practice tip: You can add value for your clients if you provide them with well-drafted consent forms they can use to collect and document member approvals. You can also add value by drafting the operating agreement to provide easy-to-follow procedures for voting and documenting votes.

Manager meetings: Most LLC statutes provide the same flexibility for manager meetings when manager approval is necessary. Formal meetings are not required. When the law or the operating agreement requires or envisions manager meetings, default rules usually allow for the liberal use of teleconferencing, proxies and consents in lieu of meetings.

If the parties have decided to have the LLC managed by more than one manager, you should consider whether the operating agreement should require regular meetings and whether there should be other formal decision-making processes.

5C-201(f) CLASSES OF MEMBERS AND CLASSES OF MANAGERS:

To refresh your memory, when we discussed voting in the corporation, we discussed voting by different classes of shares. A corporation might have, for example, common stock, a class of preferred stock with limited voting rights, and a class of stock with no voting rights.[153]

For the LLC, **you generally have the flexibility to draft different classes of membership interests with varying voting rights** to fit your clients' needs. Some LLC statutes are silent on the matter of different classes of membership interests with different voting rights. Silence in LLC statutes with respect to structuring an LLC in a particular way usually does not mean you cannot structure it as such. It does mean, however, that you must draft it carefully, and in detail, because there will be no default rules to rely upon in the event an issue arises that the operating agreement does not address.

In other jurisdictions, you may find general provisions allowing different classes of membership voting interests, but such provisions will likely be short on specifics and details. Delaware law, for example, provides:

> A limited liability company agreement may provide for classes or groups of members having such relative rights, powers and duties as the limited liability company may provide . . .. A limited liability company agreement may provide that any member or class or group of members shall have no voting rights.[154]

Once again, if you draft an operating agreement with several classes of membership interests having different voting rights, make sure you draft the

---

[153] See §5A-207(a), above.

[154] DLLCA §18-302.

details. Use your knowledge of the default rules of corporate law with respect to class voting to help you spot the issues for which you need to draft. For example:

> Under what situations will a class have a right to vote?

> Will membership interests that generally have no voting rights be allowed to vote when the proposal attempts to impair, alter, or dilute the class's economic rights?

> When a class has a right to vote, will it vote with the other classes, or will it vote separately (effectively giving the class a right to veto the transaction)?

Finally, it is conceivable in manager-managed LLCs that the parties might want to give **different voting rights to each of the managers**. Once again, this contrasts sharply with corporate law, which does not allow for disparate voting rights among directors. Most LLC statutes are silent on the matter, which generally means there is no reason why you cannot do it. Delaware specifically permits it.[155]

5C-201(g) APPRAISAL RIGHTS:

To quickly refresh your memory: When shareholders in a corporation have a right to vote on certain fundamental transactions, such as a merger or a sale of substantially all of the corporation's assets, they will often have appraisal rights (also called dissenters rights).[156] By exercising her appraisal rights, the shareholder forces her corporation to buy her out at fair market value and she will, therefore, not be forced to go along with the transaction.

LLC statutes generally do <u>not</u> provide appraisal rights for members, but you may draft them into an LLC operating agreement. Drafting appraisal rights will protect a minority member from a transaction she does not believe will maximize the value of her membership interests.[157]

5C-202 AUTHORITY IN LLCS:

The general principles of agency law apply to LLCs and their members, managers, and other agents. A putative agent of the LLC will bind the LLC if she has express, implied, or apparent authority.

---

[155] DLLCA §18-404.

[156] See Chapter 9, §5A-207(b), above and Chapter 9, §§9A-200 and 9A-600.

[157] Delaware specifically authorizes the operating agreement to provide contractual appraisal rights. DLLCA §18-210.

The main agency issue for LLCs is **whether a member or a manager has apparent authority to bind the LLC simply based on her status as member or manager**. In other words, is a third party reasonable in believing that a member of an LLC or a manager of an LLC has the authority to bind the LLC simply because she is a member or manager of the LLC?

5C-202(a) AUTHORITY IN THE MEMBER-MANAGED LLC:

Each member of a member-managed LLC usually has the apparent authority to bind the LLC simply based on her status as member. ULLCA (1994) §301, for example, provides:

> [E]ach member is an agent of the limited liability company for the purpose of its business, and an act of a member . . . for apparently carrying on in the ordinary course of business or business of the kind carried on by the company binds the company.

The language is intentionally similar to the relevant provisions of the Revised Uniformed Partnership Act ("RUPA") that defines the authority of partners, which we discussed earlier in this Chapter.[158]

The effect of this provision is that a third party is reasonable in believing a member can bind the LLC to a transaction, provided, however, the third party:

(1) knows of the LLC;
(2) knows the person with whom she is dealing is a member; and
(3) reasonably believes the member's actions were for "**carrying on in the ordinary course of business or business of the kind carried on by the company.**"

Most jurisdictions follow the approach of ULLCA by providing that each member of an LLC has the apparent authority to bind the LLC simply because she is a member. **However, some jurisdictions take another approach and provide that a member does not have apparent authority simply because she is a member.** Iowa's LLC law, for example, provides:

> A member is not an agent of a limited liability company solely by reason of being a member.[159]

Indeed, the 2006 version of RULLCA takes the same approach as Iowa: members are not agents of the LLC simply because of their status as member.[160] Make sure you are familiar with the approach of your jurisdiction.

---

[158] See §5B-203(a), above.

[159] Iowa Code §489.301.

[160] RULLCA (2006) §301 states: "A member is not an agent of a limited liability company solely by reason of being a member."

5C-202(b) AUTHORITY IN THE MANAGER-MANAGED LLC:

The main issue raised for manager-managed LLCs is: **who has the apparent authority to bind the LLC?**

In some jurisdictions, the decision to make the LLC a manager-managed LLC results in stripping members of any apparent authority that is based solely on membership status. Instead, each manager in manager-managed LLCs has the apparent authority to bind the LLC simply because she is a manager.

For example, ULLCA provides:

> In a manager-managed company . . . [a] member is not an agent of the company . . . solely by reason of being a member. Each manager is an agent of the limited liability company for the purpose of its business, and an act of a manager . . . for apparently carrying on in the ordinary course of business of business of the kind carried on by the company binds the company . . . .[161]

Several commentators have criticized this provision for creating excessive transaction costs in the market. They argue that the rule puts a burden on third parties to investigate whether the LLC is registered as a member-managed LLC (in which case she can safely believe the member has authority to bind the LLC) or a manager-managed LLC (in which case she cannot safely believe the member has apparent authority to bind the LLC simply because she is a "member").

The rule does indeed shift the risk of unauthorized member transactions in manager-managed LLCs to third parties contracting with LLCs. However, **the third party will shift the cost of the risk** to the LLCs with which she transacts business by:

(a) refusing to deal with members,

(b) asking for proof of a member's authority to bind the LLC, or

(c) adjusting its price to compensate her for the risk or for the costs of researching whether the LLC is member-managed or manager-managed.

The interesting effect of this rule, however, is that it benefits manager-managed LLCs at the expense of member-managed LLCs.

Here is the argument:

(1) The rule benefits *manager-managed* LLCs by protecting them from unauthorized member transactions;

---

[161] ULLCA §301(b).

257

(2) The rule shifts the costs of unauthorized member transactions in manager-managed LLCs to third parties; and

(3) Third parties will naturally shift some of these costs to LLCs that are represented members in their transactions. Naturally, this will impact ***member-managed*** LLCs more than manager-managed LLCs because members are the default agents of member-managed LLC.

The costs, however, might be insignificant, if the secretary of state's website makes researching this information rather easy.

5C-203 LLC MEMBER INFORMATION RIGHTS:

A member needs access to information about the business and affairs of the LLC to properly monitor her investment in the company. In addition, if she is active in the management of the company, she will need access to information about the company's business and its financial condition in order to make good decisions.

Because the law anticipates that the members of many LLCs will be active in the day-to-day business of their companies, LLC members general have broad information rights. Most state LLC statutes contain mandatory provisions granting members the right to access the records of the LLC.

Some LLC statutes take their cue from partnership statutes and provide a category of **information that must be provided to a member without the request of the member**.

> ### *Illustration:*
>
> RULLCA requires the LLC to provide information to a member, without demand, if the information is "**material to the proper exercise of the member's rights and duties.**"[162]

All other information must be provided to a member upon request, but only to the extent the request is not unreasonable or improper.

Generally, the operating agreement may require the LLC to maintain specific information or it may set reasonable standards for the members to gain access to the LLC's records. State LLC statutes often require the LLC to maintain certain records and documents at the LLC's principal office. Typically, these statutes might require the LLC to maintain **relevant financial records** and the **basic organizational documents**. You should expect that the law of your

---

[162] RULLCA (2006) §420(a)(2)(A).

jurisdiction will require an LLC to maintain the following documents at its principal office:

A copy of the articles of organization, as amended;

A copy of the operating agreement;

Copies of the minutes of recent meetings of the members or managers;

A list of the members;

Copies of the LLC's recent income tax returns; and

Copies of recent financial statements for the LLC.

In contrast, RULLCA does not expressly require an LLC to maintain any specific documents, information, or records. However, RULLCA's requirement that the LLC shall provide its members with information reasonably necessary to allow them to exercise their rights and duties creates an implicit requirement for the LLC to maintain adequate records.

CHAPTER 6
FIDUCIARY DUTIES

UNIT 6A
FIDUCIARY DUTIES IN THE CORPORATION:

UNIT 6B
FIDUCIARY DUTIES IN THE PARTNERSHIP:

UNIT 6C
FIDUCIARY DUTIES IN THE LLC:

6C-200 **FIDUCIARY DUTIES IN MANAGER-MANAGED LLCS:**

6C-300 **WAIVING FIDUCIARY DUTIES IN LLCS:**

_____

UNIT 6A

FIDUCIARY DUTIES IN THE CORPORATION

6A-100 FIDUCIARY DUTIES IN THE CORPORATION – GENERAL INTRODUCTION:

6A-101 THE SET-UP:

The shareholders of a corporation have entrusted their money to the corporation's management. They rely on the management to increase their wealth by increasing the corporation's wealth. In connection with this relationship among the shareholders, the management, and the corporation, the shareholders are concerned with three basic issues:

Bad decisions: The management might make poor investment decisions, which would adversely affect the corporation and diminish the value of the shareholders' interest in the corporation.

Shirking: The management might not dedicate as much time and effort to the business and affairs of the corporation as the shareholders might want.

Stealing: The management might embezzle money from the corporation. In addition, there are numerous ways the management can cause the company to engage in transactions that benefit the management at the expense of the shareholders.

> **Self-dealing:** The directors can cause the company to sell corporate assets to themselves at a price below market value. They can also cause the corporation to buy assets from the directors and prices above market value.

> **Kickback:** The directors can cause the company to enter into transactions with third parties because the third parties promise some sort of benefit to the directors.

> **Usurping an opportunity:** The director might take business opportunities that the company could take.

> **Personal use of corporate assets:** A director might use the corporate car, for example to take a personal trip.

266

The fiduciary duties of directors and officers are designed to address these concerns. In a sense, the fiduciary duties serve two functions:

> **Fiduciary duties instruct directors and officers** that they must make good decisions, they must not shirk, and they must not steal from the corporation; and

> **Fiduciary duties provide shareholders with a cause of action** to sue directors for their misfeasance or malfeasance.

There is one very important theme the student of corporate law should keep in mind as she studies fiduciary duties: **fiduciary duties are generally very protective of directors**. In other words, only the most egregious cases of director or officer misconduct or inaction will result in liability for the directors or officers in question.

This chapter discusses the fiduciary duties of directors and officers (and to a lesser extent, the fiduciary duties of controlling shareholders). When reading this chapter, please remember that the **fiduciary duties of directors and officers are almost identical**. When reference is made in this chapter to the fiduciary duty of directors, you can assume that it also applies to officers and *visa versa*. There one major area where fiduciary duty law treats officers in a manner that it significantly different from directors – the exculpation clause, which is discussed below.[163]

6A-102 **LABELING THE FIDUCIARY DUTIES:**

When we discuss of the fiduciary duties of directors and officers, we generally refer to them in these terms:

> **The duty of care:** The duty to make decisions on an informed basis and after adequate deliberations.

> **The duty of loyalty:** The duty not to steal from the corporation – either through blatant theft or through transactions designed to siphon funds away from the corporation. Essentially the duty of loyalty requires a director or officer to put their personal pecuniary interests second to those of the corporation.

> **The duty to monitor:** The duty to stay informed about the business and affairs of the corporation- including the activities of the officers and employees- and to take action when necessary.

---

[163] See §6A-209, below.

The duty of good faith: The duty to serve the interests of the corporation honestly.

The labels are legal jargon that helps lawyers, judges, legal scholars, and corporate officers and directors to engage in discourse on fiduciary duties with a common vocabulary. By all means, **learn the labels and use them liberally in your discussions of fiduciary duties**, but please remember that it is **far more important for you to learn the nature of fiduciary duties**, the fact patterns that implicate possible breaches of fiduciary duties, and the standards of liability that apply to the various fact patterns.

6A-103 STANDARDS OF LIABILITY:

It is easy to remember that a director or officer of a corporation owes a particular fiduciary duty to the corporation. However, it is **important for you to recognize what standard of liability applies** to a fact pattern implicating a breach of a particular fiduciary duty.

It may be helpful to make an analogy to a cause of action that you have discussed in your torts class. A plaintiff may sue a defendant for the wrongful death of a victim. Of course, the label "wrongful death lawsuit" describes the cause of action in broad strokes, but does not give us a lot of information about whether the defendant will be liable. You might remember from your torts class that a defendant will be liable if she negligently or recklessly caused the death of the victim, or if she acted knowingly or with intent to cause the death. The "wrongful death" label is helpful, but the standard of liability is more important.

The same holds true for breaches of fiduciary duties. If a director's conduct meets the standard of liability (e.g., she was "reckless"), she has breached her fiduciary duty to the corporation. The key lies in understanding which standard of liability applies to each of the various fiduciary duty fact patterns.

6A-103(a) DUTY OF CARE – STANDARD OF LIABILITY:

Directors and officers owe a duty of care to the corporation when making decisions. Directors and officers will not be liable for breaching their duty of care unless their decision-making process **was reckless (or grossly negligent)**.

Please notice that the law **focuses on the decision-making process**, not the decision itself. Courts do ask whether a decision was bad, and they do not care whether the decision turned out poorly for the company. Good business decisions can result in bad outcomes. Risk is an inherent part of doing business.

To determine whether the directors have breached their fiduciary duty of care, you must **focus on whether the decision-making process was reckless.** The factors that you should consider are the **length and depth of the deliberations** leading up to the decision and the **quantity and quality of the information** used to make the decision.

6A-103(b) DUTY OF LOYALTY/CONFLICT OF INTEREST – STANDARD OF LIABILITY:

A director or officer will **breach her fiduciary duty of loyalty if she is conflicted (i.e., interested) in the transaction and cannot prove the transaction was fair to the corporation.** In other words, a director or officer will not be liable to the corporation simply because she has a conflict of interest in the transaction in question. Her conflict creates a presumption of liability, but she will overcome the presumption if she can prove the transaction was fair to the corporation.

A director or officer is **conflicted** or **interested** in the transaction in question if she has a **financial interest we reasonably expect would influence her decision.** In order to **prove the transaction was fair** to the corporation, and avoid liability, the defendant must usually show **substantive fairness** (i.e., the price was fair) and **procedural fairness** (e.g., the negotiations were fair).

In addition, if the transaction went through a proper **ratification process,** the conflicted director **will not be liable and will not need to prove fairness.** Ratification is the **approval of the transaction by non-conflicted directors or non-conflicted shareholders** after the conflicted director has disclosed her conflict of interest and other material information about the transaction.

6A-103(c) DUTY OF LOYALTY/CORPORATE OPPORTUNITY – STANDARD OF LIABILITY:

A director or officer will be liable for taking a **business opportunity that belonged to the corporation.** She will be able to **avoid liability if she shows it was fair for her to take the opportunity.**

A court will examine various factors to determine whether it was fair for the directors to take the opportunity. We discuss these factors in detail below,[164] but they essentially provide standards to determine whether the opportunity belonged to the corporation.

In addition, if the **non-conflicted directors or non-conflicted shareholders** gave the defendant director permission to take the opportunity, she **will not be liable and will not need to prove fairness.** This process is analogous to the **ratification process** for self-dealing transactions discussed immediately above.[165]

---

[164] See §6A-203(b), below.

[165] See §6A-103(b), above.

6A-103(d) DUTY TO MONITOR – STANDARD OF LIABILITY:

As we already discussed above, when a shareholder challenges the board's business decisions in court, the judge will determine the director's liability under the duty of care standard – i.e., did the board engage in a reckless decision-making process? However, as you may recall from the materials you studied in Chapter 5, the board of directors will not decide on every corporate action. The board of directors will only meet several times throughout the year to decide on major strategic decisions. The officers and employees of the corporation make most day-to-day decisions. The board has a duty to monitor the officers and employees who make these day-to-day decisions.

The duty to monitor involves two general fact patterns:

(1) The board **failed to prevent or detect** conduct by the officers or employees that caused harm to the corporation.

> ***Illustration 1:***
>
> The employees of XYZ Inc. have been engaging in illegal anti-competitive activities that have subjected the corporation to heavy fines. A shareholder sues the board of directors for failing to detect and stop the activity.
>
> ***Illustration 2:***
>
> The head of the IT department of XYZ Inc. has been purchasing computers for the corporation from a company that he owns (self-dealing). A shareholder sues the board of directors for failing to detect and stop the self-dealing activity.

(2) The board **failed to consider a transaction** and such failure eventually causes harm to the corporation.

> ***Illustration:***
>
> XYZ Inc. failed to renew its business license. The license expired, which resulted in fines for the corporation, a temporary stoppage of business, and extra expenses to have the license renewed on an expedited basis. A shareholder sues the board of directors for failing to renew the license (i.e., for failing to keep on top of the matter).

The standard of liability for these types of fiduciary duty claims is **bad faith**.

What type of conduct constitutes bad faith? It would be bad faith if the director or officer **intended to cause harm** to the corporation, but that is highly unlikely in most situations. It would also be bad faith if the board **consciously disregarded a duty to act**.

In practical terms, a lawsuit against directors or officers for breaching their duty to monitor is most likely a losing lawsuit for the shareholder. It would be difficult to prove that the directors intended to cause harm to the corporation or consciously disregarded a duty to act.

We might think of situations where the board carelessly or even recklessly failed to consider a matter, or detect or prevent certain activities by the employees. But it is hard to imagine that a shareholder-plaintiff would be able to show that the board knew they should have taken action (i.e., renew the business license) and consciously disregarded it (i.e., "To hell with the business license, let's go to the beach instead").

6A-103(e) DUTY OF GOOD FAITH - STANDARD OF LIABILITY:

There is considerable debate on whether the duty of good faith is a separate fiduciary duty. In Delaware, at least, the current trend is to characterize the duty of good faith as a subset of the duty of loyalty.

It does not really matter whether you characterize good faith as free standing fiduciary duty or a subset of the duty of loyalty. In either case, there are certain fact patterns that will implicate liability for failing to act in good faith.

   (1) The director or officer intended to harm the corporation.

   (2) The director or officer consciously disregarded a duty to act.

6A-103(f) WASTE:

Waste is not a separate fiduciary duty. I suppose you could say that the **duty not to waste corporate assets** a fiduciary duty. In any case, directors and officers will be liable if they waste corporate assets.

You may think of waste as a standard of liability. If the board's action constitutes "waste," the directors will be liable for breaching their fiduciary duties. The board's action will be waste if **no rational business person under the same circumstances would have made the same decision**.

Don't fall into the trap of asking whether the decision was rational or reasonable. A director or officer will only be liable for her decision if **no other rational person in the world would have made the same decision in the same circumstances**. The standard is very protective of directors and officers. It is a very high burden for the shareholder-plaintiff to overcome.

I like to use the following standard to help me with my analysis of waste: **How close was the board's decision to literally burning cash or giving away corporate assets for free?**

6A-104 THE BUSINESS JUDGMENT RULE:

Lawyers, judges, and legal scholars frequently cite the business judgment rule. The rule is stated in several different formulations, but the gist is always the same:

> **A court will not second guess a decision by directors unless the plaintiff can demonstrate the directors breached their fiduciary duties.**

In simple terms, this means the shareholder-plaintiff must come to court alleging something more than a bad decision by the directors. She must allege and present a prima facie case that the defendant directors breached one of their fiduciary duties.

The business judgment rule is often stated as a rebuttable presumption. The court will presume the directors were disinterested, acted in good faith and with due care. Unless the shareholder plaintiff can plead facts and present a prima facie case that shows otherwise, her lawsuit will be dismissed for failure to state a cause of action (usually via the court's application of the business judgment rule). She must present a prima facie case showing the defendant directors were conflicted, failed to act in good faith, engaged in a reckless decision-making process, or committed waste, etc.

6A-105 BAD DECISIONS:

We have already stated that the board does not breach its fiduciary duties simply by making a bad decision. In other words, even if the directors made a decision that turns out to be disastrous for the corporation, they will not be liable. This principle is the essence of the business judgment rule – we will not second guess the business decisions of the board unless it has breached one of its fiduciary duties.

A shareholder plaintiff must allege and present a prima facie case of something more than a bad decision. Even if she can present very convincing evidence that the board should have (or easily could have) made another decision that was far superior to their actual decision, she will still not win her case. She must make out a prima facie case that the board breached its fiduciary duties - i.e., the directors were reckless in their decision making process, the directors were self-dealing or usurping a corporate opportunity, the directors acted in bad faith, or committed waste.

6A-106 EXCULPATION CLAUSE:

Legal protection of directors extends beyond the lenient liability standards of fiduciary duty breaches. Most state corporate law statutes also allow corporations to adopt a **provision in their articles of incorporation exculpating directors** (but not officers) **for breaching the fiduciary duty of care**.

If a corporation has an exculpation clause in its articles of incorporation, any director who engages in a reckless decision-making process in breach of her duty of care, would not be liable to the corporation, or its shareholders, for monetary damages.

Generally, exculpation clauses in the articles may only:

(1) Exculpate directors, not officers; and

(2) Exculpate directors for breaches of the duty of care, not the duty of loyalty, bad faith or waste.

6A-107 FIDUCIARY DUTIES OF CONTROLLING SHAREHOLDERS:

When a corporation has a controlling shareholder, the law imposes the same fiduciary duties on the controlling shareholder as it does for directors and officers. For example, a shareholder (or group of shareholders working together) that controls a majority of a corporation's voting power will owe a fiduciary duty to the corporation and the corporation's minority shareholders.

The cases that involve the fiduciary duties of controlling shareholders generally focus on duty of loyalty issues – namely, **self-dealing** and **taking a corporate opportunity**.

6A-108 SUMMARY OF THE GENERAL INTRODUCTION TO FIDUCIARY DUTIES IN THE CORPORATION:

Before you move on to the detailed explanations, make sure you understand the following terms and concepts:

Duty of care

Duty of loyalty

Duty to monitor

Duty of good faith

Waste

Bad decisions

Exculpation clause

Fiduciary duties of controlling shareholders

6A-201 PROTECTING DIRECTORS AND OFFICERS:

The standards of liability for breaches of fiduciary duties are very protective of corporate directors and officers. As a general proposition, directors and officers will only be personally liable for fiduciary duty breaches when their conduct is egregious. The justification for the high-level of protection of directors and officers is that the shareholders would prefer their directors and officers to receive this type of protection, at least on an *ex ante* basis.

6A-202 DUTY OF LOYALTY – CONFLICTED TRANSACTIONS:

6A-202(a) CONFLICTED/INTERESTED DIRECTORS:

In general terms, a director or officer is **conflicted** or **interested** or **has a conflict of interest** if she will directly or indirectly benefit in the transaction.

A **direct conflict** occurs where the director is transacting business with the corporation.

> *Illustration:*
>
> The corporation sells a tract of land to the director.

An **indirect conflict** occurs where the director or officer has a significant financial interest in an entity that transacts business with the corporation.

> *Illustration:*
>
> Director X is a director of ABC Inc. She also owns 58% of XYZ LLC. ABC Inc. enters into a licensing agreement with XYZ LLC.

Similarly, a director is conflicted if the another promises a benefit to the director if the corporation enters into a transaction (colloquially known as a **kickback**). The potential benefit for the director impairs her ability to review and make a decision about the transaction in an independent and impartial manner.

A director will also be conflicted when a **close relative transacts business with the corporation**. Of course, the analysis is very fact specific, but the basic idea is that a benefit to the close relative is an indirect benefit to the director.

Finally, there are other situations where a director will be indirectly conflicted even though she has **no direct or indirect *financial*** interest in the transaction. If a person sits on the board of directors of two corporations that transact business with each other, the director is conflicted even if she is not a shareholder of either corporation.

Illustration:

Bob is a director of XYZ Corp. He is also a director of ABC Inc. XYZ Corp. and ABC Inc. begin negotiations to merge the two companies. Bob is conflicted in the transaction.

In this situation, courts focus on the director's conflicting duties, not the benefit the director might receive. Arguably, the director stands to gain nothing from the transaction, but she owes a fiduciary duty to serve the best interests of each of the corporations. When parties transact business, there are many circumstances where their interests will not be aligned. It would be a most difficult task for the directors to serve the best interests of both corporations.

Once again, labeling the transaction as a "direct conflict" or an "indirect conflict" is not as important as understanding the situations that give rise to conflicts. Indeed, there are standards for determining whether a director is conflicted.

Under the RMBCA, a director is conflicted if she is a **party to the transaction** (direct conflict) or if has "a **material financial interest** [in the transaction] known to her." The RMBCA defines "material financial interest as:

> [A] **financial interest** in a transaction that would **reasonably be expected** to **impair the objectivity** of the director's judgment when participating in the action on the authorization of the transaction[166]

The comments to the RMBCA make it clear that this is an objective standard, not a subjective one. In other words, the court should not ask whether the defendant director's objectivity was actually impaired, but whether we would reasonably expect the objectivity of a reasonable director in similar circumstances to be impaired.

6A-202(b) RATIFICATION:

A director or officer who was conflicted in a corporate transaction will normally have to prove the transaction was fair to the corporation in order to avoid personal liability for breaching her fiduciary duties. However, if the transaction was **approved by disinterested directors or shareholders**, the director will not be liable and will not be required to prove the transaction was fair to the corporation. The approval of a conflicted transaction by disinterested shareholders or directors is normally called **ratification**.

---

[166] RMBCA §8.60(4).

When a conflict-of-interest transaction is approved by the non-conflicted shareholders or directors, the court will defer to the judgment of the non-conflicted shareholders or directors. More specifically, the court will defer to the decision of those who approved the transaction, apply the business judgment rule to the transaction in question, and dismiss the lawsuit against the conflicted director if the transaction in question:

> Was **approved** (before or after the fact)

> By **shareholders** or **directors** (at least two directors),

> Who were **disinterested** (i.e., not conflicted in the transaction), **independent** (i.e., not dominated or controlled by the conflicted directors)

> After **receiving full disclosure** about the transaction (i.e., disclosure of the nature of the conflict and all other material facts about the transaction).

6A-202(c) THE STATUTES:

Many state corporate law statutes provide that a transaction will not be void simply because directors or officers were conflicted in the transaction, provided the transaction was approved by disinterested directors, shareholders, or if the transaction was fair to the corporation. These statutes are often silent about several matters. First, they provide the transaction will not be void, but they give no instruction on whether the conflicted director or officer will be liable for monetary damages. Second, they do not indicate whether the plaintiff-shareholder or defendant director will have the burden of proving the fairness of the transaction.

Courts have filled in the gaps in most jurisdictions. In other jurisdictions, corporate law statutes on conflicted transactions are more detailed. The RMBCA has very detailed provisions that address conflicted transactions and their ratification.[167]

6A-202(d) THE RATIFICATION PROCESS:

A valid ratification of a conflicted transaction requires approval of **disinterested and independent directors or shareholders**, after receiving **full disclosure** from the conflicted party.

Timing of the ratification approval: The ratification approval by the disinterested directors or shareholders can be **before the fact** – i.e., approval

---

[167] RMBCA Subchapter F, §§8.60-8.70.

of the conflict before entering into the transaction – or **after the fact** – approval of the conflict after the transaction has already occurred.

Disinterested and independent: The ratification approval of the transaction usually requires approval by directors or shareholders who are disinterested **and** independent.

Disinterested simply means the directors or shareholders approving the transaction were **not conflicted** in the transaction.

Independent means the directors or shareholders approving the transaction must also be independent from the conflicted director(s). Courts have said that directors are not independent if they are **dominated by, controlled by, or beholden to the conflicted director(s)**.

The essence of **dominance and control** is that the relationship between the conflicted director and the non-conflicted director is one where the conflicted director's influence over the non-conflicted director sterilizes her objectivity and impartiality. Familial ties can be an indicator of control and dominance, as can other close personal relationships. The key is not whether the personal relationship exists, but whether the nature of the relationship shows dominance or control.

A non-conflicted director may be **beholden** to the conflicted director when the **conflicted director has the power to withdraw or withhold some material benefit** from the non-conflicted director.

The **burden to show** the non-conflicted director lacked the requisite independence is generally **on the plaintiff challenging the transaction**. If the decision was made by the entire board of directors, the plaintiff might be required to prove that a majority of the directors were not independent to nullify the effects of the ratification.

The **RMBCA** provides a more detailed standard to determine the independence of a non-conflicted director who approves a conflicted transaction. The RMBCA calls the non-conflicted and independent director a "**qualified director.**" As you read the RMBCA provision below, please note that it addresses whether the director was **disinterested** [in part (i)], **independent** [in part (ii)], and provides a definition of material relationship:

[A qualified director is] not a director (i) as to whom the transaction is a director's conflicting interest transaction, or (ii) who has a material relationship with another director as to whom the transaction is a director's conflicting interest transaction[168]

---

[168] RMBCA §1.43(a)(3)

"Material relationship" means familial, financial, professional, employment or other relationship that would reasonably be expected to impair the objectivity of the director's judgment when participating in the action[169]

Quorum and approval: In many jurisdictions, the quorum requirement for the ratification of a conflicted transaction is reduced from the normal majority of the directors to **a majority of disinterested/independent directors.** The board might establish an independent committee of non-conflicted directors to make the decision. In many jurisdictions, the law requires that **no fewer than two disinterested/independent directors** ratify the conflict, regardless of whether the decision comes in a meeting of the full board or a special committee.

State law does not always require the disinterested/independent directors to meet outside the presence of the conflicted director(s). The Kentucky Business Corporation Act, for example, specifically provides that the presence or the vote of a conflicted director will not affect the validity of the ratification.[170] However, as a practical matter, the presence of a conflicted director at a meeting to ratify the conflicted transaction might tend to show that she dominated the other directors. The RMBCA requires the disinterested/independent directors to deliberate and vote outside the presence and without the participation of the conflicted or non-independent directors.[171]

Full disclosure: Ratification of the transaction requires the conflicted director to make full disclosure to the disinterested directors or shareholders. If full disclosure is not made, the disinterested directors are not informed, and their approval of the transaction will not act as a ratification of the conflict.

Full disclosure generally requires the conflicted director to disclose:

(1) **The nature of her interest in the transaction** – In other words, she must disclose how she is conflicted.

(2) **All relevant material facts about the transaction** – In other words, the conflicted director is not permitted to have an informational advantage in her conflicted transaction with the corporation. The ratification process is **not an arm's length bargaining** process. In an arm's length bargaining process, parties do not generally have to disclose all the

---

[169] RMBCA §1.43(b)(1).

[170] KBCA §6A-310(3).

[171] RMBCA §8.62(a)(1).

279

material information they have to the other party. They are allowed to have an informational advantage over the other party.

However, if the conflicted director desires the protection of the business judgment rule, **she must give up any bargaining advantage** she has over the corporation. Here is an example:

> ***Hypothetical transaction:*** The purchase and sale of a plot of land. Seller knows that a major local employer is shuttering its business, which will reduce property values in the area. Buyer is not aware of this information.

>> ***Disclosure in arm's-length bargaining:*** Seller does not have to disclose to the buyer that the local employer is ceasing its operations. It is the buyer's duty to discover this type of information for herself.

>> ***Disclosure by a conflicted director during the ratification process:*** If the director is selling the land to the corporation, in order to be protected in ratification process, she must disclose the information about the local employer's plan to shutter its business because it is relevant and material to the corporation's decision to purchase the land.

6A-202(e) FAIRNESS:

If the conflicted director did not submit the transaction to the board or shareholders for ratification, or if the ratification process was somehow tainted (i.e., the directors or shareholders who ratified it were not disinterested, independent or receive full disclosure from the conflicted director), she will be required to **prove the transaction was fair**. Courts may use different names for fairness review: *entire fairness; intrinsic fairness; fair and reasonable; just and reasonable*, etc.

Delaware courts have said that fairness review requires the defendant director to show fair price and fair dealing, which means fairness has elements of both **substantive fairness (fair price)** and **procedural fairness (fair dealing)**. Why not simply allow the director to prove the price was fair?

> **Range of fair price:** There is always a range of fair prices. The price any party can obtain or pay within the range of fair price depends on its relative negotiating power in an arm's-length process. We cannot be certain the price is fair in this particular transaction unless the deal was arms-length.

Necessity of the deal: A good price on services, goods, or real estate is not relevant if the corporation did not need the services, goods or real estate.

However, price may be the deciding factor in many cases. The Delaware Supreme Court has stated: "in a non-fraudulent transaction we recognize that price may be the preponderant consideration outweighing other features of the [transaction]."[172] Although this statement by the court confirms our understanding that a fair price will sometimes win the day over a less than perfect process, it still begs the question: What is a fraudulent transaction? If approval by conflicted directors alone is not fraudulent, what other factors might make a transaction fraudulent?

What factors are important to a **review of the procedural fairness of a transaction**? In one famous case,[173] the Delaware Supreme Court enumerated several factors relevant to the fairness of the bargaining process in a self-dealing transaction. A court should consider **how the transaction was timed, initiated, structured, negotiated, disclosed, and approved**.

6A-202(f) THE RELATIONSHIP BETWEEN FAIRNESS AND RATIFICATION:

Some courts seem to conflate fairness and ratification into one test. The fairness of the transaction will depend on whether it was approved by disinterested and independent directors who received full disclosure from the conflicted directors or officers. In other jurisdictions, fairness and ratification are two different issues – you need two show either fairness or ratification.

Conflict-of-interest provisions in corporate law statutes generally make ratification and fairness two separate issues. The statutes normally state that a transaction will not be void if ratified by directors, ratified by shareholders, OR if it was fair. They envision situations where a defendant director can escape liability by showing fairness, even though there was a deficient ratification process or no ratification process at all. However, many of these conflict-of-interest statutes often only expressly address whether the transaction is void because of the conflict, not whether the conflicted directors are liable for monetary damages. Because these statutes do not expressly address liability, courts might legitimately adopt other standards to determine the liability of a director for breaching her duty of loyalty.

Some issues that are common to fairness and ratification will naturally overlap. The procedural fairness review of the conflicted transaction will necessarily include an analysis of the fairness of the bargaining process. Facts such as whether those approving the transaction were independent, disinterested and informed are relevant to procedural fairness as well as ratification. Of course,

---

[172] *Weinberger v. UOP*, 457 A.2d 701 (Del. Sup. Ct. 1983).

[173] Id.

for the fairness standard to have any meaningful separate existence from the ratification standard, fairness review should not require the same level of independence and information sharing as the ratification process demands. In theory, the court should be looking for **a process more akin to arms-length bargaining** in fairness review than the more strict process we expect in ratification.

We would expect a **court's review of the ratification process** to focus on the **disinterestedness** and **independence** of the directors or shareholders approving the transaction, as well as whether they received **information** that removed any informational advantage the conflicted party might otherwise enjoy. We would expect the court to refrain from any determination about whether the price was fair, or whether the ratification process was fair, except a review of the disinterestedness, independence, and disclosure of information that is necessary for ratification.

We would expect a **court's fairness review** to focus on **fair price** and **fair dealing**, with the **assumption that those who approved the transaction were <u>not</u> disinterested, independent, or did not receive full disclosure from the conflicted party**. Of course, when analyzing the issue of fair dealing, it would be difficult for a court not to consider the fact that the parties who approved the transaction were not disinterested or independent, or the fact that they did not have perfect information, but those facts should not control the court's review of fairness if it conflates "fairness" and "ratification." Indeed, advice from independent advisors or a market test might demonstrate a fair process when the decision-makers are not independent or disinterested.

6A-202(g) CORPORATE LOANS TO DIRECTORS AND OFFICERS:

Corporate loans to directors or officers are self-dealing transactions that often receive special treatment in state corporate law statutes. In addition, corporate loans to entities in which the corporation's directors or officers have financial interests might also be subject to similar treatment. Some corporate law statutes allow these loans only if they go through an approval process similar to ratification – approval by disinterested and independent shareholders or directors. This process is different from ratification for other self-dealing transactions because the statutes do not normally contemplate an opportunity to prove fairness if the statutorily prescribed procedures are not met.

Publicly-traded corporations are subject to more stringent federal standards regarding loans to officers and directors. The Sarbanes-Oxley Act prohibits public companies from making loans to directors and officers.

6A-202(h) COMPENSATION OF DIRECTORS AND OFFICERS:

Setting the compensation for officers and directors will often involve conflicts of interest. Some officers of the corporation might also serve on its board of directors. Executive officers who sit on the board of directors are called **inside**

directors. When the board determines executive compensation plans, the inside directors should recuse themselves from the deliberations and the voting, allowing the other directors to approve the compensation plan. This ratification process would protect the inside directors from any duty of loyalty lawsuits regarding their compensation.

In contrast, in many closely-held corporations, each director is also an executive officer, which means all the directors are interested when they set executive compensation. This situation only becomes an issue when the corporation has minority shareholders other than those who sit on the board. In those circumstances, a few clever boards have tried an alternating board approval process in an attempt to ratify the approvals:

> A and B decide C's compensation, B and C decide A's compensation, and A and C decide B's compensation.

I have read reports of two cases where the directors used this type of alternating approval. In one case, the court held that this was a legitimate ratification process, but in the other, the court held that it was not. I would have to agree with the court that found it was not a legitimate ratification process. When the implicit (or even explicit) agreement is *"I will approve your compensation if you approve mine,"* the directors are clearly interested in their decisions to approve the other directors' compensation. It is no different from a "kickback." The only options in these situations are to submit the decision to disinterested shareholders for their ratification, or to prove the fairness of the compensation if it is ultimately challenged by an unhappy shareholder.

6A-202(i) DISINTERESTED DIRECTORS AS DEFENDANTS:

The disinterested/non-conflicted directors who ratify a self-dealing transaction will often be defendants themselves. Do these directors risk any liability for approving a conflicted transaction?

Duty of care claim: The disinterested directors might be liable under a duty of care claim. This claim would allege that they did not approve the transaction after a careful decision-making process. As we will discuss below, it is very difficult for a shareholder-plaintiff to make a successful duty of care claim.[174]

Duty of loyalty claim: The disinterested directors might be liable under a duty of loyalty cause of action. This type of claim would allege that the disinterested directors were so dominated, controlled by or beholding to the conflicted directors, that they were also conflicted.

---

[174] See §6A-204 et seq., below.

283

There is support in caselaw for the proposition that an otherwise disinterested director might be considered conflicted simply by virtue of being under the very strong influence of the conflicted director. As one court has stated:

> The key issue is not simply whether a particular director receives a benefit from a challenged transaction not shared with the other shareholders, or solely whether another person or entity has the ability to take some benefit away from a particular director, but whether the possibility of gaining some benefit or the fear of losing a benefit is likely to be of such importance to that director that it is reasonable for the Court to question whether valid business judgment or selfish consideration animated that director's vote on the challenged transaction.[175]

The RMBCA approach is in accord. Under the RMBCA, there is a point where a director is so dominated by, controlled by, or beholden to the conflicted director that she is also conflicted, and can be liable for breach her duty of loyalty for ratifying the transaction.[176] However, under the RMBCA approach, the dominated director has the opportunity to escape liability if she can show she reasonably believed the transaction was in the best interests of the corporation.[177]

Duty to monitor claim: Finally, in cases where the disinterested/independent directors approve a transaction without discovering a fellow director had a conflict of interest, it seems like the only possible causes of action against the disinterested directors are **duty to monitor** and duty of care claims. As we will see below, it is difficult for a plaintiff-shareholder to make a successful duty of care or duty to monitor claim.[178]

6A-202(j) EXCULPATION CLAUSES AND THE DUTY OF LOYALTY:

Most state corporate law statutes allow a corporation to include a clause in its articles of incorporation exculpating directors, but not officers, for any liability to the corporation or its shareholders for fiduciary duty breaches. However, **the exculpation clause cannot exculpate directors for breaches of the duty of loyalty**.

The relevant Delaware provision specifically mentions the duty of loyalty:

> [T]he certificate of incorporation may also contain . . . [a] provision eliminating or limiting the personal liability of a director to the

---

[175] *Orman v. Cullman,* 794 A.2d 5, 25 fn. 50 (Del.Ch. 2002).

[176] RMBCA 8.31(a)(2)(iii)(A).

[177] RMBCA 8.31(a)(2)(iii)(B).

[178] For a discussion of a duty of care cause of action, see §6A-204 et seq., below. For a discussion of a duty to monitor cause of action, see §6A-205 et. seq., below.

corporation or the stockholders for money damages for breach of fiduciary duty as a director, provided that such provision shall not eliminate or limit the liability of a director: (i) For any breach of the director's **duty of loyalty** to the corporation or its stockholders . . .[179]

The relevant provision of the RMBCA does not specifically mention the duty of loyalty, but the language prohibiting exculpation for certain types of fiduciary duty breaches covers conduct that implicates breaches of the duty of loyalty:

> The articles of incorporation may set forth . . . a provision eliminating or limiting the personal liability of a director to the corporation or the stockholders for money damages for any action taken, or any failure to take action, as a director, except for liability for . . . the amount of a financial benefit received by the director to which he is not entitled . . .[180]

A director who has breached her duty of loyalty cannot rely on an exculpation clause in the corporation's articles of incorporation, even if the clause is drafted broadly to include duty of loyalty claims.

6A-202(k) CONFLICTED TRANSACTIONS – FLOWCHARTS:

The following flowcharts and their explanations summarize the law of conflicted transactions.

Flowcharts and explanations begin on the next page.

---

[179] DGCL §102(b)(7) (emphasis added).

[180] RMBCA §2.02(b)(4).

DUTY OF LOYALTY – CONFLICTED TRANSACTION FLOWCHART:

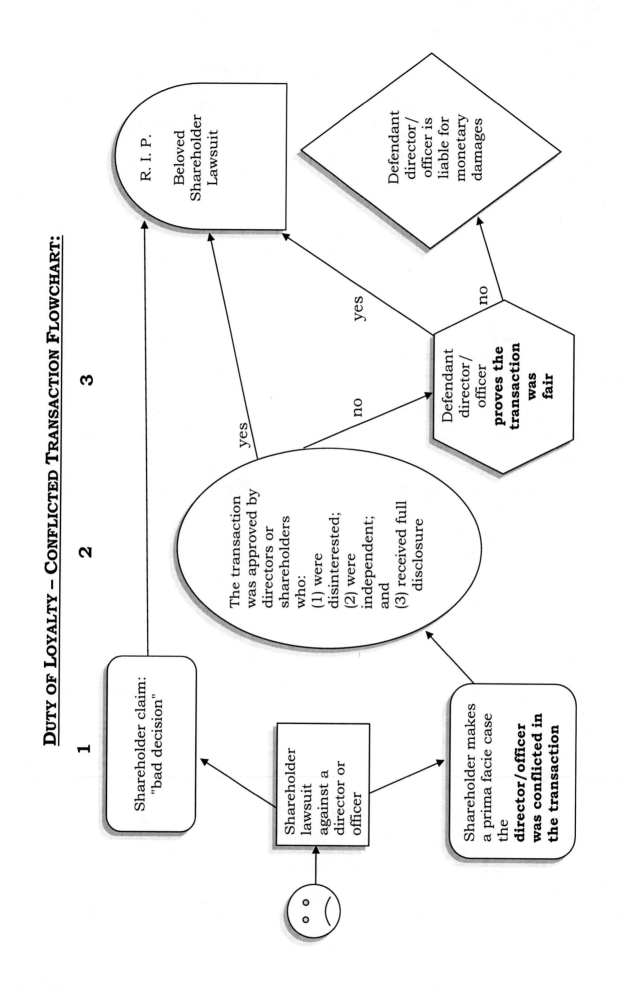

DUTY OF LOYALTY – CONFLICTED TRANSACTION FLOWCHART EXPLANATION:

1)   When a shareholder brings a lawsuit against a director for a breach of her fiduciary duties, the lawsuit is quite often a derivative lawsuit. We will discuss derivative lawsuits in detail in Chapter 8. There may be instances where the board of directors decides to cause the corporation to bring suit against the director who allegedly breached her fiduciary duties. In such a case, the shareholder will not need to bring the derivative suit.

If the shareholder pleads facts that merely allege the director(s) made a business decision that turned out poorly, the court will apply the business judgment rule and dismiss the lawsuit.

However, if the plaintiff can make out a prima facie case that a director was conflicted in the transaction, the court will not immediately apply the business judgment rule. The shareholder's suit against the conflicted director survives for the moment – at least until the next step in the flowchart. If the shareholder has also named the non-conflicted directors as defendants, the court should dismiss the lawsuit against them (unless the shareholder can show they breached some other fiduciary duty).

2)   If the transaction in question was **approved** (before or after the fact) **by the shareholders** or **directors** (at least two directors) who were **disinterested** (i.e., not conflicted in the transaction), **independent** (i.e., not dominated or controlled by the conflicted directors), after **full disclosure from the conflicted directors** about the transaction (i.e., disclosure of the nature of the conflict and all other material facts about the transaction), the court will defer to the decision of those who approved the transaction, apply the business judgment rule, and dismiss the lawsuit against the conflicted director.

If the transaction was **not approved** by shareholders or directors who were disinterested and independent, after full disclosure from the conflicted directors, the lawsuit survives to the next step in the flowchart.

3)   The conflicted director has one more chance to escape liability. If she can **prove the transaction was fair to the corporation**, despite her conflict, she will not be liable to the corporation or the shareholders for breaching her duty of loyalty. If she cannot prove the transaction was fair to the corporation, she will be liable.

DUTY OF LOYALTY – CONFLICTED TRANSACTION FLOWCHART (ALTERNATE):

1

2

3

Shareholder claim: "bad decision"

Shareholder lawsuit against a director or officer

Shareholder makes a prima facie case the **director/officer was conflicted in the transaction**

The transaction was approved by directors or shareholders who:
(1) were disinterested;
(2) were independent; and
(3) received full disclosure

yes → **3A** Shareholder-plaintiff **proves the transaction was <u>unfair</u>**

no → **3B** Defendant director/officer **proves the transaction was fair**

R. I. P. Beloved Shareholder Lawsuit

Defendant director/officer is liable for monetary damages

no

yes

no

yes

288

DUTY OF LOYALTY – CONFLICTED TRANSACTION FLOWCHART (ALTERNATE) EXPLANATION:

A court might adopt this alternate approach **when a controlling shareholder engages in a conflicted transaction with the corporation** (see 6A-211(c), below). The alternate flow chart for duty of loyalty-self dealing is the same as the regular flowchart for the duty of loyalty-self dealing except with respect to the burden of proving fairness when the transaction has been approved by disinterested shareholders or directors. The explanation below notes where the alternate flowchart differs from the regular flowchart.

1)   Same as regular duty of loyalty-self dealing flowchart.

2)   If the transaction in question was **approved** (before or after the fact) **by the shareholders** or **directors** (at least two directors) who were **disinterested** (i.e., not conflicted in the transaction), **independent** (i.e., not dominated or controlled by the conflicted directors), after **full disclosure from the conflicted directors** (i.e., disclosure of the nature of the conflict and all other material facts about the transaction), the court will *give the plaintiff-shareholder an opportunity to prove that the transaction was unfair to the corporation* (step 3A).

If the transaction was **not approved** by shareholders or directors who were disinterested and independent, after full disclosure from the conflicted directors, the court will give the defendant-director the opportunity to prove the transaction was fair to the corporation (step 3B).

3A)   If the plaintiff-shareholder can prove the transaction was unfair to the corporation, the defendant-director will be liable for breaching her fiduciary duties.

If the plaintiff-shareholder is not able to prove the transaction was unfair to the corporation, the court will dismiss the lawsuit against the conflicted director.

3B)   Same as step 3 in the regular duty of loyalty-self dealing flowchart.

289

6A-203 DUTY OF LOYALTY – TAKING A CORPORATE OPPORTUNITY:

6A-203(a) THE SET-UP:

A director or officer might come across a business opportunity and take it for herself. The issue in these circumstances is whether her fiduciary duties to the corporation prohibited her from taking the opportunity. After all, her fiduciary duties require her to put the corporation's interest before her own interests **with respect to the business of the corporation**.

> ### *Illustration:*
>
> Imagine you are a director of ABC Corp. You drive by an electronics store that is selling a 52 inch HD TV with all the bells and whistles for an incredibly low price. The TV was a floor model, but it is in mint condition. You buy it, take it home, and look forward to watching baseball games in HD.
>
> Should you have allowed the corporation to take the opportunity to buy the TV before you did? Was this transaction somehow related to the business of the corporation?

Director and officer liability to their corporations for taking a business opportunity depends on whether we can fairly characterize the business opportunity as belonging to the corporation.

6A-203(b) THE ANALYSIS:

There are several tests courts use to determine whether a director or officer will be liable for taking a business opportunity, but they generally focus on one or more of the factors we discuss in this subsection. The student of corporate law should approach the corporate opportunity analysis as you would approach the fairness analysis in a conflicted transaction – i.e., **unless there was a valid ratification, the defendant director must prove it was fair for her to take the corporate opportunity**. In corporate opportunity cases, however, fairness depends on the application of the following factors:

> **Line of business** – Was the business within one of the corporation's lines of business? The answer to this question is important, but it might not be dispositive of the matter because corporations do not take or want every business opportunity within their line of business, they might also expand their businesses to take opportunities outside their current lines of business.

Expectancy – A corporation might have an expectancy in an opportunity if, for example, it was pursuing or planning to pursue this opportunity or a similar opportunity. In addition, a court might find that a corporation had an expectancy in an opportunity if the corporation received an offer for the opportunity or an invitation to bid for it.

Individual capacity vs. corporate capacity – It is conceivable that it would be fair for a director or officer to take an opportunity within the corporation's line of business if it came to her personally, and not in connection with her position with the corporation. We might treat officers and directors differently in these situations. Directors and officers often serve different roles in corporations: directors monitor, advise, and ultimately decide, but are often not active in creating business for their corporations. Indeed, the paradigm in U.S. public corporations is part-time boards that meet only several times a year, relying on the executive officers to bring in business and manage it. The directors have jobs, businesses, and professional lives aside from their work for the corporation. In other words, they have personal capacities with respect to business opportunities – maybe even those within the corporation's line of business.

In contrast, executive officers are hired to create and manage the business of the corporation. They are supposed to seek out opportunities for the corporation. In essence, they have no personal capacities with respect to business opportunities – at least with respect to business opportunities within the corporation's line of business or to which it had an expectancy.

Corporate rejection – Has the corporation rejected the opportunity at some point in the past? A corporation's rejection of the opportunity in the past should not absolutely determine that the director or officer could freely take the opportunity. A corporation might change its mind about the opportunity after its rejection, or it might have rejected it as a bargaining strategy.

Corporate incapacity – Did the corporation have the financial wherewithal to take the opportunity? If the corporation did not have the ability to take the opportunity, the defendant directors or officers should not be liable for taking it themselves. However, when considering whether the corporation had the financial ability to take the opportunity, you should remember to look beyond the cash balance in the corporation's bank account. You should also consider whether the corporation could have financed the opportunity by selling assets, taking out loans, issuing debt securities, or selling more stock.

Competing with the corporation – On many occasions, if the director or officer takes the opportunity, she will be directly competing with the corporation. Under the common law rules of agency law, an agent has a duty to refrain from competing with her principal unless the principal gives permission. The same principle applies to the director of a corporation. Unless the corporation gives the director permission, she is under a duty not to compete with the corporation. When a court considers whether it is fair to the corporation to allow the director or officer to take the opportunity, it should consider whether the opportunity will cause the director or officer to be in competition with the corporation.

If the corporation did not expressly allow the director or officer to take the opportunity through a board or shareholder ratification**Error! Bookmark not defined.** process, the defendant director or officer has the burden to show it was fair to the corporation for her to have taken the opportunity.

6A-203(c) RATIFICATION:

Of course, we can imagine that a corporation might allow a director or officer to take a corporate opportunity. The corporation should go through a formal ratification process, just like the ratification process for conflicted transactions. The decision to allow the director or officer to take the opportunity should be made by directors or shareholders who are **independent** and **disinterested**, after **full disclosure** from the director or officer who wants the opportunity.

If there is a valid ratification, the court should apply the business judgment rule to the decision. The defendant director will not be liable to the corporation for taking a corporate opportunity.

6A-203(d) CORPORATE OPPORTUNITY – FLOWCHART:

The following flowchart and its explanation summarize the law of corporate opportunity.

Flowchart and explanation begin on the following pages.

This page is intentionally blank

DUTY OF LOYALTY – CORPORATE OPPORTUNITY FLOWCHART:

1   2   3

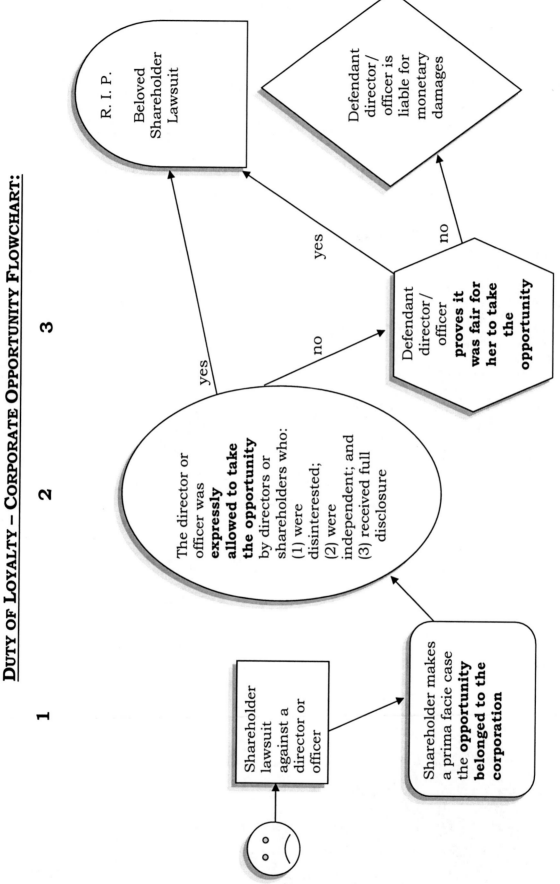

Shareholder lawsuit against a director or officer

Shareholder makes a prima facie case the **opportunity belonged to the corporation**

The director or officer was **expressly allowed to take the opportunity** by directors or shareholders who: (1) were disinterested; (2) were independent; and (3) received full disclosure

yes → R. I. P. Beloved Shareholder Lawsuit

no → Defendant director/officer **proves it was fair for her to take the opportunity**

yes → R. I. P. Beloved Shareholder Lawsuit

no → Defendant director/officer is liable for monetary damages

DUTY OF LOYALTY – CORPORATE OPPORTUNITY FLOWCHART EXPLANATION:

1)   When a shareholder brings a lawsuit against a director for taking a corporate opportunity, the lawsuit is a derivative lawsuit. We will discuss derivative lawsuits in detail in Chapter 8. There may be instances where the board of directors decides to cause the corporation to bring suit against the director who allegedly breached her fiduciary duties. In such a case, the shareholder will not need to bring the derivative suit.

If the plaintiff can make out a prima facie case that a director took a corporate opportunity, the court will not immediately apply the business judgment rule. Her suit against the defendant-director survives for the moment – at least until the next step in the flowchart. If the shareholder has also named the directors who did not participate in taking the opportunity as defendants, the court should dismiss the lawsuit against them (unless the shareholder can show they breached some other fiduciary duty).

2)   If the taking of the opportunity by the defendant-director was **approved** (before or after the fact) **by the shareholders or directors** (at least two directors) who were **disinterested** (i.e., not conflicted in the transaction), **independent** (i.e., not dominated or controlled by the conflicted directors), after **full disclosure from the conflicted directors** (i.e., disclosure of all material facts about the opportunity), the court will defer to the decision of those who approved the transaction, apply the business judgment rule, and dismiss the lawsuit against the defendant director. If the taking of the opportunity was **not approved** by shareholders or directors who were disinterested and independent, after full disclosure from the conflicted directors, the lawsuit survives to the next step in the flowchart.

3)   The defendant director has one more chance to escape liability. If she can **prove it was fair for her to take the opportunity**, she will not be liable to the corporation for breaching her duty of loyalty. Factors:

Expectancy – Did the corporation have an expectancy in the opportunity?
Line of business – Was the opportunity within the corporation's line of business?
Individual capacity vs. corporate capacity – Did the opportunity come to the director or officer personally or in her official corporate capacity? (should we treat executives differently from directors?)
Corporate rejection – Did the corporation reject the opportunity at some point in the past?
Corporate incapacity – Did the corporation have the financial wherewithal to take the opportunity? (remember to ask whether the corporation could have gotten financing in the form of loans or equity investment).
Competition with the corporation - If we allow the director or officer to take the opportunity, would she be competing with the corporation?

6A-204 **DUTY OF CARE:**

6A-204(a) **THE DECISION-MAKING PROCESS:**

A bad decision by the board of directors or the officers, without something more, does not equate to a breach of the duty of care. The duty of care focuses on the decision-making process, not the decision itself. Even if we assume an unhappy shareholder could prove that the board's decision was foolish, excessively risky, not in the best interests of the corporation, not as good as other possible alternatives, or caused great harm to the corporation, she still has not proven a breach of the duty of care. The board will only breach its duty of care if it engages in an **extremely flawed decision-making process**.

When a shareholder sues directors or officers for a breach of the duty of care, she must show that there was more than just a decision that turned out badly for the corporation. She must show the process leading up to the decision was flawed. The court's analysis of whether there was a breach of the duty of care will center on **information and time**:

1) The information the board considered in formulating its decision;
2) How the information was gathered; and
3) The time spent considering and deliberating the information.

You will often come across cases where the plaintiff-shareholder makes a very convincing argument that the board's decision was foolish or far less beneficial to the corporation than a possible alternative. Despite the convincing arguments, the courts apply the business judgment rule and dismiss these cases. For any chance of success, the plaintiff must show the board's process was highly flawed.

Illustration:

Imagine XYZ Corp.'s single line of business is the production of a highly inflammable material. It has one production plant. The board of directors has decided not to renew the fire insurance policy for the plant. Several weeks later, an accidental fire destroys the entire plant.

A shareholder sues the board for breaching its duty of care.

What is your analysis of the shareholder's prospect for success?

> Make sure you **do not fall into the trap** the fact pattern has set for you. The facts are designed to make you think the board made **a bad decision**. The fact that the corporation had one line of business and one production plant means the company had

everything invested in the plant – surely the board should protect the plant by taking out appropriate fire insurance.

The fact that the company produced a highly inflammable product would lead you to think that the board's decision not to take out fire insurance was a poor one.

The fact that a fire destroyed everything gives you a justification for your feelings that the board made a bad decision – after all the decision turned out badly for the corporation.

However, you must keep in mind that directors and officers do not breach their duty of care by making bad decisions.

Once you have avoided falling into the trap, you must now scour the facts to find if there is anything that supports a claim for a breach of the duty of care – keeping in mind that the duty of care **focuses on the process the board used to come to its decision**.

Here, the facts simply state that "the board of directors decided not to renew the fire insurance policy." There are no facts provided with respect to what information the board considered in making its decision, how it gathered that information, and how the board deliberated the issue. The plaintiff-shareholder will need to make a prima facie case that the board breached its duty of care. **The directors do not have the burden to show their decision-making process was not flawed**. If the shareholder cannot plead any facts that show a flawed decision-making process, the court will dismiss her case. These pleading requirements are discussed in greater detail in Chapter 8.[181]

6A-204(b) STANDARD OF LIABILITY:

Of course, stating that the duty of care analysis centers on a flawed decision-making process, not a bad decision, just raises the next question: How flawed must the process be for the directors (of officers) to be liable for breaching the duty of care? Generally the standard is **gross negligence or recklessness**. In other words, a merely careless or negligent decision-making process will not be enough to hold the directors liable for breaching the duty of care. They will only be liable if **their decision-making process was a serious or gross departure** from what a reasonable board would do under the same circumstances.

The RMBCA provides the following **standard of conduct**; which, sounds like a simple negligence standard:

---

[181] See Chapter 8, §8A-103(c).

297

The members of the board of directors or a committee of the board, when becoming informed in connection with their decision-making function . . ., shall discharge their duties with the care that a person in a like position would **reasonably believe appropriate** under similar circumstances.[182]

The RMBCA's standard of liability provision also seems to use language that would hold a director liable for mere negligence:

A director shall not be liable to the corporation or its shareholders . . . unless a party asserting liability in a proceeding establishes that . . . the challenged conduct consisted of or was the result of . . . a decision which the director did not **reasonably believe** to be in the best interests of the corporation, or . . . as to which the director was not informed to an extent the director **reasonably believed** appropriate in the circumstances . . .[183]

This language stands in contrast to the **gross negligence standard of liability the Delaware courts apply**.

Some jurisdictions have adopted a standard of conduct for directors that clearly differs from the express standard of liability. Ohio's General Corporation Law, for example, provides the following **standard of conduct** for directors:

A director shall perform the director's duties . . . in good faith, in a manner the director reasonably believes to be in or not opposed to the best interests of the corporation, and with the **care that an ordinarily prudent person** in a like position would use under similar circumstances.[184]

However, under Ohio law, the **standard of liability** is the following:

A director shall be liable in damages . . . only if it is proved by clear and convincing evidence . . . that a director's action or failure to act involved an act or omission undertaken with deliberate intent to cause injury to the corporation . . . or with **reckless disregard** for the best interests of the corporation.[185]

From these two provisions, we can see that Ohio has different standards for conduct and for liability. The standard of conduct is the use of "care that an ordinarily prudent person in a like position would use." We expect that the

---

[182] RMBCA §8.30(b) (emphasis added).

[183] RMBCA §8.31(a)(2) (emphasis added).

[184] OGCL §1701.59(B) (emphasis added).

[185] OGCL §1701.59(D) (emphasis added).

board's decision-making process will be one that a reasonable board would employ under the same circumstances. However, the standard of liability is not one of negligence (i.e., reasonable care); rather it is "reckless disregard." Under Ohio law, if a board makes a decision based on a negligent process, they have not met the legal standard of conduct – i.e., we are very disappointed in them – but they will not be held liable for any harm they caused to the corporation.

6A-204(c) INFORMATION AND DELIBERATION:

As we discussed earlier, the duty of care analysis centers on the process the board used to make its decision, not the decision itself. In determining whether the board fulfilled its duty of care, the shareholder-plaintiff would need evidence of the information the board reviewed, how it gathered the information, what information it lacked and the reason it lacked the information, and the time and effort the board put into deliberating the information. **The greater the magnitude of the decision, the more is required of the board**. The lawyer advising the board will need to assist the board in gathering information, deliberating the issues, and documenting the decision-making process.

In many cases, especially in public corporations, the members of the board are not full-time employees of the corporation, nor are they experts in every aspect or detail of the company's business. When they are called on to make a decision on a particular matter, they lack information and must rely on the information provided by the employees and outside experts. Normally, state **corporate law statutes protect directors who rely on representations, reports, or other information supplied by outside experts or the company's management**, even when the information provided is flawed or incorrect. However, the directors will not be justified in relying on information provided to them by experts and management when they should have known the information was incomplete or flawed. In other words, the directors have a **duty to ask questions** when the information they receive should raise doubts about its completeness, veracity, accuracy, etc.

Here are two famous examples:

> *Smith v. Van Gorkom*[186] is probably the most famous duty of care case in U.S. corporate law. In this case, the board of directors of Trans Union was deliberating a merger between Trans Union and another company. The shareholders of Trans Union would receive $55 per share in the merger. The court eventually found that the Trans Union board had breached its duty of care by approving the merger after a grossly negligent decision-making process. Specifically, the board had no basis for determining that $55 per share was a fair price.

---

[186] 488 A.2d 858 (Del. Sup. Ct. 1985)

In its defense, the board said that the Trans Union CEO and management team had designed the merger and presented it to the board with the $55 per share price. The board argued it was justified in relying on the management's "report." In response, the Delaware Supreme Court stated:

> [The CEO's] oral presentation of his understanding of the terms of the proposed Merger Agreement, which he had not seen, and [the CFO's] brief oral statement of his preliminary study regarding the feasibility of a leveraged buy-out of Trans Union do not qualify as §141(e)[187] "reports" for these reasons: The former lacked substance because [the CEO] was basically uninformed as to the essential provisions of the very document about which he was talking. [The CFO's] statement was irrelevant to the issues before the Board since it did not purport to be a valuation study. At a minimum for a report to enjoy the status conferred by §141(e), it must be pertinent to the subject matter upon which a board is called to act, and otherwise be entitled to good faith, not blind reliance. Considering all of the surrounding circumstances – hastily calling the meeting without prior notice of its subject matter, the proposed sale of the Company without any prior consideration of the issue or necessity therefor, the urgent time constraints imposed by [the other party to the transaction], and the total absence of any documentation whatsoever – the **directors were duty bound to make reasonable inquiry** of [the CEO] and [the CFO], and if they had done so, the inadequacy of that upon which they now claim to have relied would have been apparent.

In this passage, the court was saying that the information provided to the board merely stated a price, and did not state a method for determining the price or provide any support for why the price was fair. In other words, it was not a report about the fairness of the $55 price, and the directors could not rely on the report to justify its failure to determine the price was fair to the shareholders. In addition, the circumstances of the transaction put the directors on notice that they should make further inquiry about the information the officers were providing.

In *Hanson Trust PLC v. ML SCM Acquisition, Inc.*,[188] the board of directors was careful enough to get a fairness opinion from an investment bank.[189] However,

---

[187] Editor's note: DGCL §141(e) provides, in relevant part: "A member of the board . . . shall . . . be protected in relying in good faith upon . . . information, opinions, reports or statements . . . by any of the officers or employee . . . or by any other such person as to matters the member reasonably believes are within such person's professional or expert competence . . . ."

[188] 781 F.2d 264 (N.Y. 1986).

[189] A fairness opinion is an opinion by an investment bank that the shareholders or the corporation will receive fair consideration in a transaction, usually a merger of some kind.

the court held that the board was not justified in relying on the fairness opinion because it was conclusory and did not provide a basis for its opinion or supporting documentation.

6A-204(d) EXCULPATION CLAUSES AND THE DUTY OF CARE:

As a reminder, we discussed in the introduction that most jurisdictions allow a corporation to amend its articles of incorporation to include a clause exculpating directors (but not officers) for certain breaches of their fiduciary duties. In practice the clauses often look like this:

> Limitation of Directors' Liability: The liability of the directors of this corporation for monetary damages shall be eliminated to the fullest extent permissible under applicable law.

In the section on duty of loyalty claims, we discussed that the **exculpation clause cannot apply to breaches of the duty of loyalty**.[190] That is to say, if a director engages in self-dealing, takes a corporate opportunity, or otherwise breaches her duty of loyalty, the exculpation clause will not protect her from liability. Instead, she will have to show valid ratification or prove the fairness of the transaction.

Duty of care claims are another matter. The law was specifically designed to allow corporations to adopt exculpation clauses that protect directors for breaches of their duty of care. **The directors of a corporation with an exculpation clause in its articles will not be liable to the shareholders or the corporation for breaches of their duty of care**. The board is effectively immune from any duty of care claims, even if its decision-making process was reckless.

Because of the exculpation clause, shareholders who sue directors for some perceived harm to the corporation will attempt to characterize their claims as breaches of the duty of loyalty or the duty of good faith. Indeed, there is a blurred line between a reckless decision-making process, which is a breach of the duty of care, and a conscious disregard of a duty to act, which is a breach of good faith.[191]

---

[190] See §6A-202(j), above.

[191] For a discussion of the duty of good faith, see §6A-206, below.

6A-204(e) FAIRNESS:

When a corporation does not have an exculpation clause in its articles, its directors can still **escape liability for breaches of their duty of care by proving the transaction was fair** to the corporation.[192] The process is analogous to fairness review in duty of loyalty claims, where a director argues she should not be liable to the corporation because the transaction was fair to the corporation, even though she was conflicted.[193] In the duty of care context, the directors will argue that despite their generally poor efforts, they somehow achieved a fair result for the corporation and its shareholders.

6A-204(f) RATIFICATION:

In our discussion of self-dealing and corporate opportunity transactions that implicated the duty of loyalty, we said that ratification of the transaction would protect the conflicted director from liability, provided independent and disinterested directors or shareholders voted to approve the transaction after full disclosure from the conflicted director.[194] In the duty of care context, there is some legal support that the shareholders can ratify the board's duty of care breach. In *Smith v. Van Gorkom*,[195] the court seems to indicate that the directors would have been protected from the duty of care claim had the shareholder vote been informed.

One should approach the possibility a court would validate shareholder ratification of a transactions where the directors breached their duty of care with some skepticism. It is one thing to allow shareholder ratification in duty of loyalty cases. In those situations, the directors are saying to the shareholders:

> "Please approve this transaction. We think it is good for the corporation, but we cannot make the decision ourselves because we are conflicted."

There seems to be a significant difference in the ratification of a duty of care breach, where the directors are saying to the shareholders:

> "Please approve this transaction. We have not really done our homework on this transaction, so we will leave it up to you."

The law requires the shareholders ratification of a transaction to be informed. In duty of loyalty claims, the conflicted directors are required to disclose the nature of their conflict. By analogy, in duty of care cases, the directors would,

---

[192] See *Cede & Co. v. Technicolor, Inc.*, 634 A.2d 345, 361 (Del. 1993)

[193] See §6A-202(e), above.

[194] See §6A-202(d), above.

[195] 488 A.2d 858 (Del. Sup. Ct. 1985)

be required to disclose the nature of their recklessness. It seems implausible that a board would consider making such a disclosure, even if it was able to recognize and it had been reckless.

6A-204(g) JUSTIFICATION FOR PROTECTING DIRECTORS AND OFFICERS FOR BREACHES OF THE DUTY OF CARE:

As you have most likely discerned, the law on the duty of care is very protective of directors and officers. What justifies such protection of corporate directors and officers?

Courts will not hold directors liable for their decisions that turn out poorly for the corporation. Business decisions necessarily involve risk. The greater the risk, the greater the potential return. A failed project, a bad investment, or any decision that results in the corporation losing money does not mean the decision was a bad decision. Consider the following hypothetical fact pattern:

> The board of directors of XYZ Corp. has the opportunity to make an investment of $10,000,000. The CFO and outside consultants have determined that there is a 20% chance that the company will lose its entire $10,000,000, but there is an 80% chance the company will make $30,000,000 (i.e., return of its principal $10 million, plus another $20 million).

Clearly the investment opportunity is a good one. Indeed, it is a fantastic opportunity (at least I attempted to make it a fantastic opportunity). Remember, however, there is a real prospect that the company will lose everything. If the board decides to make the investment and the project eventually fails, has the board made a bad decision? No. The decision to invest was sound. *Ex post* (i.e., in hindsight) it looks like a bad decision, because its failure is certain. *Ex ante* (i.e., at the time the decision was made) it was a very good decision. One of the reasons the law does not hold directors and officers liable for decisions that turn out poorly is that such decisions are not necessarily bad decisions *ex ante*.

Assuming you are willing to concede that we should not hold directors liable for decisions that turn out poorly *ex post*, you might argue that we should hold them liable for decision that were poor decisions *ex ante*. There are two reasons for not taking such an approach:

> The first reason is that our examination of whether the board's decision was a poor one will be colored by the fact we know the decision turned out poorly. Judges might tend to determine that a decision was poor *ex ante* simply because the result was bad *ex post*.

> The second reason we do not examine whether the decision was bad *ex ante* is that judges are not business experts. This argument is often

303

phrased in terms of "administrative competence." The board of directors and the officers are in a much better position to evaluate whether the course of action will be best for the company on an *ex ante* basis than the court.

Of course, you might further argue that even though judges are not business experts, they are not experts in any situation where they are asked to determine whether a person acted negligently. For example, judges are not medical experts, but they routinely evaluate medical decisions made by physicians. The attorneys for each side can call experts to help the judge (or the jury- whichever is acting as the fact finder) to evaluate whether the physician's conduct was reasonable. We could do the same for business decisions, but would it provide an overall benefit to society?

There are costs to our current approach of refusing to evaluate the quality of business decisions. The corporation and the shareholders will bear the costs of the board's bad decisions. However, there are also benefits to our current approach. Society does not bear the cost of long and numerous trials, where courts try to determine whether the board could have made a better business decision. In addition, society does not bear the costs of incorrect decisions by the courts. It does bear the costs of incorrect decisions by corporate directors and officers, but we believe that they have a comparative advantage in making those decisions. In other words, we think that the directors and executive officers of corporations would make fewer bad decisions than the courts.

Of course, if courts do not police the bad decisions of directors, one might argue that directors have less incentive to make good decisions. In response to that argument, we might question whether the threat of legal sanction is necessary to incentivize directors and officers to make good decisions. Indeed, there are strong arguments that directors and officers already have sufficient incentives to make good business decisions:

> Directors and officers are often shareholders in their corporations, so they will benefit from good business decisions and suffer from poor business decisions. In closely-held corporations, this will almost always be the case. In public corporations, directors and officers are often provided with stock or stock options as part of their compensation. An economist or corporate law scholar would say that stock ownership of directors and officers helps **align their incentives** with the shareholders of the corporation.

> Directors and officers in large, public corporations are also subject to a market for reputation. Directors often sit on the boards of several public companies. Executive officers are often directors of other public corporations. Directors and officers need to position themselves for other opportunities. Involvement in a bad business decision or a poorly-

managed company would harm their reputations and impede their future opportunities.

Finally, social and moral pressures encourage directors and officers to make good decisions. You make good decisions when you are given responsibility because: (1) if you do not, others would not respect you; and (2) something inside of you tells you that you are not a good person if you do not.

On top of this all is the fact the shareholders in public corporations can protect themselves against risks of poor management in any one company with a diversified portfolio. In the end, we believe that shareholders, *ex ante,* would prefer a high level of protection for directors and officers for their decisions. The benefits of protecting the directors outweigh the costs, resulting in an increase of shareholder wealth on an *ex ante* basis.

6A-204(h) **DUTY OF CARE – FLOWCHART:**

The following flowchart and its explanation summarize the law of the duty of care.

Flowchart and explanation begin on the next page.

DUTY OF CARE FLOWCHART:

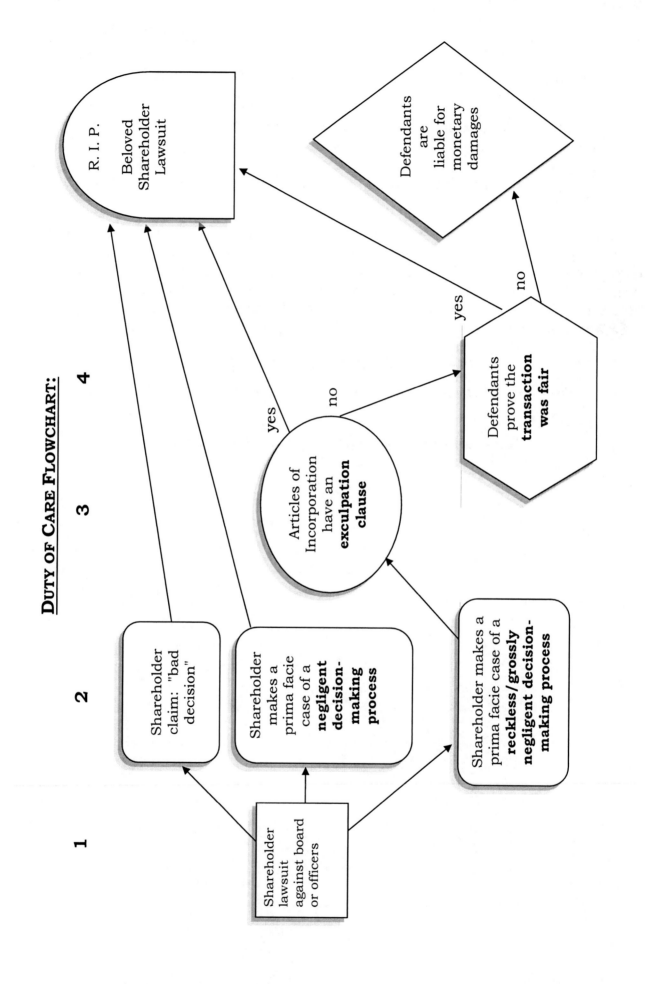

DUTY OF CARE FLOWCHART EXPLANATION:

1) When a shareholder brings a lawsuit against a director for a breach of her fiduciary duties, the lawsuit is quite often a derivative lawsuit. We will discuss derivative lawsuits in detail in Chapter 8. There may be instances where the board of directors decides to cause the corporation to bring suit against the director who allegedly breached her fiduciary duties. In such a case, the shareholder will not need to bring the derivative suit.

2) If the shareholder pleads facts that merely allege the directors made a business decision that turned out poorly, the court will apply the business judgment rule and dismiss the lawsuit.

If the shareholder pleads facts that the directors engaged in a negligent decision-making process, the court will apply the business judgment rule and dismiss the lawsuit.

However, if the shareholder pleads facts that the directors engaged in a **grossly-negligent (reckless) decision-making process,** the court will not immediately apply the business judgment rule. Her suit against the defendant-director survives for the moment – at least until the next step in the flowchart.

3) If the corporation's articles of incorporation have an **exculpation clause,** the court will dismiss the lawsuit.

If the corporation's articles of incorporation do not have an exculpation clause, the lawsuit survives to the next step in the flowchart.

4) The directors have one more chance to escape liability. If they can **prove the transaction was fair to the corporation,** despite their grossly-negligent decision-making process, they will not be liable to corporation or the shareholders for breaching their duty of care.

If they cannot prove the transaction was fair to the corporation, they will be liable.

6A-205 **Duty to monitor:**

6A-205(a) The set-up:

The duty of care and the business judgment rule apply in circumstances where the directors or executive officers actually make decisions. However, we know from our discussions in Chapter 5 that the board of directors in most corporations will not meet to review and decide on every corporate matter. Much is left to the discretion of the executive officers. Indeed, in larger corporations, even the executive officers are not involved in all day-to-day business decisions. Much of corporate decision-making is delegated to mid-level management and lower-level corporate employees.

The employees cause harm to the corporation by making poor decisions, shirking their duties, violating the law, engaging in self-dealing, or taking corporate opportunities. Shareholders will often sue the board for failing to engage in proper oversight of the employees and the corporation's business, claiming the board should be liable for failing to discover and prevent the employees' acts of misfeasance and malfeasance. This type of cause of action does not fit squarely into the common duty of care claim, where the directors will be liable for reckless or grossly negligent decision-making processes. The issue is monitoring, not decision-making. However, if the board actually made a decision not to monitor, a court might indeed review that under the auspices of the duty of care and the business judgment rule.

Another fact pattern that implicates the duty to monitor (or "duty of oversight") involves some important matter that the board never considers or that falls through the cracks. For example, the board might forget to renew an important lease or fail to consider a good business opportunity. Once again, we cannot base director liability on a reckless decision-making process because the board did not decide to refuse to renew the lease or reject the business opportunity – they simply did not consider these matters.[196]

6A-205(b) Information and reporting systems:

In order to allow directors to effectively monitor the business and activities of the entire organization, large corporations set up **information and reporting systems**. As the name indicates, these systems are designed to gather information and to report it to those people who are responsible for monitoring and decision-making. Information and reporting systems cover areas such as

---

[196] Conceptually, this situation may implicate the duty to monitor. The board relies on the officers and employees to bring such matters to the board's attention.

accounting, human resources, manufacturing, distribution, customer relations, legal compliance etc.

Businesses will have specific compliance systems for laws that apply to their particular business needs. For example, if your corporation is a financial institution subject to the Bank Secrecy Act, it would behoove you to set up some sort of Bank Secrecy Act compliance system. Similarly, if your corporation regularly engages in international transactions that require the approval of foreign regulators, you should seriously consider setting up a Foreign Corrupt Practices Act compliance system.

6A-205(c) DUTY TO MONITOR – STANDARD OF LIABILITY:

Courts have generally held that a board of directors will not be liable for breaching its duty to monitor unless it **failed to act in good faith**. This standard is more difficult for a plaintiff to prove than duty of care's recklessness standard.

6A-205(d) ABSENT OR UNQUALIFIED DIRECTORS:

There are times where directors do not sufficiently understand the corporation's business or do not attend board meetings. When corporate officers make poor decisions or steal from the corporation, shareholders often try to hold these absent or unqualified directors liable. The shareholder's claim in these cases is that the defendant director could have prevented the harm if she had attended meetings, paid attention to the business, and understood the business.

Courts have generally held that **directors have a duty to attend board meetings, to keep apprised of the corporation's business and affairs, and to understand at least the basics of the corporation's business**. However, absent or unqualified directors are rarely found liable for any harm the corporation suffered under their less than stellar leadership because of the issue of causation. It is difficult for the plaintiff-shareholder to show that the defendant director would have been able to detect the problem or prevent the harm if she had been the informed, attentive director that we expect.

6A-205(e) WARNING SIGNS OR "RED FLAGS":

Sometimes, information will be available to the board that raises the potential likelihood that there is some problem with the corporation's business that requires attention. To show that the board breached its oversight responsibilities when there are warning signs or red flags about potential problems, the plaintiff must make a prima facie case that **the board consciously disregarded a duty to act**. In other words, the plaintiff must show that the board knew it had a fiduciary duty to act and consciously ignored that duty. This standard is very protective of directors and places a **heavy burden on the plaintiff-shareholder to make a prima facie case**.

What constitutes a conscious disregard of the board's duty to act? It might be easier to conceptualize using hypothetical fact patterns.

> The board of directors becomes aware that certain executive officers are engaged in an ongoing scheme to embezzle from the company. The board does nothing. It does not even discuss the matter.

Under these circumstances, we would expect the board to act in response to the information, but it did nothing at all. It did not even meet to discuss the matter. We might not be surprised if a court found the directors liable under those circumstances. However, if we change the facts somewhat, board liability becomes doubtful.

> The board of directors becomes aware that certain executive officers embezzled money from the company last year. The board meets to discuss whether they should contact the attorney general to bring a criminal complaint against the offenders. In the end, the board decides not to pursue a criminal complaint.

The board's decision against pursuing a criminal complaint does not indicate a conscious disregard of a duty to act. They acted by deciding to do nothing. Deciding not to act is a valid business decision that deserves the protection of the business judgment rule. The situation is analogous to a board decision to forgo a business opportunity. Once the board decides on a matter, they will be protected by the business judgment rule unless they were conflicted, dominated, engaged in a reckless decision-making process, committed waste, or acted in bad faith. Take a step back and think of possible business reasons for the board's decision to not make a criminal complaint:

> The amount of the embezzlement was not significant.

> The bad publicity would hurt the company's reputation.

> The embezzlers have already resigned and returned the money.

It will be very difficult for a plaintiff to show that a director breached its duty to monitor the business in conscious disregard of a duty to act, even when there are warning signs or red flags. The case of *In re Citigroup*,[197] demonstrates the difficulty of showing the directors breached their duty to monitor in the face of certain clear business risks.

In *In re Citigroup*, the shareholders of Citigroup brought suit against the board for failing to monitor the corporation's investments in mortgage backed securities and collateralized debt obligations. The value of mortgage backed securities ("MBS") and collateralized debt obligations ("CDO") are based on residential real estate mortgages. The plaintiff alleged that the board ignored

---

[197] *In re Citigroup Inc. Shareholder Derivative Litigation*, 964 A.2d 106 (Del. Ch. Ct. 2009).

clear signs that the residential real estate mortgage market was unstable and increasingly risky. The failure of the board to decrease Citigroup's exposure from MBS and CDO investments was a conscious disregard of a duty to act that caused Citigroup to suffer great losses when the residential real estate market collapsed.

The Delaware chancery court dismissed the plaintiff's claim for failure to allege facts that the board acted in bad faith. The plaintiff merely alleged that the directors were aware of the risks, and that the investments ultimately failed, causing great harm to the corporation. The court held that because all business decisions involved risk, alleging that the board knew of the risk, simply stated a truism of business. Alleging the investment failed and caused harm to the corporation simply pointed out the potential unfortunate consequences of any business decision, even very good decisions.

6A-205(f) No warning signs or "red flags":

Delaware courts have held that even when there are no warning signs of potential issues that require board attention, the board nevertheless has a duty to monitor, and may be liable to the corporation for failing to discover or prevent some injury to the corporation. Specifically, the board is under a duty to establish some sort of information and reporting system, designed to detect the misfeasance and malfeasance of corporate officers and employees and to keep the directors informed about of the corporation's business.

Delaware courts have stated a board is under a duty to set up adequate information and reporting systems that the board deems reasonable. However, a board will only be liable when there has been a "sustained or systematic failure of the board to exercise oversight – such as an utter failure to attempt to assure a reasonable information and reporting system exists."[198]

You may be wondering what kind of action or inaction qualifies as a "sustained or systematic" failure to implement information and reporting systems. Because the alliteration is attractive, "sustained or systematic failure" is oft quoted, but it really provides little practical guidance. A simple failure by the board to establish an information and reporting system is not enough to hold the board liable.

The Delaware Supreme Court has made it clear that only the most egregious action or inaction by the board could ever result in any potential liability for the board. In *Stone v. Ritter*, the Delaware Supreme Court stated:

> We hold that *Caremark* articulates the necessary conditions
> predicate for director oversight liability: (a) the directors utterly
> failed to implement any reporting or information system or controls;

---

[198] *In re Caremark International Inc. Derivative Litigation*, 698 A.2d 959 (Del. Ch. 1996).

or (b) having implemented such a system or controls, consciously failed to monitor or oversee its operations, thus, disabling themselves from being informed of risks or problems requiring their attention. In either case, **imposition of liability requires a showing that the directors knew that they were not discharging their fiduciary obligations**. Where directors fail to act in the face of a known duty to act, thereby demonstrating a conscious disregard for their responsibilities, they breach their duty of loyalty by failing to discharge that fiduciary obligation in good faith.[199]

6A-205(g) <u>DUTY TO MONITOR – PLAINTIFF'S PROSPECTS OF SUCCESS:</u>

It is clearly difficult for a plaintiff-shareholder to be successful in a failure to monitor case against the board of directors, mainly because it is difficult to show that the board acted in bad faith. It may be easy to show that the board acted carelessly, negligently, or even recklessly in failing to monitor the business of the corporation, but it is difficult to show that the board acted in bad faith. Generally, bad faith requires a showing that the defendant director or officer acted (1) with the intent to harm the corporation, (2) knowingly illegally, or (3) in conscious disregard to a duty to act. In *In re Citigroup*, the court discussed plaintiff's burden in these cases:

> [T]he burden required for a plaintiff . . . to show bad faith is even higher [than the burden to show gross negligence in a duty of care case]. Additionally, as former-Chancellor Allen noted in *Caremark*, director liability based on the duty of oversight 'is **possibly the most difficult theory in corporation law upon which a plaintiff might hope to win a judgment**.' [200]

6A-205(h) <u>EXCULPATION CLAUSES AND THE DUTY TO MONITOR:</u>

In most jurisdictions, a corporation may amend its articles of incorporation to include a clause that exculpates directors (not officers) for breaches of their fiduciary duties.[201] However, the exculpation clause may not indemnify a director for any conduct that was not in good faith.

In the unlikely event that a director is held liable for breaching her duty to monitor, she will not be able to rely on the exculpation clause. Liability for the duty to monitor requires a showing that the directors failed to act in good faith. Because her conduct was not in good faith, the law will not allow an exculpation clause in the corporation's articles to provide any protection for the

---

[199] *Stone v. Ritter*, 911 A.2d 362 (Del. 2006).

[200] *In re Citigroup Inc. Shareholder Derivative Litigation*, 964 A.2d 106 (Del. Ch. Ct. 2009).

[201] See §6A-209 et seq., below.

director, even if the language of the clause is drafted broadly enough to include breaches of good faith.

The relevant provision of the Delaware General Corporation Law specifically prohibits exculpation for acts or omissions not in good faith:

> [T]he certificate of incorporation may also contain . . . [a] provision eliminating of limiting the personal liability of a director to the corporation or the stockholders for money damages for breach of fiduciary duty as a director, provided that such provision shall not eliminate or limit the liability of a director: . . . (ii) for any acts or omissions **not in good faith** or which involve intentional misconduct or knowing violation of the law . . . .[202]

In contrast, the relevant provision of the RMBCA, does not specifically mention the good faith. Indeed, under the RMBCA there may be room to argue that directors are entitled to exculpation if they have breached their duty to monitor, even though they acted in conscious disregard of a duty to act. The relevant RMBCA provision reads as follows:

> The articles of incorporation may set forth . . . a provision eliminating of limiting the personal liability of a director to the corporation or the stockholders for money damages for any action taken, or any failure to take action, as a director, except for liability for . . . an **intentional infliction of harm** on the corporation or the shareholders . . .[or] an **intentional violation of a criminal law**.[203]

Under the RMBCA provision, an exculpation clause in a corporation's articles would not exculpate a director for liability in connection with her failure to monitor unless her failure was because of her intent to cause harm to the corporation or her intent to violate a criminal law.

6A-206 DUTY OF GOOD FAITH:

6A-206(a) WHAT CONSTITUTES BAD FAITH?

Generally, to show a director or officer acted in bad faith, the plaintiff must make out a prima facie case that the director or officer:

(1) Acted in knowing violation of the law;
(2) Acted with the intent to harm the corporation; or

---

[202] DGCL §102(b)(7) (emphasis added).

[203] RMBCA §2.02(b)(4).

(3) Acted in conscious disregard of a duty to act.

Of three categories of bad faith listed above, it may be easiest to prove the directors knowingly violated a law, if the facts permit. However, it seems that even a knowing violation of the law may sometimes not constitute a breach of the duty of good faith. Companies like UPS and FedEx probably view parking tickets as simply a cost of doing business. Would the board be acting in bad faith if they allowed the executive officers to create a policy that encourages drivers to double-park when necessary in order to make a delivery?

As for the other two categories of bad faith, the prospects of success for plaintiff are quite remote. It is probably extremely rare that a director or officer would act with the intent to harm the corporation. Even in those rare situations, it might be difficult to prove the director had the requisite intent. Finally, as we have discussed above with respect to the duty to monitor, a conscious disregard to act in the face of a duty to act is difficult for plaintiff to prove.[204]

6A-206(b) IS "GOOD FAITH" AN INDEPENDENT DUTY?

There has been some debate among academics with regards to whether the duty of good faith is a distinct fiduciary duty, independent of the duty of care and duty of loyalty. In dicta, the Supreme Court of Delaware has apparently decided that the duty of good faith is a subset of the duty of loyalty.[205] The court's reason was that you could not be "loyal" to the corporation if you failed to act in good faith.[206] This reasoning, however, is somewhat suspect. The same reasoning would make the duty of care a subset of the duty of loyalty. After all, you could not be "loyal" to the corporation if you engaged in a reckless decision-making process.

In the end, it really does not matter much whether good faith is a subset of the duty of loyalty. There are fact patterns that involve directors and officers benefiting themselves at the expense of the corporation and its shareholders. self-dealing, corporate opportunity, kickbacks, and embezzlement implicate the duty of loyalty because the fiduciary receives some sort of benefit at the expense of the corporation. We normally characterize these cases as **breaches of the duty of loyalty**.

---

[204] See §6A-205 et seq. above.

[205] *Stone v. Ritter*, 911 A.2d 362 (Del. 2006) ("It follows that because a showing of bad faith conduct, in the sense described in *Disney* and *Caremark*, is essential to establish director oversight liability, the fiduciary duty violated by that conduct is the duty of loyalty."). "

[206] "As the Court of Chancery aptly stated in *Guttman*, '[a] director cannot act loyally towards the corporation unless she acts in the good faith belief that her actions are in the corporation's best interest.' " *Stone v. Ritter*, 911 A.2d 362 (Del. 2006).

There are other fact patterns that where directors and officers engage in conduct that we consider egregious, although the director of officer does not receive any benefit. We have generally characterized these cases as **breaches of good faith**, and it is likely that everyone will continue to think of them in that way even if the Delaware judiciary considers them to be a subset of the duty of loyalty.

6A-207 **WASTE:**

As we stated in the introduction, directors have an obligation not to waste corporate assets. We introduced the standard for determining whether the board committed waste as: **no rational business person under the same circumstances would have made the same decision**.

It is important for you to remember that the standard to determine director liability for waste does not ask whether the directors made an unreasonable decision. The standard does not consider what a reasonable board would have done. If we used those standards, we would simply be second guessing business decisions by the board of directors, which would eviscerate the business judgment rule.

The waste standard only applied in very limited circumstances, such as when the corporation receives no real consideration or benefit in a transaction. You can think of waste as a very narrow exception to the business judgment rule's overarching principle that we will not second guess the board's business decisions. The waste standard second guesses a bad decision by the board, but only when that decision is tantamount to giving money away[207] or burning it. Waste claims are rarely successful, but in Delaware, the court might look at executive compensation more closely under the waste standard.[208]

6A-208 **"DUTY" TO DISCLOSE:**

There is no separate duty on the part of the board to make disclosures to shareholders. As we saw in Chapter 5, shareholders have access to certain financial information and other books and records upon demand.[209] Otherwise, the board is under no duty to make periodic disclosures to the shareholders. In a public company, however, the corporation is required to make periodic

---

[207] Remember, however, the board is allowed to make donations to legitimate charities.

[208] See *In re Citigroup Inc. Shareholder Derivative Litigation*, 964 A.2d 106 (Del. Ch. Ct. 2009), where the court decided not to dismiss a waste claim against an executive's compensation where it might have been "disproportionately large."

[209] See Chapter 5, §5A-211 for a discussion of shareholder information rights.

disclosures to the market pursuant to federal securities laws. Generally, the board or any one of the directors only has a "duty" to disclose information in connection with some vote by the directors or shareholders.

6A-209 EXCULPATION CLAUSE:

6A-209(a) SCOPE OF EXCULPATION CLAUSES:

By now, you should be aware that the corporate law of most states allows a corporation's articles of incorporation to limit a director's liability for breach of her fiduciary duties. Generally, the law does not allow the articles to limit the liability of officers or controlling shareholders for breach of their fiduciary duties.

Most corporate law statutes prohibit exculpation for waste, breaches of the duty of loyalty, or any conduct by the director that was not in good faith. As a practical matter, the exculpation clause can only exculpate directors for breaches of their fiduciary duty of care. Thus, in duty of care cases, where the defendant directors are protected by an exculpation clause in the corporation's articles, plaintiff's lawyers might attempt to portray a breach of the duty of care as a breach of good faith.

In the famous case of *In re Walt Disney Co. Derivative Litigation*,[210] Disney shareholders sued their directors for approving a compensation package for a Disney executive. When Disney fired the executive without cause after only fourteen months, the executive was entitled to approximately $130 million under the contract.

The evidence showed that the directors might have been a bit sloppy in the approval of the compensation package and in making the decision to dismiss him without cause. The shareholder-plaintiffs argued that the directors did not act in good faith. The definition of good faith that they advocated for was:

> 'directors violate their duty of good faith if they are making material decisions without adequate information and without adequate deliberation'

The court rejected this definition of good faith, spotting it as an attempt to frame facts implicating a possible breach of the duty of care as a breach of good faith. The court stated:

> [The plaintiff's] verbal effort to collapse the duty to act in good faith into the duty to act with due care, is not unlike putting a rabbit into the proverbial hat and then blaming the trial judge for making the insertion.

---

[210] 906 A.2d 27, (Del. Sup. Ct. 2006).

6A-209(b) HISTORY OF THE EXCULPATION CLAUSE:

In 1985, in the case of *Smith v. Van Gorkom*,[211] the Delaware Supreme Court found that the directors of Trans Union were liable to the company's shareholders for breaching their duty of care. The board of directors approved a merger of Trans Union after a careless process. The court found that the directors engaged in decision-making process that was grossly negligent, breaching their duty of care.

The decision of the Delaware Supreme Court in *Smith v. Van Gorkom* case sent shock waves throughout the corporate world. Many never expected that Delaware courts would ever find a board of directors liable for breaching its duty of care. Others were surprised that the court found the careless process of the Trans Union board in making its decision to be gross negligence or recklessness, rather than mere negligence. In short, directors of public companies were concerned that they too might one day be held liable for breaching the duty of care.

In response the Delaware legislature amended the Delaware General Corporation Law to allow corporations to adopt exculpation clauses in their certificates of incorporation (the Delaware equivalent of the articles of incorporation). Many other states followed Delaware's lead, as did the drafters of the MBCA.

6A-209(c) TOO MUCH PROTECTION FOR DIRECTORS?

Does the exculpation clause provide too much protection for directors? One might argue that an exculpation clause provides incentive for directors to engage in very poor decision-making processes, causing harm to the corporation and reducing shareholder wealth. However, the law is designed to give shareholders the power to decide whether to adopt an exculpation clause. The law requires the exculpation clause to be in the articles of incorporation. Amendment of the articles of incorporation requires approval of the shareholders. The fact that most public corporations have exculpation clauses in their articles of incorporation demonstrates that the shareholders believe the clause is in their best interests.

Why would the shareholders believe eliminating any potential director liability for breaches of the duty of care is in the best interests of the shareholders? The rationale underlying the business judgment rule is the same rationale that justifies a shareholder belief that an exculpation clause would be in the best interests of shareholders. Greater protection for directors allows them to perform their jobs better, creating greater wealth for the shareholders. With an exculpation clause, the corporation is in a better position to attract good

---

[211] 488 A.2d 858 (Del. Sup. Ct. 1985).

317

candidates to the board. In addition, the exculpation clause allows to the board to take business risks without the fear of being held liable.

One might argue that there is no good reason for exculpating directors for their recklessness. This argument somewhat misses the point of the exculpation clause. By approving an exculpation clause, the shareholders believe that there is very little risk that the directors will engage in a reckless decision-making process. Market forces, social forces, and moral forces give the directors sufficient incentives to make careful decisions. When they make a decision that turns out poorly, the business judgment rule protects them. When they make a decision that turns out poorly and there are facts that indicate their process was careless, the business judgment rule might eventually protect them, but only after a costly court process to determine whether their process was reckless or merely negligent. Because it is unlikely that that the board engaged in a reckless decision-making process, it would be better to have these cases dismissed before the costly fact-finding stage of a lawsuit. The exculpation clause serves that purpose.

Shareholder approval of exculpation clauses in articles of incorporation creates a very strong presumption that they serve shareholder interests. Of course, this assumes that shareholder voting in public corporations is active and informed. The nature of shareholding in public corporations raises some doubt that a shareholder's voting is informed. Individual shareholders, like you and me, do not have enough invested in any one company to actually research and make an informed decision on any issue that may come up for a shareholder vote. We tend not to vote our shares at all, or simply vote in favor of management's recommendations.

However, there are fewer and fewer individual shareholders in public companies.[212] Institutional investors make up the majority of shareholders in U.S. public companies. These institutional investors include insurance companies, securities dealer, investment banks, public and private retirement systems, mutual funds, hedge funds, and private equity funds. Arguably, institutional investors have the resources and incentives to make informed voting decisions. Thus, shareholder voting in public corporations may be informed.

There is one situation where the shareholders of a public company will not get to vote on whether an exculpation clause will be adopted into the articles of incorporation. Before a private company makes its initial public offering and do the other things necessary to be a public company, it will normally amend

---

[212] Individual investors are still investing in public companies, but they do so indirectly through mutual funds, hedge funds, and public and private retirement system. For example, my university and I each contribute a certain percentage of my salary to a professionally managed retirement fund each month. I have elected to have the fund manager invest a certain percentage of my total funds in public companies in the U.S. and overseas.

its articles to include an exculpation clause. The shareholders voting on this amendment are the founders of the business and venture capitalists who provided it with the capital it needed to grow to the stage where it could consider making an IPO, not the public shareholders who will invest during the IPO. However, even though the public shareholders never voted directly on the exculpation clause, they did get to vote indirectly. If they felt the exculpation clause was unduly protective of directors, they would not purchase the corporation's shares in the IPO, or they would pay less for the shares because of the risk the exculpation clause creates. Because the corporation is trying to raise as much capital as possible, it will be sensitive to the demands of the investors. If the investors are strongly opposed to exculpation clauses, we would expect that companies making initial public offerings would not have exculpation clauses in their articles. If the investors generally favor exculpation clauses because they serve the best interests of the shareholders, we would expect them to be commonplace in new IPOs.

6A-210 FIDUCIARY DUTIES AND OTHER CONSTITUENCIES:

6A-210(a) GENERAL CONCEPT:

The fiduciary duties of officers and directors run to the corporation itself. However, saying that the directors and officers owe a fiduciary duty to the corporation does not help very much in defining the exact scope of the fiduciary duties. Naturally, the directors and officers have a duty to serve the interests of the corporation, but a corporation is a fictional person that does not have a consistent identity with respect to its interests. It is made up of many constituents that often have conflicting interests. These constituents include shareholders, employees, creditors, and the community.

There are a large number of scholars, economists, and judges who subscribe to the proposition that directors and officers have a duty to maximize shareholder wealth, even when that harms the interests of the other constituents. In other words, increasing shareholder wealth is the main and only objective of fiduciary duties. Other constituents must rely on contractual arrangements with the corporation to protect themselves. Banks and bondholders who lend money to the corporation draft detailed loan agreements to protect their interests. Employees enter into individual employment agreements with the corporation or form labor unions to protect their interests. The common shareholders, in contrast, have no detailed agreements with the corporation to protect their interests. They rely on fiduciary duties.

6A-210(b) OTHER-CONSTITUENCY STATUTES:

Several jurisdictions have enacted what is often called an "other-constituency statutes." These statutes allow directors to consider the well-being of constituents of the corporation besides than the shareholders. For example, the Ohio General Corporation Law provides:

> [A] director, in determining what the director reasonably believes to be in the best interests of the corporation, shall consider the interests of the corporation's shareholders and, in the director's discretion, may consider any of the following:
>
> > (1) The interests of the corporation's employees, suppliers, creditors, and customers;
> >
> > (2) The economy of the state and nation;
> >
> > (3) Community and societal considerations;
> >
> > (4) The long-term as well as short-term interests of the corporation and its shareholders, including the possibility that these interests may be best served by the continued independence of the corporation.[213]

If a board decided not to close down a local factory because it would be devastating to the community, even though it would increase the wealth of the shareholders, the statute would protect the board from shareholder lawsuits. Similarly, the statute would protect a board from shareholder lawsuits if the board decided not to take on a project because it would leave the corporation with little cash, putting the creditor's claims at risk.

> **Note:** In either of the above examples, the board could easily frame their decision as one that is best for the future of the corporation, and thus best for the shareholders:
>
> > "Closing the plant would harm our reputation, making it more difficult to sell our products."
> >
> > "Taking on a project that would make creditors uneasy would adversely affect our ability to get loans in the future."
>
> The statute eliminates the board's need to justify its decision as a course of action that maximizes shareholder wealth.

It is hard to make any definitive conclusions about the affect these statues actually have on corporations, their shareholders, and the other corporate constituents, but we can speculate on how it might affect shareholder investment. As a thought experiment, put yourself in the position of a sophisticated investor that is considering how much it should pay for 100 shares of XYZ Inc. You have been through XYZ's financial statements, you

---

[213] Ohio General Corporation Law §1701.59(E).

know the industry, and you have estimated future profits for XYZ. Based on that information, you have come up with a price for XYZ.

Would the price you would be willing to pay for the shares change if the company was incorporated in a jurisdiction that had an other-constituency statute like Ohio's? Arguably, yes. Under a statute like Ohio's, the directors of XYZ are not legally required to put shareholder wealth above all other interests. Arguably, you would discount the price you were willing to pay because shareholder wealth is not paramount. In contrast, you would probably pay a higher price for XYZ shares if it was incorporated in a jurisdiction that required the directors to maximize the wealth of the shareholders over all other constituent interests.

Although other-constituency statues may allow the board to favor one or more constituency over the shareholders, the background of these statutes presents an even more complex story. **The statutes were created in response to hostile takeovers.** Hostile takeovers occur when one corporation, the "surviving corporation" would like to take over another corporation, the "target corporation," through a friendly merger. The board of the target corporation rejects the friendly merger overtures of the surviving corporation. When the target corporation is a public company, the surviving corporation can take measures to attempt force the merger. This process is called a hostile takeover.

The term hostile takeover simply means that the surviving corporation is trying to do the merger without the approval of the target's board. Effectively, the surviving corporation tries to remove the target's directors and replace them with directors who will approve the merger. It can accomplish this goal by acquiring sufficient shareholder voting power in the target through a tender offer (i.e., buying target shares on the market) and soliciting proxies from target's shareholders.[214]

There are defensive measures the target's board can take to frustrate the hostile takeover. Why would target's board frustrate the hostile takeover? There are two possibilities:

(1) **Target's board is protecting the shareholders** - Target's board believes that the surviving corporation is undervaluing the target corporation.

(2) **Target's board is protecting itself** - Target's directors and executive officers want to entrench themselves to keep their jobs. When a merger occurs, the surviving corporation usually fires the board and executive officers of the target corporation. In fact, many times a company will try to acquire another corporation only when it believes

---

[214] For more information on hostile takeovers, see Chapter 9, §9A-404(d).

the target corporation is underperforming because of poor management.

If the target's directors adopt defensive measures to protect themselves and the management team, they are breaching their fiduciary duty of loyalty; they are putting their interests over the interests of the shareholders. If the directors are trying to protect shareholder interests, they are fulfilling their fiduciary duties. However, it is very difficult to determine whether the board is thwarting the hostile takeover to protect itself or the shareholders.[215]

In most cases, the surviving corporation is offering the shareholders of the target a premium above the market price of their shares. Under such circumstances, the shareholders would wonder how thwarting the merger could benefit them. After all, they will be better off with the merger than without. The board's response would be that the premium offered is not sufficient.

State legislatures are also concerned with hostile takeovers. The takeover of a corporation with significant operations within the state often means the loss of jobs for the local economy. Other-constituency statutes allow directors to consider factors other than the maximization of shareholder wealth when defending against hostile takeovers, such as serving the interests of the local community. However, one might argue that these statutes merely give the directors a justification for entrenching themselves and serving their own interests when defending against a hostile takeover.

Some other-constituency statutes only apply to board decision regarding mergers and takeovers. Others only apply to decisions made by the directors of public corporations. Still others apply to all board decisions in all corporations, large and small.

Questions remain about the efficiency of other-constituency statutes:

(1) They might merely serve to provide the directors and officers with a pretense to protect and entrench themselves;

(2) They might provide the board with greater freedom to protect shareholders from underpriced merger offers;

(3) They might serve to shift wealth from shareholders to employees and local communities; and

---

[215] For more information on fiduciary duties in hostile takeovers, see Chapter 9, §9A-700.

(4) They might benefit other constituencies, but in so doing reduce costs for the corporation (wages, taxes, etc) and ultimately benefit shareholders.

6A-210(c) FIDUCIARY DUTY TO CREDITORS IN INSOLVENCY?

Strictly speaking, the board owes its fiduciary duties to the corporation. As we have discussed above, this normally means the board has a duty to protect the residual claimants- the shareholders. The creditors/fixed claimants, protect their interests through contract.

There is debate about whether the fiduciary duties of the directors of an insolvent corporation shift to the creditors, rather than the shareholders. In other words, when a corporation is insolvent, are the directors required to protect and promote creditor wealth over shareholder wealth? To understand why this might be the case, let's look at an insolvent corporation:

> XYZ Inc. is insolvent. It has assets of $100,000 and liabilities of $120,000.[216] Under these circumstances, there is no residual claim for the shareholders.[217] If the company were to liquidate today, the shareholders would receive nothing.

> The creditors' claims are $120,000. If the company were solvent the creditors' claims would be fixed at $120,000. They would receive no more and no less. However, with insolvency, the creditors' claims have lost their "fixed" nature. When the corporation is insolvent the creditors' claims become more like residual claims. If the board makes poor decisions, the $100,000 available to pay creditors' claims will dwindle to $85,000 for example. If the board makes good decisions, the $100,000 available to meet creditors' claims will increase to $115,00, for example.

Imagine you are on the board of directors of XYZ Inc. and you have two potential projects to invest in:

> **Project #1 - high risk, high return:** XYZ invests $20,000. There is a 20% chance that XYZ will see a return of $150,000 (return of the original $20,000, plus profit of $130,000).

> **Project #2 - low risk low return:** XYZ invests $20,000. There is a 70% chance that XYZ will see a return of $40,000 (return of the original $20,000, plus profit of $20,000).

---

[216] There are several possible definitions for insolvency. For the purposes of this discussion, the most intuitive definition is that the company's liabilities exceed its assets.

[217] For an explanation, see Chapter 2, § 2-109(f).

You as a director know the shareholders would prefer Project #1 because only Project #1 gives the shareholders a chance to recover some of the residual. Project #1, has the potential to bring the company out of insolvency and restore a significant amount of the residual claim to the shareholders.

Project #1 is unappealing to the creditors. They are not concerned with restoring a significant amount of the residual to the shareholders. In addition, Project #1 puts a large amount of the creditors' claims at risk for the benefit of the shareholders. If project #1 is successful, the creditors will only benefit by $20,000 of the potential $130,000 return. The shareholder would benefit by the remaining $110,000. Essentially, Project #1 is risking the creditors' money to give the shareholders a potential return of $110,000. The shareholders risk nothing in Project #1.[218]

The creditors find Project #2 much more attractive. Its potential return is not as great as Project #1, but it has a much better chance to restore the company's financial position to where it would be able to meet all of its fixed claims.

Which project do you take if you are on the board of XYZ? If your duty is to protect the fixed claim (i.e., your duty runs to the creditors), you should select Project #2. If your duty runs to the shareholders, you select Project #1.

There is one major Delaware Supreme Court opinion on this issue. In the *Gheewala* case,[219] the Delaware Supreme Court held that **when a corporation has become insolvent, the creditors can sue the directors for any injury the directors cause to the corporation because of a breach of their fiduciary duties.**[220] The court reasoned that "the creditors take the place of the shareholders as the residual beneficiaries of any increase in value."[221]

---

[218] More accurately, they risk going deeper into insolvency, making the possibility of ever seeing a residual more remote.

[219] North America Catholic Educational Programming Foundation Inc., v. Gheewala, 930 A.2d 92 (Del. Sup. Ct. 2007).

[220] The court said the creditors have standing to bring a **derivative lawsuit** against the directors for any injury to the corporation caused by a breach of fiduciary duties. Normally, the shareholders have standing to bring derivative lawsuits. We will discuss derivative lawsuits in Chapter 8, §8A-100 et seq.

[221] Gheewala made it clear that the creditors only had this right when the corporation was insolvent, not when it was near insolvency or in the zone of insolvency.

Some commentators have read *Gheewala* to mean that fiduciary duties shift to the creditors when a corporation is insolvent. Instead of protecting shareholder interests and promoting shareholder wealth, the board is required to protect the interests of creditors. However, a more narrow reading of *Gheewala* suggests that the board's fiduciary duties do not shift from shareholders to creditors, simply because, under normal circumstances, the board's owes its fiduciary duties to the corporation, not the shareholders. When the corporation becomes insolvent, the board still owes its fiduciary duties to the corporation, not the creditors.

Of course, based on all we have learned in this chapter about the various divergent stakeholders and constituencies of the corporation, it is naïve to suggest that there is one thing that is best for the corporation itself, without considering one of more of its stakeholders. As a practical matter, in most cases, the court will never have to decide whether the board is required to promote shareholder interests of creditor interests. When the directors are disinterested, they will be protected by the business judgment rule. They are under no burden to prove the propriety of their business decisions or demonstrate whose interests it serves. Only when the board is foolish enough to state that it is favoring creditors over shareholders or shareholders over creditors will it matter whose interests the business decision serves.

In a contemporary Delaware Court of Chancery decision that was affirmed by the Delaware Supreme Court, the Delaware judiciary made it clear that **the same principles that protect the directors from shareholder fiduciary duty lawsuits protect them from creditor fiduciary duty lawsuits**. In the *Trenwick* case,[222] the court of chancery adopted a very narrow reading of *Gheewala*. The court stated that even in insolvent corporations, the board is "expected to seek profit for stockholders, even at risk of failure." Under Gheewala, creditors may have standing to bring derivative lawsuits when the board breaches its fiduciary duties to the corporation, but according to the court in *Trenwick*, a "strategy [that] results in continued insolvency and an even more insolvent entity does not give rise to a cause of action." In other words, according to *Trenwick*, **shifting fiduciary duties in insolvent corporations is not an issue when the board makes disinterested business decisions**, even if they involve a high level of risk for the corporation or they ultimately cause the corporation to go deeper into insolvency.

---

[222] *Trenwick America Litigation Trust v. Ernst & Young*, 906 A.2d 168 (Del. Ch. 2006) , affirmed by the Delaware Supreme Court in *Trenwick America Litigation Trust v. Billett*, A.2d 438 (Del. Sup. Ct. 2007).

6A-211 FIDUCIARY DUTIES OF CONTROLLING SHAREHOLDERS:

6A-211(a) GENERAL CONCEPT:

In a corporation with a controlling shareholder, the concerns of the minority shareholders shift from the conduct of the directors and the executive officers to the conduct of the controlling shareholder. In the typical large public corporation in the U.S., the shareholders are dispersed. It is relatively rare for a single shareholder or group of shareholders to have shareholdings large enough to control the corporation. However, there are public companies in the U.S. where one shareholder or a shareholder group can control the company. Of course, in large private corporations and closely-held corporations, there is often a controlling shareholder or controlling group of shareholders.

At one end of the spectrum there are public companies where shareholdings are widely dispersed among a great number of shareholders. These shareholders cannot exercise direct control over the corporation's operations or management. Centralized management in the form of the board of directors becomes the apparatus for managing the corporation's business and affairs. The shareholders elect the directors and the directors are given a tremendous amount of discretion to manage the corporation's operations. Because dispersed shareholders suffer from the free-rider problem and from a collective action problem, they cannot engage in effective monitoring. As a result, the directors and officers have a tremendous amount of power and discretion. Of course, with power comes the ability to abuse power and engage in opportunism. When a corporation has dispersed shareholders, its directors and officers are in a position to engage in opportunism – benefitting themselves at the expense of the corporation and the shareholders.

On the other end of the spectrum, there are private companies and, to a lesser extent public companies, with controlling shareholders. A controlling shareholder is in a much better position to monitor and control the directors than dispersed shareholders. The controlling shareholder will have the voting power to elect a majority of the board in virtually all cases, and the power to elect the entire board in most cases.[223] The controlling shareholder will be able to remove directors more easily when they fall out of line. The controlling shareholder will also have more of an incentive to invest in monitoring the directors and officers. Although she also suffers from the free-rider problem, the costs of the problem are less acute for her.

Illustration:

Shareholder X only owns 0.1% of the shares of ABC Inc. Shareholder X invests a significant amount of time and effort monitoring the directors

---

[223] See Chapter 5, §5A-202(a) for an explanation of why a straight-voting scheme allows the majority shareholder to elect the entire board of directors.

and officers of ABC Inc. Her efforts increase the productivity of the corporation, and result in the value of the corporation increasing by $1,000,000.

What rewards does Shareholder X reap from her efforts? The value of her shares increases by $1,000. The value of the other shareholders' shares increases by $999,000.

The other shareholders are free-riding on her efforts. She has very little incentive to continue monitoring the company's directors and officer.

Compare with the following:

Shareholder Y owns 51% of the shares of ABC Inc. Shareholder Y invests a significant amount of time and effort in monitoring the directors and officers of ABC Inc. Her efforts increase the productivity of the corporation, and result in the value of the corporation increasing by $1,000,000.

What rewards does Shareholder Y reap from her efforts? The value of her shares increases by $510,000. The value of the other shareholders' shares increases by $490,000.

The other shareholders are free-riding on her efforts, but she still captures enough of the benefit her efforts produce to give her the incentives to continue monitoring the company's directors and officer.

In a corporation with a controlling shareholder, the threat of director and officer opportunism is significantly lower because the directors and officers do not have the broad discretion they would have in a corporation with dispersed shareholders. They answer to the controlling shareholder, who is an active monitor of their conduct. The ultimate control and discretion has shifted to the controlling shareholder, who may use that control to benefit herself at the expense of the minority shareholders.

6A-211(b) DEFINING CONTROLLING SHAREHOLDERS:

There are no strict standards for determining when a shareholder will be considered a controlling shareholder. It is a fact-specific analysis. The court will probably look at whether the shareholder controls voting power sufficient to elect a majority of the board of directors. A corporation may issue shares with extra voting rights, diminished voting rights, or no voting rights. When analyzing whether a shareholder is a controlling shareholder, we look at the voting rights her shareholdings give her, not the economic rights.

327

Illustration:

Shareholder B owns 10,000 shares of "Common Stock B" in XYZ Inc. Her shareholdings only entitle her to 20% of the residual, but they give her preferred voting rights that allow her to elect a majority of the board.

Shareholder B is a controlling shareholder.

In a public corporation, a shareholder might be a controlling shareholder with far less than a majority of the voting power. A shareholder with 40%, 30%, or even 20% of the voting power of a public company will normally be able to elect a majority of the board and control the corporation because the other shareholders suffer from a collective action problem. Although the other shareholders would constitute a majority if they worked together as a group, the economic realities of their situation prevents them for doing so – the costs of communicating and cooperating are prohibitively high.

Once again, there is no bright-line standard for determining what percentage of voting power a shareholder needs in a public corporation to exert control. Academics performing empirical studies on the opportunism of controlling shareholders in public companies often use 20% as a benchmark. Twenty percent may be a good number to keep in the back of your mind as a rule of thumb, but the real question one should ask is **whether the shareholder's voting power actually allows her to elect a majority of the board**, even if she does not control a majority of shareholder voting power. The analysis is specific to the facts of each particular case.

6A-211(c) THE FIDUCIARY DUTIES OF CONTROLLING SHAREHOLDERS:

Controlling shareholders have fiduciary duties to the corporation and the minority shareholders. These fiduciary duties are similar to the fiduciary duties of directors and officers, but litigation on controlling shareholder fiduciary duties **revolves around duty of loyalty claims**. In practical terms, the controlling shareholder's duty of care in decision-making is not a major concern for minority shareholders because the interests of controlling shareholders and minority shareholder are most often aligned on this issue. In addition, it is likely the controlling shareholder does not have a duty to monitor, or at least there has been no judicial precedent on the issue. Once again, the interests of the controlling shareholders are closely aligned on the oversight of the management team and the corporation's operations.

The greatest concern for minority shareholders is that the controlling shareholder will divert corporate assets to herself. Litigation on the fiduciary duty of controlling shareholders **focuses on the common duty of loyalty claims – self dealing and corporate opportunity**. The details of the duty of loyalty claims you learned for claims against directors and officers are relevant to claims against controlling shareholders. Specifically:

Approval of the transaction by **disinterested/independent directors or shareholders** (i.e., "ratification") will give the controlling shareholder some protection in both self-dealing and corporate-opportunity claims.[224]

BUT, keep in mind that the directors of the corporation are often employed or dominated by the controlling shareholder, in which case they will not be disinterested or independent. It is unlikely that a court would consider a director to be under the domination of a controlling shareholder simply because she was elected by the controlling director, but other facts may show that the controlling shareholder dominates or controls the director in some other way.

In addition, shareholder ratification is only valid if the transaction is approved by disinterested/independent shareholders. The term of art that corporate lawyers often use is **"approval by a majority of the minority."** This term means that the holders of a majority of the shares not controlled by the controlling shareholder voted in favor of the transaction.

Finally, in Delaware, valid director or shareholder ratification in duty of loyalty claims against controlling shareholders does not automatically result in the application of the business judgment rule. Instead, the complaining minority shareholder is given an opportunity to prove the unfairness of the transaction.[225] In Delaware, valid ratification of a controlling shareholder self-dealing transaction does not provide absolute protection for the controlling shareholder; rather it simply relieves the controlling shareholder from the burden of proving the fairness of the transaction, shifting it to the complaining shareholder to prove unfairness.

In cases, where director or shareholder ratification did not occur or was flawed, the controlling shareholder will have an opportunity to escape liability by **proving the transaction was fair** to the corporation in self-dealing cases, and proving it was fair to the corporation for her to take the opportunity in corporate opportunity cases.[226]

6A-211(d) SPECIFIC EXAMPLES OF CONTROLLING-SHAREHOLDER SELF-DEALING:

A controlling shareholder can engage in self-dealing by **causing the corporation to purchase goods or services from the controlling**

---

[224] See §6A-202(b), above.

[225] See DUTY OF LOYALTY – CONFLICTED TRANSACTION FLOWCHART (ALTERNATE) EXPLANATION in §6A-202(k), above.

[226] See §6A-202(e), above, for a discussion of fairness review in self-dealing litigation. See §6A-203(b), above, for a discussion of fairness review in corporate opportunity litigation.

shareholder a company the controlling shareholder owns. Similarly, a controlling shareholder can engage in self-dealing by **causing the corporation to sell goods or services to the controlling shareholder** or a company that controlling shareholder owns. In either case, the controlling shareholder will realize private benefits of control at the expense of the minority shareholders only if the transaction is not fair to the corporation. If a minority shareholder challenges a self-dealing transaction in court, the controlling shareholder will bear the burden of proving the transaction was fair to the corporation, unless the transaction was properly ratified by the minority shareholders or by disinterested and independent directors.

Another common controlling shareholder self-dealing fact pattern involves mergers. You will not learn the details of mergers until Chapter 9, but to understand how a **controlling shareholder can use a merger to exploit minority shareholders**, you need only understand the most basic aspects of a merger transaction. When two corporations merge, one corporation survives ("surviving corporation") and the other is merged out of existence ("target corporation"). The surviving corporation acquires the business of the target corporation, as well as its assets and liabilities. Even though the target corporation does not survive the merger, its business, assets and liabilities survive and within the surviving corporation.[227]

The shareholders of the target corporation must approve the merger. They will often receive shares in the surviving corporation as consideration for the merger. In other merger transactions, the shareholders of the target corporation receive cash in the merger, which is commonly called a cash-out merger.

Now imagine you are the controlling shareholder of Target Co., owning 75% of the outstanding shares, and you want to get rid of those pesky minority shareholders. How can you use a merger to do so?

Step 1: You form a corporation called New Co. You are the only shareholder of New Co. You plan to merge Target Co. into New Co. (If the controlling shareholder is a corporation, it does not need to set up New Co. It can simply merge the target into itself.)

Step 2: You receive approval of the merger from the shareholders of Target Co. Of course, this will not be an obstacle since you control 75% of the outstanding shares of Target Co. As long as you vote your shares in favor of the merger, shareholder approval is certain.

Step 3: Target Co. is merged into New Co. The shareholders of Target Co. receive cash in the transaction.

---

[227] We discuss mergers in greater detail in Chapter 9.

Step 4: You change the name of New Co. to "Target Co.," or something similar.

You have successfully eliminated the minority shareholders and acquired control of 100% of the business of Target Co. Of course, there is a question about whether you have exploited the minority shareholders by cashing them out this way. The answer depends on the price you paid them for their shares. Theoretically, if you paid them a fair price for their shares, you have not exploited them because you have compensated them for the future profits of Target Co.[228] However, if a minority shareholder challenges the merger in court, you will have the burden of proving both fair price **and** fair dealing, unless the transaction was properly ratified by the minority shareholders or by disinterested and independent directors.

6A-211(e) SALE OF CONTROL PREMIA:

When a controlling shareholder sells her controlling interest in the corporation to a third party, she will often be able to obtain a price above market price:

Illustration 1:

XYZ Inc. is a publicly traded corporation listed on the NYSE. Its shares are currently trading at around **$20 per share**. Parent Co. owns 55% of the outstanding shares of XYZ Inc. Buyer makes an offer to Parent to purchase its 55% controlling interest for **$25 per share.**

Buyer has offered a price with a control premium of $5 per share for the controlling interest.

Illustration 2:

ABC Inc. is a private company with around 40 shareholders. **Sharon owns 55%** of the outstanding shares of ABC Inc. A private equity fund is interested in purchasing Sharon's controlling interest. Sharon, the private equity fund, and their respective attorneys, accountants, and investment bankers negotiate the sales price. The parties agree that the entire company is worth **$20 million**. The private equity fund offers Sharon **$12 million for her 55% controlling interest**.

The private equity fund has offered a price that includes a control premium of $1,000,000 for Sharon's controlling interest.

When a controlling shareholder sells her shares for a control premium, minority shareholders often cry foul. Should the law allow a controlling shareholder to sell her control stake for a premium? Your first reaction might be that anyone, including a controlling shareholder, has the right to sell her

---

[228] See Chapter 4, §4D-503.

331

property for any price a buyer is willing to pay. However, after you analyze why the buyer is willing to pay a control premium, your thoughts on the matter might change.

Why would a buyer pay more per share for a controlling interest than a non-controlling interest? You may have a sense that control is worth extra, and you would be right, but why is control worth extra? There are two possible explanations for why a buyer would pay a premium for control:

> Explanation #1 – **Buyer adds value:** The buyer believes the company, will be more profitable under her control. The buyer has better ideas, a better management team, or its business has certain synergies with the target corporation that will make the target corporation more profitable. The value of a business is based on its ability to make profits in the future.[229] If the buyer strongly believes she will make the company more profitable in the future, she will be willing to pay more than the current valuation of the company, which is based on potential future profits under the current management and controlling shareholder.

> Explanation #2 – **Private benefits of control**: The control premium represents the benefits of exploiting the minority shareholders. The controlling shareholder can use her control to divert corporate assets to itself through self-dealing, taking corporate opportunities, excessive compensation packages, unreasonable perquisites, etc.

If the reason for the control premium is buyer-adds-value, the control premium is completely legitimate. If the reason for the control premium is private-benefits-of-control, it is illegitimate because it merely quantifies the breach of the controlling shareholder's fiduciary duties.

The law essentially provides that a controlling shareholder cannot sell its control stake for a control premium if the control premium represents the private benefit of control. Often, courts state the rule as follows:

> **A controlling shareholder may not sell her control stake for a premium if she knows or has reason to know that the buyer will exercise control to the detriment of the corporation or the minority shareholders.**

As you have probably been able to spot, the real difficulty lies in trying to determine whether the premium represents buyer's added value or buyer's private benefits of control.

---

[229] See Chapter 4, §4D-300.

6A-211(f) LIFE WITHOUT MINORITY SHAREHOLDERS:

The presence of minority shareholders generates agency costs. Even the most honest and diligent controlling shareholders will need to take extra measures to ensure transactions are fair to the minority shareholders and to demonstrate to the minority shareholders that there is no opportunism. Even so, there will be complaints from minority shareholders and lawsuits that challenge self-dealing transactions with the controlling shareholder. The controlling shareholder may be able to show ratification or prove fairness, but the corporation would still bear the costs of litigation and settlement.

Compare the following two situations:

Situation 1:

Parent Co. owns all the outstanding shares of Supply Inc. Parent owns 60% of Retail Inc.

Supply Inc. sells 10,000 widgets to Retail Inc. for $100,000.

If you were a minority shareholder in Retail Inc., you would look at this transaction with suspicion. Parent Co. has an incentive to use her control of Retail to make it pay a high price for the widgets, diverting corporate funds from Retail to Supply. Parent only has 60% of Retail's equity, but has all of Supply's equity.

For example, if Supply makes a $30,000 profit on the transaction, Parent's wealth is increased by $30,000. If Supply makes only a $20,000 profit on the transaction, saving Retail $10,000, Parent's wealth is only increased by $26,000 (100% of Supply's $20,000 profit plus 60% of the $10,000 saved by Retail).

To protect itself, Parent could submit the transaction to Retail's directors for ratification, but director ratification might not have the desired effect because Parent probably controls all of the directors. Parent could submit the transaction to Retail's minority shareholders for ratification, but the process would be time consuming and costly. Alternatively, Parent could take steps to make sure the transaction would pass fairness review, or it could simply make Retail purchase widgets from another source.

Situation 2:

Parent Co. owns all the outstanding shares of Supply Inc. and all of the outstanding shares of Retail Inc.

Supply Inc. sells 10,000 widgets to Retail Inc. for $100,000.

In this situation, there are no minority shareholders to consider, so there are none of the related costs.[230]

---

[230] The IRS, however, might be interested in the transaction. Parent Co. may be using the pricing to shift profits from the subsidiary with a higher tax rate to the subsidiary with the lower tax rate. This strategy is called "transfer pricing."

UNIT 6B

FIDUCIARY DUTIES IN THE PARTNERSHIP

6B-100 FIDUCIARY DUTIES TO THE PARTNERSHIP:

Most of the fiduciary duties you explored in the corporate context are the same for the partnership. Partners owe the partnership the fiduciary duties of loyalty, care, and good faith.

6B-101 THE DUTY OF LOYALTY:

Partners owe a fiduciary duty of loyalty to the partnership. They may not use partnership property for their private benefit, they may not engage in self-dealing, they may not take partnership opportunities, and they may not compete with the partnership.

6B-101(a) SELF-DEALING:

Your understanding of self-dealing in the corporate context should guide your understanding of self-dealing in the partnership context. In short, a partner may not engage in any transaction where she is **conflicted** (i.e., interested) without the consent of the other partners. Situations where a partner is conflicted include the following transactions:

(1) A transaction between the partnership and **the partner**;

(2) A transaction between the partnership and **an entity the partner controls**;

(3) A transaction between the partnership and **an entity in which the partner has a financial interest** (to the extent we would expect the partner's financial interest in the entity to affect the partner's impartiality);

(4) A transaction between the partnership and **a close relative the partner** (to the extent we would expect the relationship to affect the partner's impartiality); and

(5) A transaction between the partnership and **a person who controls the partner**.

As you may recall, corporate law allows self-dealing transactions if the board of directors ratifies them. Partnership law is similar. Transactions where a partner has a conflict of interest **can be ratified or waived by the informed**

335

consent of the other partners. Because ratification of a conflicted transaction is considered an extraordinary transaction, the law probably requires **the consent of all partners**, in contrast to corporate law, which usually requires a vote of the majority of independent and non-conflicted directors. Of course, the partners may change this default rule in their partnership agreement, and require something less than unanimous consent.[231]

In addition, partnership law does not expressly give conflicted partners a chance to prove the **fairness of the transaction** in order to escape liability. As you may recall, under corporate law, a conflicted director or officer could escape liability by showing that the either (1) independent and non-conflicted directors ratified the transaction **or** (2) the transaction was fair to the corporation. In contrast, **there is nothing in RUPA, UPA, or precedent to support a fairness defense for a conflicted transaction**.

6B-101(b) PARTNERSHIP OPPORTUNITY:

Similar to the doctrine of corporate opportunity, a partner may not take an opportunity that belongs to the partnership.[232] A partner may only take a partnership opportunity **if all partners consent**, unless the partnership agreement provides otherwise. The partners may agree to a lower approval standard in their partnership agreement.

Without the consent of the other partners, the partner who takes an opportunity can only avoid liability by showing the opportunity did not rightfully belong to the partnership. The factors relevant to whether the opportunity belonged to the partnership should be the same factors we covered in detail in our discussion of corporate opportunity:[233]

> **Line of business** – Was the business within one of the partnership's lines of business?

> **Expectancy** – Did the partnership have an expectancy in the opportunity?

> **Individual capacity vs. official capacity** – Did the opportunity come to the partner in her personal capacity or in her official partnership capacity?

> **Partnership rejection** – Has the partnership rejected the opportunity at some point in the past?

---

[231] See §6B-204, below.

[232] See §6A-203 et seq., above, for a detailed discussion of taking a corporate opportunity.

[233] See §6A-203(b), above.

Partnership incapacity – Did the partnership have the financial wherewithal to take the opportunity?

Competing with the partnership - If the partner takes the opportunity, will she be directly competing with the partnership?

6B-101(c) THE DUTY NOT TO COMPETE WITH THE PARTNERSHIP:

A partner may not compete with the partnership. In fact, any agent has a duty not to compete with her principal. We only touched upon this concept briefly in the context of the corporation,[234] but it is an issue for all business organizations and all agent-principal relationships, not just in the partnership.

Once a partner resigns or otherwise dissociates[235] herself from the partnership, she is no longer obligated to refrain from competing with the partnership. Before she resigns, she may not compete with the partnership, but she may start planning to compete with the partnership. There is a somewhat vague line between *competing with the partnership* and *planning to compete with the partnership*.

As part of her planning to compete with the partnership, before she leaves the partnership a partner rents office space, hires employees, etc. She generally may not solicit the partnership's clients or try to lure away the partnership's employees. After she leaves the partnership, she is free to compete with the partnership, including the solicitation the partnership's clients and employees, but she may not use the partnership's proprietary or confidential information, such as customer lists.

6B-102 THE DUTY OF CARE:

As you may remember from earlier discussions in this chapter, the standard of liability for breaching the duty of care for directors and officers of a corporation is **gross negligence in the decision-making process**.[236] You should expect the partnership law of your jurisdiction to provide a similar standard for partners in a partnership. For example, RUPA provides:

---

[234] In §6A-203(b), we briefly discussed a director or officer's duty not to compete with the corporation when we explored the factors relevant to the corporate opportunity doctrine.

[235] We will discuss partner dissociation in Chapter 7, §7B-302 et seq.

[236] See §6A-204 et seq., above

A partner's duty of care to the partnership and the other partners . . . is limited to refraining from engaging in grossly negligent or reckless conduct, intentional misconduct, or knowing violation of the law.[237]

Some courts will even apply the business judgment rule to business decisions in the partnership context.

6B-103 THE DUTY OF GOOD FAITH:

Not surprisingly, partners violate their fiduciary duties to the partnership if they act in **knowing violation of the law** or with **the intent to harm the corporation**. RUPA does not characterize these acts falling within a duty of good faith, but within the duty of care.

A partner's duty of care to the partnership and the other partners . . . is limited to refraining from engaging in grossly negligent or reckless conduct, intentional misconduct, or knowing violation of the law.[238]

6B-200 FIDUCIARY DUTIES IN THE PARTNERSHIP – SPECIAL ISSUES:

6B-201 THE DUTY TO PROVIDE INFORMATION:

In Chapter 5, we discussed a partner's duty under RUPA to provide the other partners with "any information concerning the partnership's business and affairs **reasonably required for the proper exercise of the partners rights and duties** . . .."[239] RUPA does not characterize this duty as a "fiduciary" duty, but one can see how it is closely related to the duties of care and loyalty, especially where information and disclosure are important to fulfilling one's fiduciary duties.

---

[237] RUPA §404(c).

[238] RUPA §404(c).

[239] RUPA §403(c).

6B-202 FIDUCIARY DUTIES TO CO-PARTNERS:

Maybe the most interesting issues with respect to fiduciary duties of partners are related to the scope of a partner's fiduciary duties to her fellow partners. In the corporate context, fiduciary duties run from the directors and officers to the corporation.[240] Shareholders do not owe fiduciary duties to other shareholders, unless they are controlling shareholders, in which case they owed a fiduciary duty to the corporation and the minority shareholders.[241] Effectively, the controlling shareholder in a corporation has a fiduciary duty not to deny the minority shareholders their share of the current and future profits of the corporation.

In the partnership context, a partner owes a fiduciary duty to her fellow partners. A fiduciary relationship requires the fiduciary to put her interests aside in favor of the interests of the person to whom the duty is owed. To better understand how fiduciary duties between partners create interesting issues, let's look at two transactions between partners.

Transaction 1 – Sale of a house:

A and B are partners in an accounting firm. A is looking to sell his house and B is in the market for a new home.

A and B enter into a contract for the sale of A's house.

Query: If A owes B a fiduciary duty, as partners, does A have a duty to treat B better than she would any other buyer? For example, is A required to disclose that the house has certain latent defects that the law does not require her to disclose to any other buyer? Does A have to give B the lowest price she is willing to take, or can she try to get as high a price as B is willing to pay?

You would probably be correct in concluding that A does *not* owe B a fiduciary duty in this context, even though they are partners. The transaction is unrelated to their relationship as partners or to the partnership's business and affairs.

Transaction 2 – Sale of partnership interests:

A and B are partners in an accounting firm. A is looking to sell his partnership interest.

A and B enter into a contract for the sale of A's partnership interest.

---

[240] See §6A-210(a), above.

[241] See §6A-211 et seq., above.

Query: If A owes B a fiduciary duty, as partners, does she have a duty treat B better than she would any other buyer? For example, is A required to disclose that she knows that the partnership is about to lose a big account? Does she have to give B the lowest price she is willing to take, or can she try to get as much of her asking price as B is willing to pay?

You would probably be correct in concluding that A owes B a fiduciary duty in this context, because they are partners and the transaction is related to their relationship as partners. Once you conclude that A owes a fiduciary duty to B, defining the exact scope of her fiduciary duty is a bit more difficult.

6B-202(a) RIGHT TO VOTE ONE'S SELF INTEREST *VS.* THE DUTY OF GOOD FAITH:

RUPA has two provisions that help us understand the scope of a partner's fiduciary duty to another partner. First, RUPA provides that **a partner does not violate her fiduciary duties simply by pursuing her own interests**.[242]

Scenario 1:

Assume a partnership agreement provides that the partnership will only make a distribution if a majority of the voting interests approves.

> Partner A has voting control under the partnership agreement. Partner A is wealthy. She has more than enough savings and other income to support her lavish lifestyle. She thinks it is best for her if the partnership retains the money and uses it to expand the business.

> Partner B is not wealthy. Her savings are depleted and she needs money for a new roof. She thinks it is best for her if the partnership makes a cash distribution to the partners.

Each partner is free to vote to further her own interest, even if she has more voting power than her fellow partners and even if she has voting control.

On the other side of the coin is RUPA's requirement that partners **discharge their duties and exercise their rights in a manner consistent with good faith and fair dealing**.[243] Under RUPA, the scope of good faith and fair dealing is not clear. The comments to RUPA §404 state:

> The meaning of "good faith and fair dealing" is not firmly fixed under present law. . . . It was decided to leave the terms undefined . . . and

---

[242] RUPA §404(e)

[243] RUPA §404(d)

allow the courts to develop their meaning based on the experience of real cases. [244]

The undefined state of good faith and fair dealing makes it necessary for use to try to predict how a court would apply good faith and fair dealing when the partners deal with each other. It might help if we performed a thought experiment based on the illustration immediately above. When might a court find that a partner's vote on distributions violated good faith and fair dealing?

Scenario 2:

Assume the partnership agreement provides that the partnership will only make a distribution if a majority of the voting interests approves.

Partner A has voting control under the partnership agreement. Partner A is wealthy. She has more than enough savings and other income to support herself. She knows Partner B needs cash desperately.

Partner A knows that if the partnership does not make a distribution, Partner B's financial situation will compel her to sell her partnership interest at a low price, which will allows A to purchase B's interest at a discounted price.

Has Partner A violated RUPA's requirement of good faith and fair dealing?

To help answer that question, we might want to parse out good faith and fair dealing is three contractual contexts:

The pre-contract bargaining context:

Generally, when parties are negotiating to enter into a contract the standard of good faith and fair dealing provides minimal protection for the parties. The law expects the parties to protect their own interests. The principle of good faith and fair dealing only prevents the most egregious opportunistic behaviors, such as lies, misrepresentations, and active concealment of latent defects.

The contractual performance context:

When the parties have already entered into a contract, the implied duty of good faith and fair dealing in the performance of the contract is a somewhat higher standard than we see in the bargaining context. In the contractual performance context, parties have a greater duty to refrain from engaging in opportunistic behavior. A party has a more stringent duty to correct the other party when she is mistaken, to cooperate when the contract is silent or ambiguous, and to refrain from taking advantage

---

[244] RUPA §404, comment 4.

of the other party when situations arise that were not contemplated by the parties at the time of contracting.

The long-term/relational contract:

When the parties have entered into a long-term contract, we expect them to adhere to an even higher standard of good faith and fair dealing. The nature of a long-term contractual relationship means that the parties are expecting a close working arrangement over a long period of time. In addition, the long-term nature of the relationship makes it difficult to draft every possible contingency into the written contract. Many matters will be left to the discretion of each of the parties. It is this high level of discretion that especially calls for some sort of default implied duty to ensure the parties exercise discretion for their mutual benefit.

For these reasons, parties have higher expectations regarding the scope of good faith and fair dealing in these long-term/relational contracts. They expect good faith and fair dealing to include a duty to refrain from engaging in opportunistic behavior at the expense of the other party, even when the contract provides them with a tremendous amount of discretion to do so.

We could say that the partnership is the ultimate long-term/relational contract. Partners have a tremendous amount of discretion to bind the partnership to ordinary matters. Partners also have voting discretion on all extraordinary matters and ordinary matters where there is a difference of opinion among the partners. As such, partners expect that the duty of good faith and fair dealing allows each partner to vote her own interest, but not to cause intentional harm to the interests of her co-partners and not to engage in opportunistic behavior.

6B-202(b) ANALOGY TO SELF-DEALING:

It may be helpful for you to approach situations that might implicate the duty of good faith and fair dealing with an analogy to self-dealing transaction. **When a partner uses control and discretion to cause a transfer of wealth to herself from her co-partner**, she has breached her duty of good faith and fair dealing.

Let us re-visit the scenario we discussed in 6B-202(a), above:

Scenario:

Assume the partnership agreement provides that the partnership will only make a distribution if a majority of the voting interests approves.

Partner A has voting control under the partnership agreement. Partner A is wealthy. She has more than enough savings and other income to support herself. She knows Partner B needs cash desperately.

If Partner A uses her voting to control to prevent a distribution because she feels the money is better used to expand the business, she has not caused a transfer of wealth from Partner B to herself. Partner A benefits from the transaction and Partner B suffers from it, but there is no transfer of wealth from B to A.

In contrast, if Partner A uses her voting control to place Partner B in a situation where she will have no choice but to sell her partnership interest at a discount, Partner A has caused a transfer of wealth from Partner B to herself when she purchases B's partnership interests. In this case, the transfer of wealth can be measured by the difference between the fair market value of the B's partnership interest and the price Partner A actually paid.

6B-202(c) **FREEZE-OUT – FACT PATTERNS:**

In business organization law, when a one owner, or a group of owners, exercises its control to cause a transfer of wealth to those in control from those not in control, we often call it a **freeze-out**. The duty of good faith and fair dealing is implicated in cases of freeze-out.

Consider the following examples of freeze-outs:

Example 1 – expelling a partner without cause:

Some partnership agreements may allow the partners to **expel a partner, without cause**, and buy out her partnership interest. Normally, the partnership agreement will expressly provide the price the partnership will pay for the expelled partner's interest.

If the partnership agreement calls **for a price below the fair market value**, the expulsion of the partner and the buy-out of her partnership interest are highly suspicious. The partners in control may have violated their duty of good faith and fair dealing by freezing out the expelled partner.

A buy-out of the expelled partner at a price below fair market value results in a **transfer of wealth from the expelled partner to the remaining partners**. The remaining partners receive the expelled partner's share of the partnership's future profits without paying her for it.[245] Their duty of good faith and fair dealing requires them to exercise their right to expel her in good faith and with fair dealing. If they expelled her without cause, there is a strong inference that they did so simply to take her full economic interest in the partnership without having to compensate her fully for it.

---

[245] Any price below fair market value does not compensate the expelled partner fully for her share of the partnership's future profits. See Chapter 4, §§4D-300 and 4D-500 et seq.

The remaining partners might have good reason to expel the partner. She might have committed an act of serious misfeasance or malfeasance, in which case we are less suspicious of the partners' decision to expel her. Similarly, there might be an honest reason for expelling the partner that did not rise to the level of expulsion for cause, but still merits expelling her. For example, they have lost confidence in her abilities, or they are worried about her emotional state. Once again, under these circumstances we are not as suspicious about their conduct.

Example 2 – purchase of a co-partner's partnership interest:

One partner will often have the opportunity to purchase the partnership interest of another partner. The opportunity may arise out of an option to purchase upon the expulsion of a partner, as discussed immediately above in example 1. The opportunity may also arise from a desire of one partner to withdraw from the partnership and exit her investment. When one partner is selling her partnership interest to another, one of them may have superior information that the other would consider important.

For example, maybe the buying-partner knows the partnership is about to land a new, lucrative account. If the selling-partner is unaware of this information, the price she negotiates for her partnership interest will be lower than fair market value because it will not account for the future profits of the new lucrative account. Because of the informational asymmetries, the buying-partner is able to cause a transfer of the future profits of the new lucrative account to herself without compensating the selling-partner.

Similarly, the selling-partner might have superior information. For example, the selling-partner might know the partnership is about to lose a lucrative account. If the buying-partner is unaware of this information, the price she negotiates for the partnership interest will be higher than fair market value because it will include the future profits of the lucrative account the partnership will lose. The selling-partner is able to cause a transfer of wealth to herself from the buying-partner. The price she receives for her partnership interest will be higher than the fair market value because it includes the value of the lost account.

In normal arm's-length contract negotiation situations, we generally do not impose a duty on the parties to disclose information. We expect buyers and seller to protect themselves. The law requires them to refrain from making misrepresentations, but does not require them to make disclosures to the other party, except in very limited circumstances. However, between partners we impose a higher standard of good faith and fair dealing.

344

The duty of good faith and fair dealing between partners likely requires the partner with superior information about the partnership's business to disclose it to the other partner in a transaction involving the sale of a partnership interest. The case is even stronger when we consider a partner's right to information about the partnership and a partner's duty disclose information to the other partners.[246] RUPA Section 403 provides:

> Each partner and the partnership shall furnish to a partner . . . without demand, any information concerning the partnership's business and affairs reasonably required for the proper exercise of the partner's rights and duties under the partnership agreement or this [Act] . . . [247]

Example 3 – decisions about distributions:

When the partners vote on distributions, they may not use this power to intentionally put other partners in a position where they will have to sell their partnership interests at a discount.[248]

6B-202(d) FREEZE-OUT AND PRICE:

You may have noticed that the price of the partnership interest was an important variable in the freeze-out fact patterns we discussed above. Fair market value represents the present value of the future profits of the business. A purchase of a partnership interest at a price below fair market value results in a transfer of the present value of the future profits from the selling partner to the purchasing partner.[249] When the purchase price was below fair market value, we easily spotted a transfer of wealth.

Price is a proxy for good faith. Good faith is a state of mind. Unless the partner admits she did not act in good faith, a court must make its determination based on the circumstances. The fact that a partner caused a transfer of wealth from the affected partner to herself is likely the main basis for our inference of bad faith. However, if the partner paid fair market value for the partnership interest, there was no transfer of wealth, leaving us very little to justify an inference that she did not act in good faith.

Of course, fair market value is actually a range of prices. The selling partner might have sold at the lower end of the fair market value range, which would result in a transfer of wealth to the purchasing partner. If the purchasing

---

[246] See §6B-201, above.

[247] RUPA §403(c)

[248] See §6-202(b), above.

[249] See Chapter 4, §4D-503 for illustrations on this concept.

partner had observed reasonable standards of fair dealing, the selling partner might have sold at the more favorable end of the fair market value range. In other words, a transfer of wealth could occur even when the price for the partnership interests was at fair market value because it might be at the lower end of fair market value. Because courts are probably poorly equipped to make these fine distinctions in valuation, they rely on fair dealing as a proxy for wealth transfers within the range of fair market value.[250]

6B-203 WAIVING FIDUCIARY DUTIES:

The parties to a partnership agreement might want to limit or eliminate their fiduciary duties. The law permits the partners some flexibility to define the scope of their fiduciary duties in their partnership agreement, but they may not eliminate them completely. Delaware law allows the partnership agreement to define and limit fiduciary duties unless it is unreasonable.[251] RUPA Section 103(b) follows the same approach.

It is quite common for partnership agreements to define what business opportunities partners can take without breaching the duty of loyalty. In addition, you might see partnership agreements that specifically address how to approve self-dealing transactions.

6B-204 FIDUCIARY DUTIES IN LIMITED PARTNERSHIPS (LPs):

[Reserved]

---

[250] See §6A-202(e), above, discussing how the element of fair dealing plays an important role in ensuring fair price in fairness review for duty of loyalty claims.

[251] Delaware General Partnership Law §15-103(f).

UNIT 6C

FIDUCIARY DUTIES IN THE LLC

6C-100 ANALOGY TO PARTNERSHIP:

The fiduciary duties in LLCs closely follow the fiduciary duties in partnerships. Members in member-managed LLCs owe the LLC the same fiduciary duties that partners owe the partnership.[252] A member may also owe a duty of good faith and fair dealing to her fellow members, depending on jurisdiction. A member's duty of good faith and fair dealing to her co-members raise the same issues we discussed with respect to a partner's duty of good faith and fair dealing to her co-partners.[253]

There are only two areas where fiduciary duties in LLCs require a separate discussion from the fiduciary duties in partnerships:

Fiduciary duties in manager-managed LLCs; and

Waiving fiduciary duties in LLCs.

6C-200 FIDUCIARY DUTIES IN MANAGER-MANAGED LLCs:

In manager-managed LLCs, the managers owe fiduciary duties to the LLC and its members. The members in manager-managed LLCs will generally not owe any fiduciary duties to the LLC or the other members, except the duty of good faith and fair dealing.[254]

6C-300 WAIVING FIDUCIARY DUTIES IN LLCs:

In many jurisdictions, LLCs have far greater freedom to define, limit and even eliminate fiduciary duties. Delaware law, for example, allows an operating

---

[252] See for example RULLCA §409(a)-(d). See §6B-100 et seq., above, for a discussion of fiduciary duties in partnerships.

[253] See RULLCA §§409(a) and 409(d). See §6B-203 et seq., above for a discussion of partner's duty of good faith and fair dealing to her co-partners

[254] See RULLCA §409(d) & (g). See §6B-203 et seq., above for a discussion of partner's duty of good faith and fair dealing to her co-partners

agreement to eliminate completely any and all fiduciary duties, but it may not eliminate the duty of good faith and fair dealing.[255]

RULLCA's provision allowing exculpation for fiduciary duty breaches is similar in scope to the exculpation clauses a corporation might have in its articles of incorporation.[256] In other words, the operating agreement may exculpate a member or manager for breaches of the duty of due care, but not for the duties of loyalty or good faith.[257] In addition, RULLCA prohibits the operating agreement from eliminating or varying the duty of good faith and fair dealing.[258]

---

[255] DLLCA §18-1101(c).

[256] See §6A-209 et seq., above.

[257] RULLCA §110(g).

[258] RULLCA §110(b)(5).

CHAPTER 7

CLOSELY-HELD BUSINESS ENTITIES

UNIT 7A
<u>CLOSELY-HELD CORPORATIONS:</u>

7A-100   **SPECIAL ISSUES IN CLOSELY-HELD CORPORATIONS – INTRODUCTION:**

7A-200   **FIDUCIARY DUTIES IN CLOSELY-HELD CORPORATIONS:**

     7A-201   TRADITIONAL FIDUCIARY DUTIES:

     7A-202   DUTY OF GOOD FAITH AND FAIR DEALING – THE BASICS:

         7A-202(a)   EXERCISE OF CONTROL:

         7A-202(b)   FREEZE-OUT AND REASONABLE EXPECTATIONS:

     7A-203   DUTY OF GOOD FAITH AND FAIR DEALING – THE DETAILS:

         7A-203(a)   DUTY OF GOOD FAITH AND FAIR DEALING – TERMINATING THE EMPLOYMENT OF A SHAREHOLDER:

         7A-203(b)   DUTY OF GOOD FAITH AND FAIR DEALING – DECISIONS REGARDING DIVIDENDS:

     7A-204   THE MASSACHUSETTS APPROACH:

     7A-205   ALTERNATE APPROACH:

     7A-206   DUTY OF GOOD FAITH WITHOUT A TRANSFER OF WEALTH:

     7A-207   REMEDIES FOR FIDUCIARY BREACHES IN THE CLOSELY-HELD CORPORATION:

         7A-207(a)   TYPICAL REMEDIES:

         7A-207(b)   INVOLUNTARY DISSOLUTION:

7A-300   **TRANSFER OF SHARES:**

     7A-301   CONTINUITY OF OWNERSHIP:

     7A-302   LIQUIDITY AND EXIT:

     7A-303   THE SPECIFIC TERMS OF A BUY-SELL AGREEMENT:

         7A-303(a)   TRIGGERING EVENTS – THREE DS AND A BEER:

         7A-303(b)   TRIGGERING EVENTS – THE DETAILS:

         7A-303(c)   PURCHASE METHODS:

         7A-303(d)   PRICE:

         7A-303(e)   DIFFERENT PRICES FOR DIFFERENT TRIGGERING EVENTS:

         7A-303(f)   OTHER PROVISIONS:

     7A-304   TRANSFER RESTRICTIONS AND THIRD PARTY TRANSFEREES:

     7A-305   FUNDING THE BUY-SELL AGREEMENT:

     7A-306   TAXES AND THE BUY-SELL AGREEMENT:

7C-400 DEADLOCK IN THE LLC:

UNIT 7A

CLOSELY-HELD CORPORATIONS:

7A-100 SPECIAL ISSUES IN CLOSELY-HELD CORPORATIONS – INTRODUCTION:

As we discussed in earlier chapters, there are special tax issues and control issues for closely-held corporations.[259] In addition, there are three other major issues that are common in the context of the closely-held corporation: (1) the scope of fiduciary duties; (2) the transfer of shares; and (3) deadlock

The scope of fiduciary duties: Unit 6A discussed the fiduciary duties directors, officers, and controlling shareholders. The same fiduciary duties apply to the directors, officers, and controlling shareholders of closely-held corporations as well as large and publicly-traded corporations. However, the shareholders of a closely-held corporation also owe each other a **duty of good faith and fair dealing** that is analogous to the fiduciary duties partners owe one another in a partnership.[260]

In this unit, we will further explore the duty of good faith and fair dealing of the shareholders in closely-held corporations.

The transfer of shares: As a default rule, state corporate law statutes allow a shareholder to **freely transfer** her shares, even when her fellow shareholders oppose the transfer. A default rule permitting the free-transferability of shares is crucial to the shareholders of public corporations, but it might not be ideal for the shareholders of closely-held corporations. Shareholders in closely-held corporations approach the selection of their co-owners more like the partners in a partnership. Because the shareholders will often work closely with each other and because they might each bring specific skill-sets to the business, the benefits of maintaining the continuity of the shareholders might outweigh the benefits of shareholdings that are freely-transferable. For this reason, the shareholders of a closely-held corporations often enter **agreements that limit their rights to transfer their shares**.

The second issue related to the transfer of shares in a closely-held corporation is the **lack of liquidity**. Even when the shareholders are allowed to transfer their shares, there is usually no market for their shares. Essentially, the only

---

[259] For tax issues, see Chapter 3, §§3A-400 et seq., 3A-500 et seq., and 3A-600 et seq. For control issues, see generally Chapter 5, Unit 5A.

[260] See Chapter 6, §6B-202 et seq.

potential purchasers of their shares are their fellow shareholders and the corporation itself. For this reason, the shareholders of a closely-held corporation often enter **agreements that require the corporation or other shareholders to purchase their shares** upon the occurrence of specific events.

In this unit, we will further explore how shareholders in closely-held corporations draft their buy-sell agreements to address the free transferability of shares and the lack of liquidity.

Deadlock: When a disagreement between two sides in a closely-held corporation results in a stalemate, how does the law address this issue and how can the parties draft their shareholders agreement to address this possibility?

7A-200 FIDUCIARY DUTIES IN CLOSELY-HELD CORPORATIONS:

7A-201 TRADITIONAL FIDUCIARY DUTIES:

In Chapter 6, we discussed the traditional fiduciary duties of directors, officers, and controlling shareholders. These same fiduciary duties apply in the context of the closely-held corporation: the **directors and officers** of the closely-held corporation have fiduciary duties of **care, loyalty, oversight, and good faith**.[261] Naturally, a shareholder who is a director or officer in a closely-held corporation has the fiduciary duties that come with her office. In addition, the **controlling shareholder** of a closely-held corporation owes a fiduciary duty of loyalty to the corporation and the minority shareholders.[262]

7A-202 DUTY OF GOOD FAITH AND FAIR DEALING – THE BASICS:

In many jurisdictions, the shareholders of a closely-held corporation also owe each other a **duty of good faith and fair dealing** similar to the statutory duty of good faith and fair dealing that partners in a partnership owe each other. The duty of good faith and fair dealing in closely-held corporations is normally not statutory; rather, it is a common-law creation. It functions to **prevent a shareholder or group of shareholders from exercising control to freeze-out another shareholder**.

---

[261] See Chapter 6, §§6A-201 through 6A-209 for a discussion of these fiduciary duties.

[262] See Chapter 6, §6A-211 et seq. for a discussion of the fiduciary duties of controlling shareholders.

A freeze-out is where a **control person** or a **control group** denies a non-control person the **reasonable expectations** she may have from her investment in the business.

7A-202(a) EXERCISE OF CONTROL:

The duty of good faith and fair dealing in the closely-held corporation will only become an issue when a shareholder **exercises control** over the corporation. It is important to keep in mind that we are not necessarily looking for a shareholder who holds a majority of the stock. Instead, we are looking for circumstances where **any one shareholder, or several shareholders working together, can control the fate of any single corporate decision.** Of course, a shareholder who controls a majority of the stock and the board would usually be able to control any single corporate decision, but **there may be circumstances where a minority shareholder can exercise control over a corporate decision.**

A minority shareholder will have an opportunity to control a corporate decision when the shareholders agreement, the articles, bylaws, or the law give her control, usually in the form of a veto right:

Illustration 1:

The shareholders agreement requires approval of the shareholders representing 90% of the outstanding shares for any transaction exceeding $200,000.

Any shareholder (or group of shareholders) that holds more than 10% of the shares can veto a transaction exceeding $200,000.

Illustration 2:

The articles give Class C common shareholders the right to vote as a class on any merger transaction.

Those who control Class C common stock can veto any merger

Illustration 3:

The bylaws require the affirmative vote of 75% of the outstanding shares to approve any dividend.

Minority shareholders can work together as a group to vote down any dividend proposal.

In addition, a shareholder might exercise control through her position as director or executive officer of the company.

7A-202(b) FREEZE-OUT AND REASONABLE EXPECTATIONS:

Shareholders in closely-held corporations have expectations that are different from the expectations of the shareholders in public corporations. The shareholders of public corporations have minimal expectations regarding their control and economic rights. They expect the right to elect directors and vote on fundamental transactions. They also expect the right to share in any dividend, but only if the board decides to issue a dividend.

In contrast, the shareholders of a closely-held corporation might have reasonable expectations to one or more of the following:

Salaries from employment with the corporation

Dividends

Control

Traditional fiduciary duties and the business judgment rule provide little or no protection for the reasonable expectations of minority shareholders. Here are some illustrations:

Illustration 1:

In a closely-held corporation, a shareholder in control of the board of directors fires a minority shareholder from her position with the corporation. The minority shareholder is an employee-at-will.

If the minority shareholder challenges the action under traditional fiduciary duty law, she will have a possibly insurmountable burden. The firing of an employee is a business decision. Unless the decision involved self-dealing, the business judgment rule protects the decisions of the board of directors (and the controlling shareholder). In this case, self-dealing is not immediately apparent.

Illustration 2:

In a closely-held corporation, a group of shareholders with control of the board decides not to issue a dividend to any of the shareholders. The minority shareholders are unhappy with the decision.

Traditional fiduciary duty law provides no protection to the minority shareholders. The board has discretion to issue or withhold dividends. The business judgment rule protects this decision, unless there is self-dealing. In this case, self-dealing is not immediately apparent.

Illustration 3:

In a closely-held corporation, a group of shareholders with a majority of the outstanding shareholdings decides not to elect a minority shareholder to the board of directors. Traditional fiduciary duty law provides no protection to the minority shareholder. Shareholders are free to elect whomever they wish to the board.

7A-203 DUTY OF GOOD FAITH AND FAIR DEALING – THE DETAILS:

You have probably already spotted the conundrum that courts face in these situations: If we apply the business judgment rule and defer to the controlling shareholder's decision, the minority shareholder receives no protection. On the other hand, if we review all decisions that adversely affect the minority shareholders, we virtually eviscerate the business judgment rule and the board and the corporation will bear the burden of showing their decision was fair. Neither approach seems ideal.

As a practical matter, the courts must address the two issues. These are the same two issues we discussed in the context of the duty of good faith and fair dealing in the partnership in Chapter 6:[263]

> (1) Did the decision by the controlling shareholder cause a **transfer of wealth** from the minority shareholder to the controlling shareholder?
>
> and
>
> (2) Did those in control act in **bad faith**?

Although the duty of good faith and fair dealing could arise in any number of possible circumstances, there are **two common fact patterns**:

> Terminating the employment of a shareholder; and
>
> Decisions to issue or not issue dividends.

7A-203(a) DUTY OF GOOD FAITH AND FAIR DEALING – TERMINATING THE EMPLOYMENT OF A SHAREHOLDER:

Common fact pattern: In a closely-held corporation, a shareholder in control of the board of directors fires a minority shareholder from her position with the corporation. She is an employee-at-will. Courts will have to struggle with two issues:

---

[263] See Chapter 6, §6B-202 et seq. for a discussion of these issues in the partnership context.

<u>Issue 1</u>: Did the decision by the controlling shareholder cause a transfer of wealth from the minority shareholder to the controlling shareholder?

The corporation has one less salary expense. Fewer expenses translates into higher profits, and higher profits means a greater residual for the shareholders. Because every shareholder benefits by the increase in the residual, including the minority shareholder who was fired, it is hard to see how the decision to fire the minority shareholder results in a transfer of wealth to the controlling shareholder.

However, if we look at this through the lens of the closely-held business, the potential for a transfer of wealth becomes more evident. In many closely-held corporations, the shareholders expect to receive a "salary," which they view it as part of their return on their investment. When a shareholder loses her job and her salary, she loses that part of her return on her investment. In addition, she does not fully recapture the increased profit that results from eliminating her salary because she shares those savings with all the other shareholders.

Illustration:

The minority shareholder owns 25% of ABC Corp. She is also the CFO, receiving a salary of $100,000 year. The controlling shareholders, who own 75% of ABC, cause the board to fire the minority shareholder.

The corporation now saves $100,000 in expenses each year by eliminating the minority shareholder's salary, which means profits will increase by $100,000 each year.

Because the minority shareholder owns 25% of the corporation, $25,000 of the $100,000 increase in profits that results from her employment termination will inure to her benefit. In contrast, if she still had her job, she would capture the full $100,000 as salary.

Because the controlling shareholders own 75% of the corporation, $75,000 of the $100,000 increase in profits inure to their benefit. In contrast, if the minority shareholder still had her job and salary, the controlling shareholders would not capture any of the $100,000.

Thus, firing the minority shareholder results in a transfer of $75,000 of wealth per year from Mary to the controlling shareholders.

Of course, if the controlling shareholders had to hire a new CFO to replace her for the same salary, there would be not transfer of wealth.

When you analyze whether the termination of a shareholder from her employment with the corporation results in a transfer of wealth, you should also consider **whether she also loses her shareholdings.** The shareholders of a closely held corporation often enter into a shareholders agreement that gives the corporation or the other shareholders the **right to purchase shares of the terminated shareholder.**[264] If the controlling shareholders exercise the right to purchase the terminated shareholder's shares, does that result in a transfer of wealth from the terminated shareholder to the other shareholders? The answer depends on the purchase price.

You may remember from earlier discussions in Chapter 4 that there are many different ways to value a business.[265] There are lower valuations that do not reflect the true market value of the business, such as book value and liquidation. Book value and liquidation value do not reflect true market value of the business because they do not take into account the potential future earnings of the business.

If the controlling shareholders (or the corporation) **purchase the terminated shareholder's shares at book value or liquidation value,** the terminated shareholder has lost her share of the future earnings of the company without compensation, and the controlling shareholders have acquired it without paying for it. **This scenario results in a transfer of wealth.**[266]

In contrast, if the controlling shareholders (or the corporation) **purchase the terminated shareholder's shares based on the fair market value of the corporation,** the terminated shareholder has been fairly compensated for her share of the future earnings of the company. **In this scenario there is NO transfer of wealth.**

Issue 2: Did those in control act in bad faith?

The minority shareholder might have been an incompetent CFO. If so, the controlling shareholders might not have acted in bad faith by firing her. Could they show that she was incompetent as the CFO? Could they also show that her position as CFO was intended to be a real position, rather than just a vehicle to give the minority shareholder a portion of her return in the form of a salary. Do the other shareholders receive salaries? Are they competent in their positions? If the minority shareholder's position and salary were simply a means to provide her a return, it seems irrelevant that she performed incompetently as the CFO.

---

[264] See §7A-303 et seq., below.

[265] See Chapter 4, §4D-500 et seq.

[266] See Chapter 4, §4D-503 for illustrations on this concept.

In other words, firing her for incompetence was merely a pretext for freezing her out.

7A-203(b) DUTY OF GOOD FAITH AND FAIR DEALING – DECISIONS REGARDING DIVIDENDS:

Common fact pattern: In a closely-held corporation, a group of shareholders with control of the board decides not to issue a dividend to any of the shareholders. The minority shareholders are unhappy with the decision.

Issue 1: Did the decision by the controlling shareholder cause a transfer of wealth from the minority shareholder to the controlling shareholder?

When shareholders do not receive dividends, the residual claim increases. For example, if a corporation makes a $50,000 profit, but does not issue a dividend, the shareholders' residual (i.e., owners' equity on the balance sheet) increases by $50,000. Because all shareholders, including the minority shareholder, benefit from an increase in the residual, it is not immediately apparent how a decision to withhold dividends would cause a transfer of wealth to the controlling shareholders.

However, the controlling shareholders might give themselves dividends disguised in other forms: They might receive salaries, director's fees, trips to board meetings in exotic locations, company cars, company smart phones, etc. Because the minority shareholder does not share in these **disguised dividends,** the controlling shareholders have caused a transfer of wealth to themselves from the minority shareholder.

> *Illustration:*
>
> The minority shareholder owns 25% of ABC Corp. She receives no salary or other perquisites from the company. The controlling shareholders, who own 75% of ABC, decide that the company will not issue a dividend – let's just say that the dividend would have been $100,000 total, so that we have a number to work with.
>
> The residual claim of the corporation would increase by $100,000 because it does not issue a dividend. However, assume that the controlling shareholders decide to increase their total salaries and board fees by an additional $70,000 per year.
>
> If the corporation had issued the $100,000 dividend, the minority shareholder would have received $25,000 (she owned 25% of the corporation). In contrast, she received nothing of the $70,000 increase in salaries and board fees.
>
> Even if the corporation had simply retained the $100,000, the minority shareholder would have received $25,000 because she

360

has the residual claim to 25% of the retained earnings, although she would not have received any cash.

However, the controlling shareholders' actions of issuing themselves disguised dividends of $70,000 results in a much smaller residual claim for the minority shareholder – just $7,500, which is 25% of the $30,000 retained earnings. The controlling shareholders have managed to capture $92,500 of the $100,000 profits for themselves (i.e., $70,000 in salaries and fees plus 75% of remaining $30,000 in retained earnings).

Of course, a court would need to determine whether the salary and fee increases were indeed disguised dividends, or were they actually legitimate increases in salaries and board fees.

Issue 2: Did those in control act in bad faith?

If the controlling shareholders did not receive disguised dividends, it is hard to see how their actions are not in good faith. It would also help their cause if they could articulate a legitimate reason for retaining earnings, rather than distributing them. Did they have plans for the company to acquire new assets or take on new projects that require capital?

7A-204 THE MASSACHUSETTS APPROACH:

The approach of Massachusetts courts in these cases has received significant attention, but other courts have not consistently followed Massachusetts's lead. Massachusetts courts use a **burden-shifting test** when minority shareholders allege a freeze-out by the controlling shareholder in a closely-held corporation:[267]

> **The minority shareholder must make a prima facie case that the controlling shareholder acted in bad faith** (i.e., intent to freeze out the minority).

> The burden then shifts to the **controlling shareholder to show some legitimate business purpose** for her actions.

> Finally, the burden might then shift back to **the minority shareholder to show the corporation could have achieved the legitimate business purpose in a way that would have been less harmful** to minority interests.

---

[267] See *Wilkes v. Springside Nursing Home, Inc.*, 353 N.E.2d 657 (Mass. 1976).

You can see how this approach forces the court to explore the two major issues we have already discussed – (1) transfer of wealth; and (2) bad faith:

The first part of the test – **the minority shareholder must show bad faith** – requires the minority shareholder to show facts that raise the possible specter of bad faith, namely that the action by the controlling shareholder results in a **transfer of wealth** from minority shareholder to majority shareholder. Without this transfer of wealth, there is no need to question the good faith of the controlling shareholder.

The second part of the test – **the controlling shareholder must show a legitimate business purpose** – allows the controlling shareholder a chance to show she did not act in **bad faith**.

The third part of the test – **the minority shareholder must show that the legitimate business purpose could have been achieved in less harmful manner** – allows the minority shareholder a chance to rebut the controlling shareholder's arguments of **good faith** by showing the controlling shareholder legitimate business interest was just a **pretext**.

_____

7A-205 ALTERNATE APPROACH:

Other courts, such as Delaware, rely on the **traditional fiduciary duties of directors or controlling shareholders** to police the possible oppression of minority shareholders. In these jurisdictions, the minority shareholder must frame her cause of action as a duty of loyalty claim.

Where a shareholder with control of the board of directors fires a minority shareholder from her employment-at-will position with the corporation, the minority shareholders must frame the issue as a duty of loyalty issue.

She will have to make an argument that the controlling shareholder had a material financial interest in the decision to fire the minority shareholder. For example, she will try to convince the court that one less salary means lower expenses and greater profits for the corporation. However, because the shareholders all share the profit in proportion to their shareholdings, the increased profit inures to the benefit of both the minority and controlling shareholders. Without more, her duty of loyalty claim is specious at best.

The duty of loyalty claim has a much better chance if the shareholder can demonstrate that the salaries the shareholders received were **disguised dividends**. In other words, at least part of the "salary" the minority shareholder received for her employment with the corporation represented a return on her investment. By firing the minority employee, the controlling shareholder is effectively issuing dividends to herself in another form, and not the minority shareholder.

7A-206 DUTY OF GOOD FAITH WITHOUT A TRANSFER OF WEALTH:

Up to this point, we have discussed the duty of good faith and fair dealing in closely-held corporations in the context of an exercise of control by the controlling shareholders that results in a transfer of wealth from the minority shareholders to the controlling shareholders. However, there is a possibility that a court would protect minority shareholders even without a clear case for a transfer of wealth. If you run into such a case, consider the following explanations:

(1) There was an implicit transfer of wealth; or
(2) Denial of the minority shareholder reasonable expectations alone is sufficient.

Cases where it appears that the **denial of reasonable expectations alone**, without a transfer of wealth, is a sufficient basis for relief for a minority shareholder may be **better understood as contractual interpretation cases**, rather than good faith and fair dealing cases. At its most fundamental nature, the closely-held corporation is a long-term relational contract among the shareholders. The articles of incorporation and the bylaws are the basic contractual documents. If the parties have been careful, they will also have a shareholders' agreement that further describes the rights and obligations of the shareholders to one another and the corporation.

As you remember from your study of contract law, a party is liable for breaching of a contract regardless of whether she had a good reason for breach or whether the breach caused a transfer of wealth. We should look at the contract between the shareholders of a closely-held corporation the same way.

Illustration 1:

The shareholders of a closely-held corporation expressly agreed that each shareholder would have employment with the corporation, unless terminated for cause.

If the controlling shareholders use their control to fire the minority shareholder without cause, they have breached their contractual promise. It is not relevant whether they benefitted from some sort of transfer of wealth because of the firing.

363

Illustration 2:

The shareholders of a closely-held corporation expressly agreed that the corporation would issue dividends every year the corporation realized a profit.

If the controlling shareholders use their control to withhold a dividend in a year the corporation realized a profit, they have breached their contractual promise. It is not relevant whether they benefitted from some sort of transfer of wealth because of the decision.

In the two illustrations above, the contractual aspects of the cases were clear because they both stipulated that the shareholders "expressly agreed." In contrast, however, what if the shareholders had been less careful in describing their agreement? What if the articles and bylaws were boilerplate forms, and there was no written shareholders' agreement, or a shareholders agreement that only addressed a few basic issues? It is conceivable that the shareholders still had "*understandings*" about employment or dividends, although they did not expressly incorporate those understandings in the articles, bylaws, or the written shareholders' agreement.

One of the most basic doctrines of contract law is that the "contract" is not the written contract, but what the parties actually agreed upon. If they actually agreed to guaranteed employment or a specific dividend policy, this is their contract, even if it is not in their written agreement. Moreover, implicit promises and understandings between parties to a contract are also part of their "contract," even if not expressed orally or in their written agreement. When a court discusses the **reasonable expectations** of the shareholders of a closely-held corporation, we might translate that to mean the **implicit agreements and understandings** of the shareholders.

When the shareholders have implicit understanding that form their reasonable expectations, **we might anticipate that a court would decide the matter based on contract interpretation**, not based on the duty of good faith and fair dealing between the shareholders of closely-held corporations. **However, courts might decide some of these cases based on good faith and fair dealing for two possible reasons**:

(1) Lawyers for the aggrieved minority shareholders will make pleadings alleging both express and implicit contractual understandings, as well as good faith and fair dealing. The court's ultimate decision might not carefully distinguish between the contractual claims and the good faith claim or clearly state which doctrine was the basis for the decision.

(2) When the aggrieved minority shareholder wants to allege an express or implicit understanding that was not part of the written documents, the parol evidence rule becomes an obstacle. When there is any sort of

written agreement, the parol evidence rule will often prevent admission of evidence of any prior or contemporaneous understandings between the parties that is not expressly part of the written documents. Under some circumstances, the parol evidence rule will allow admission of the prior or contemporaneous understanding. In any case, a court might not view the duty of good faith and fair dealing to be subject to the parol evidence rule. Thus, if a particular judge is sympathetic to the aggrieved shareholder's claim, she might decide the case under the doctrine of good faith and fair dealing to avoid application of the parol evidence rule.

7A-207 REMEDIES FOR FIDUCIARY BREACHES IN THE CLOSELY-HELD CORPORATION:

7A-207(a) TYPICAL REMEDIES:

In the context of the closely-held corporation, remedies for the breach of fiduciary duties may differ from what we would expect in the public corporation.

In the **public corporation**, a defendant director that is liable for breaching her fiduciary duties will pay money damages to the corporation for its harm and/or disgorge any profits to the corporation.

In the **closely-held corporation**, the court might fashion other remedies when the controlling shareholder breaches her fiduciary duties to the minority.

The court might require the controlling shareholder to **disgorge any profits to the minority shareholders**, instead of to the corporation.

Similarly, the court might require the controlling shareholder to cause the corporation to give **equal treatment to the minority shareholders** – i.e., give the minority the same benefits the controlling shareholder received.

7A-207(b) INVOLUNTARY DISSOLUTION:

In most cases where the controlling shareholder systematically engages in oppression of the minority shareholder, the minority shareholder would simply prefer to get out of the situation. It is costly for the minority shareholder to challenge or sue the controlling shareholder every time the controlling shareholder abuses her control. The minority shareholder would prefer that the controlling shareholder or the corporation buy her out.

However, under state corporate law statutes, a shareholder does not have a right to demand the corporation, or the other shareholders, to buy her out. The only time a shareholder might have a right to force the corporation to buy her out is when the corporation undergoes a fundamental change, such as a merger, in which case the shareholder might have appraisal rights.[268] Other than that, a shareholder cannot simply say "I want out - - you must buy my shares."

The only way a shareholder can exit her investment is by finding a willing buyer for her shares. However, a cause of action for involuntary dissolution might give her the result she desires.

Involuntary dissolution simply means a court-ordered dissolution, usually at the request of one or more shareholders.[269] A court will only order the dissolution of a corporation under rare circumstances.[270] In some states, courts will grant a minority shareholder's request for involuntary dissolution to obtain a judicial order for dissolution **if the controlling shareholders have abused their control or mistreated the minority shareholder**.

Under the RMBCA, a court may order dissolution of the corporation at the request of a shareholder when those in control of the corporation **have engaged in oppressive conduct**.[271] Older versions of the RMBCA do not mention "oppressive conduct." Instead, in states that adopted earlier versions of the MBCA, the court may dissolve the corporation if those in control of the corporation **have acted in a manner that is illegal or fraudulent.**

The complaining shareholder must convince the court that the controlling shareholder breached the duty of good faith and fair dealing, and that the court should consider that breach to be "oppressive conduct" or "illegal or fraudulent activity," whichever the case may be under the particular corporate law statute.

Even if the minority shareholder can win on her dissolution claim, dissolution of the corporation and liquidation of its assets is probably not her preferred remedy. As we discussed in Chapter 3, the liquidation value of a business is normally low compared to its fair-market value as a going concern.[272] The company's true value is not in the assets alone, but in how it uses those assets to create a profit.

Illustration:

XYZ Corp has various assets that are worth $100,000. XYZ Corp uses these assets to generate $75,000 in profit each year. If the corporation dissolves and liquidates its assets, the shareholders will get $100,000. If

---

[268] For a discussion of appraisal rights, see Chapter 9, §§9A-102 and 9A-600.

[269] See Chapter 9, §9A-300 for a discussion of voluntary dissolution – where the shareholders vote to dissolve the corporation.

[270] See §7A-207(b), below, discussing involuntary dissolution when there is a deadlock.

[271] RMBCA §14.30(a)(2).

[272] See Chapter 4, §4D-501.

the corporation can sell itself as a going concern, its market value is worth more than $100,000 (clearly, a business that can generate $75,000 per year in profit is more than $100,000).

The minority shareholder would prefer to have the controlling shareholder buy her out, rather than see the corporation dissolved and liquidated. There are two possible ways the minority shareholder can use involuntary dissolution to persuade or force the controlling shareholder to buy her out:

Bargaining chip: The minority shareholder can use the threat of involuntary dissolution as a bargaining tool to get controlling shareholder to buy her out. The controlling shareholders would generally prefer to avoid the dissolution of the company and the liquidation of its assets. Indeed, the RMBCA expressly allows the controlling shareholder to purchase the minority shareholders' interest in order to avoid involuntary dissolution.[273]

Court-ordered buy out: Some courts may order a controlling shareholder who engaged in oppressive conduct to purchase the minority interest at fair-market value instead of ordering dissolution, even when the statute does not expressly authorize such a remedy. Courts have justified this approach by relying on their **powers of equity**: If the law allows them the power to order the drastic remedy of dissolution, equity allows them to fashion a less drastic remedy, such as forcing the controlling shareholder to purchase all of the minority shareholder's interest in the corporation.[274]

7A-300 TRANSFER OF SHARES:

The shareholders of a closely-held corporation should enter into what is often called a **buy-sell agreement** to address two issues:

Continuity of ownership; and

Need for liquidity.

The buy-sell agreement can be a stand-alone contract or it can be part of a larger shareholders agreement that addresses vote-pooling and other business and governance issues.

---

[273] RMBCA §14.34

[274] *Alaska Plastics Inc. v. Coppock*, 621 P.2d 270 (Alaska 1980).

7A-301 <u>**CONTINUITY OF OWNERSHIP:**</u>

Shares in a corporation are freely transferable, like any other type of personal property. A shareholder may **voluntarily transfer** her shares by selling them, hypothecating[275] them, or leaving them to her heirs in her will. A shareholder may **involuntarily transfer** her shares when they become part of her estate if she becomes bankrupt or dies intestate, or if a creditor forecloses on shares that the shareholder used as collateral for a loan.

The transferee of the shares becomes a shareholder in the corporation, with all appurtenant rights. In a large public corporation, the exit of the current shareholder and the admittance of a new shareholder creates no issues. However, in the closely-held corporation, exit and admittance of shareholders are major events.

The closely-held corporation is a corporation in name, but a partnership in spirit. The shareholders of the closely-held corporation often want to have control over the exit of current "partners" and the entrance of new "partners."

To illustrate the matter, imagine that you are a shareholder of a closely-held corporation. You have likely chosen your fellow shareholders carefully because their skills add value to the business, and you have a good working relationship with them. They have probably chosen you for the same reasons. If one of your fellow shareholders transfers her shares, not only has the business lost an asset, you now have to develop and manage a relationship with the new shareholder.

State corporate law statutes typically **do not allow shareholders to place an absolute prohibition on the transfers of shares**, but they allow some transfer restrictions, which are discussed in detail below.

7A-302 <u>**LIQUIDITY AND EXIT:**</u>

The term **liquidity** simply refers to how easy or difficult it is for you to turn an asset into cash. For example, my certificate of deposit with the bank is very liquid; I can turn it into cash at any time by surrendering it to the bank, even if I might have to pay a penalty for early withdrawal. In contrast, the 3½ acres of wooded land I bought several years ago has proved to be much less liquid – I have been unable to sell it for more than two years.

I also own shares in several public companies. These investments are almost as liquid as cash. If I wish to sell, I can simply log on to my online brokerage account, click on "sell at market price," and normally within a few minutes my

---

[275] Pledging the shares as collateral to secure a debt.

shares are sold and my account is credited with the respective cash (less brokerage fees). A shareholder in a public corporation can normally **exit her investment** (i.e., convert her investment into cash by selling her shares), with a relatively simple online transaction.

It is not as easy for a shareholder in a closely-held corporation to exit her investment. Imagine you are a shareholder in a closely-held corporation and you need cash to build your dream house, send your child to college, or pay medical bills, etc. You would like to be able to exit your investment by selling all or a portion of your shares so that you will have the cash you need. There are two obstacles for you to sell your shares:

(1) You and your fellow shareholders may have put **transfer restrictions on your shares**; and

(2) There is really **no ready market for your shares**. Shares in a closely-held corporation are very different from shares in a publicly company. There is a large, fluid market for shares in a public company. Public companies often list their shares on national stock exchanges, such as the New York Stock Exchange or Nasdaq, promoting the development of a robust market for their shares. There is no similar market for shares in closely-held corporations.

Even if there were some sort of national exchange for shares in closely-held corporations, who would buy them? Investing in a closely-held business puts you at risk for fraud, poor management, sloppy bookkeeping, and questionable corporate governance. In other words, the information costs for investing in a closely-held corporation are quite high.

If you are a shareholder in a closely-held corporation, the **potential market for your shares consists almost entirely of your fellow shareholders**. The information costs are much lower for your fellow shareholders because they are already familiar with the operations, financial condition, management and governance of the company. They might be willing to purchase your shares and you might be willing to purchase their shares.

7A-303 **THE SPECIFIC TERMS OF A BUY-SELL AGREEMENT:**

A buy-sell agreement addresses continuity of ownership and liquidity in the closely-held corporation. Three broad issues provide the basic outline of the buy-sell agreement:

Triggering Events: What types of events should trigger the purchase or sale of shares?

369

Purchase Methods: When one of the events occurs, what happens to the shareholders shares? Does the corporation re-purchase them? Is it mandatory or an option? Do the other shareholders purchase them? Is it mandatory or an option? Is a third party allowed to acquire the shares and become a new shareholder?

Price: When the corporation or the other shareholders have an obligation or an option to purchase the shares, what price will they pay?

7A-303(a) TRIGGERING EVENTS – THREE Ds AND A BEER:

Buy-sell agreements usually address the following events, which are discussed in greater detail immediately below:

Death: What happens to a shareholder's shares when she dies? Do they just pass to her heirs, making the heirs shareholders?

Disability: What happens to a shareholder's shares if she becomes disabled?

Divorce: What happens to a shareholder's shares if she divorces?

Bankruptcy: What happens to a shareholder's shares if she becomes unable to pay her personal debts and goes through formal bankruptcy or other similar processes where her shares might be sold to help pay her debts?

Employment (and/or Expulsion): What happens to a shareholder's shares if she resigns from her employment from the company or if she is terminated?

Exit: What happens if a shareholder simply wants to exit her investment (i.e., liquidate or sell her shareholdings) because she needs the cash or simply wants to pursue other opportunities?

Retirement: What happens to a shareholder's shares if she retires from her position in the company?

A useful mnemonic device to remember these events is:

DDD BEER or **Three Ds and a beer.**

A former student said he was able to remember this device because after the end of his first semester in law school, he had three Ds and a beer.[276]

---

[276] Thank you Brian S.

7A-303(b) <u>Triggering Events – the Details:</u>

Each of the events raises an issue of continuity, liquidity, or both.

Death: What happens to a shareholder's shares when she dies? Do they just pass to her heirs, making the heirs shareholders? The death of a shareholder raises **both continuity and liquidity issues**.

> With regard to continuity, the surviving shareholders might not want to work with the deceased shareholder's spouse, children or other heirs. With regard to liquidity, the deceased shareholder might prefer to leave her heirs cash, instead of an illiquid investment fraught with potential business risks and internal governance issues.
>
> ***Sample clause 1:***
>
> Within 30 days after the death of any Shareholder, the Corporation shall purchase from the Decedent's estate all the shares owned by the decedent at the price and on the terms and conditions specified in this Agreement.
>
> ***Sample clause 2:***
>
> Upon the death of a Shareholder ("Deceased Shareholder"), the Deceased Shareholder's estate shall sell the Deceased Shareholder's shares to the remaining Shareholders and each other Shareholder shall buy Deceased Shareholder's shares in proportion to his or her respective ownership of all outstanding Shares (excluding the Deceased Shareholder's shares), or in such other proportion the remaining Shareholders otherwise agree to.

Disability: What happens to a shareholder's shares if she becomes disabled? Does she remain a shareholder? The disability of a shareholder raises **both continuity and liquidity issues**.

> With regard to **continuity**, the disabled shareholder might not have the ability to make the non-monetary contributions to the business that originally made her an attractive co-investor, such as her skills in management, finance, or negotiation.
>
> With regard to **liquidity**, the disabled shareholder might prefer to have cash immediately, instead of an illiquid investment in a closely-held business.

Sample clause 1:

If a Shareholder becomes either physically or mentally disabled and a physician or qualified mental health professional has issued an opinion that the disability will continue for twelve-months or longer, the remaining Shareholders will have an option to purchase all of the shares of the disabled Shareholder.

Sample clause 2:

Upon the physical or mental disability of a Shareholder that results in the inability of the Shareholder to perform his normal duties of employment for the Corporation for a period of six months or more ("Disabled Shareholder"), the Corporation shall purchase the Disabled Shareholder's shares, and the Disabled Shareholder or his legal representative shall sell the Disabled Shareholder's shares to the Corporation.

Divorce: What happens to a shareholder's shares if she divorces? Does her ex-spouse get half of the shares, making him a shareholder? The divorce of a shareholder raises **both continuity and liquidity issues**.

With regard to **continuity**, if the divorcing shareholder is required by law or agreement to transfer half of her shareholdings to the spouse, the spouse becomes a shareholder in the corporation. The other shareholders might not want to work with the shareholder's spouse.

With regard to **liquidity**, the divorcing shareholder and the divorcing shareholder's spouse might both prefer the spouse to have cash for any shareholdings to which he may be entitled.

> **Practice tip:** The shareholders' spouses should be parties to the buy-sell agreement and formally sign it. Naturally, they will only need to agree to the parts of the buy-sell agreement that may affect the community property rights that spouses might enjoy.

Sample clause 1:

If a Shareholder's shares are transferred involuntarily due to divorce or voluntarily as part of a divorce settlement, the other Shareholders shall have the option, but not the obligation to purchase all or some of the shares owned by the Shareholder.

Sample clause 2:

If the marital relationship of a Shareholder is terminated by divorce, and the Shareholder does not succeed to any interest the Spouse may have in the Shareholder's shares because of the marital relationship or otherwise ("Spouse's Interest"), the Shareholder shall purchase and the Spouse shall sell to the Shareholder the Spouse's Interest.

Bankruptcy: What happens to a shareholder's shares if she files for personal bankruptcy or goes through some similar proceeding? Do the shares become part the bankruptcy estate, making the bankruptcy trustee or subsequent transferee a shareholder? The bankruptcy of a shareholder raises **both continuity and liquidity issues**.

With regard to **continuity**, the surviving shareholders might not want to work with the ultimate transferee of the shares in the bankruptcy proceedings.

With regard to **liquidity**, the bankrupt shareholder (and her creditors) might prefer to have cash to satisfy her creditors' claims, instead of an illiquid investment in a closely-held business.

> **Practice tip:** Typically, the agreement will cover not only formal bankruptcy proceedings, but also other bankruptcy-like events such as, **assignment for the benefit of creditors; appointment of a trustee, receiver, or liquidator** for the person or for substantially all of the person's property.

Sample clause:

If a Shareholder (1) files a voluntary petition under any federal or state bankruptcy, insolvency or related law (2) is subject to an involuntary petition under any federal or state bankruptcy, insolvency or related law; (3) is subject to the appointment of a receiver, (4) makes an assignment for the benefit of creditors; or (5) is subject to attachment, assignment or other collection action with respect to his/her shares, the other Shareholders shall have the option to purchase all or a portion of the Shareholder's shares. Each surviving Shareholder shall purchase the available shares in proportion to his or her existing ownership interests, not including the shares owned by the selling Shareholder.

Employment (and/or Expulsion): What happens to a shareholder's shares if she resigns from her employment from the company or if she is terminated? Do we still want her as a shareholder? The end of a shareholder's employment with the corporation by firing or resignation raises **both continuity and liquidity issues**.

With regard to **continuity**, the other shareholders might not want the terminated shareholder to have any part in the business because the terminated shareholder will no longer make the non-monetary contributions to the business that originally made her an attractive co-investor.

With regard to **liquidity**, the terminated shareholder might be frozen out of all or some of the return on her investment. As we have discussed, a shareholder in a closely-held corporation will probably receive all or part of her return on her investment in the form of a salary.[277] When she is no longer employed by the corporation, she is frozen out of her return. She would like the corporation or other shareholders to purchase her shareholdings, so that she can reap some return on her investment, or at least retrieve her capital so she can find an alternative investment that will provide her an opportunity to receive a return.

> **Practice tip:** Typically, the agreement among the shareholders will expressly provide that a shareholder's employment may only be terminated for cause. For-cause termination reduces the potential for the controlling shareholder or the control group from freezing out a minority shareholder from investment returns that come in the form of salaries and employment benefits.[278]

Sample clause:

If a Shareholder's employment with the Corporation is terminated for any reason, the remaining Shareholders shall have the option, but not the obligation, to purchase all of the shares held by the terminated Shareholder at the price and on the terms provided in this Agreement.

Exit: What happens if a shareholder simply wants to exit her investment (i.e., liquidate or sell her shareholdings) because she needs the cash or simply wants out? She might have already found a willing buyer for her shares, or maybe she is hoping the other shareholders or the corporation will buy her out. The exit of a shareholder raises **both continuity and liquidity issues**.

---

[277] See §7A-202(b), above.

[278] See §7A-202(b), above.

374

With regard to **continuity**, if the exiting shareholder has a willing third-party buyer, the other shareholders might not want to work with the buyer.

With regard to **liquidity**, a shareholder who needs cash will have trouble finding a third party to buy her shares. She would like the corporation or other shareholders to purchase her shareholdings.[279]

Retirement: What happens to a shareholder's shares if she retires from her position in the company? Will she remain a shareholder through her golden years? The retirement of a shareholder raises **both continuity and liquidity issues**. Indeed, the continuity and liquidity issues with the retirement of a shareholder overlap with the employment and exit of a shareholder.[280]

With regard to **continuity**, if the retiring shareholder has a willing third-party buyer, the other shareholders might not want to work with the buyer. In addition, if the shareholder retires, she will no longer make the non-monetary contributions to the business that originally made her an attractive co-investor.

With regard to **liquidity**, the retiring shareholder would often prefer cash over an illiquid investment in a closely-held corporation. In addition, after retiring, she no longer receives a salary, which might represent all or a significant portion of her return on investment. Because she will most likely have difficulty finding a willing third-party buyer for her shares, she would like the corporation or other shareholders to purchase her shareholdings.

7A-303(c) PURCHASE METHODS:

There are several methods to deal with a shareholder's shares upon the occurrence of any of these triggering events:

Cross purchase: One or more of the other shareholders purchase the shares.

Sample clause:

Within 60 days after the death of a Shareholder, the surviving Shareholders shall purchase from the Decedent's estate all the shares owned by the Decedent.

Redemption: The corporation purchases shares.

---

[279] See §7A-302, above.

[280] "Three Ds and a BEE" was not as easy to remember as "Three Ds and a BEER."

Sample clause:

Within 60 days after the death of a Shareholder ("Deceased Shareholder"), the Corporation shall purchase from the Deceased Shareholder's estate all the shares owned by the Deceased Shareholder.

Hybrid/Combination: Some combination of cross purchase and redemption.

Sample clause:

Within 60 days after the death of a Shareholder ("Deceased Shareholder"), the Corporation will have the option to purchase from the Deceased Shareholder's estate all the shares owned by the Deceased Shareholder. If the Corporation declines to exercise this option, in whole or in part, the surviving Shareholders will have the option to purchase any remaining shares of stock owned by the Deceased Shareholder.

Third party purchase: The shareholder is allowed to transfer her shares to an outside third party.

If the agreement provides for a cross purchase, redemption, or combination of the two, it must state whether the other shareholders or the corporation are **obligated to purchase** the shares or whether they simply have an **option to purchase** the shares.

Obligation: The corporation or other shareholders have an obligation to purchase the shares upon the occurrence of the triggering event.

Option: The corporation or the other shareholders have a right, but no obligation to purchase the shares.

When the option contemplates a **current or pending offer from a third party**, the option will often take the form of a right of first refusal or a right of first offer:

Right of first refusal: If a third party offers to purchase a shareholder's shares, the corporation/other shareholders have the right to purchase the shares (at a set price or by matching the third party's offer, depending on how the agreement is drafted).

Sample clause:

When a Shareholder (the "Selling Shareholder") intends to accept a bona fide offer from a third party ("Third Party Offer") to purchase all or any portion of the Selling Shareholder's shares in the Corporation ("Offered Shares"), the Selling Shareholder shall provide the other Shareholders ("Offeree Shareholders") a copy of the Third Party Offer.

The Offeree Shareholders have the right, exercisable within thirty days of the receipt of the copy of the Third Party Offer, to purchase the Offered Shares from the Selling Shareholder at the same price and upon the same terms and conditions that are contained in the Third Party Offer ("Right of First Refusal").

If the total number of Offered Shares that the Offeree Shareholders intend to purchase exceeds the actual number of Offered Shares, the sale and purchase of the Offered Shares to the Offeree Shareholders will occur in the proportion to the number of shares owned by each Offeree Shareholders to the total number of shares of the Company owned by all of the Offeree Shareholders.

If the total number of Offered Shares that the Offeree Shareholders intend to purchase is less than the actual number of Offered Shares, the Offeree Shareholders are deemed to have refused to exercise the Right of First Refusal.

If the Offeree Shareholders do not exercise the Right of First Refusal before the expiration of Right of First Refusal, the Selling Shareholder is free to accept the Third Party Offer and complete the sale of the Offered Shares to the third party upon the terms and conditions set forth in the Third Party Offer. The completion of such sale must occur within 180 days of the expiration of the Right of First Refusal.

Right of first offer: If a shareholder wants to sell her shares, she must first offer them to the corporation/other shareholders at a specific price **before offering them to a third party**. The shareholder may only offer to sell to a third party after the other shareholders or the corporation has refused to purchase the shares.

Sample clause:

If a Shareholder ("Offering Shareholder") desires to dispose of any of her shares in the Corporation during her lifetime ("Offered Shares"), she shall first offer to sell her shares to the other Shareholders ("Offeree Shareholders") by giving them written notice specifying the purchase price, terms of payment and the number of shares offered for sale ("Offer").

Each of the Offeree Shareholders will have the option for thirty (30) days after receipt of the Offer to purchase her proportionate share of the Offered Shares. If any Offeree Shareholders declines to purchase her full proportionate share of the Offered Shares, the remaining Offeree Shareholders may purchase by the remaining Offered Shares.

If the Offeree Shareholders do not agree to purchase 100% of the Offered Shares before the expiration of thirty-day time period, the Offering Shareholder shall be under no obligation to sell any of the Offered Shares to Offeree Shareholders, but may dispose of such shares in any lawful manner; provided, however, the Offeror Shareholder shall not sell the Offered Shares on terms and conditions more favorable than the Offer without first giving the Offeree Shareholders the right to purchase the Offered Shares on the new terms and conditions.

7A-303(d) PRICE:

When a buy-sell agreement calls for the remaining shareholders or the corporation to purchase the selling shareholder's shares, it must establish a price. The buy-sell agreement will normally take one or more of the following general approaches to setting a price for the shares:[281]

Book value: A valuation of the shares based on the book value of the corporation is generally a **low valuation** of the business.

> ***Sample clause:***
>
> The Book Value of the Corporation means the amount of Total Shareholders' Equity as set forth in the Corporation's balance sheet, prepared in accordance with the accounting principles adopted by the Corporation and consistent with Generally Accepted Accounting Principles.
>
> The Book Value of each Share is determined by dividing (a) the Book Value of the Corporation, by (b) the number of Shares outstanding.

Adjusted book value: A valuation of the shares based on the liquidation value of the corporation is generally a **low valuation** of the business, although it will normally be higher than book value.

---

[281] See Chapter 4, §4D-500 et seq. for a more detailed discussion of valuation methods.

Sample clause:

The Adjusted Book Value of the Corporation means the net worth of the Corporation based on the assets and liabilities on the Corporation's balance sheet, prepared in accordance with the accounting principles adopted by the Corporation and consistent with Generally Accepted Accounting Principles, adjusted to take into account the fair market value of the Corporation's assets and liabilities.

The Adjusted Book Value of each Share is determined by dividing (a) the Adjusted Book Value of the Corporation, by (b) the number of Shares outstanding.

Fair market value: A valuation of the shares based on the fair market value of the corporation is a **higher valuation** of the business compared to book value, adjusted book value, and liquidation value.

When the parties choose "fair market value" or "fair value" as the purchase price, they must agree how to determine this value. There are a few approaches:

Formula: The parties can come up with a set formula to calculate the fair market value. The formula may be based on the discounted cash flow we learned in Chapter 4.[282] It may be based on a multiple – e.g., 3 times the company's profits.

> ***Sample clause:***
>
> The Fair Value of the Corporation is three times the Corporation's EBITDA for the most recently concluded fiscal year based on the Corporation's financial statements prepared in accordance with accounting principles adopted by the Corporation and consistent with Generally Accepted Accounting Principles.
>
> The Fair Value of each Share is determined by dividing (a) the Fair Value of the Corporation, by (b) the number of Shares outstanding.

Experts/Appraisal: Sometimes the buy-sell agreement will leave the decision up to a valuation expert, such as a certified public accountant. Others will require each party to choose her own expert to determine the fair market value of the company, and then a third expert will make the final decision.

---

[282] See Chapter 4, §4D-300 et seq. for a more detailed discussion of discounted cash flow.

Sample clause 1:

The purchase price of the Shares is the value of the shares set by appraisal. Within fourteen days after an event requiring the determination of purchase price, the Corporation and the selling Shareholder shall mutually select a qualified appraiser to appraise the Corporation and determine a value for its Shares.

Sample clause 2:

The Purchasing Shareholder and the Selling Shareholder shall each name one appraiser, who will work together to determine the value of the Selling Shareholder's Shares. If the two appraisers cannot agree upon the value, they shall appoint a third appraiser. If the third appraiser agrees with either of the original appraisals, the value of such appraisal is binding on the parties. If the third appraiser does not agree with either of the original appraisals, the arithmetic mean of the original two originally appraised values will be binding on all parties.

Agreed Price: One approach is for the parties to meet regularly to agree upon the purchase price for the buy-sell agreement.

Sample clause:

The Corporation and the Shareholders agree that unless and until a new value is established as herein provided, the value of the Shares is One Thousand Dollars ($1,000.00) per share.

Within thirty days following the end of each fiscal year, the Corporation and the Shareholders shall agree upon the value of each share of stock. If the parties fail to determine a value for a particular year, the last stipulated value will control.

Practice note: I once asked a local attorney which valuation method he preferred when he drafted a buy-sell agreement. He said he preferred having the parties meet once a year to agree on a price. He told me that this gave him an opportunity to remind the shareholders about the terms of the buy-sell agreement each year. In addition, he said it helped him maintain regular contact with the corporation and the shareholders (the agreement provided that the meetings would take place in his office).

7A-303(e) DIFFERENT PRICES FOR DIFFERENT TRIGGERING EVENTS:

Buy-sell agreements will often have different purchase prices for different triggering events. For example, the price for a shareholder's shares upon her death might be based on the fair market value of the company, while the price for a resigning shareholder's shares might be based on the book value of the company.

As the lawyer who is drafting the buy-sell agreement, you must determine what price to use. Let's go through a simple series of scenarios designed to get you to think about why a lawyer might choose a specific price in buy-sell agreement.

The set up:

Imagine you are drafting a buy-sell agreement. Your client is one of the shareholders. You could ask your client what price she would prefer for each of the possible triggering events, but this is not the best approach. Your client might not fully understand the reasons for and the consequences of the various choices. Even if your client does understand, it is your job to create a draft agreement that will provide a basis for your discussions with your client before sending a proposed draft to the other shareholders and their legal counsel.

As you consider each of the following scenarios, you must keep in mind that the shareholders want to create a purchase price structure for the buy-sell agreement that provides the shareholders with the proper incentives to invest in the success of the business.

Scenario 1 – resignation:

The buy-sell agreement will address what happens to the shares of a shareholder who resigns from her employment with the corporation.

If you draft the agreement to **require the corporation to purchase the resigning shareholder's shares at fair market value**, which is a high valuation, you will give the shareholders negative incentives. Your object is to draft an agreement that will maximize the shareholders' incentives to make individual efforts to contribute to the success of the business and to be cooperative with the other shareholders. However, if a shareholder has the opportunity to receive fair market value if she resigns, resignation might become a more attractive option than working hard and trying to resolve conflicts with other shareholders.

Of course, if you draft the agreement so that the corporation or the other shareholders have an option, not a requirement, to purchase the resigning shareholder's shares at fair market value, a shareholder's incentives to resign in order to be cashed out at a high valuation are mitigated. However, she now has some incentives to become the problem shareholder, hoping that the other shareholders will buy her out. Although the other shareholders might offer less than fair market value, drafting fair market value in the buy-sell agreement gives the resigning shareholder negotiating power.

In contrast, if the buy-sell agreement gives the **other shareholders the option to purchase the resigning shareholders at book value** the shareholders have a disincentive to resign from her employment with the corporation.

Sample clause:

Any Shareholder may voluntarily resign from her positions with the Corporation ("Resigning Shareholder"). The remaining Shareholders will have the option to purchase the Resigning Shareholder's Shares for the Book Value of the Shares.

Scenario 2 – death:

The buy-sell agreement will address what happens to the shares of a shareholder who dies.

You should first consider what objectives your client has in protecting and providing for her family when she dies. She would prefer her family to receive the highest amount possible. The other shareholders would want the same. All the shareholders would probably favor requiring the corporation to purchase the deceased shareholder's shares at fair market value, based on their desires to protect and provide for their families.

You should also consider the well-being of the corporation and the surviving shareholders, which may include your client. If they are required to purchase the deceased shareholder's shares at fair market value, will the corporation have sufficient funds to operate? If the corporation takes out a life insurance policy on each of the shareholders, it can fund the repurchase of the deceased shareholder's shares without creating a financial crisis for the corporation.

Finally, you should consider whether drafting a mandatory purchase of the deceased shareholder's shares at fair market value would create negative incentives for the shareholders. Generally, people have an incentive to avoid death for obvious reasons, so one would not expect a shareholder to use death as a pretense to forcing the corporation to buy her out at fair market value.

Sample clause:

Upon the death of a Shareholder, the Shareholder's estate, or beneficiary or beneficiaries, as the case may be, have the right to require the Corporation to purchase the Shares of the deceased Shareholder at the Fair Market Value of the Shares.

Keep in mind that what your client wants *ex ante* might differ from what she wants *ex post*. You will draft the buy-sell agreement (and any other contract) based on what is best for your client *ex ante*, but clients tend to look at the effect of contractual provisions *ex post*, unfortunately.

Illustration:

You represent one shareholder in a closely-held corporation. It is your task to draft the buy-sell agreement she will sign, along with the other shareholders. You draft a buy-sell agreement that gives the corporation and the other shareholders an **option** to purchase the shares of any shareholder who resigns her employment with the corporation, at **book value**.

Ex ante, this is best for your client because it gives the shareholders proper incentives to work hard on the business and resolve internal conflicts.

Imagine that sometime after the parties have signed the buy-sell agreement, your client's relationship with the other shareholders deteriorates. Your client feels the other shareholders are acting incompetently and she wants to exit her investment. She discovers that if she resigns from her job with the corporation, the most she will receive is the book value of her shares (and she might not even receive that much because neither the corporation nor the other shareholders are required to buy her shares). From your client's perspective *ex post*, you have not drafted an agreement that best serves her interests.

Practice tip: Ultimately, you can only draft an agreement that best serves your client's interests *ex ante*, but clients do not always understand this. To avoid these types of problems with your clients, you might walk your client through the draft agreement to explain how it operates.

7A-303(f) OTHER PROVISIONS:

There are other provisions you might see in a buy-sell agreement or other shareholders agreement:

Drag along right: A "drag along" is an agreement between two shareholders providing that if either one finds a third party to buy her shares, she may force the other shareholder to sell to the third party, usually at the same price.

Illustration:

Bob and Mary are the only two shareholders of a closely-held corporation. Bob holds 51% of the outstanding shares, and Mary holds the remaining 49%. They have a shareholders' agreement that provides:

If a third-party purchaser makes a bona fide offer to one or more Shareholders that individually or in the aggregate hold more than fifty percent of the Corporation's outstanding Shares ("Offeree Shareholder(s)") to purchase all of the Shares of the Corporation ("Offer"), the Offeree Shareholder(s) have a right to require the remaining Shareholders to sell all of their Shares in the Company to the third party purchaser.

The terms on which the remaining Shareholder(s) are required to sell their Shares must be the same terms the Offeree Shareholder(s) receives for their Shares.

This drag-along provision provides a controlling shareholder with a better opportunity to sell her controlling interest. Most buyers of closely-held corporations want to acquire 100% control. They do not want to have to deal with minority shareholders. The drag-along allows the controlling shareholder to deliver 100% of the stock without owning 100%.

Tag along right: A "tag along" is an agreement between two or more shareholders providing that if one finds a third party to buy her shares, she must include the other shareholders in the sale to the third party along with her own shares.

Illustration:

Bob and Mary are the only two shareholders of a closely-held corporation. There are 1,000 shares issued and outstanding. Bob holds 501 of the outstanding shares, and Mary holds the remaining 499. They have a shareholders' agreement that provides:

> If a third-party purchaser makes a bona fide offer to one or more Shareholders that individually or in the aggregate hold more than fifty percent of the Corporation's outstanding Shares ("Offeree Shareholder(s)") to purchase more than fifty percent of the outstanding Shares of the Corporation ("Offer"), the remaining Shareholders have a right to require the Offeree Shareholders to include their Shares in the sale to the third party, in proportion with their relative shareholdings and on the same terms and conditions as the Offeree Shareholder.

A third party wants to acquire a controlling interest in the corporation by purchasing 501 of the outstanding shares, and begins negotiations with Bob. The above provision will give Mary the right to include a portion of her shares in the sale of shares to the third party. As Bob negotiates with the third party, he must keep in mind that if he agrees to sell his

501 shares to the third party, effectively he will be required to include approximately 250 of Mary's shares and only 251 of his owns shares.

The tag along provision provides some liquidity for the minority shareholder, where she would otherwise have none. It also provides the minority shareholder an opportunity to share in any control premium the third party is willing to pay[283] because the tag-along usually requires the minority interest be purchased at the same price as the control interest.

Solomon's choice (or "Russian roulette" or "Shotgun buyout"): The Solomon's choice clause is an agreement between shareholders that creates a mechanism whereby a Shareholder A can force Shareholder B to make a choice between either selling all her shares to Shareholder A or purchasing all of Shareholder A's shares. In either case, one of the parties will be bought out and the other will remain a shareholder in the corporation.

Usually, the Solomon's choice clause is triggered by a deadlock between the shareholders of some other major disagreement about the management of the business or the governance of the corporation. However, it could also be triggered after a certain period of time or at-will by one of the shareholders, depending on how the clause is drafted. The Solomon's choice clause has a very ingenious design:

Step 1: Shareholder A offers to buy all of Shareholder B's shares for x dollars per share.

Step 2: Shareholder B must now decide between two alternatives:

(1) She must sell all of her shares to Shareholder A at the price Shareholder A offered (and Shareholder A will then be obligated to purchase Shareholder B's shares at that offered price); or

(2) She must purchase all of Shareholder A's shares at the price Shareholder A offered for her shares (and Shareholder A will then be obligated to sell her shares to Shareholder A at that price).

Illustration:

Bob and Mary are the sole shareholders of XYZ Corp. Their shareholders agreement has a Solomon's choice clause that is triggered by a disagreement between the shareholders regarding certain, specific major business decisions. The clause provides:

A shareholder ("Initiating Shareholder") may offer to purchase all of the Shares of other shareholder ("Responding

---

[283] See Chapter 6, §6A-211(e), discussing controlling shareholder sale of the control premium.

Shareholder") at a specified price per share ("Offer Price").
The Responding Shareholder shall choose between:

(1) Accepting the offer, and selling its Shares to the Initiating
Shareholder at the Offer Price, in which case the
Initiating Shareholder shall purchase all of the
Responding Shareholder's Shares at the Offer Price;

or

(2) Rejecting the Offer, and purchasing all the Initiating
Shareholder's Shares at the Offer Price, in which case the
Initiating Shareholder shall sell all of its Shares to the
Responding Shareholder at the Offer Price.

Bob and Mary have a major disagreement regarding one of the
events specified in the Solomon's choice clause. Bob offers to
purchase all of Mary's shares for $10 per share. Mary must now
make a choice – she can either sell all her shares to Bob for $10
per share; or she can purchase all Bob's shares for $10 per share.
After Mary makes her choice and the parties complete the transfer,
there will only be one remaining shareholder, Bob or Mary.

The design of the Solomon's choice clause encourages the offering shareholder
to offer a fair purchase price for the other shareholder's shares. If she offers a
price too low, the other shareholder will reject the offer and purchase the
offering shareholder's shares at the same low price.

Illustration:

Bob and Mary are the sole shareholders of XYZ Corp. Their
shareholders agreement has a Solomon's choice clause that has
been triggered by an event specified in the agreement.

Bob wants to take advantage of the situation to buy Mary out at a
low price. He and his advisors estimate that the corporation's fair
market value translates into a per share value of about $9 to $11.

If Bob offers to purchase Mary's shares at the low price of $5 per
share, he runs the risk that Mary will reject his offer; which will
obligate Bob to sell his shares to Mary at the bargain price of $5
per share.

One major shortcoming of the Solomon's choice clause is that it always **favors
the party with the better access to capital**. In other words, it usually favors
the wealthier party.

386

Illustration:

Bob and Mary are the sole shareholders of XYZ Corp. Their shareholders agreement has a Solomon's choice clause that has been triggered by an event specified in the agreement.

Bob wants to take advantage of the situation to buy out Mary at a low price. He and his advisors estimate that the corporation's fair market value translates into a per share value of about $9 to $11. Bob also knows that Mary does not have the cash to purchase Bob's shares for anywhere close to fair market value.

Bob offers to purchase Mary's shares for $7.50 per share.* Mary would like to reject Bob's offer, but she cannot raise the funds to purchase Bob's shares. Her only choice under the Solomon's choice clause is to accept Bob's offer.

*__Note:__ Bob cannot offer a price that is too low. The lower the price, the better the chance Mary will be able to convince someone to lend her the capital.

You might recognize the **potential good faith and fair dealing issue** that the exercise of the Solomon's choice clause presents. There is a possibility a court would find the offeror has breached her duty of good faith and fair dealing when she made an unreasonably low offer in an attempt to take advantage of the offeree's poor financial situation.[284]

7A-304 **TRANSFER RESTRICTIONS AND THIRD PARTY TRANSFEREES:**

A shareholder's transfer of her shares in violation of a contractual transfer restriction is obviously a breach of contract, for which the shareholder will be liable, but what happens to the shares? Can the other shareholders prevent the transfer to the third party purchaser and refuse to enter the name of the transferee in the shareholder ledger? Can the third party purchaser force the corporation to recognize the transfer?

Generally, the law will protect the good faith third-party purchaser. If the third party is aware there is a transfer restriction on the shares, the law will not require the corporation to recognize the transfer. To put third parties on notice that the shares are subject to a transfer restriction, the parties will place a legend on the actual share certificates. Here are two examples:

THE SHARES REPRESENTED BY THIS CERTIFICATE ARE SUBJECT TO THE TERMS OF A SHAREHOLDERS AGREEMENT. NO SALE,

---

[284] See §7A-203 et seq., above, and Chapter 6, §6B-202 et seq.

TRANSFER, ASSIGNMENT, HYPOTHECATION, PLEDGE, OR ANY OTHER DISPOSITION OF THE SHARES REPRESENTED BY THIS CERTIFICATE IS PERMITTED, EXCEPT IN ACCORDANCE TO THE TERMS OF THE SHAREHOLDERS AGREEMENT.

or

THESE SHARES ARE SUBJECT TO TRANSFER RESTRICTIONS UNDER A BUY-SELL AGREEMENT AMONG THE CORPORATION AND ITS SHAREHOLDERS,

The RMBCA expressly states that the transferee will be bound to a valid transfer restriction if noted **conspicuously** on the share certificate.[285] Normally, to make the notation conspicuous, it is drafted in all capital letters or in bold type.

7A-305 FUNDING THE BUY-SELL AGREEMENT:

Another important issue for the buy-sell agreement is how the corporation or other shareholders will fund their purchase of a shareholder's shares pursuant to the agreement. There are several common funding options for buy-sell agreements: insurance products, sinking funds, and installment payments.

> **Insurance products:** For a purchase of shares upon the **shareholder's death**, the corporation can take out a life insurance policy for each of the shareholders and use the proceeds to purchase the shares. If the buy-sell agreement envisions a cross-purchase, the shareholders can take out life insurance policies on each other. The buy-sell agreement might require the corporation to pay the premium for these life insurance policies.
>
> ### Sample clause 1:
>
> In order to assure that all or a substantial part of the purchase price for the shares of a Deceased Shareholder will be available immediately in cash upon his death, the Corporation shall procure and maintain insurance upon the life of each Shareholder.
>
> ### Sample clause 2:
>
> Each Shareholder will take out, and be the beneficiary of, a life insurance policy for the life of each other Shareholder. The death benefit of the policy shall be an amount reasonably calculated to

---

[285] RMBCA §6.27(b)

fully pay for the Shareholder-beneficiary's share of the Purchase Price for the Deceased Shareholder's Shares.

Each Shareholder shall take any action that is reasonably necessary to maintain all of the insurance policies she is required to maintain under this provision, and will not cancel them or allow them to lapse without the prior written consent of each other Owner. Each Shareholder shall pay every premium on any life insurance policy that she is required to maintain under this provision.

Certain life insurance products will have a cash value that can be redeemed before the death of the insured. These types of policies can help fund the purchase of shares under a buy-sell agreement for events other than the death of a shareholder.

There are also insurance products that will cover the **disability** of a shareholder and help fund a purchase of a disabled shareholder's shares. Of course, it is important to make sure the definitions of disability under the policy and the buy-sell agreement are consistent with one another.

Sinking fund: The buy-sell agreement might require that the company create an accounting reserve to cover redemptions for any event specified under the agreement.

Installment payments: The buy-sell agreement might allow the purchaser to pay for the shares in installments and at an appropriate rate of interest. This method is particularly useful when the corporation or the shareholders may not have the cash reserves that would allow them to purchase the shares.

> *Sample clause:*
>
> The Purchasing Shareholder shall pay the Selling Shareholder twenty-five percent of the Purchase Price in cash immediately upon the transfer of the Shares and the remaining portion in sixty equal monthly installments of principal and interest compounded annually at the prime rate as listed in the Wall Street Journal on the date of the transfer of Shares.
>
> The Purchasing Shareholder shall execute a negotiable promissory note as evidence of this debt that allows prepayment in whole or in part of the principal balance of the note at any time without penalty or premium. Payments will be applied to interest first.

389

7A-306 **TAXES AND THE BUY-SELL AGREEMENT:**

There are quite a few income tax issues related to the structure and drafting of a buy-sell agreement. Most of these tax issues are best left to an advanced taxation course that covers business entity taxation. However, since you are already familiar with pass-through taxation for S-corps, you should be aware of how the buy-sell agreement might affect the S-corp entity.

Prohibited transfers in S-corps: Remember that there are certain conditions that a business organization must meet to qualify for S-corp status.[286] Several of these qualifications are related to **the identity of the shareholders**:

Shareholders must be **citizens or resident aliens**

Shareholders must be **natural persons** (with a few exceptions for non-profit entities, certain trusts and estates, and single-member LLCs).

In addition, an S-corp may have **no more than 100 shareholders**, with special counting rules for family members.

The buy-sell agreement should prohibit any transfer of shares that would undermine the corporation's S-corp status. Although the law generally disfavors absolute prohibitions on the transfer of property, the RMBCA expressly allows absolute prohibitions "to maintain the corporation's status when it is dependent on the number or identity of shareholders."[287]

Sample clause:

Shareholder shall not transfer Shares to any person if the transfer might reasonably be expected to result in a termination of the Corporation's subchapter S election. Any transfer in violation of the provision is void.

Buyout rights for shareholders in S-corps: You will also recall that an S-corporation may only have one class of shares with respect to economic rights.[288] Typically, the IRS has focused on whether the articles, bylaws, and shareholder agreements provide all the shares with the same rights to distributions and liquidation rights. However, the redemption rights under buy-sell agreements might also undermine the corporations S-corp status if they effectively create more than one class of stock.

---

[286] See Chapter 3, §3A-404.

[287] RMBCA §6.27(c)(1)

[288] See Chapter 3, §3A-404.

Illustration:

Alice and Carol are the only two shareholders of a closely-held corporation. They each hold 100 shares. They have elected Subchapter S taxation in order to receive pass-through tax treatment.

Their buy-sell agreement provides that the corporation will purchase Alice's shares upon her death at **fair market value**, and Carol's shares upon her death for **book value**. These redemption provisions in the buy-sell agreement create different buyout rights for shares held by Alice and Carol.

Does the corporation runs the risk of losing its S-corp status because of the different redemption prices under the buy-sell agreement?

Under relevant tax regulations, buy-sell agreements will not undermine S-corp status unless two conditions are met:[289]

1) A principal purpose of the agreement is to circumvent the one-class requirement of Subchapter S; and

2) The purchase price at the time the agreement is entered into is "significantly in excess of or below the fair market value of the stock."

The regulations provide some more guidance on what price is considered to be "significantly in excess of or below" fair market value. According to the regulations, buy-sell agreements that provide a purchase price or redemption price for stock at **book value** or **between fair market value and book value** are **not** considered to have a price that is significantly in excess of or below the fair market value of the stock.[290] Furthermore, the regulations state that bona fide agreements for the purchase or **redemption of stock at death, divorce, disability, or termination of employment are disregarded** in determining whether shares confer identical liquidation and distribution rights.[291]

Under our illustration, it seems that Alice and Carol's buy-sell agreement will not undermine the corporation's S-corp status because it creates different economic rights. It uses book value as the price to redeem Carol's shares, which the regulations provide will not create a second class of stock. Furthermore, the agreement between Alice and Carol is a bona fide agreement for redemption of stock at death, which should be disregarded under the regulations in determining whether there is more than one class of stock.

---

[289] I.R.C. Reg. §1.1361-1(1)(2)(iii)(A).

[290] I.R.C. Reg. §1.1361-1(1)(2)(iii)(A).

[291] I.R.C. Reg. §1.1361-1(1)(2)(iii)(B).

Once again, it is important for you to work with your client's tax advisors if you do not have the requisite expertise.

7A-400 DEADLOCK IN THE CLOSELY-HELD CORPORATION:

7A-401 DEFINING DEADLOCK:

A deadlock arises when the corporation must choose between two or more courses of action, but the board of directors or the shareholders cannot decide on any one of the choices. A deadlock can occur when none of the possible potential courses of action receives support of the majority of directors. This can happen when there are an even number of directors on the board, or when only an even number are voting due to absences or abstentions.

When the vote belongs to the shareholders, a deadlock can occur when none of the possible potential courses of action receives support of the majority of shares. Alternatively, a shareholder voting agreement might give any one shareholder a veto right on certain important decisions. When the shareholders each veto the proposed courses of action, there is a deadlock.

Please note that simply disagreeing with the majority decision does not constitute a deadlock.

> ### *Illustration:*
>
> Mary is a shareholder of ABC Inc. She owns 30% of the outstanding shares and controls one of five seats on the board of directors. Bob owns the remaining 70% of the outstanding shares and controls four of the five seats on the board of directors.
>
> The board is considering entering into a rather risky transaction. Mary is firmly against the transaction, but Bob thinks the transaction is the best course of action for the company.
>
> Mary tries to convince Bob not to pursue the transaction. She is not successful. Bob tries to convince Mary that entering the transaction is a good opportunity for the company, but he is not successful.
>
> There is a disagreement between the two shareholders, BUT **there will be no deadlock**. Bob's control of four board seats allows him to control the decision.

In the strictest definition of the term, when there is deadlock, the status quo must not be an option.

392

Illustration:

Bob and Mary are shareholders of XYZ Corp. They share equal power on the board of directors. XYZ's leases a storefront where its sells its widgets. The lease expires at the end of the month, but it has an option to renew the lease agreement. Bob wants to renew the lease, but Mary wants to lease new premises in the next town.

The parties must decide between renewing the current lease and finding a new place to lease. The status quo would leave them without a place of business at the end of the month.

7A-402 DEADLOCK AND DISSOLUTION:

Under most state corporate law statutes, a shareholder may seek a court-ordered dissolution of the corporation when there is a deadlock, but the court will only grant such an application in the most extreme cases of deadlock. Under the RMBCA, deadlock alone is not a sufficient justification for a court-ordered dissolution of the corporation at the request of one or more of the shareholders.[292]

The RMBCA envisions that **if the board is deadlocked on an issue, the issue will be submitted to the shareholders for them to resolve.**[293] Of course, in a closely-held corporation, the board members and the shareholders are often one and the same, so there is a possibility that the shareholders will also be deadlocked on the matter. However, there are many circumstances where shareholders share equal voting power as members of the board of directors, but not as shareholders.

Illustration:

In a closely-held corporation, Bob and Mary are the only two shareholders. Bob holds 60 shares. Mary holds 40 shares. The shareholders' agreement, articles, and the bylaws all provide that the board will consist of two members. In the shareholders' agreement, Bob and Mary agree that each of them would hold a board seat.

The corporation's lease is about to expire. The board must decide between renewing the lease and finding a new location for the business. Bob favors renewing the lease. Mary favors finding a new location. The board is deadlocked because Mary and Bob have equal voting power on

---

[292] See RMBCA §14.30(a)(2)

[293] RMBCA §14.30(a)(2)(i).

the board. However, when the matter goes to the shareholders to resolve the deadlock, Bob will prevail – he holds 60% of the voting power.

If the shareholders are unable to resolve the deadlock, under the RMBCA, a court may only grant a request from one of the shareholders to dissolve the company if **"irreparable injury** to the corporation is threatened or being suffered, or the business and affairs of the corporation **can no longer be conducted to the advantage of the shareholders** generally, because of the deadlock." [294]

Courts are generally cautious about granting dissolution and have interpreted this requirement very narrowly. For example, if the deadlock simply results in a less profitable business, most courts would not consider the circumstances to implicate **irreparable injury** or indicate that the business could no longer be run to the advantage of the shareholders.

7A-403 DRAFTING FOR DEADLOCK:

Drafting a shareholders' agreement to address deadlock is very difficult. I learned this fact very early in my career. My first job as an attorney was as an associate in a large corporate law firm in the heart of the financial district in Manhattan. I felt completely lost. Everything was overwhelming to me. I felt like I did not understand anything I was doing. On my third day on the job, I was flying back to New York after working on a deal that completely baffled me. I was very stressed out. The woman sitting next to me on the plane began talking to me, and when she found out that I was a lawyer, she told me the story of how she and her husband had entered into a "partnership" with another couple.

The two couples had a disagreement that turned into a deadlock, effectively crippling operations. She and her husband sued the lawyer for malpractice. Her mention of a malpractice lawsuit merely enhanced the deep anxiety I was already feeling about my competence as a lawyer.

Her lawyer had drafted a "partnership agreement," but the lawyer settled the lawsuit, admitting that the partnership agreement lacked a crucial clause that would have resolved the problem. I was on the edge of my seat. I was completely lost as a new attorney, but now I had the opportunity to learn something crucial – the magic contract clause that would resolve deadlocks in closely-held businesses. If I knew nothing else, at least I would know this. I asked her what the missing clause was. She said she did not remember.

------

[294] RMBCA 14.30(a)(2)(i).

I now know that there is no magic contractual provision to deal with deadlock in closely-held businesses. There are several options, but none of them is perfect:

Avoid equal distribution of power: If possible, do not allocate an equal number of shares or board seats between two parties and avoid creating an even number of director seats. These strategies become difficult when the parties have made equal investments in the corporation. They also do not necessarily address the alliances that will naturally form when there are more than two shareholders or shareholder groups.

Use a Solomon's choice provision: As we discussed above,[295] the Solomon's choice clause eliminates deadlock by allowing one party to buy the other out, but it disadvantages the party without the cash to purchase the other party's shares. If you draft the Solomon's choice with an installment purchase option, the cash-poor party will be under less of a disadvantage.

Give one shareholder the deadlock-breaking vote: A shareholder's agreement can give the chairman of the board a deadlock-breaking vote. Normally, the chairman will be one of the shareholders. The benefit of this arrangement is that it reduces the costs of deadlock. The cost of this arrangement is that it increases risk for the shareholder that does not have the tie-breaking vote.

Require non-binding mediation: Although non-binding mediation does not ensure the problem will be resolved, having a third party work with the shareholders could promote some sort of solution.

Require binding mediation or arbitration: Requiring some sort of binding alternative dispute resolution procedure ensures the deadlock will be resolved. However, this solution will put an important business or governance decision in the hands of an outside arbitrator or mediator.

7A-404 DEADLOCK AND GOOD FAITH AND FAIR DEALING:

The duty of good faith and fair dealing does not help resolve deadlock situations. In deadlock situations, each side has a right to insist on its preferred course of action. As the stalemate progresses, the business might suffer harm. One might argue that a shareholder has a duty to capitulate when there is a deadlock in order to prevent the harm to the corporation. However, if that were the case, both sides would be under a duty to capitulate.

---

[295] See §7A-303(f), above.

There is a **well-known case** that illustrates the problem of requiring a shareholder duty to capitulate in the context of a deadlock.

In the case of *Smith v. Atlantic Properties Inc.*,[296] there were four shareholders in a C-corp. The shareholder's agreement gave each shareholder a **right to veto any distribution** to the shareholders.

The corporation had enjoyed profitable years and had to make a decision about what to do with the profits. The IRS notified the corporation that it had two choices: it could distribute its profits with dividends to the shareholders, or it could use its profits to make capital investments in the business, such as buying new equipment or repairing its buildings.[297] If they did neither, the IRS would levy stiff fines against the company.

Three of the four shareholders wanted to issue dividends. Because the corporation was a C-corp, the shareholders would pay income taxes on any distributions they received from the corporation. The fourth shareholder, Dr. Wolfson, did not want the corporation to issue dividends. He was in a higher tax bracket than the other three shareholders. It made more sense for his overall individual financial well-being for the company to use the profits to repair its existing buildings, rather than distributing the profits as a dividend.

Dr. Wolfson used his veto power in accordance with the terms of the shareholders' agreement to prevent the corporation from issuing a dividend. The other three shareholders tried to persuade him to allow the corporation to distribute the profits to the shareholders, but he would not move from his position.

In the end, the IRS fined the corporation because it did not issue a dividend or make capital investments. The three shareholders sued Dr. Wolfson, claiming he breached his fiduciary duty of good faith and fair dealing to the other three shareholders. The court agreed with the three shareholders, but commentators have been very critical of the court's decision. Can you see why?

One can easily focus on the selfish decision by Dr. Wolfson and the harm it caused to the corporation. However, there was an equally selfish decision by the other three shareholders: they insisted on distributing the profits, rather than making capital investments. It was better

---

[296] 422 N.E.2d 798 (Mass. 1981).

[297] C-corps are taxed at the entity level and the shareholder level. If a C-corp retains all its earnings and does not distribute them to the shareholders, the shareholders never pay tax on those earnings, reducing the federal government's tax revenue. See Chapter 3, §§3A-402 and 3A-403(a).

financially for the three shareholders to have the corporation distribute the profits, rather than re-invest them, just as it was better for Dr. Wolfson to have the corporation re-invest the profits, rather than distribute them.

It seems that each side shared equal blame for the resulting fines. Maybe we would look at Dr. Wolfson's actions differently if the IRS only gave one choice – distribute the profits, or otherwise face fines – but under the actual facts, there was another courses of action that the corporation could have taken in order to avoid the fines.

However, for some reason, the court held that Dr. Wolfson breached his fiduciary duties to the three. Did the court get it wrong? You know how the common law works: If a court makes a decision that appears incorrect, we try to find the reasons. In its opinion, the court stated that Dr. Wolfson acted out of "spite" for the other three shareholders, and not for any legitimate reason. Clearly, a deliberate attempt to harm the three other shareholders would be bad faith.

It is possible that Dr. Wolfson was acting out of spite, but not very likely. We have all seen situations where a relationship between individuals has deteriorated to the point where the original issue is no longer important and all that remains is a desire to injure the other party. But how likely is that the situation here? We know that Dr. Wolfson had legitimate tax reasons for opposing the dividend. We also know that the corporation had buildings that were in need of repair. Both of these facts lend support to the view that Dr. Wolfson was not acting out of spite.

The court may have found support for its finding that Dr. Wolfson acted out of spite in the fact that Dr. Wolfson did not come up with any kind of concrete plan for making the capital investments. However, should we look this fact as an indication of spite and bad faith on his part? I would think that any plan to make investments in the business would require the input and cooperation of all the shareholders. It should not fall on the shoulders of one shareholder. In addition, it is not as if the other three shareholders came up with a detailed plan for their preferred course of action. A distribution of profits does not require a detailed plan. When it comes to distributions, a dollar amount is a sufficiently detailed plan, in most cases. If a proposal with sufficient detail is a prerequisite of good faith, the simpler, less complicated proposals will always meet this requirement, but will not necessarily be the better course of action. We cannot support a rule that favors simple courses of action just because they require less detail.

Ultimately, deadlock seems a poor fit for an application of the duty of good faith and fair dealing unless one shareholder is acting out of spite.

UNIT 7B

<u>CLOSELY-HELD PARTNERSHIPS:</u>

7B-100 <u>SPECIAL ISSUES IN CLOSELY-HELD PARTNERSHIPS – INTRODUCTION:</u>

Because general partners bear personal liability for the debts of the partnership, the general partnership is always closely-held. The special issues that partnerships encounter are the same general issues that closely-held corporations encounter, although partnership default rules often address the issues differently from the default rules of corporate law. Just as we saw in Unit 7A of this chapter, an attorney providing advice in the context of a closely-held business must carefully consider fiduciary duties, transfer of ownership interests, and deadlock.

7B-200 **FIDUCIARY DUTIES IN PARTNERSHIPS:**

In Chapter 6, Unit 6B, we discussed the fiduciary duties partners owed to the partnership and each other.[298] Of particular importance in that discussion was the **duty of good faith and fair dealing** the partners owe one another. This duty is virtually the same as the duty of good faith and fair dealing among the shareholders of closely-held corporations.[299]

7B-300 **TRANSFER OF PARTNERSHIP INTERESTS:**

There are two important default rules for partnerships that are vastly different from those for corporations:

1) A partner may not transfer her partnership interests to a third party without the **consent of each of her partners**, although she may assign her economic rights to a third party.

2) A partner may, at any time, withdraw from the partnership and force the partnership to pay her for her partnership interest.

---

[298] See Chapter 6, §6B-202 et seq.

[299] See §7A-202 et seq., above.

7B-301 <u>TRANSFER TO A THIRD PARTY REQUIRES THE CONSENT OF EACH PARTNER:</u>

Continuity of ownership is even more crucial in the partnership than in the closely-held corporation because the partners are not protected with limited liability. In the partnership, each partner is jointly and severally liable for the debts of the partnership. This potential for personal liability means the partners will choose their co-partners carefully. They will choose people they trust will not cause unwise or unnecessary liabilities. They will also choose partners with personal wealth that is sufficient to meet their respective share of the partnership debts.

RUPA does not specifically state that a partner may not transfer her partnership interest without the consent of the other partners, but it explicitly states that the admission of a new partner requires the consent of all the partners.[300] As a result, a partner can **freely transfer her economic rights to a third party**, but the third party will not become a partner unless all of the other partners consent. The partners may change this rule by agreement.

As we have already discussed, the ownership interests in partnerships, corporations, LLCs, and any other business organization are comprised of **control rights and economic rights**. In the partnership, **a partner may freely transfer or assign her economic rights, but not her control rights**. In other words, a partner may freely transfer her rights to receive her share of partnership profits to a third party (e.g. through a contract, a will, etc.), but that third party would not become a partner. In contrast, a shareholder in a corporation may freely transfer her shares, which include both the economic rights and whatever control rights that shareholders have. Of course, a general partner's default control rights are far more extensive than the default control rights of a shareholder.

As a practical matter, you must understand how the default rules of partnership law operate when your client is involved in the transfer of a general partnership interest. If you represent the buyer, make sure your client receives what she is expecting. If she is expecting to become a full partner, the transaction should have as a condition precedent to the approval of all the other partners. If you represent the selling partner, you also need to protect your client with the same condition precedent.

Because the default rule protects the continuity of the partners, the partnership does not need a clause in the buy-sell agreement prohibiting the transfer of partnership interests. However, most partnership agreements do indeed have such a clause because the partners will look to the partnership

---

[300] RUPA §401(i).

agreement to understand their rights and obligations; they normally will not look to the relevant statute.

The partners may change the default transfer rule by unanimous agreement. In fact, the portion of the partnership agreement that deals with the transfer of partnership interests might look very much like the buy-sell agreement among the shareholders of a closely-held corporation.

7B-302 DISSOCIATION – TERMINATION OF PARTNER STATUS:

One very distinct characteristic of the partnership, compared to the corporation, is the number of ways a partner's status as partner can be terminated. Under RUPA, the termination of a partner's status is called "**dissociation**." The older approach under the UPA was to call the termination of partnership status "dissolution." Because most states have adopted RUPA, we will use the term "dissociation."

Dissociation is directly related to the issues of **continuity of ownership** in the partnership because dissociation terminates one's status as partner. Dissociation is also closely related to **liquidity** because, under the default rules, **partner dissociation requires the partnership to buy out the dissociated partner's partnership interest**.

7B-302(a) CAUSES FOR DISSOCIATION:

To get a better idea of how dissociation operates in a partnership, first consider how it works in a corporation. If you were a shareholder in XYZ Corp., how would you dissociate yourself from the corporation? The only way for you to terminate your status as shareholder is to transfer all of your shares, either voluntarily or by the operation of law (i.e., intestate transfer, bankruptcy, foreclosure by a secured creditor).

The situation in a partnership is very different. Under the default partnership rules of RUPA, **a partner's transfer of her partnership interest does NOT automatically result in termination of the partner's status**. When a partner "transfers" her partnership interest, she does not transfer the right to become a partner to the transferee. The transferee will only become a partner when each of the other partners consents to admitting the transferee as a new partner.[301]

---

[301] See §7B-301, above.

It helps to think of the **partnership interest as two separate interests**:

(1) **Economic interest:** The right to receive distributions from the partnership. Under RUPA, this economic interest is called the **partner's transferable interest**.

(2) **Control interest:** The right to be a "partner" and participate in the management of the partnership.

Actually, a shareholder's shares include the same two interests. When a shareholder "transfers" her shares, she transfers both interests as a bundle, and the transferee receives both the economic interest and the control interest that shareholders enjoy.

In contrast, **when a partner "transfers" her partnership interests to a third party, she is only assigning her economic rights**, which is called the "transferable interest" under RUPA. The transferee will only become a partner, with full partner participation and control rights, if the other partners unanimously consent to it. The other partners are under no obligation to consent, unless their partnership agreement otherwise provides.

Although the transfer of one's economic interest does not automatically result in one's dissociation from the partnership, there are several events under the default rules of RUPA that automatically result in dissociation. You will notice how the following list resembles the trigger events (DDD BEER)[302] a buy-sell agreement will normally address:

The **death** of a partner results in dissociation of that partner.[303]

> When the partner is a legal person, such as a corporation, LLC, non-profit entity, or some other organization, filing its articles of dissolution or equivalent with the secretary of state or other relevant authority is the functional equivalent of the death of a partner who is a natural person.[304]

The **disability** of a partner results in dissociation of that partner.

> You should note that RUPA separates dissociation because of disability to two categories: ". . . appointment of a guardian or general conservator for the partner; or . . . a judicial determination

---

[302] See §7A-303(a), above.

[303] RUPA §601(7)(i).

[304] The one major difference is that under RUPA 601(4)(iii), the legal-entity partner will have 90 days to revoke it articles of dissolution to avoid dissociation. The partner that is a natural person will not be able to revoke her death to avoid dissociation.

402

that the partner has otherwise become incapable of performing the partner's duties under the partnership agreement."[305]

The **bankruptcy** etc. of a partner results in dissociation of that partner.

Of course, similar to what we see in a typical buy-sell agreement, dissociation is triggered by proper bankruptcy proceedings and other bankruptcy-like events, such as executing an assignment for the benefit of creditors, or the appointment of a trustee receiver or liquidator for the partner or the partner's property.[306]

The **withdrawal** of a partner from the partnership results in dissociation of that partner.

A partner may withdraw at will and dissociate from the partnership, even if the partnership agreement provides otherwise. RUPA provides that a partner is dissociated as soon the partnership has notice of her "express will to withdraw."[307] We will discuss this right to withdraw at will in further detail, below.[308]

The **expulsion** of a partner results in dissociation of that partner.

You should take note that under RUPA, the partnership can only expel a partner according to the terms of a partnership agreement, and under certain limited circumstances when the other partners unanimously vote to expel a partner.[309] The parallel category in the buy-sell agreement in the closely-held corporation is the termination of a shareholder's employment with the company.

In all of the above cases, **when a partner dissociates, the default rules of RUPA require the partnership to purchase the dissociated partner's interest** in the partnership. We will discuss the purchase price in greater detail, below.[310]

7B-302(b) WITHDRAWAL AT-WILL (DISSOCIATION-AT-WILL):

Partnership law allows a partner to withdraw from the partnership at any time, regardless of a provision in the partnership agreement to the contrary. The

---

[305] RUPA 601(7)(ii)&(iii).

[306] RUPA §601(6). See §7A-303(b), above, for a discussion of drafting for these types of events in the buy-sell agreement.

[307] RUPA §601(1).

[308] See §7B-302(b), below.

[309] RUPA §601(4).

[310] See §7B-302(c), below.

withdrawal of the partner results in her dissociation. In other words, a partner may dissociate from the partnership even if the partnership is for an unexpired duration or even if the partnership agreement expressly prohibits a partner from withdrawing.

An important consequence of dissociation by voluntary withdrawal is that **the law requires the partnership to buy out the partnership interest of the withdrawing partner, even when her withdrawal breaches the partnership agreement**. However, when a partner withdraws in breach of the partnership agreement, she will be liable for any damages her breach causes to the partnership.

Illustration 1:

Betty is a partner of Partnership X. Pursuant to the partnership agreement, the partnership's duration is seven years. In year three, Betty notifies the partnership that she is withdrawing from the partnership immediately.

Betty has successfully dissociated from the partnership. Under RUPA default rules, she is no longer a partner and the partnership is obligated to buy out her partnership interest.

However, Betty has breached the partnership agreement and will be liable to the partnership for any injury her breach causes.

Illustration 2:

Harry is a partner of Partnership Y, a firm that develops real estate. Pursuant to the partnership agreement, the partnership will continue until the last condominium is sold on Project Y. Before the last condominium is sold, Harry notifies the partnership that he is withdrawing from the partnership immediately.

Harry has successfully dissociated from the partnership. Under RUPA default rules, he is no longer a partner and the partnership is obligated to buy out his partnership interest.

However, Harry has breached the partnership agreement and will be liable to the partnership for any injury his breach causes.

Illustration 3:

Claudia is a partner of Partnership Z. The partnership agreement expressly prohibits any partner from withdrawing from the partnership. Claudia notifies the partnership that she is withdrawing from the partnership immediately.

Claudia has successfully dissociated from the partnership. Under RUPA default rules, she is no longer a partner and the partnership is obligated to buy out her partnership interest.

However, Claudia has breached the partnership agreement and will be liable to the partnership for any injury her breach causes.

There is a strong policy reason for allowing a partner to withdraw even when the partnership agreement provides otherwise: **the risk of personal liability for the actions of co-partners justifies allowing the partner to escape the relationship that creates the potential for liability**. The same rationale allows a principal to terminate an agent even when the termination would result in a breach of a contract between the principal and agent. The principal will be liable for the breach, but will be allowed to terminate the relationship.

7B-302(c) PRICE:

Any time the law requires the partnership to purchase a partnership interest from a dissociated partner, the default purchase price is very important. As we discussed immediately above, under the default rules of RUPA, any time a partner dissociates from the partnership, the partnership must purchase her partnership interest. Under RUPA, there is only one standard of valuation for the purchase price of a partnership interest, regardless of the reason for the partner's dissociation. RUPA, §701(b) provides:

> The buyout price of a dissociated partner's interest is the amount that would have been distributable to the dissociating partner . . . if, on the date of dissociation, the assets of the partnership were sold at a price equal to the greater of the liquidation value or the value based on a sale of the entire business as a going concern without the dissociated partner . . . .

Hopefully, you were able to glean the valuation method that RUPA adopts for the dissociating partner's interest. Under RUPA, the dissociating partner receives her share of the **liquidation value OR going-concern value of the partnership, whichever is greater**. Remember, the going-concern value of the partnership is another way of expressing the fair market value of the partnership business.

The partners might want to change this valuation method in the buy-sell section of their partnership agreement. As we discussed in Unit 7A, above, a high valuation for all types of dissociation, including voluntary withdrawal or expulsion, for example, might provide the partners with the wrong incentives.[311]

---

[311] See §7A-303(e), above.

Under UPA, the exit of a partner from the partnership for any reason was called **dissolution** of the partnership. For example, the death, disability, bankruptcy, or withdrawal of a partner caused the dissolution of the partnership.

The UPA's use of the term "dissolution" in the context is a bit confusing. I know that I found it confusing when I was a law student. To me, dissolution meant the end of the existence of the partnership, which seemed like an inefficient result when only one of the partners exited. Dissolution of the partnership under those circumstances also went against intuition and my basic understanding of the world. I knew that many law firms were partnerships that continued even though partners often left the partnership.

It is better to think of dissolution as a term of art with a special meaning that does not necessarily mean the end of the partnership business. The default rule under the UPA was that the remaining partners could continue the partnership business.

Illustration:

A partnership exists between Alvin, Bertha, and Carol.

Alvin dies.

The partnership of Alvin, Bertha, and Carol is dissolved, but the partnership of Bertha and Carol could continue the original partnership business.

Of course, this approach under the UPA created a conceptual problem, which in turn created real legal issues for the continuing partnership. The issue was whether the continuing partnership was the original entity or a new entity. If it was a new entity, what happened to the property owned by the original partnership and to the contractual rights and obligations of the original partnership? Courts had to the address these issues as they arose and created common law rules to fill in these conceptual gaps.

Thankfully **RUPA takes a more intuitive approach**. Under RUPA, when a partner withdraws from the partnership for any reason, it results in dissociation of the partner, not dissolution of the partnership.[312]

---

[312] See §§7B-302(a)&(b), above.

7B-303 CREDITOR ATTACHMENT OF PARTNERSHIP INTERESTS:

A partner will have her own creditors and her own personal debts that are unrelated to the partnership's business.

Illustration:

Alvin is a partner in the partnership of Alvin, Bertha, Carol and Danny. Alvin borrows money from Bank in his own name for his personal use.

Alvin defaults on the bank loan. Bank obtains a judgement against Alvin and tries to enforce it by attaching Alvin's personal property, including his partnership interests.

A partner's partnership interest, like any other personal property, is subject to attachment by the partner's personal creditors. A court will issue a **charging order** in favor of the creditor against the partner's partnership interest. There are four important aspects of the charging order:

(1) A charging order **gives the creditor the right to receive distributions** the partnership makes to the debtor-partner.

(2) A charging order **does not make the creditor a partner**. In other words, the creditor has no rights to participate in management of the partnership business or in partnership decisions, nor do the partners owe the creditor any fiduciary duties.

(3) A charging order means that the **debtor-partner no longer enjoys her economic rights** (they now belong to the creditor), but she still has management rights. RUPA provides that the **other partners can expel the debtor-partner**, if they choose, because she no longer has any economic rights.[313]

(4) A creditor with a charging order may request the court to **foreclose on the charging order**. Foreclosing on the charging order simply means the court can order the sale of the partnership interests, but only the economic interests. The creditor will receive the proceeds of the sale. The purchaser of the foreclosed partnership interest does not become a partner – she merely acquires the right to receive any distribution the partnership makes.

Illustration:

Alvin is a partner in the partnership of Alvin, Bertha, Carol and Danny. Alvin defaults on a $200,000 personal loan he received

---

[313] RUPA §601(4)(ii).

from Bank, with $150,000 unpaid. The court issues a charging order in favor of Bank against Alvin's partnership interests.

The partnership is entering into a new lease, which according to the partnership agreement, requires the unanimous approval of all the partners.

> Bank has no right to vote. The charging order did not make Bank a partner.

> Alvin still has a right to vote, despite the charging order. The charging order did not strip Alvin of his partnership control rights.

The partnership makes a $15,000 distribution to each partner.

> Bank has a right to receive the $15,000. The charging order gives Bank the right to the economic rights of Alvin's partnership interest.

Bank wants to foreclose on the charging order because it does not believe the partnership will make significant distributions in the near future. In the foreclosure sale, Investor purchases the interest subject to the charging order for $100,000.

> Bank has a right to receive the $100,000.

> Investor now has the economic rights of Alvin's partnership interest, but Investor is not a partner.

> Alvin is still a partner, still has control rights, but has no economic rights. Under RUPA default rules, the partners could expel Alvin because he no longer has any economic rights.

7B-400 DEADLOCK IN THE PARTNERSHIP:

The deadlock issues in the partnership are virtually the same as they are in the closely-held corporation,[314] but the default rules for partnerships might increase the chances of deadlock.

First, in the partnership, the default rule for partner voting is that each partner has one vote regardless of her capital investment in the partnership business. This **one-partner-one-vote default rule increases the chances of deadlock**

---

[314] See §7A-400 et seq., above.

when there is an even number of partners, especially when there are only two partners.

Second, the ability of any partner to withdraw from the partnership at-will through the **dissociation process somewhat changes the deadlock dynamic.** The partners on either side of the deadlock might dissociate and demand to be bought out, which might cause a financial burden for the partnership and the remaining partners. Indeed, one side's dissociation might prompt the other side's dissociation, leaving the partnership no other option but to dissolve and liquidate – a result that neither side desires because they might not capture the partnership's value as a going concern.[315] One might argue that the right to dissociate gives each side an incentive to resolve the deadlock through compromise. Naturally, if the partnership agreement limits the partners' rights to dissociate or provides a low buy-out price upon dissociation, there is less incentive to dissociate when a deadlock occurs.

---

[315] They might not be able to sell the business as a going concern.

UNIT 7C

CLOSELY-HELD LLCS:

7C-100 SPECIAL ISSUES IN CLOSELY-HELD LLCS – INTRODUCTION:

Most LLCs are closely-held, with a relatively small number of members. Closely-held LLCs encounter the same issues that closely-held corporations and general partnerships encounter; namely special issues with respect to fiduciary duties, transfer of ownership interests, and deadlock. The default rules of the various state LLC statutes may take different approaches to these issues. However, once an attorney has an understanding of how corporate law and partnership law address these issues, she will know what to expect from a particular jurisdiction's LLC statute.

7C-200 FIDUCIARY DUTIES IN CLOSELY-HELD LLCS:

In Chapter 6, Unit 6C, we discussed the fiduciary duties members have to each other and the LLC.[316] The scope of the **duty of good faith and fair dealing** is an important issue for closely-held LLCs, just as it is for closely-held corporations and partnerships.

7C-300 TRANSFER OF MEMBERSHIP INTERESTS – LLCS:

An **operating agreement** for an LLC with more than one member will normally have the same **buy-sell provisions** introduced and discussed in Unit 7A.[317] Of course, the default rules for the transfer of membership interests are the baseline for drafting the buy-sell provisions of the LLC operating agreement.

---

[316] See Chapter 6, Unit 6C.

[317] See §§7A-303 through 7A-306, above.

7C-301 TRANSFER TO A THIRD PARTY AND CONSENT OF EACH MEMBER:

In most jurisdictions, the default rules treat the transfer of LLC membership interests the same way the law treats the transfer of partnership interests. In other words, **a member may assign her economic rights to a third party, but that third party may not become a member unless every other member consents.** The partners may change this rule by unanimous agreement. Some jurisdictions might treat LLC membership interests like shares in a corporation, allowing members the right to freely transfer their economic and control rights without the consent of the other members. A well-drafted buy-sell agreement will carefully define how the parties will the treat transferability of membership interests, regardless of the existing default rules.

7C-302 DISSOCIATION (WITHDRAWAL) FROM THE LLC:

In many jurisdictions, a member may have the same rights as a partner to dissociate from the LLC and demand to be bought out. However, in other jurisdictions, the member does not have a right to dissociate at will.

Under RULLCA, dissociation by withdrawal by a member places the member in limbo. **When a member withdraws from the LLC, her status changes from member to quasi-transferee:** Her dissociation causes her to lose her membership status and the rights she had as member. **Her control rights are extinguished**, and the other members no longer owe her any fiduciary duties. Her status becomes equivalent to that of a transferee of a membership interest. In other words, **she maintains her economic rights only**.

In addition, **when a member dissociates under RULLCA, she has no right to require the LLC to purchase her interest**. In other words, under RULLCA, a member's withdrawal from the LLC is tantamount to abdicating her control rights, without any chance of actually discontinuing her economic relationship with the LLC. If we assume the member's reason for withdrawal was dissatisfaction with how the other members were managing the business, her withdrawal will make things worse – she has given up the control rights that provided her only avenue to influence the company's business. If we assume her reason for her withdrawal was majority oppression, her dissociation will make things worse for her – not only has she relinquished her control rights, she has also given up her rights to any fiduciary duties.

When you draft a buy-sell provision in a RULLCA jurisdiction, or when you advise a client on withdrawal from an LLC, you must consider that the RULLCA default rules place a dissociating member in an untenable position – she is left powerless and cannot exit her investment.

411

7C-303 CHARGING ORDERS ON LLC MEMBERSHIP INTERESTS:

A member's personal creditor may attach her membership interest though a charging order issued by the court. The process for a charging order on an LLC membership interest is virtually the same as for a charging order on a partnership interest.[318] The creditor does not become a member in the LLC because of the charging order. The creditor only has the right to receive distributions that belong to the membership interest. Upon foreclosure of the charging order, the membership interest is sold, the creditor receives the proceeds of the sale, and the purchaser membership interest does not become a member unless all the other members consent.

7C-400 DEADLOCK IN THE LLC:

The potential for deadlock and the drafting issues it raises for the LLC are no different from those issues we addressed earlier in this chapter regarding deadlock in the corporation and partnership.[319]

If the jurisdiction's LLC statute or the operating agreement calls for one vote for each member, regardless of the relative amount of capital investment, the situation more closely resembles the default rules of general partnerships. In addition, if the statute or the operating agreement allows a member to dissociate by withdrawing at will, the deadlock dynamics will have an extra variable. [320] The attorney must recognize and draft for the potential for deadlock accordingly.

Similarly, if the jurisdiction's LLC statute or the operating agreement calls for voting based on the proportion of capital investment, the situation more closely resembles the default rules of the corporation.[321] Once again, the attorney must recognize and draft for the potential for deadlock accordingly.

---

[318] See §7B-303, above.

[319] See §7B-400, above.

[320] Id.

[321] Id.

CHAPTER 8
LITIGATION

UNIT 8A

CORPORATIONS – LITIGATION:

8A-100 SHAREHOLDER LAWSUITS AGAINST DIRECTORS AND OFFICERS:

8A-101 SHAREHOLDER LAWSUITS - DERIVATIVE OR DIRECT?

   8A-101(a) DERIVATIVE LAWSUITS:

   8A-101(b) DIRECT LAWSUITS:

   8A-101(c) DISTINGUISHING DIRECT AND DERIVATIVE LAWSUITS:

   8A-101(d) CONFUSION AND UNCERTAINTY:

   8A-101(e) DIRECT OR DERIVATIVE – WHY IS THE DISTINCTION IMPORTANT?

   8A-101(f) DERIVATIVE LAWSUITS IN CLOSELY-HELD CORPORATIONS:

8A-102 INCENTIVES TO BRING SHAREHOLDER DERIVATIVE LAWSUITS:

8A-103 THE DEMAND PROCESS:

   8A-103(a) DEMAND – THE BASIC PRINCIPLES:

   8A-103(b) THE DEMAND PROCESS – THE DETAILS:

   8A-103(c) PLEADING PARTICULARIZED FACTS:

   8A-103(d) THE TRIAL OF THE DERIVATIVE CLAIM:

8A-104 THE SPECIAL LITIGATION COMMITTEE ("SLC"):

   8A-104(a) USING AN SLC TO GET A DERIVATIVE CLAIM DISMISSED:

   8A-104(b) JUDICIAL REVIEW OF THE SLC'S DECISION:

   8A-104(c) THE SLC WHEN EVERY DIRECTOR IS DISABLED:

8A-105 FEE-SHIFTING PROVISIONS:

8A-200 INDEMNIFICATION OF DIRECTORS AND OFFICERS:

8A-201 INDEMNIFICATION GENERALLY:

   8A-201(a) MANDATORY INDEMNIFICATION:

   8A-201(b) PERMISSIVE INDEMNIFICATION:

   8A-201(c) INDEMNIFICATION PURSUANT TO CONTRACT:

   8A-201(d) D&O INSURANCE:

8A-202 INDEMNIFICATION OF DERIVATIVE AND DIRECT SHAREHOLDER LAWSUITS:

   8A-202(a) INDEMNIFICATION IN SHAREHOLDER DERIVATIVE LAWSUITS:

   8A-202(b) INDEMNIFICATION IN SHAREHOLDER DIRECT LAWSUITS:

8A-203 ADVANCEMENT OF EXPENSES:

UNIT 8B
PARTNERSHIPS – LITIGATION:

8B-100 **PARTNER LAWSUITS AGAINST CO-PARTNERS AND THE PARTNERSHIP:**

8B-101 GENERAL PARTNERSHIPS AND LIMITED LIABILITY PARTNERSHIPS:
    8B-101(a) DERIVATIVE LAWSUITS IN GENERAL PARTNERSHIPS:
    8B-101(b) AN ACTION FOR ACCOUNTING – DIRECT OR DERIVATIVE CLAIMS:
    8B-101(c) AN ACTION FOR ACCOUNTING AS THE EXCLUSIVE REMEDY:

8B-102 LIMITED PARTNERSHIPS:
    8B-102(a) LIMITED PARTNER DERIVATIVE LAWSUITS:
    8B-102(b) LIMITED PARTNER DIRECT LAWSUITS:
    8B-102(c) GENERAL PARTNER LAWSUITS:

UNIT 8C
LLCs – FIDUCIARY DUTY LITIGATION:

8C-100 **MEMBER LAWSUITS AGAINST CO-MEMBERS, MANAGERS, AND THE COMPANY:**

8C-101 LLC MEMBER DERIVATIVE LAWSUITS:
8C-102 DRAFTING OUT OF DERIVATIVE LAWSUITS IN THE LLC:
8C-103 LLC MEMBER DIRECT LAWSUITS:

UNIT 8A

CORPORATIONS – LITIGATION:

8A-100 SHAREHOLDER LAWSUITS AGAINST DIRECTORS AND OFFICERS:

8A-101 SHAREHOLDER LAWSUITS - DERIVATIVE OR DIRECT?

A shareholder lawsuit against officers, directors, or the entire board of directors will be either **derivative** or **direct**. The most important distinction between direct and derivative lawsuits is that **a shareholder will have more control over a direct lawsuit than a derivative lawsuit**.

For reasons discussed below, a **derivative lawsuit** still belongs to the corporation. Thus, the corporation, not one individual shareholder, should have the ultimate right to decide whether pursuing the lawsuit is in the best interests of the corporation.

Of course, when we say the *corporation* should have the right to decide whether to pursue the lawsuit, we must remember that the board of directors makes decisions for the corporation and might not be able to act impartially when deciding whether to sue the board, one or more of its members, or one or more officers. In some instances, the corporation will not have the final word on whether to continue pursuing the lawsuit. One might think of a shareholder derivative lawsuit as a narrow exception to the board's control over corporate decisions.

The **direct lawsuit**, in contrast, completely belongs to the plaintiff-shareholder. The corporation will not have a right to decide whether pursuing the lawsuit serves the best interests of the corporation.

8A-101(a) DERIVATIVE LAWSUITS:

A shareholder derivative lawsuit is often said to be **in the right of the corporation** or **on behalf of the corporation**. The shareholder steps into shoes of the corporation and sues a third party who has caused harm to the corporation. Usually the third party is one or more of the corporation's directors or officers who have allegedly breached their fiduciary duties.

In a shareholder derivative lawsuit, the shareholder's claim against the director or officer is effectively the following:

416

"You have caused injury to the corporation and have, thereby, caused injury to me in proportion to my shareholdings in the corporation".

The shareholder's injury is "derivative" because she suffers an injury, indirectly, through the injury to the corporation.

Illustration:

Sally is a shareholder of ABC Corp. She owns 100 of the 100,000 outstanding shares (i.e., 0.1%). Oliver is an officer of ABC Corp. Oliver steals $1,000,000 from the corporation. The corporation's harm is $1,000,000. Sally's derivative harm is $1,000 (the value of her shareholdings will decrease by that much).

Procedurally, the corporation is a nominal defendant in an equity suit to force it to sue the third party. The director or officer that allegedly caused harm to the corporation by breaching her fiduciary duties is the real defendant. If the shareholder wins the derivative lawsuit, recovery goes to the corporation and the shareholder-plaintiff will be reimbursed for her expenses (the largest of which are her attorney's fees).

Illustration:

Sally Shareholder wins her derivative lawsuit against Oliver Officer. Oliver must re-pay ABC Corp. $1,000,000 (in addition to damages for any other injury he may have caused to the corporation). ABC Corp must reimburse Sally for her attorney's fees and other expenses.

8A-101(b) DIRECT LAWSUITS:

In a shareholder's direct lawsuit, the corporation's directors or officers have directly impinged upon the rights of the shareholders.

Often the right will be **a right that corporate law provides to the shareholders**:

Illustration:

ABC Corp has been merged into another corporation. Under the law, the shareholders of ABC have a right to vote on the merger, but the board never called a shareholder meeting to vote on the merger. Sally Shareholder sues the board. (You will note that there is no allegation that the corporation has suffered any harm).

In other circumstances **the right will be one that the corporation's articles or bylaws provide to the shareholders**:

Illustration:

Under the articles of incorporation of ABC Corp, holders of common "A" shares are to receive a dividend of $3.00 before the holders of common "B" receive any dividend. The board of directors declared a dividend of $1.00 for "A" shares and $1.00 for "B" shares. Sally, an A shareholder, sues the board. (You will note that there is no allegation that the corporation has suffered any harm).

8A-101(c) DISTINGUISHING DIRECT AND DERIVATIVE LAWSUITS:

Generally, shareholder lawsuits against directors, officers, or controlling shareholders for breaches of fiduciary duties are **derivative lawsuits**. For example:

Shareholder sues the directors for breaching their duty of care in making a decision to purchase a factory. The claim by the plaintiff-shareholder is that by breaching its duty of care, the board has harmed the corporation and, as a result of the corporation's injury, the value of the shareholder's interest in the corporation has been impaired.

Shareholder sues the directors for breaching their duty to monitor employees for possible illegal activities. The shareholder's claim is that the board's failure to monitor has caused harm to the corporation directly and, as a result of the corporation's injury, the value of the shareholder's interest in the corporation has been impaired.

Minority shareholder sues the controlling shareholder for a self-dealing transaction, where the corporation contracted for services from a company owned by the controlling shareholder. The claim by the plaintiff-shareholder is that the controlling shareholder breached its duty of loyalty by profiting itself at the corporation's expense. The self-dealing caused harm to the corporation and, thereby, impaired the value of the minority shareholder's interest in the corporation.

The key to spotting a derivative action: **articulating some sort of harm to the corporation.** If you cannot, then the legal action is not a derivative lawsuit; rather it is a direct lawsuit.

In a **direct lawsuit**, the shareholder's rights are directly violated. One court has presented the test for a direct cause of action as follows:

The shareholder-plaintiff must show "the duty breached was owed to the stockholder and that he or she can prevail without showing an injury to the corporation."[322]

---

[322] *Tooley v. Donaldson, Lufkin, & Jenrette, Inc.*, 845 A.2d 1031 (Del. 2004)

Here are some examples of corporate issues that would normally give a shareholder a right to a **direct lawsuit**:

Voting issues. If the board fails to get a vote when required by law, the articles of incorporation, or the bylaws, or if the board abuses or manipulates the voting process, shareholders have a direct cause of action against the board.

> *Reasoning:* Shareholders have a right to vote when the law or the corporation's governing documents grant such a right. Conduct by the board of directors or the executive officers that impairs shareholder voting rights directly injures the shareholders and does not injure the corporation. (However, if the shareholder claims that the corporation should receive some monetary compensation, a court might consider the lawsuit to be derivative).

Inadequate consideration for the shareholders of an acquired corporation. The shareholders in a corporation that has been merged out of existence might argue that they did not receive adequate consideration in the merger because their directors breached their fiduciary duties (e.g., care, loyalty, disclosure, etc.).

> *Illustration:*
>
> The shareholder-plaintiffs in one of the most famous corporate law cases, *Smith v. Van Gorkom*,[323] made this type of claim. In this case, Trans Union was merged into another corporation. Trans Union's shareholders received $55 per share as consideration for the merger. The shareholders sued the board and the CEO in a direct lawsuit, claiming that because the Trans Union board was reckless in its decision-making process, the Trans Union shareholders did not receive adequate consideration in the merger.
>
> This case is a direct shareholder claim because it is not possible to articulate any harm to the corporation. Trans Union was merged into another corporation, but corporate law does not consider this to be an injury. It is the Trans Union shareholders, and only the shareholders, who have been harmed by the board's misfeasance.

Shareholder claims to dividends. A shareholder's right to a dividend will be defined in the corporation's articles of incorporation. When a shareholder claims that she did not receive the dividend she was entitled to, or that the board ignored her dividend preference, she is making a direct claim. However, if the shareholder's claim that the board's

---

[323] 488 A.2d 858 (Del. 1985). See Chapter 6, §§6A-204(c) and 6A-209(b) for a discussion of *Smith v. Van Gorkom.*

issuance of a dividend left the corporation without sufficient funds, she is making a derivative claim because she is alleging harm to the corporation.

Claims regarding other shareholder rights provided by law or by the corporation's governing documents. For example:

A claim for involuntary dissolution.

A claim regarding dissenter's rights.

A claim regarding the shareholders' rights to call a special meeting.

A claim regarding the shareholders' rights to remove directors.

A claim regarding the shareholders' rights to propose a bylaw amendment.

A claim that the corporation engaged in an ultra vires transaction.

It may be **helpful to think of direct claims as addressing the contractual rights of shareholders**. "Contractual rights" in this instance are broadly defined to include the rights shareholders have pursuant to statutes, the common law, the articles of incorporation, or the bylaws.

8A-101(d) CONFUSION AND UNCERTAINTY:

It is sometimes difficult to determine whether a claim is direct or derivative. In many cases where courts struggle to determine whether the claim is direct or derivative, the claim is specious. When a claim does not articulate a valid cause of action, it will often be difficult to determine whether it is derivative or direct. The court might be able to dismiss the claim for failure to state a cause of action, but that does not solve the direct or derivative issue.

Another source of confusion is the way some courts determine whether a claim is direct or derivative. These courts base the determination on the type of remedy the plaintiff is seeking. If the plaintiff is seeking an **equitable remedy** (i.e., an injunction) and **not a legal remedy** (i.e., monetary damages), the claim will be a **direct lawsuit**.

I must admit that this approach makes little sense to me. It seems illogical to hold that one remedy is derivative and the other direct. A court might protect a corporation's interest through legal or equitable remedies. Similarly, a court might protect a shareholder's rights through legal or equitable remedies

Because I do not fully understand this approach, I normally go through the general test first – asking whether I can articulate any harm to the corporation – and then I remind myself that the plaintiff's election of equitable or legal

420

redress might influence a court's decision on whether the claim is direct or derivative.

8A-101(e) DIRECT OR DERIVATIVE – WHY IS THE DISTINCTION IMPORTANT?

As we have already discussed, the most important difference between shareholder direct lawsuits and shareholder derivative lawsuits is control over the lawsuit. The **shareholder has total control over her direct lawsuit.** In contrast, the shareholder has limited control over the shareholder derivative suit. **The corporation's board of directors may be able to wrest control of the derivative lawsuit away from the shareholder.**

The derivative lawsuit is a lawsuit in the right of the corporation and, as we have learned, the board of directors makes decisions for the corporation. The shareholders only participate in a limited number of corporate decisions, usually in response to a proposal by the board. Thus, control over whether the corporation should pursue litigation belongs to the board, not one or more shareholders. Indeed, a decision regarding whether to bring a lawsuit is like any other business decision – it has its costs and benefits – and the board is in a much better position than the shareholder to evaluate those costs and benefits.

However, there is a **natural conflict in most shareholder derivative lawsuits.** The typical shareholder derivative lawsuit alleges a breach of fiduciary duties by the corporation's directors. Because the directors are the defendants, their decision not to pursue the claim is different from a decision not to pursue a claim against a supplier or a customer, for example. The directors in a fiduciary duty lawsuit are conflicted because they are deciding on whether to sue themselves and/or their fellow directors. The law addresses this conflict through the **demand process**, which is discussed in detail below.

8A-101(f) DERIVATIVE LAWSUITS IN CLOSELY-HELD CORPORATIONS:

In many jurisdictions, **courts treat all shareholder lawsuits in closely-held corporations as direct lawsuits.** Minority shareholder claims alleging freeze-outs discussed in Chapter 7 might be categorized as direct suits.

There are several possible justifications for treating freeze-out claims as direct, rather than derivative. In a freeze-out claim, the minority shareholder is not necessarily claiming that the controlling shareholder's actions harmed the corporation. Rather, the claim is that the controlling shareholder denied the minority shareholder of something to which she is entitled – i.e., her reasonable expectations.

Indeed, you can see how the determination of whether the claim is direct or derivative may depend on how the claim is framed.

Illustration:

The controlling shareholder is also the CEO of the corporation. She uses her control of the board to cause the corporation to increase her compensation as CEO.

> *Analysis:* Framing the claim as a traditional duty of loyalty/self-dealing claim that implicates harm to the corporation would make the claim a derivative claim. In contrast, the minority shareholder might frame the issue as a freeze-out, claiming the increase in compensation is a **constructive dividend** that should be issued to all shareholders. This argument presents the claim as a direct injury to the rights of the minority shareholder (i.e., the right to receive a pro rata share of any dividend), rather than as injury to the corporation (i.e., excessive compensation).

Framing the claim as a constructive dividend or as a denial of the minority shareholder's reasonable expectations would most likely make the claim direct, rather than derivative. In addition, the minority shareholder might base her claim as a breach of a shareholders' agreement between the controlling shareholder and minority shareholder, if there is one, instead of breach of fiduciary duties. This contractual claim is most likely a direct claim.

Finally, even where a court does not characterize a fiduciary duty claim in a closely-held corporation as a direct claim, the court might direct any monetary recovery to the minority shareholder, pro rata, instead of the corporation.

Illustration:

The controlling shareholder owns 80% of the stock in the corporation. The minority shareholder owns 30%. The controlling shareholder diverts $100,000 of corporate assets to herself through self-dealing transactions, usurpation of corporate opportunities, and hidden perquisites. The court might require the controlling shareholder to compensate the minority shareholder $30,000.

8A-102 INCENTIVES TO BRING SHAREHOLDER DERIVATIVE LAWSUITS:

Why would a shareholder bring a shareholder derivative lawsuit? In economic terms, we would say that she has very little incentive to do so because she bears all of the downside risk but stands to gain little of the potential benefit.

The **plaintiff-shareholder must bear the expenses** of the derivative lawsuit herself. She will only be entitled to reimbursement of her expenses by the corporation **if she wins the lawsuit** or if she is able to **negotiate a settlement** with the corporation or the other defendants that compensates her for her litigation expenses. Providing even further disincentive for her is the fact that if she is successful in her derivative lawsuit, any **recovery goes directly to the corporation**.

Thus, the shareholder bears the risk of the lawsuit, without the possibility of any direct personal gain. Of course, she will benefit indirectly from any gains the corporation receives from the shareholder derivative suit, whether it is monetary gain or improved corporate governance, but she will share that gain with the other shareholders.

Illustration:

Plaintiff-shareholder owns .001% of the outstanding shares of the corporation. Her shareholder derivative lawsuit against several directors for breach of the duty of loyalty is successful, and the directors must pay the corporation $10 million in damages. The plaintiff-shareholder will indirectly benefit from the recovery. The value of her shares should increase by $100 (.001% of $10 million) after the corporation collects its judgment.

The plaintiff-shareholder suffers from the **free-rider problem**. She bears all the risks herself, but the other shareholders will gain from her success, without any efforts or risks on their own part. The other shareholders are free-riders. **This free-rider problem creates disincentives for any shareholder to bring a derivative lawsuit**.

There are circumstances where a shareholder might be willing to bear the cost of the free-rider problem. For example, if she has a large percentage of shareholdings in a corporation, the benefit she would receive from a successful lawsuit might outweigh the costs of the risks associated with the derivative lawsuit.

More troublesome, however, is the situation where the shareholder stands to receive some sort of **private benefit** (i.e., a benefit that other shareholders will not receive) from the shareholder derivative lawsuit. If the shareholder's potential private benefit from a derivative lawsuit is sufficiently enticing, she has an incentive to bring a derivative lawsuit even when it is not in the best interests of the corporation. Under these circumstances, the derivative lawsuit becomes a **strike suit** – where settling the lawsuit (i.e., "paying off" the plaintiff) is less costly for the defendant than litigating the matter.

Law firms are the driving force behind many shareholder derivative lawsuits involving publicly-traded corporations. These law firms often seek a nominal plaintiff (i.e., a shareholder of the corporation), sue the board, and hope for a settlement that will include substantial legal fees. This type of settlement may provide no real benefit to the shareholders of the corporation. On the other hand, the costs are real. Not only will the corporation bear the costs of the plaintiff's legal expenses, but a significant amount of time and other corporate resources will be used to defend and settle the lawsuit. These types of settlements are often called **collusive settlements**.

It is fair to say that courts, policy-makers, and corporate boards are concerned with the potential for strike suits and collusive settlements in shareholder derivative lawsuits. A number of legal rules and procedures have developed in an attempt to reduce incentives to bring strike suits, while not discouraging meritorious derivative suits. You can judge for yourself whether the law has struck the proper balance.

> **Contemporaneous ownership requirements:** Most state corporate law statutes or relevant civil procedure statutes require the plaintiff-shareholder to be a shareholder at the time of wrongdoing and to maintain ownership throughout the lawsuit.[324] This rule serves to help ensure the plaintiff's interests are aligned with the shareholders of the corporation and that she has continuing incentives to vigorously pursue the lawsuit.

> Some jurisdictions may have statutory or common-law exceptions to the contemporaneous-owner rules. When learning the law of the jurisdiction where you practice, you should look for exceptions such as:

>> *Exception for continuing wrong:* The plaintiff-shareholder acquired shares while the wrongful conduct was still in progress.

>> *Exception for non-disclosure:* The plaintiff-shareholder acquired shares before the wrongful act was disclosed.

> An interesting consequence of the contemporaneous-ownership rule is that the shareholders of a corporation that no longer exists after a merger might lose their right to bring a shareholder derivative suit. The shareholders of the corporation that is merged out of existence cannot hold shares continuously throughout the lawsuit because they no longer hold shares in the original corporation. Consider the following situations:

>> **Situation 1:** The directors of Zed Corp. engage in self-dealing, and embezzlement. Zed Corp. is subsequently merged into Alpha Corp.

>>> If Zed shareholders received Alpha shares in the merger, they have standing to sue the former directors of Zed derivatively. Alpha acquired all of Zed's rights, including its rights to sue former directors for breaching fiduciary duties,

---

[324] Record ownership or beneficial ownership? Some states require record ownership.

and Zed's former shareholders are now shareholders of Alpha.[325]

If Zed shareholders did not receive Alpha shares in the merger (i.e., they received cash or debt securities in the merger), they now have no standing to sue the former directors of Zed.

Situation 2: Zed Corp. is merged into Alpha Corp. *In connection with the merger process*, the board breaches its duties of care and loyalty.

This claim is most likely a direct claim,[326] so the rule requiring ownership throughout the lawsuit is not applicable. Even when a court considers the lawsuit to be derivative in nature, some courts will allow former shareholders in the merged corporation to maintain a derivative lawsuit when the fiduciary duty breaches occurred in connection with the merger.

After considering the above examples, you might have been able to see the potential use of a merger to extinguish a shareholder derivative lawsuit. Here's the situation:

Imagine you are a director who is a defendant in a shareholder derivative lawsuit. You could return to your normal, carefree life if only this pesky shareholder lawsuit would magically disappear. You suddenly realize that if all the shareholders, including the plaintiff-shareholder, were cashed out in a merger, the derivative lawsuit would be dismissed because the plaintiff would no longer be a shareholder.

Will the law allow the defendants to use a cash-out merger to quash the shareholder derivative lawsuit? The answer is probably yes, but with a major proviso. If the shareholder-plaintiff is cashed out in a merger during the derivative suit proceedings, her case will be dismissed, even if the merger was simply a pretense to terminate the lawsuit. However, the defendants have now likely opened themselves to a lawsuit for breach of their duty of good faith in connection with the merger transaction.

Adequate representative requirements: A court will determine whether the plaintiff-shareholder adequately represents the interests of the shareholders. A court might consider a plaintiff to be an inadequate representative if: (1) she has a **conflict of interest** (e.g., the lawsuit

---

[325] See Chapter 9, 9A-401, et seq.

[326] See §8A-101(c), above.

involves a contract with another corporation and she has major shareholdings in the other corporation); (2) she is **controlled by her legal counsel** or her attorney is not competent to handle the case; or (3) the court determines her **efforts in pursuing the case will be lacking**.

Security requirements: Some jurisdictions require the plaintiff-shareholder to post a security (in the form of a bond) for expenses the corporation and the defendants may incur in defending the suit. The plaintiff will forfeit this bond if she loses the derivative lawsuit. In many of these jurisdictions, if the plaintiff-shareholder owns a certain percentage of the company's shares (typically 5% or more), she will not need to post a bond. The amount of the security is normally left to the discretion of the court.

Settlement approval by court: To reduce the potential for collusive settlements, courts will review any proposed settlement between the defendants and the plaintiff, and will approve it only if it is reasonable.

8A-103 THE DEMAND PROCESS:

Demand is **the process where the board of directors has the opportunity to gain control of a derivative lawsuit**. Stripped down to its essence, the demand process provides the board an opportunity to move for dismissal of the shareholder derivative lawsuit because the board has determined it does not serve the corporation's best interests.

8A-103(a) DEMAND – THE BASIC PRINCIPLES:

Before we get into the details of the demand process, let us first discuss whether a court should defer to the board's decision to dismiss a derivative lawsuit because it is not in the best interest of the corporation.

We start out with the basic principle of the business judgment rule we discussed in earlier chapters: we should defer to the decision of the board of directors UNLESS it was conflicted, acted in bad faith, or was grossly negligent in its decision making process.[327]

Do you think a court should defer to the board's request to dismiss the derivative lawsuit in the following situations?

Situation 1: A supplier has breached a contract with ABC Corp. and ABC's board has not pursued the claim against the supplier.

---

[327] See Chapter 6, §6A-104.

A shareholder of ABC Corp. brings a shareholder derivative lawsuit against the supplier.

The board of directors of ABC Corp. asks the court to dismiss the lawsuit.

> ***Analysis:*** Without any other facts, **the court should defer to the judgment of the board**. The board may have many reasons for not suing the supplier: the expenses of the lawsuit might outweigh any potential recovery; the company might want to maintain good relations with the supplier; the board might feel a non-judicial resolution is preferable; the board might not want the company to appear to other potential suppliers and customers as excessively litigious, etc.
>
> Whatever the reasons, the board is in a much better position than the shareholders and the court to determine whether the lawsuit against the supplier is in the best interests of the corporation.
>
> The decision to refrain from suing a supplier is like any other business decision by the board – it deserves the same sort of deference we saw in earlier discussions of the business judgment rule.[328]

Situation 2: Oliver, a mid-level manager in charge of the ABC Corp.'s accounting department, embezzles $1,000,000 from the company. ABC's board has not pursued a claim against Oliver.

A shareholder of ABC Corp. brings a shareholder derivative lawsuit against Oliver.

The board of directors of ABC Corp. asks the court to dismiss the lawsuit.

> ***Analysis:*** At first blush, this fact pattern might seem different from the one involving the supplier's breach of contract in Situation 1, immediately above. Did you read this fact pattern and say to yourself: "Clearly when an employee embezzles money from the corporation, the board should cause the corporation to sue the culprit."? If you did, you fell for the trap.
>
> There might be numerous reasons why the board would choose not to sue an employee who embezzled from the company. This fact pattern was designed to entice you to lose sight of the principles we discussed in Situation 1 – namely, we should defer to the board's decision because they

---

[328] See Chapter 6, Unit 6A.

are in the best position to judge if the lawsuit is in the best interests of the corporation.

Situation 3: ABC Corp. buys a tract of land from Zed LLC.

ABC Corp has 9 directors on its board of directors. Five of the directors are the sole owners of Zed LLC.

A shareholder of ABC Corp. brings a shareholder derivative lawsuit against the board of directors for breach of the duty of loyalty.

The board of directors of ABC Corp. asks the court to dismiss the lawsuit.

> ***Analysis:*** In this situation, we have some legitimate reasons for NOT deferring to the board of directors. A majority of the directors was conflicted in the underlying transaction and faced potential liability in the derivative lawsuit. When there is significant potential that any board member will face liability in the derivative lawsuit, we should not defer to her decision to dismiss the derivative lawsuit against herself because she cannot act impartially in making that decision (i.e., she is conflicted). When a majority of the board members cannot act impartially in making a decision, the court should not defer to the board's decision.

Through the demand process, the board will have a chance to ask the court to dismiss the shareholder derivative lawsuit. **A court will defer to the board's decision unless there is a substantial likelihood that the directors will be liable in the underlying transaction.**

8A-103(b) THE DEMAND PROCESS – THE DETAILS:

The demand process ultimately results in a decision by the court regarding **whether the board of directors faced a substantial likelihood of liability in the underlying transaction,** in which case, the court would not dismiss the lawsuit at the board's request. The specter of potential liability for the directors raises serious doubts that the directors could make a disinterested and independent decision about the lawsuit.

Jurisdictions generally adopt one of two different approaches to demand: **Universal Demand** or **Demand Excused.** These two approaches might vary from each other, but their functions are the same: each approach provides the board a chance to ask the court to dismiss the lawsuit and requires the court to determine whether the board of directors faces a substantial likelihood of liability in the underlying transaction.

In a **Universal-demand** jurisdiction, a shareholder must ALWAYS formally demand the board of directors to sue *before* she can sue derivatively. In other words, the shareholder must demand the board take legal action and only if the board rejects the demand or fails to act on it within a reasonable time, may the shareholder bring a derivative action in court.

In a **Demand-excused** jurisdiction, a shareholder is excused from first making demand on the board of directors if demand would be **futile**.

The universal-demand and demand-excused approaches are essentially the same because they both require the court to eventually ask:

> **Do we have serious doubts that the board will make an impartial, disinterested, and independent decision regarding whether the derivative lawsuit serves the best interests of the corporation?**

Here is a step-by-step analysis of each of the processes:[329]

Universal-demand jurisdiction:

Step 1:   The shareholder makes demand on the board to sue one or more directors or officers.

Step 2:   The board **rejects demand** or does not respond to the demand within a reasonable time. (If the board accepts demand, the corporation then takes control of the suit and we stop at this step).

Step 3:   The shareholder brings a derivative lawsuit against one or more directors or officers.

Step 4:   The board asks the court to dismiss the suit because it rejected demand (i.e., "We rejected demand because we determined that the lawsuit was not in the best interest of the corporation. Please defer to our decision.")

Step 5:   The shareholder asks the court not to dismiss the lawsuit because the board **wrongfully rejected** (or "**wrongfully refused**") her demand (i.e., "Please don't defer to the board's decision.")

Step 6:   The court determines if the board wrongfully rejected demand.

            A court will determine that the board wrongfully rejected demand when the court has **serious doubts the board was disinterested and independent when it rejected demand**.

---

[329] These step-by-step analyses are generalized for the sake of illustration; actual practices may vary from jurisdiction to jurisdiction.

The court requires the shareholder to plead particularized facts that allege:

1) A majority of the directors were conflicted in the **underlying transaction** (i.e., the transaction that the shareholder is suing about) or were dominated or controlled by a conflicted party; or

2) The board's actions in the **underlying transaction** were waste, in bad faith, or grossly negligent.

Demand-excused jurisdiction:

Step 1:   The shareholder sues one or more directors or officers without making demand.*

Step 2:   The board asks the court to dismiss the suit because the shareholder never made demand (i.e., "We are the board and we should determine whether the lawsuit is in the best interests of the corporation.")

Step 3:   The shareholder asks the court not to dismiss the lawsuit, claiming **demand on the board was excused** because it was futile (i.e., "The board should not have a chance to determine whether the lawsuit is in the best interests of the corporation because they could not act impartially.")

Step 4:   The court determines if demand on the board was excused. A court will determine that demand on the board was excused if demand would have been futile. Demand would be futile if there are **serious doubts the board was disinterested and independent** with respect to the demand. The court requires the shareholder to plead particularized facts that allege:

1) A majority of the directors were conflicted in the **underlying transaction** (i.e., the transaction that the shareholder is suing about) or were dominated or controlled by a conflicted party; or

2) The board's actions in the **underlying transaction** were waste, in bad faith, or grossly negligent.

*__Note:__ In a demand-excused jurisdiction, a shareholder might choose to make demand even though it would be excused. She might make demand, although not required, to give the board a chance to make things right, or she might simply not have all the facts that would allow her to know that demand was excused. In many jurisdictions, the shareholder will still be able to argue that demand was wrongfully rejected if and when the board does reject demand. However, in Delaware, if a shareholder makes demand, she has conceded that the board was able to deal with the demand in an impartial and independent manner. Thus, she will no longer be able argue the board's rejection of demand was wrongful. This approach may seem unfair, but the shareholder-plaintiff can avoid the problem by not making demand in the first place. Thus, in Delaware, shareholders NEVER make demand on the board. Instead, they immediately sue and argue demand was futile.

You can see that under either the universal-demand approach or the demand-excused approach, **the case comes down to whether the board is able to make an impartial and independent decision to sue the defendant officers or directors.**

Often the directors making the decision will be defendants. However, as far as the law is concerned, **being a defendant to a shareholder derivative lawsuit does not mean a director is unable to deal with the decision to sue herself in an impartial manner.** Thus, a shareholder cannot simply sue all the directors and claim that they could not deal with the demand impartially because they were defendants. In fact, plaintiffs will often sue all the directors as a matter of course and let the court sort out who is liable.

Illustration:

Imagine you are a director. You are considering whether to sue yourself by accepting demand. The court will only consider you incapable of impartially deciding on whether to sue yourself if there is a substantial likelihood you will be liable in the underlying lawsuit.

Of course, there will be a substantial likelihood you will be liable in a shareholder derivative lawsuit if you were conflicted in the transaction that is the subject matter of the lawsuit, or if your actions with respect to the underlying transaction were waste, in bad faith, or grossly negligent.

My preferred formulation of the test is the following:

The court requires the shareholder to plead particularized facts that allege:

1) A majority of the directors were conflicted in the **underlying transaction** or were dominated or controlled by a conflicted party; or

2) The board's actions in the **underlying transaction** were waste, in bad faith, or grossly negligent.

Courts might phrase the test differently, but the import is the same as the two-part test I prefer. Here are some examples of different formulations of the test:

> "The basis for claiming excusal would normally be that: (1) a majority of the board has a material financial or familial interest; (2) a majority of the board is incapable of acting independently for some other reason such as domination or control; (3) the underlying transaction is not the product of a valid exercise of business judgment."[330]

> "Where . . . plaintiffs complain of board inaction and do not challenge a specific decision of the board, there is no "challenged transaction," . . .. [T]o show demand futility where the subject of the derivative suit is not a business decision of the board, a plaintiff must allege particularized facts that 'create a reasonable doubt that, as of the time the complaint is filed, the board of directors could have properly exercised its independent and disinterested business judgment in responding to a demand.' "[331]

> "(1) Demand is excused because of futility when a complaint alleges with particularity that a majority of the board of directors is interested in the challenged transaction. Director interest may either be self-interest in the transaction at issue . . . , or a loss of independence because a director with no direct interest in a transaction is 'controlled' by a self-interested director. (2) Demand is excused because of futility when a complaint alleges with particularity that the board of directors did not fully inform themselves about the challenged transaction to the extent reasonably appropriate under the circumstances . . . . The 'long-standing rule' is that a director 'does not exempt himself from liability by failing to do more than passively rubber-stamp the decisions of the active managers'. . . . (3) Demand is excused because of futility when a complaint alleges with particularity that the challenged transaction was so egregious on its face that it could not have been the product of sound business judgment of the directors."[332]

8A-103(c) PLEADING PARTICULARIZED FACTS:

In the battle over whether demand was excused or wrongfully rejected, courts require the shareholder plaintiff to plead **particularized facts** that the board could not deal with demand in an impartial manner because they faced

---

[330] *Grimes v. Donald*, 673 A. 2d 1207 (Del. 1996).

[331] *In re Citigroup Inc. Shareholder Derivative Litigation*, 964 A.2d 106 (Del. Ch. Ct. 2009).

[332] *Marx v. Akers*, N.E.2d 1034 (1996).

substantial likelihood of liability in the shareholder derivative lawsuit (i.e., the demand was excused or rejection of demand was wrongful).

The requirement for particularized facts in the derivative lawsuit pleadings is a departure from the less stringent **traditional notice-pleading standards**. Traditional notice pleading merely requires the plaintiff to make a short statement of the cause of action; the particular facts will come out during trial and discovery.[333]

In contrast, the **pleadings of a shareholder derivative lawsuit must do more than simply state the directors breached their fiduciary duties in the underlying transaction**. The shareholder's pleadings must give facts detailing how the directors breached their fiduciary duties in the underlying transaction.

Although the shareholder-plaintiff's pleadings surrounding the demand process must include particularized facts, the shareholder will not have the benefit of discovery to help her with her pleadings. She will eventually have a right to discovery, but only if she can make it past the enhanced pleading requirements for shareholder derivative lawsuits.

To gather the facts necessary to make her pleadings sufficiently particularized, the shareholder-plaintiff must be creative. As a shareholder, she will have access to corporate books and records[334] and any press releases by the company. If the corporation is a public corporation, she will also have access to the information in the corporation's filings with the Securities and Exchange Commission.

8A-103(d) THE TRIAL OF THE DERIVATIVE CLAIM:

If a shareholder-plaintiff can get past the initial pleadings at the demand stage of her shareholder derivative lawsuit, the case will then go to trial. In trial, as more facts come out, the defendants might be found not liable. For example, the facts in a duty of loyalty claim might show that there was no material conflict or the board or shareholders properly ratified the transaction.[335] In a duty of care claim, the facts might show that the board was not reckless in its

---

[333] Those of you who are current on the latest developments of notice pleading will probably be aware of two relatively recent cases – *Ashcroft v. Iqbal,* 129 S. Ct. 1937 (2009) and *Bell Atlantic Corp. v. Twombly,* 550 U.S. 544 (2007) – where the U.S. Supreme Court seemed to require pleading of particularized facts- not just a simple statement of the cause of action. These two cases may mean a shift from traditional notice pleading to something more like we see in shareholder derivative lawsuits. I am not up to date on the latest developments of civil procedure, so I refrain (happily) from opining on the importance of *Iqbal* and *Twombly.*

[334] See Chapter 6, §5A-211 for a discussion of shareholder access to corporate books and records.

[335] See Chapter 6, §6A-202, et seq.

decision-making process. Similarly, during the trial, the defendants might persuade the fact-finder that the transaction was entirely fair.

The issues of ratification and fairness will generally not come up as a defense to the shareholder derivative lawsuit until the issues of demand and demand excusal have already been settled. In other words, if the shareholder-plaintiff pleads particularized facts demonstrating a majority of the board was conflicted in the underlying transaction, the board will not be able to plead ratification as a defense during the demand-pleading process. Their ratification defense will have to wait until trial. Likewise, any argument that the transaction was entirely fair will also have no bearing during the demand-pleading process; it will also have to wait until the trial.

However, the issue of whether there is an exculpation clause in the corporation's articles[336] will be relevant at the demand stage, at least with respect to a duty of care lawsuit. Indeed some courts will require the shareholder-plaintiff's pleading to state that there is no exculpation clause in the corporation's articles or that although there is an exculpation clause, it would not apply to the alleged fiduciary duty breach.

––––––––––

8A-104 THE SPECIAL LITIGATION COMMITTEE ("SLC"):

If you remember from our discussions in Chapter 5, the board is generally authorized to delegate authority to a committee of directors.[337] The board might choose to appoint a committee to determine whether a derivative lawsuit is in the best interests of the corporation. This committee is often called a special litigation committee ("SLC").

8A-104(a) USING AN SLC TO GET A DERIVATIVE CLAIM DISMISSED:

The board often creates an SLC when the **board is disabled**. A board is disabled when demand on the board would be futile. Use of the SLC in the context of a disabled board is controversial. If the SLC determines that the derivative lawsuit is not in the best interests of the corporation, should the court defer to the SLC's determinations and dismiss the lawsuit?

To provide better context for the issues surrounding the use of an SLC when there is a disabled board, let us use the following hypothetical situation:

> ABC Inc. entered into a transaction where 6 of its 9 directors were conflicted.

––––––––––

[336] See Chapter 6, §6A-209, et seq.

[337] See Chapter 5, §5A-507, et seq.

A - Universal-demand jurisdiction: A shareholder makes demand on the board to sue the 6 conflicted directors for breach of their fiduciary duties in connection with the underlying transaction. The board needs to decide whether to accept demand (i.e., decide to sue the 6 conflicted directors) or reject demand.

B - Demand-excused jurisdiction: A shareholder brings a shareholder derivative lawsuit against the 6 conflicted directors without making demand. The board needs to decide whether to ask the court to dismiss the lawsuit, or to allow the corporation to sue the 6 conflicted directors.

Under these circumstances, demand would clearly be wrongfully refused (in A) or futile (in B) because a majority of directors were conflicted in the underlying transaction.

Now imagine the board forms an SLC to determine whether the lawsuit is in the best interests of the corporation. The board appoints the three non-conflicted directors to the SLC and the SLC eventually determines that the derivative lawsuit is not in the corporation's best interest.

Should the court defer to the SLC's determination?

Pro: The three members of the SLC are disinterested. We have always deferred to the business judgment of disinterested directors.

Con: The three SLC members may be disinterested, BUT are they really independent? It seems like there is a strong **structural bias**.

The term **structural bias** refers to pressures and expectations inherent in an organizational structure that tend to have a negative impact on unbiased decision making. For example, if we work closely together during the week and play tennis with each other on the weekends, I might not report your unethical business activities to the corporation's compliance officer.

The structural bias problem may be especially acute in the SLC context. It might be unrealistic to expect directors who serve on the SLC to make a completely unbiased decision about suing one or more of their fellow directors.

8A-104(b) JUDICIAL REVIEW OF THE SLC'S DECISION:

This brings us back to the original question: Will courts defer to the SLC's decision to dismiss the derivative lawsuit? Not surprisingly, courts take different approaches.

Delaware courts will apparently do a **strict review of the SLC's decision,** using a two-step process to review the SLC's decision:

Step 1: The defendants have the burden to show the members of the SLC were **disinterested, independent**,* and made a **good faith and reasonable investigation**.

>*In *In re Oracle Corp. Derivative Litigation*,[338] the Delaware Supreme Court made it clear that in determining whether the SLC members were independent, the court would consider subtle problems of independence and structural bias. This approach is arguably a general departure from the traditional test of independence we have seen for ratification of conflicted transactions, which merely asks whether the directors were dominated or controlled by the conflicted directors.[339]

Step 2: The **judge will apply her own "independent business judgment"*** about the merits of the lawsuit and whether the company should pursue it or not.

>*Notice the departure from traditional principles of the competence of courts. One of the justifications for the business judgment rule is that judges are not competent to second guess the business judgments of directors – after all, judges are not business experts. However, maybe with respect to lawsuits, judges do indeed have a certain amount of "business" acumen that makes deference to the SLC less justified. A judge is arguably in a good position to judge the merits of a lawsuit, its chances of success, and maybe even the potential legal expenses. On the other hand, judges may be in a poor position to judge the harm the lawsuit might cause to the corporation's reputation or the cost of employee resources the corporation will need to divert away from its everyday businesses to the lawsuit.

Other jurisdictions, such as New York, are more deferential to the decisions of the SLC, limiting their inquiry to whether the SLC was independent and whether its investigation was adequate and appropriate. In sharp contrast, Iowa generally rejects the idea that the board has the capacity to appoint an SLC when the majority of the board members are disabled.[340]

---

[338] 824 A.2d 917 (Del. Ch. 2003).

[339] See Chapter 6, §6A-202(d).

[340] *Miller v. Register and Tribune Syndicate, Inc.*, 336 N.W.2d 709 (Iowa 1983).

8A-104(c) THE SLC WHEN EVERY DIRECTOR IS DISABLED:

The example above assumed that only six of the nine directors of ABC Corp. were conflicted in the underlying transaction that gave rise to the shareholder derivative suit. Three directors were available to serve as members of an SLC.

What if, however, **all of the directors had been conflicted**, or if there was a substantial likelihood that each of the directors would be liable for some breach of other fiduciary duties in connection with the underlying transaction? Could the board create and staff an SLC under such circumstances?

There are three possible ways to form an independent SLC when the entire board is disabled (unless you are in a jurisdiction, like Iowa, that does not recognize the board's power to do so):

(1) New directors have been elected after the transaction in question. The board appoints the new directors to an SLC.

(2) Old directors have resigned after the transaction in question and new directors have been appointed to fill the vacancies. The board appoints the new directors to an SLC.

(3) The board votes to expand the size of the board, creating vacancies. The board votes to fill those vacancies with new directors.[341] The board appoints the new directors to an SLC.

8A-105 FEE-SHIFTING PROVISIONS:

Imagine the board of directors amended the bylaws to include a provision that required the **unsuccessful shareholder-plaintiff in an intra-company lawsuit to pay the corporation's attorney's fees and other expenses**. This type of provision is often called a **fee-shifting provision**. Because it applies all "intra-company" lawsuits, it applies to both derivative and direct shareholder lawsuits that address corporate governance issues.

The benefit of a fee-shifting provision is that it will discourage frivolous and non-meritorious lawsuits against the board and the executive officers. The corporation usually bears the costs of these lawsuits through indemnity and advancement of expenses.[342] The corporation also bears the costs of these lawsuits indirectly when the attention of its officers and directors is directed toward the lawsuit, and away from the business.

---

[341] See Chapter 5, §5A-502(b).

[342] See §8A-200 et seq., below.

The cost of a fee-shifting provision is that it will discourage valid claims whose chances of success in court are less than certain because of an uncertainty in the law or the difficulty of proving the facts. Shareholder direct and derivative lawsuits are important mechanisms for policing the conduct of directors and officers.

In response to this controversy, the Delaware General Assembly passed the following amendments to the Delaware General Corporation Law:[343]

> The certificate of incorporation may not contain any provision that would impose liability on a stockholder for the attorneys' fees or expenses of the corporation or any other party in connection with an internal corporate claim . . . .[344]

> The bylaws may not contain any provision that would impose liability on a stockholder for the attorneys' fees or expenses of the corporation or any other party in connection with an internal corporate claim . . . .[345]

You will note that these amendments prohibit fee-shifting provisions in the bylaws **or** the articles of incorporation (called the "certificate of incorporation" in Delaware and many other states). Because the board is allowed to amend the bylaws without the approval of the shareholders in most instances,[346] we can readily see the propriety of a rule that prohibits the board from unilaterally imposing fee-shifting burdens on shareholders through the bylaws. However, because the shareholders must approve any amendment to the articles,[347] a rule prohibiting a fee-shifting provision in the articles is a bit more suspect.

If the shareholders agree that a fee-shifting provision in the articles is in the best interests of the corporation and its shareholders, why not allow it? You will remember that Delaware law, and most other state corporate law statutes, allow a provision in the articles of incorporation that exculpates directors for breaches of their fiduciary duty of care.[348] If the law allows shareholders to approve exculpation clauses in the articles, why not fee-shifting provisions?

We might look at exculpation clauses and fee-shifting provisions as having different levels of adverse impact on the corporate governance of public companies. Most, if not all, duty of care lawsuits would ultimately fail because of the difficulty of proving recklessness in the board's decision-making

---

[343] Delaware State Senate, 148th General Assembly Senate Bill No. 75 (April 29, 2015). Signed into law by Delaware Governor Jack Markell on June 24, 2015, effective from August 1, 2015.

[344] Amending §102 of the DGCL by adding new 102(f).

[345] Amending §109(b) of the DGCL.

[346] See Chapter 5, §5A-206(b).

[347] See Chapter 5, §5A-207 et seq.

[348] See Chapter 5, §6A-204(d).

process.[349] In that sense, exculpation clauses simply dispense with doomed lawsuits much earlier in the litigation process, reducing costs for the corporation and its shareholders. If you subscribe to that theory, the exculpation clauses have little or no adverse impact on corporate governance – the only adverse impact is the dismissal of the very rare case where the plaintiff could have proved the directors engaged in a reckless decision-making process.

In contrast, we might argue that the rather broad stroke of a fee-shifting provision dooms far more beneficial lawsuits than the exculpation clause. The threat of bearing the costs of the corporation's attorney's fees and other expenses discourages not only strike and other nuisance lawsuits that bring no value to the shareholders, it also discourages two categories of lawsuits that we might consider to be in the best interests of the corporation and its shareholders: (1) lawsuits that might bring beneficial change to the corporation through settlement, even though the prospects of winning on the merits is poor for the shareholder-plaintiff, and (2) lawsuits that make novel arguments that could change common law corporate governance doctrines, but are not supported by current precedent when the plaintiff-shareholder is weighing the threat of the fee-shifting provision.

Of course, looking at a prohibition on fee-shifting provisions in isolation might not be the best way to evaluate its efficiency. We might perform a more holistic evaluation of fee-shifting prohibition with the entire mix of corporate governance rules and market forces that protect shareholders and police director and officer misconduct. Maybe fee-shifting provisions would push the delicate corporate governance balance too far in favor of directors and officers – the proverbial straw that breaks the camel's back.

8A-200 INDEMNIFICATION OF DIRECTORS AND OFFICERS:

8A-201 INDEMNIFICATION GENERALLY:

Corporate law statutes typically permit corporations to **indemnify** directors and officers for **expenses they incur in legal proceedings that are related to their positions in the company**. Under certain narrow circumstances, corporate law statutes will require the corporation to indemnify an officer or director for her legal expenses.

Legal proceeding is usually broadly defined to include:

> Criminal prosecutions

---

[349] See Chapter 5, §6A-209 et seq.

Administrative actions and hearings

Civil lawsuits

Appeals

Arbitrations

Mediations and other alternative dispute resolutions

Investigations

Threatened legal proceedings

Legal expenses usually covers:

Attorney fees

Investigation expenses

Other litigation expenses

In addition to permitting a corporation to indemnify a director or officer for her legal expenses, the law may permit a corporation to indemnify a director or officer for monetary liability, depending on the circumstances.

Liability usually includes any adverse financial outcome of the legal proceedings, such as:

Fines

Penalties

Civil judgments

Monetary settlements

8A-201(a) MANDATORY INDEMNIFICATION:

Depending on the statute, the law usually requires a corporation to indemnify an officer or director for **legal expenses** incurred in a legal proceeding if she is wholly successful on the merits or otherwise.

> **Wholly successful on the merits:** If she is found not guilty in a criminal proceeding or not liable in a civil lawsuit, for example, the corporation *must* indemnify her for the legal expenses she incurred defending herself.

> **Wholly successful otherwise:** If the director or officer is successful because the statute of limitations has run, the corporation has settled on her behalf, or due to some other technicality, the corporation *must*

indemnify her. Courts often interpret the "wholly successful otherwise" language of mandatory indemnification to include any situation where the director or officer emerges **unscathed** financially from a legal proceeding.

There are situations where the director or officer would not be entitled to indemnification even though she would consider the outcome to be a success. For example:

> She settled a lawsuit for a small amount

> She entered into a plea bargain with the prosecutor

> She incurred costs responding to a governmental investigation, but the investigation never resulted in any kind of legal action – i.e., she never had the chance to be successful

Under these circumstances, the law will not require the corporation to indemnify her, but it will permit the corporation to indemnify her if she qualifies for permissive indemnification.

8A-201(b) PERMISSIVE INDEMNIFICATION:

A director or officer may still be eligible to receive indemnification from the corporation for her **legal expenses and liability** even though she has not been successful on the merits or otherwise. For example:

> She was adjudged liable

> She was found guilty

> She settled the lawsuit

> She paid a fine, etc.

> She never had her day in court, so to speak, because the investigation never resulted in a formal lawsuit, prosecution, or administrative action, etc.

Corporate law statutes normally **permit** a corporation to indemnify a director or officer for her liability and legal expenses **if she acted in good faith and in a manner she reasonably believed to be in the best interests of the corporation**. For criminal actions there is usually an additional requirement that **she had no reason to believe her actions were illegal**.

Permissive indemnification is subject to several important provisos. Under most corporate law statutes, the corporation **may not indemnify** the director or officer under the following circumstances:

> She is adjudged **liable** in a claim **by or in the right of the corporation**;

or

She is adjudged **liable** for receiving an **improper benefit**.

Effectively, these two provisions **prohibit indemnification of an officer or director who has lost a derivative lawsuit** (in the right of the corporation)[350] **or has lost any duty of loyalty claim** (received an improper benefit), even if the director or officer acted in good faith and in a manner she reasonably believed to be in the best interests of the corporation.

If the director or officer has **settled the claim** alleging an improper benefit or she has settled a claim by or in the right of the corporation, she has not been adjudged liable. In most states, the law **allows the corporation to indemnify her for her legal expenses, but not for the amount of the settlement.**

8A-201(c) INDEMNIFICATION PURSUANT TO CONTRACT:

Most corporate law statutes expressly allow parties to contractually define indemnification and advancement of expenses for directors and officers. For example, Delaware law provides:

> The indemnification and advancement of expenses provided by, or granted pursuant to, the other subsections of this section shall not be deemed exclusive of any other rights to which those seeking indemnification or advancement of expenses may be entitled under any **bylaw, agreement**, vote of stockholders or disinterested directors, or otherwise, . . .[351]

The RMBCA has a similar provision.[352] As alluded to in the Delaware provision, indemnification agreements may appear in traditional contracts between the corporation and its directors of officers, or they **may appear in the corporation's bylaws or articles**.

A word of caution on contractual indemnification: Although both the Delaware and RMBCA provisions seem to allow unfettered latitude to deviate from the statutory indemnification provisions, it is likely that the courts will impose limitations on how far the indemnification agreement can modify the statute.

A court would probably not allow parties to draft out of the requirement that the director or officer acted in good faith and a in manner she reasonably believed to be in the best interests of the corporation. In other words, the

---

[350] The provision applies not only to shareholder derivative lawsuits against the director or officer (i.e., "in the right of the corporation"), but also when the board decides to cause the corporation to sue the director or officer (i.e., "by the corporation").

[351] DGCL §145(f) (emphasis added).

[352] RMBCA §8.58(a).

parties may use contractual indemnification to **change the statutory permissive indemnification provisions to mandatory contractual indemnification provisions, but only if the director or officer acted in good faith and a manner she reasonably believed to be in the best interests of the corporation**.

Similarly, a court would probably **not allow a contractual provision** that permits or requires indemnification for a director or officer who **is liable for receiving an improper benefit or adjudged liable in a derivative lawsuit, or when the corporation is the plaintiff**. Of course, if the director or officer was successful on the merits or otherwise, the statute would require the corporation to indemnify her regardless.

In summary, it is unlikely a court would enforce the following contracts, bylaws, or articles:

> A promise by the corporation to indemnify a director or officer even though she did not act in good faith or in a manner she reasonably believed to be in the best interests of the corporation (and, in a criminal case, even if she had reason to believe her actions were illegal).

> A promise by the corporation to indemnify a director or officer who loses a shareholder derivative lawsuit (or a lawsuit where the corporations is the plaintiff); or

> A promise by the corporation to indemnify a director who received an improper benefit.

Effectively, the contract for indemnification may only make permissive indemnification mandatory.

8A-201(d) D&O INSURANCE:

Most corporate law statutes expressly allow the corporation to purchase **Directors and Officers Insurance**. D&O insurance is rather common. The corporation may purchase a D&O policy indemnifies directors and officers when the corporation could indemnify them. In addition, the law usually allows the corporation to purchase a D&O insurance policy that would indemnify the director or officer for liability arising from conduct that makes the director or officer ineligible for indemnification from the corporation. Thus, assuming an insurance company is willing to underwrite the policy, a corporation could take out a D&O insurance policy that would indemnify its directors or officers for liability arising from:

> A judgment against her in lawsuit by or in the right of the corporation and her related legal expenses

Her settlement of a lawsuit by or in the right of the corporation[353]

A lawsuit regarding conduct where she did not act in good faith or in a manner she reasonably believed to be in the best interests of the corporation

A judgment against her arising from conduct that resulted in her receiving an improper benefit.

8A-202 INDEMNIFICATION OF DERIVATIVE AND DIRECT SHAREHOLDER LAWSUITS:

8A-202(a) INDEMNIFICATION IN SHAREHOLDER DERIVATIVE LAWSUITS:

As discussed above,[354] corporate law indemnification statutes tend to treat indemnification for derivative lawsuits[355] differently from other civil lawsuits. It would be circular for the corporation to indemnify the defendant for the monetary damages the court requires the defendant to pay the corporation.

When the civil suit against a director or officer is a derivative lawsuit and the director or officer is **adjudged liable**, the corporation is **not permitted to indemnify her at all**. In contrast, in other civil lawsuits the corporation would be permitted to indemnify the director or officer for her legal expenses and her liability if she acted in good faith and in a manner she reasonably believed to be in the best interests of the corporation.

If the director or officer **settles the derivative lawsuit**, the corporation is permitted to indemnify her **legal expenses, but not the settlement amount**, as long as she acted in good faith and a manner she reasonably believed to be in the best interest of the corporation. In contrast, in other civil lawsuits the corporation would be permitted to indemnify the director or officer for her legal expenses and her settlement amount if she acted in good faith and in a manner she reasonably believed to be in the best interests of the corporation.

---

[353] Remember, if the lawsuit is by or in the right of the corporation, the corporation may NOT indemnify the director or officer for any settlement amount, but may indemnify her for her related legal expenses (if she acted in good faith and a manner she reasonably believed to be in the best interests of the corporation). In contrast, A D&O insurance policy may indemnify her for both her settlement and her legal expenses.

[354] See §8A-201(b), above.

[355] Lawsuits where the corporation sues the defendant are treated the same way as derivative lawsuits for the purposes of indemnification.

8A-202(b) INDEMNIFICATION IN SHAREHOLDER DIRECT LAWSUITS:

Most corporate law statutes treat indemnification of direct shareholder lawsuits like any other civil lawsuit.

8A-203 ADVANCEMENT OF EXPENSES:

Defending a lawsuit requires a significant outlay of money for lawyers, expert witnesses, etc. The director, or officer, who is defending herself in a lawsuit will find some solace in the prospect of indemnification from the corporation after the proceedings have concluded, but she would prefer the corporation to pay for her expenses up front.

State corporate law statutes normally allow a corporation to advance expenses to defendant directors or officers even in duty of loyalty cases, subject to important qualifications:

1. The corporation must first make a determination that it is likely that the director or officer eventually will be eligible (or entitled) to indemnification; and
2. Normally the director or officer must promise, in writing, to reimburse the corporation for any advancement of legal expenses if it turns out she does not qualify for permissive or mandatory indemnification.

State corporate law statutes allow the corporation to advance legal expenses, but do not require it. The corporation and the director or officer can make advancement of expenses mandatory through a contractual arrangement, through the bylaws, or through the articles of incorporation. However, it is likely that the law will require any sort of private arrangement that makes advancement of expenses by the corporation mandatory to be subject to the same qualifications as the permissive advancement of expenses.

UNIT 8B

PARTNERSHIPS – LITIGATION:

8B-100 PARTNER LAWSUITS AGAINST CO-PARTNERS AND THE PARTNERSHIP:

As you may remember from earlier chapters, partnerships come in several different forms.[356] The following three are probably the most common:

General Partnerships
Limited Liability Partnerships
Limited Partnerships

Lawsuits for breaches of fiduciary duties are handled the same in general partnerships and limited liability partnerships. Lawsuits for fiduciary breaches in limited partnerships are handled in a manner very similar to shareholder derivative lawsuits in corporations.

8B-101 GENERAL PARTNERSHIPS AND LIMITED LIABILITY PARTNERSHIPS:

We discussed in earlier chapters that the rules governing limited liability partnerships (**LLPs**) were substantially similar to those governing general partnerships (**GPs**). Indeed, LLPs are merely general partnerships that protect partners with limited liability under certain circumstances.

In GPs and LLPs, each partner owes a fiduciary duty to the partnership and her co-partners. When a partner breaches her fiduciary duty to the partnership, her liability to the partnership will likely be resolved in an **action for an accounting** (discussed below), not a derivative lawsuit.

8B-101(a) DERIVATIVE LAWSUITS IN GENERAL PARTNERSHIPS:

In the corporation, the board of directors decides whether the corporation will sue a third party, including one of its own officers or directors. The shareholder –derivative-lawsuit mechanism gives shareholders an opportunity to bypass the board and sue on behalf of the corporation, subject to the limitations discussed above.

---

[356] See Chapter 3, Unit 3D.

In the partnership, the partners decide whether the partnership will sue a third party, including one of its own partners. A decision by the partners to sue one of their own is most likely an **extraordinary decision**, requiring an affirmative vote of all the partners. Even if the law treats the lawsuit as an ordinary matter, requiring only a majority of the partners to approve of the action, if a majority of the partners will be defendants or are controlled by the defendants, they can effectively block the lawsuit. It is not entirely clear whether the law allows partners who would be the defendants in the lawsuit to vote against the lawsuit.

There appears to be little, if any, support in the RUPA for derivative actions in the partnership. RUPA §405 expressly allows the partnership to maintain an action against a partner. It also allows a partner to maintain an action against the partnership or another partner to enforce her own rights as a partner, which would be analogous to a direct shareholder suit in the corporation. However, the RUPA does not expressly allow a partner to sue on behalf of the partnership over the objections of the other partners. Indeed, the official comments explicitly state that the RUPA does not authorize derivative suits.

Although there are cases that allow individual partners to sue on behalf of the partnership over the objections of the other partners, two leading scholars of partnership law opine that "it is unlikely that partnership derivative suits will be recognized."[357] Without the right to resort to a derivative lawsuit, the partner who wants the partnership to sue one or more of her co-partners will be forced to accept the decision of her co-partners. She may try to argue that the proposed defendants to the lawsuit should not be allowed to vote on the decision to sue because they were conflicted.

8B-101(b) AN ACTION FOR ACCOUNTING – DIRECT OR DERIVATIVE CLAIMS:

An **action for an accounting** is an equitable remedy where a court investigates the partnership's books and transactions to determine relative rights and duties of the partners. **The action for accounting can address claims by partners that are analogous to shareholder direct claims in the corporate context.** Typical accounting actions might involve a dispute over a partner's rights to profits, a partner's rights to participate in management, a partner's rights to information, or other rights specifically granted to a partner in a partnership agreement.

An action for accounting can also be used by the partnership to hold a partner accountable for claims by the partnership, such as self-dealing, taking a partnership opportunity, using partnership property for personal purposes,

---

[357] 1 RIBSTEIN AND KEATING ON LIMITED LIABILITY COMPANIES §10:9.

and other breaches of fiduciary duties to the partnership. Of course, the fact that the partnership can use an accounting action to enforce its own rights does not answer the question about whether one partner can bring an accounting action on behalf of the partnership without the consent of the other partners. As discussed above, there is little support for these types of derivative actions in partnerships.

Many courts require a partner bringing a suit for an accounting to show she made demand on the other partners for an accounting and that her demand was refused, or to show although demand was not made, it was excused because it would have been futile. Although these requirements are reminiscent of the demand requirements for shareholder derivative suits, they apply to all accounting actions, not merely those that seek to enforce the rights of the partnership. The requirements are there to ensure that the parties exhaust internal solutions before pursuing judicial remedies.

While there may be room in some jurisdictions for a complaining partner to use an accounting action to enforce the rights of the partnership without the consent of the other partners, one must remember that the official comments to RUPA §405 explicitly state that the RUPA does not authorize derivative actions.

8B-101(c) AN ACTION FOR ACCOUNTING AS THE EXCLUSIVE REMEDY:

In many jurisdictions an action for an accounting is the exclusive remedy for solving disputes among partners. The justification for this requirement is efficiency: the court can settle all matters between partners in the same proceeding.

RUPA is much more liberal. It allows a partner to seek legal or equitable relief against the partnership or co-partner "with or without an accounting."[358] In addition, clauses in partnership agreements requiring disputes to be settled by arbitration are generally enforceable.

8B-102 LIMITED PARTNERSHIPS:

Limited partnerships (**LPs**) are more like corporations than general partnerships in many respects. An LP will have one or more general partners and one or more limited partners. The general partners bear personal liability for the obligations of the partnership and have control over the business of the partnership. The general partners of the LP serve the same function as the directors and officers of a corporation.

---

[358] RUPA §405(b).

448

The limited partners enjoy limited liability and, generally, do not participate in the management or control of the LP, except for limited voting rights. Thus, limited partners have rights similar to those of shareholders in a corporation. As such, you would not be surprised to discover that limited partners have rights to bring derivative lawsuits that are similar to the rights of shareholders in corporations.

8B-102(a) LIMITED PARTNER DERIVATIVE LAWSUITS:

A limited partner derivative lawsuit would seek recovery from one or more of the general partners for injury caused to the partnership because of breach of fiduciary duties. **Most jurisdictions allow limited partners to bring derivative lawsuits**, either by statutory provision or by common law rule. The 1976, 1985, and 2001 versions of the RULPA each expressly authorize limited partner derivative lawsuits.[359]

In addition, it is common for a jurisdiction's approach to limited partner derivative lawsuits to have **contemporaneous ownership requirements** similar to those for shareholder derivative lawsuits. Moreover, you should expect rules regarding **demand and demand futility** that closely resemble those for the shareholder derivative lawsuits.

8B-102(b) LIMITED PARTNER DIRECT LAWSUITS:

Limited partners may also initiate direct lawsuits against the general partners to assert their individual rights as limited partners. The distinction between limited partner derivative and direct claims will likely closely mirror the distinctions courts have made between shareholder direct and derivative actions. These individual rights are similar to the individual rights of shareholders we discussed earlier – e.g., voting rights, rights to distributions, rights granted by the partnership agreement, etc.

8B-102(c) GENERAL PARTNER LAWSUITS:

Usually, only limited partners may maintain derivative actions in LPs. The rights of a general partner in an LP to sue her co-partners are governed by the rules that govern general partnerships (discussed above). However, you should note that the 2001 version of the RULPA allows *any* partner to maintain a derivative lawsuit, which presumably includes general partners.[360] In a jurisdiction that has adopted the 2001 version of the RULPA, the general partner of an LP may indeed be allowed to bring a derivative lawsuit.

---

[359] See RULPA 2001 §1002.

[360] Id.

UNIT 8C

LLCs – FIDUCIARY DUTY LITIGATION:

8C-100 MEMBER LAWSUITS AGAINST CO-MEMBERS, MANAGERS, AND THE COMPANY:

You may recall that LLCs are often divided into two categories: (1) member-managed, where the members (i.e., the owners) directly manage the business and affairs of the LLC; and (2) manager-managed, where managers, not members, manage the business and affairs of the LLC.

In member-managed LLCs, the derivative lawsuit will come about when one member feels another member has caused harm to the LLC by breaching her fiduciary duties. When one member wants to sue the member who has allegedly breached her fiduciary duties, but the other members do not,[361] the member in favor of a lawsuit will have to resort to a derivative lawsuit.

In manager-managed LLCs, the managers decide on the company's litigation matters, including the decision to sue one of the managers. One or more members might desire to sue a manager for the harm the manager caused to the company by an alleged breach of her fiduciary duties, but the managers may decide not to sue. Under these circumstances, the member will have to resort to a derivative lawsuit.

Most jurisdictions allow an LLC member to maintain a derivative lawsuit to assert the rights of the LLC, regardless of whether the LLC is member-managed or manager-managed. Member derivative lawsuits in LLCs are subject to procedures and limitations similar to those for shareholder derivative lawsuits.

8C-101 LLC MEMBER DERIVATIVE LAWSUITS:

Many state LLC statutes have provisions regarding derivative lawsuits. If the jurisdiction where you practice does not have an express statutory provision, there may be common law rules that give members rights to maintain derivative-like lawsuits.

---

[361] If the lawsuit were considered to be an extraordinary matter, it would require approval of all of the members, unless the operating agreement provides otherwise. This would require the defendant-member to approve the lawsuit against herself.

451

Usually any member, even a managing member, may maintain a derivative lawsuit. Normally, **contemporaneous ownership rules** similar to those for shareholder derivative lawsuits apply to member derivative lawsuits. Similarly, **demand requirements** and other procedural aspects of LLC derivative lawsuits are analogous to those for shareholder derivative lawsuits.

When a jurisdiction's LLC statute does not clearly provide rules, we would expect courts to apply rules **similar to those for shareholder derivative lawsuits regarding**:

> Contemporaneous ownership rules

> Demand (universal, excused, etc.)

> Special litigation committees

> Reimbursing plaintiff's expenses if suit is wholly or partially successful

> Judicial approval of settlements

> Advancement of expenses to defendant-managers/members and indemnification of their expenses.

However, because LLCs are generally closely-held business organizations, we would **expect a court to look to rules that specifically address shareholder derivative lawsuits in closely-held corporations** for guidance on handling LLC derivative lawsuits.[362]

8C-102 DRAFTING OUT OF DERIVATIVE LAWSUITS IN THE LLC:

The members of an LLC might want to use their operating agreement to define member rights to maintain derivative lawsuits or to even eliminate those rights. State LLC statutes generally allow parties wide discretion to use an operating agreement to modify rights to maintain derivative actions, provide alternatives for derivative actions, or even eliminate member rights to maintain derivative actions.

RULLCA prohibits provisions in operating agreements that unreasonably restrict the right of members to maintain derivative lawsuits.[363] This approach probably permits agreements that reasonably modify member rights to

---

[362] See 8A-101(f), above.

[363] RULLCA §110(c)(9).

derivative lawsuits or that provide alternatives, such as arbitration. However, it likely precludes any agreement that completely eliminates member rights to maintain any derivative claims.

8C-103 **LLC MEMBER DIRECT LAWSUITS:**

LLC members can also bring direct lawsuits for conduct by co-members or managers that directly impinge their rights. You should expect the test for a direct cause of action, as opposed to a derivative one, to be the same as that for shareholder derivative lawsuits.

CHAPTER 9

FUNDAMENTAL TRANSACTIONS

UNIT 9A
<u>Corporations – Fundamental Transactions:</u>

UNIT 9B
PARTNERSHIPS – FUNDAMENTAL TRANSACTIONS:

UNIT 9C
LLCs – FUNDAMENTAL TRANSACTIONS:

UNIT 9A

CORPORATIONS – FUNDAMENTAL TRANSACTIONS:

9A-100 CORPORATE FUNDAMENTAL TRANSACTIONS – INTRODUCTION:

9A-101 THE FOUR CATEGORIES OF FUNDAMENTAL TRANSACTIONS:

As we discussed in Chapter 5,[364] shareholders have the right to elect directors and to approve four categories of fundamental transactions:

- Amendment of the articles of incorporation

- Voluntary dissolution

- Mergers and other business combinations

- Sale of substantially all of the corporation's assets

9A-102 COMMON ISSUES FOR FUNDAMENTAL TRANSACTIONS:

When you encounter a fundamental transaction, there are four common issues you need to consider:

Is board approval a prerequisite?

> Generally, the shareholders will only vote on a fundamental transaction after the board has first reviewed and approved the transaction.

Is shareholder approval required? If so, what are the quorum and approval requirements?

> You should approach any of the fundamental transactions assuming the shareholders get to vote, but there are exceptions.

---

[364] See Chapter 5, §5A-205.

You need to read your jurisdiction's corporate law statute to determine if one of the exceptions applies.

Once you have determined that the shareholders have a right to vote on the transaction, you should determine what the **quorum** and **approval requirements** are. Some jurisdictions have higher quorum or approval requirements for certain fundamental transactions.

Will the shareholders have appraisal/dissenters' rights?

If a shareholder opposes a fundamental transaction, she might be able to exercise **appraisal rights** (also called **dissenters' rights**). If the other shareholders approve the transaction, appraisal rights require the corporation to **purchase the dissenting shareholder's shares at fair market value**.

Are there fiduciary duty protections for shareholders?

Directors and controlling shareholders have the same fiduciary duties in fundamental transactions as they do in any transaction. The fiduciary duties that are most often at issue in a fundamental transaction are the **duty of care** and the **duty of loyalty**.

9A-103 TAX IMPLICATIONS FOR FUNDAMENTAL TRANSACTIONS:

Please keep in mind that the transactions discussed in this chapter have varying federal and state income tax consequences for the corporation and the shareholders. Attorneys structure transactions to minimize adverse income tax implications for the corporations and their shareholders. We will leave coverage of the tax consequences for a text dedicated to business-entity taxation or mergers and acquisitions.

9A-200 AMENDMENT OF THE ARTICLES OF INCORPORATION – APPRAISAL RIGHTS:

In Chapter 5, we discussed in detail when and how shareholders vote on amendments to the articles of incorporation, including when they will have a right to vote as a class and when non-voting classes will have a right to vote.[365] In that discussion, we only briefly mentioned appraisal rights for

---

[365] See Chapter 5, §5A-207 et seq.

shareholders.[366] If a shareholder has appraisal rights, she can **require the corporation to purchase her shares at fair market value** if the other shareholders approve the amendment she opposes.

State corporate law statutes take different approaches to appraisal rights for article amendments. In some jurisdictions, there are virtually no appraisal rights for article amendments. For example, the most recent version of the RMBCA only grants appraisal rights for article amendments in one very limited circumstance:

> When the amendment **"reduces the number of shares of a class or series owned by the shareholder to a fraction of a share if the corporation has the obligation or right to repurchase the fractional share so created."**[367]

This RMBCA provision refers to what is commonly called a **reverse stock split**. A stock split is where the corporation changes one share of stock into more than one share of stock. A reverse stock split is where the corporation changes one share of stock into less that one share.

Illustration 1 – stock split:

ABC Inc. has 1,000,000 shares of common stock authorized. The stock is trading for $10,000 per share on Nasdaq.

To reduce the price per share, making the stock more liquid on the market, the board of directors and the shareholders approve an amendment to the articles increasing the number of authorized shares from 1,000,000 to 300,000,000. Shareholders will receive 300 new shares for every one share they hold.

Mary holds 10,000 shares. She exchanges her 1,000 shares for 300,000 new shares.

Illustration 2 – reverse stock split:

XYZ Inc. has 1,000,000 shares of stock authorized. Because it has a relatively small number of shareholders, the board of directors decides to amend the articles reducing the number of authorized shares from 1,000,000 to 100.

Shareholders will receive one new share for every 10,000 shares they hold.

---

[366] See Chapter 5, §5A-207(b).

[367] RMBCA §13.02(a)(4).

Mary holds 55,000 shares. She exchanges her 55,000 shares for 5.5 shares.

If the amendment to the articles gives the corporation a right to purchase the fractional share, Mary and all the other common shareholders would have appraisal rights.

Why is a reverse stock split worthy of appraisal rights? A reverse stock split may seem benign, but it can be used to eliminate minority shareholders.

Illustration:

ABC Inc. has 2,000,000 shares authorized and outstanding. The controlling shareholder owns 1,500,000 shares. The remaining 500,000 shares are owned in equal proportion by five minority shareholders.

The controlling shareholder causes the board to amend the articles to **reduce the number of authorized shares from 2,000,000 shares to 4 shares**. The board resolution gives the corporation a right to purchase any fractional share.

In the exchange, the controlling shareholder receives three new shares. Each of the five minority shareholders receives 0.2 shares. The corporation purchases each of the 0.2 shares, eliminating the minority shareholders.

All of the shareholders would have appraisal rights.

Under older versions of the RMBCA, shareholders had appraisal rights for more types of amendments to the articles of incorporation. For example, in jurisdictions that have adopted earlier versions of the RMBCA, shareholders of a particular class or series of shares would have appraisal rights for article amendments that do any of the following:

(1) Alter or abolish a dividend or liquidation preference for the class or series of shares,

(2) Create, alter, or abolish a right of redemption for the class or series of shares; or

(3) Exclude or limit the right of the class or series of shares to vote on any matter.[368]

Of course, you must become familiar with the statute in your jurisdiction.

---

[368] See, for example, Kentucky Revised Statutes 271B.13-020(1)(e).

9A-300 **VOLUNTARY DISSOLUTION:**

Dissolution means the extinguishment of the corporation's legal existence. It ultimately results in the **liquidation** of the corporation's assets and the winding up of its business. After a company dissolves, the only business that the corporation may conduct is **winding up**, which consists of collecting money it is owed, liquidating its assets, paying its debts, and distributing the residual to the shareholders.

When reading the dissolution procedures of your jurisdiction's corporate law statute, you should consider how it addresses the following issues:

What are the internal procedures for voluntary dissolution?

BOARD APPROVAL: Usually the proposal for dissolution comes from the board of directors. In some jurisdictions, the shareholders are allowed to initiate a motion for dissolution.

SHAREHOLDER APPROVAL: Generally, shareholders have a right to vote on the dissolution. Some jurisdictions allow the board to dissolve the corporation without a shareholder vote, but only in limited circumstances.

APPRAISAL RIGHTS: Appraisal rights are not available.

How should the corporation in dissolution deal with known claims against the corporation?

A dissolved corporation will normally provide notice to all known claimants. Claimants must respond within a certain time, otherwise their claim will be barred.

How should the corporation in dissolution deal with unknown or contingent claims against the corporation?

For claims the corporation is unaware of, it will publish a notice of its dissolution. Persons with claims that were contingent or unknown to the corporation at the time of dissolution must enforce their claims within a certain time, otherwise their claims will be barred.

What happens if the corporation in dissolution has no assets to satisfy claims after making a distribution to the shareholders?

If the assets of the corporation are not sufficient to satisfy **claims made in a timely manner**, and the residual has already been distributed to the shareholders, the claimants may recover the distribution from the shareholders. Shareholder liability is limited to the distribution they received in liquidation.

In addition, the creditors can force the corporation into bankruptcy proceedings under bankruptcy law.

9A-400 MERGERS, CONSOLIDATIONS & OTHER BUSINESS COMBINATIONS:

9A-401 STATUTORY MERGER:

The term statutory merger usually refers to the business combination specifically provided in corporate law statutes. In a statutory merger, the **target** corporation ("T") is merged out of existence and the **surviving** corporation ("A") inherits the entire assets and liabilities of the Target.

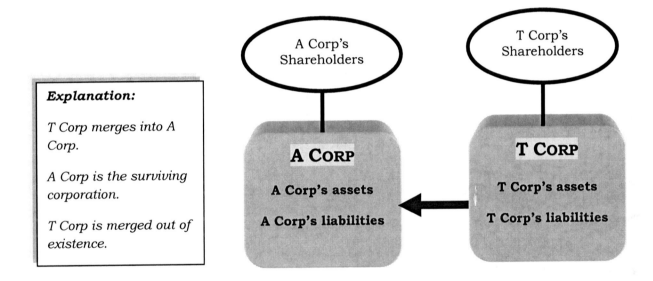

Explanation:

T Corp merges into A Corp.

A Corp is the surviving corporation.

T Corp is merged out of existence.

The illustrations on the following pages analyze the possible results of a statutory merger.

9-401(a) **STATUTORY MERGER – FORWARD MERGER 1:**

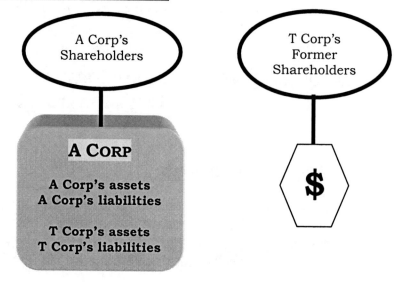

Explanation:

A Corp Survives.

A Corp inherits T Corp's assets and liabilities.

T Corp is merged out of existence.

T Corp's shareholders receive cash in the merger.

BOARD APPROVAL: The board of each corporation will approve the merger.

SHAREHOLDER APPROVAL: As a rule of thumb, we say that shareholders in the surviving corporation will not have a right to vote on the transaction. In most cases, the merger transaction is not a fundamental change for the shareholders of the surviving corporation. The surviving corporation's shareholders keep their shares in the company. The only change for the surviving corporation is the acquisition of new assets and liabilities. A company acquires new assets and liabilities on virtually every transaction, so we do not consider this transaction to be a fundamental change for the surviving corporation's shareholders.

In this case, **only T Corp's shareholders will get to vote on the transaction**. For T Corp's shareholders, the merger is a fundamental transaction because their company no longer exists. The merger fundamentally changes their original investment.

A Corp's shareholders, as the shareholders of the surviving corporation, will *not* have an opportunity to vote. For A Corp's shareholders, this merger is not a fundamental transaction. Nothing changes for A Corp's shareholders. They still have the same shares, the same number of shares, and their shareholdings have not been diluted in any way. A Corp still exists as it did before the merger, except with some additional assets and liabilities. Effectively, for A Corp, the merger was like any other business decision, such as buying a new factory or entering into a new contract. These types of business decisions are not fundamental changes, just major business decisions. Shareholders do not vote on business decisions, however major, unless they result in a fundamental change to the corporation.

APPRAISAL RIGHTS: The rule of thumb is that only shareholders who have rights to vote in the fundamental transaction will have appraisal rights. **T Corp's shareholders will have appraisal rights** because they had the right to vote on the merger. A Corp's shareholders will not have appraisal rights because they had no right to vote on the merger.

9-401(b) <u>STATUTORY MERGER – FORWARD MERGER 2:</u>

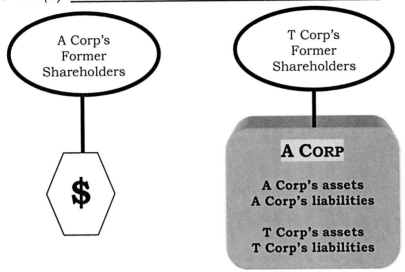

Explanation:

A Corp Survives.

A Corp inherits T Corp's assets and liabilities.

T Corp is merged out of existence.

A Corp's shareholders receive cash in the merger.

T Corp's shareholders receive A Corp stock in the merger.

<u>BOARD APPROVAL:</u> The board of each corporation will approve the merger.

<u>SHAREHOLDER APPROVAL:</u> Generally, shareholders in the surviving corporation will not have a right to vote on the transaction, but that is just simplification of the rule. The real test asks whether there is a fundamental change to the shareholders' investment.

In this transaction, the shareholders of the surviving corporation are cashed-out and the shareholders of the target corporation become the new shareholders of the surviving corporation. For each company's shareholders, this transaction fundamentally changes their original investment

In this case, both **A Corp's shareholders and T Corp's shareholders will vote on the merger**.

For A Corp's shareholders, this merger is a fundamental transaction. The merger results in A Corp's shareholders being cashed-out of their investment in A Corp. The merger fundamentally changes their original investment.

For T Corp's shareholders, the merger is a fundamental transaction because their company no longer exists and their shares in T Corp are being exchanged for shares in A Corp. The merger fundamentally changes their original investment.

<u>APPRAISAL RIGHTS:</u> Remember, the rule of thumb is that shareholders who have rights to vote in the fundamental transaction will have appraisal rights. **A Corp's shareholders and T Corp's shareholders will have appraisal rights** because they each had the right to vote on the merger.

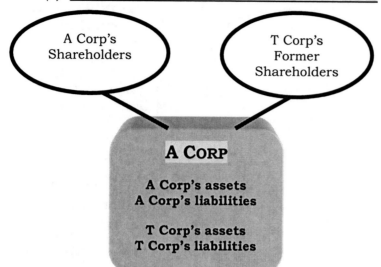

Explanation:

A Corp Survives.

A Corp inherits T Corp's assets and liabilities.

T Corp is merged out of existence.

T Corp's shareholders receive A Corp stock in the merger.

BOARD APPROVAL: The board of each corporation will approve the merger.

SHAREHOLDER APPROVAL: As we said, shareholders in the surviving corporation will normally not have a right to vote on the transaction, but we need to examine whether the transaction results in a fundamental change to the surviving shareholders' investment.

In this transaction, the shareholders of the surviving corporation are now sharing their investment in the surviving corporation with the shareholders of the target corporation. If the target shareholders acquired a large percentage of the surviving corporation, the transaction fundamentally changed the original investment of the surviving corporation's shareholders. Alternatively, if the surviving corporation's shareholders received a different class of shares in the transaction, the transaction fundamentally changed the original investment of the surviving corporation's shareholders.

In this case, **T Corp's shareholders will certainly vote on the merger**.

A Corp's shareholders might have a right to vote, depending on (1) how many A Corp shares T Corp's shareholders receive in the merger; and (2) whether A Corp's shareholders retained the same class of shares they held before the merger. The relevant corporate law statute will have specific rules addressing when the shareholders of a surviving corporation have a right to vote on the merger.

APPRAISAL RIGHTS: Remember, the rule of thumb is that shareholders who have rights to vote in the fundamental transaction will have appraisal rights. **T Corp's shareholders will clearly have appraisal rights** because they had the right to vote on the merger. We need more facts to determine whether A Corp's shareholders have a right to vote and right to appraisal.

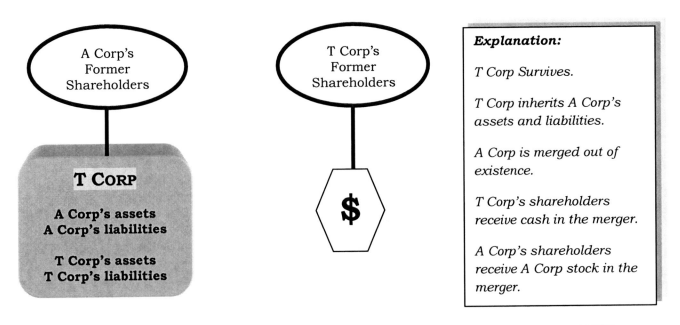

Explanation:

T Corp Survives.

T Corp inherits A Corp's assets and liabilities.

A Corp is merged out of existence.

T Corp's shareholders receive cash in the merger.

A Corp's shareholders receive A Corp stock in the merger.

This structure is often called a **reverse merger** because the target survives the merger. There must be some sort of business reason for why the parties want the target to survive.[369]

BOARD **A**PPROVAL: The board of each corporation will approve the merger.

SHAREHOLDER **A**PPROVAL: In this case, **A Corp's shareholders and T Corp's shareholders will vote on the merger**.

For A Corp's shareholders, the merger is a fundamental transaction because their company no longer exists and their shares in A Corp are being exchanged for shares in T Corp. The merger fundamentally changes their original investment.

For T Corp's shareholders, this merger is a fundamental transaction. The merger results in T Corp's shareholders being cashed-out of their investment in T Corp. The merger fundamentally changes their original investment.

APPRAISAL **RIGHTS**: Remember, the rule of thumb is that shareholders who have rights to vote in the fundamental transaction will have appraisal rights. **A Corp's shareholders and T Corp's shareholders will have appraisal rights** because they each had the right to vote on the merger.

---

[369] See §9A-408, below, for one possible reason: anti-assignment clauses in target's material contracts.

9-401(e) STATUTORY MERGER – REVERSE MERGER 2:

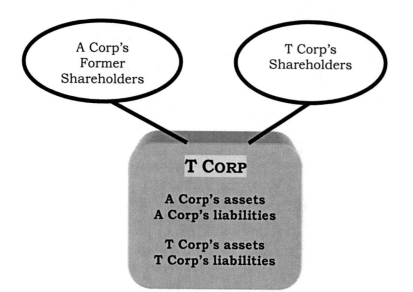

Explanation:

T Corp Survives.

T Corp inherits A Corp's assets and liabilities.

A Corp is merged out of existence.

A Corp's shareholders receive T Corp stock in the merger.

This result is just another version of the **reverse merger**, where the target is the surviving corporation

BOARD APPROVAL: The board of each corporation will approve the merger.

SHAREHOLDER APPROVAL: In this case, **A Corp's shareholders will certainly vote on the merger**.

T Corp's shareholders might have a right to vote, depending on (1) how many T Corp shares A Corp's shareholders receive in the merger; and (2) whether T Corp's shareholders retained the same class of shares they held before the merger. The relevant corporate law statute will have specific rules addressing when the shareholders of a surviving corporation have a right to vote on the merger.

APPRAISAL RIGHTS: Remember, the rule of thumb is that shareholders who have rights to vote in the fundamental transaction will have appraisal rights. **A Corp's shareholders will clearly have appraisal rights** because they had the right to vote on the merger. We need more facts to determine whether T Corp's shareholders have a right to vote and right to appraisal.

9A-402 CONSOLIDATION:

A consolidation is simply a type of merger where neither corporation is the surviving corporation. The two corporations merge to create a new corporation. For example, A Corp and B Corp merge together to create C Corp.

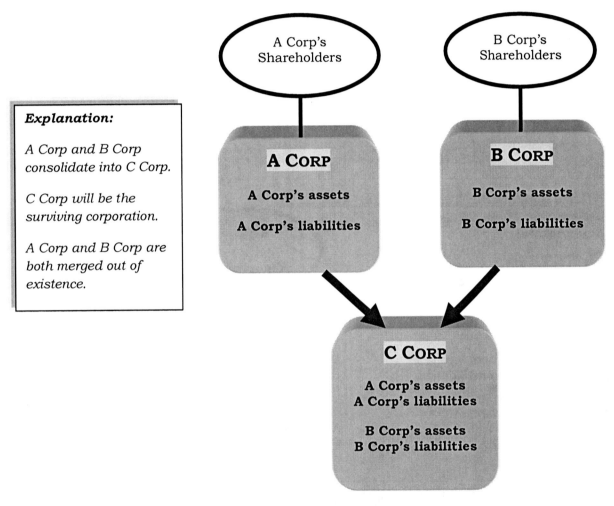

Explanation:

A Corp and B Corp consolidate into C Corp.

C Corp will be the surviving corporation.

A Corp and B Corp are both merged out of existence.

Not all jurisdictions have a consolidation provision in their corporate law statutes, but you can use the statutory merger, above, to accomplish the same goals: Set up C Corp and do the statutory merger between A Corp, B Corp and C Corp, with C Corp as the surviving corporation.

The rules for **voting and appraisal rights** in consolidations mirror those for statutory mergers. Because neither A Corp nor B Corp is the surviving corporation, **both A Corp shareholders and B Corp shareholders will have voting and appraisal rights**.

9-402(a) CONSOLIDATION – POSSIBLE RESULT 1:

A Corp's Former Shareholders

B Corp's Former Shareholders

C CORP

A Corp's assets
A Corp's liabilities

B Corp's assets
B Corp's liabilities

Explanation:

C Corp survives.

C Corp inherits A Corp's and B Corp's assets and liabilities.

A Corp and B Corp are both merged out of existence.

A Corp's shareholders and B Corp's shareholders receive C Corp stock in the consolidation.

9-402(b) CONSOLIDATION – POSSIBLE RESULT 2:

Explanation:

C Corp survives.

C Corp inherits A Corp's and B Corp's assets and liabilities.

A Corp and B Corp are both merged out of existence.

A Corp's shareholders receive C Corp stock in the consolidation.

B Corp's shareholders receive cash in the consolidation.

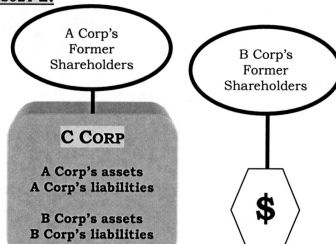

A Corp's Former Shareholders

B Corp's Former Shareholders

C CORP

A Corp's assets
A Corp's liabilities

B Corp's assets
B Corp's liabilities

$

9-402(c) CONSOLIDATION – POSSIBLE RESULT 3:

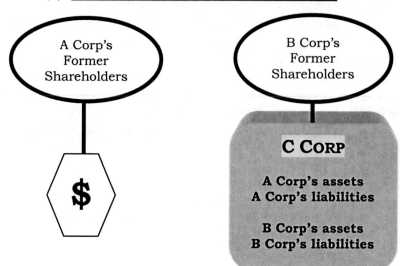

A Corp's Former Shareholders

B Corp's Former Shareholders

$

C CORP

A Corp's assets
A Corp's liabilities

B Corp's assets
B Corp's liabilities

Explanation:

C Corp survives.

C Corp inherits A Corp's and B Corp's assets and liabilities.

A Corp and B Corp are both merged out of existence.

B Corp's shareholders receive C Corp stock in the consolidation.

A Corp's shareholders receive cash in the consolidation.

9A-403 **SHORT-FORM MERGER:**

The short-form merger is a special type of statutory merger between a **parent company** and a **subsidiary company.**

When the parent owns 90% or more of the subsidiary, the parent can merge the subsidiary into the parent (or another subsidiary) without the approval of the subsidiary's board or the subsidiary's minority shareholders.

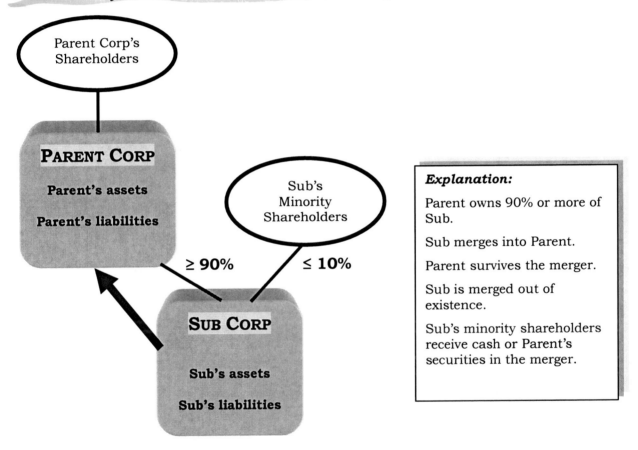

Explanation:

Parent owns 90% or more of Sub.

Sub merges into Parent.

Parent survives the merger.

Sub is merged out of existence.

Sub's minority shareholders receive cash or Parent's securities in the merger.

BOARD APPROVAL: Only the board of Parent approves the transaction. The board of Sub does not get to approve the transaction. The underlying justification is that Sub's board is controlled by the Parent, so there is no need to go through the formalities of a Sub board decision.

SHAREHOLDER APPROVAL: Sub's shareholders will not have a right to vote on the merger. Although the merger results in a fundamental change for Sub's minority shareholders, the law provides that they do not have a right to vote on the transaction.

The rules for **whether Parent corporation's shareholders have a right to vote** are the same rules governing whether the shareholders of a surviving corporation have right to vote in a regular merger. In this case, Parent's shareholders right to vote on the merger depends on (1) how many Parent shares the Sub minority shareholders received in the merger, if any; and (2) whether the Parent's shareholders retained the same class of shares they held before the merger.[370]

APPRAISAL RIGHTS: Here we find an exception to the general rule that only shareholders with a right to vote on the merger are entitled to appraisal rights. In the short-form merger, the **subsidiary's minority shareholders have appraisal rights** even though they had no right to vote on the merger.

The Parent's shareholders will only have appraisal rights if they had a right to vote on the merger.

9A-404 OTHER ACQUISITIONS:

The word "acquisition" is not a term you will normally see in a corporate law statute. It is a word used in practice that broadly refers to the acquisition of companies through mergers, consolidations, short-form mergers, and other methods. This part discusses some other methods of acquiring companies.

9A-404(a) SHARE PURCHASE:

A share purchase is not a statutory acquisition; it is a market transaction. The purchaser buys enough stock from target's current shareholders to acquire a controlling interest in the target corporation. After the completion of the transactions, the purchaser becomes the controlling shareholder.

In a share purchase, there are no shareholder votes and no appraisals rights. Each shareholder decides for herself whether she will sell to the purchaser. Most purchasers will want to acquire a control interest, at the least. Acquiring a control interest by purchasing shares can be challenging if the target does not have a single controlling shareholder, but it is still possible to negotiate individual transactions with enough target shareholders to acquire a control interest.

Many purchasers desire to acquire 100% control because of the costs and complications of dealing with minority shareholders.[371] It is often difficult to acquire 100% of the outstanding shares of a corporation through a share purchase when there is more than one shareholder because there are bound to be **hold-outs** – shareholders who refuse to sell unless they are offered a better price, usually better than the other shareholders received.

---

[370] See §9A-401(c), above.

[371] For a discussion on the costs of having minority shareholders, see Chapter 6, §6A-211(f).

The threat of hold-outs is somewhat mitigated by the negotiating power the purchaser will have if she gains control of the target. With control, she can cash-out the hold-out shareholders through a statutory merger (maybe a short-form merger) between purchaser and the target or between the target and purchaser's wholly owned subsidiary. Knowing this, hold-out shareholders have an incentive to reach some sort of settlement with the purchaser before the purchaser resorts to a cash-out merger.

In addition, if the target corporation has a controlling shareholder with a drag-along rights,[372] the purchaser can acquire 100% of target's shareholdings though negotiations with the controlling shareholder.

THE SHARE PURCHASE:

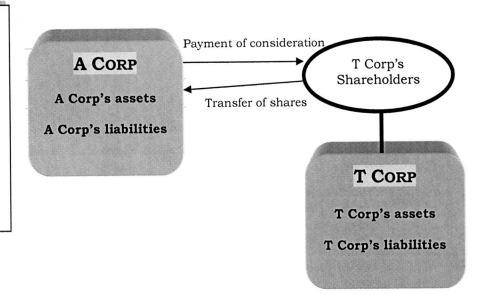

Explanation:

A Corp purchases T Corp stock from T Corp's shareholders.

A Corp may pay in cash, stock, debt securities, or any other form of consideration acceptable to T Corp's shareholders.

The illustrations on the following page analyze the possible results of a share purchase.

---

[372] For a discussion of drag-along rights, see Chapter 7, §7A-303(f).

Two possible results of the share purchase:

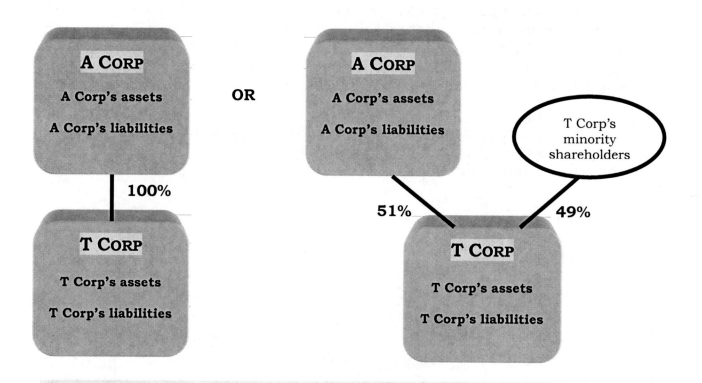

Explanation:

*In the transaction on the **left**, A Corp is able to purchase 100% of the outstanding stock of T Corp from T Corp's shareholders. A Corp becomes the parent/sole shareholder of T Corp. T Corp becomes the wholly-owned subsidiary of A Corp.*

*In the transaction on the **right**, A Corp is able to purchase a controlling interest, but is NOT able to purchase 100% of the outstanding stock of T Corp from T Corp's shareholders. A Corp becomes the controlling shareholder of T Corp. T Corp becomes the subsidiary of A Corp.*

9A-404(b) MANDATORY SHARE EXCHANGE:

A mandatory share exchange is statutory acquisition method that is a cross between the statutory merger and the share purchase. Here, unlike in the merger, the target corporation does not merge into the surviving corporation. Instead, the transaction is more like the share purchase, where the **target corporation continues to exist and the surviving corporation becomes the sole shareholder of target**.

The mandatory share exchange is like a statutory merger in the sense that **approval by a majority of the target shareholders can force all target shareholders to sell their shares** to the surviving corporation (i.e., "purchasing corporation"). You can think of the mandatory share exchange as a **statutory drag-along right**.[373] If the majority of target's shareholders approve the sale of their shares to the purchasing corporation, the remaining target shareholders are required to sell their shares to the purchasing corporation.

BOARD APPROVAL: Same as the merger - the board of each corporation will approve the merger.

SHAREHOLDER APPROVAL: Same as the merger - target's shareholders have a right to vote. The shareholders of the purchasing corporation will only have a right to vote under limited circumstances – the same circumstances that create voting rights for the shareholders in the surviving corporation of a merger.[374]

APPRAISAL RIGHTS: Same as the merger – shareholders that have a right to vote in the mandatory share exchange will also have appraisal rights.

9A-404(c) SALE OF SUBSTANTIALLY ALL THE ASSETS:

One can acquire a corporation's business by purchasing all of a corporation's assets, including its land, buildings, equipment, intellectual property, and its contracts with suppliers, customers, and key employees. This type of acquisition is different from the merger because the purchasing corporation acquires the assets only, and **does not assume or inherit the target corporation's liabilities**. In contrast, in a merger, the surviving corporation inherits the target's liabilities as well as its assets.

When a corporation sells **substantially all** of its assets **not in the regular course of business**, its shareholders usually have a right to vote and appraisal rights.

---

[373] For a discussion of drag-along rights, see Chapter 7, §7A-303(f).

[374] See §9A-401(c), above.

Substantially all of the assets: Courts have wrestled with the interpretation of the term "substantially all of the assets." You should probably not think of it as being synonymous with "most of its assets," or "a majority of its assets." Instead, interpret it to mean **"virtually all of its assets."** In other words, the selling corporation's shareholders only have a right to vote on the sale of assets when the corporation sells its land, buildings, equipment, intellectual property, and its contracts with suppliers, customers and key employees, and other assets, while only **retaining insignificant assets**.

Not in the ordinary course of business: The selling corporation's shareholders only have a right to vote on the sale of substantially all of the assets when the sale was not in the regular course of business. You can imagine a business model where a corporation might dispose of substantially all of its assets as part of its regular business. For example, a corporation buys one dilapidated house at a time, repairs and renovates it, then sells it. Although the corporation is selling virtually all of its assets, the shareholders of that corporation would not have a right to vote on the transaction because it was in the ordinary course of business.

There is one more wrinkle to a corporation's sale of substantially all of its assets. The creditors of the selling corporation may cry foul because the selling corporation is left with no assets to satisfy its debts. Of course, the selling corporation should have the consideration it received for the sale of its assets. The selling corporation usually dissolves after selling all of its assets. It uses the consideration it received in the asset sale to satisfy all of its debts, and then it distributes the remainder to its shareholders.

Sometimes, after an asset sale and dissolution of the selling corporation, maybe even many years later, the selling corporation's contingent liabilities suddenly come to fruition. Often, the contingent liability is a products liability claim related to products the selling corporation manufactured or sold before dissolution. These claims are often contingent or unknown at the time of dissolution. Because the selling corporation no longer exists, the victims cannot sue the selling corporation.

However, the purchasing corporation now owns the selling corporation's assets, including the assets related to the brands and products in question with the current claims, but it did not acquire or assume selling corporation's liabilities. In these situations, a court might invoke the **successor liability doctrine,** which will hold the purchasing corporation liable for the selling corporation's liabilities.

Not all jurisdictions subscribe to the successor liability doctrine. Even those that do subscribe will only apply it in limited circumstances. Although it is difficult to generalize under what circumstances any specific court will apply the successor liability doctrine, you should expect that **the more the asset sale looked like a merger, the more likely a court will apply the successor liability doctrine**.

For example, a sale of assets looks more like a merger when the purchasing corporation gives its own stock, instead of cash, to the selling corporation as consideration for the sale of assets. The selling corporation distributes the stock to its shareholders when it dissolves. The resulting transaction looks very much like a merger – the purchasing corporation winds up with all of the selling corporation's assets and all of the selling corporation's shareholders become shareholders in the surviving corporation.

9A-404(d) HOSTILE TAKEOVER:

A takeover or hostile takeover refers to a situation where one company, often referred to as the **bidder**, attempts to acquire a target company without the cooperation of the target's board. Because the target's board is opposed to the acquisition, it is not possible to use a merger, consolidation, mandatory share exchange, or asset sale, unless the target's board is replaced with directors who are in favor of merging with bidder.

Normally, we only see hostile takeovers of corporations whose shares are publicly traded on stock markets. The bidder will appeal to the public shareholders of the target corporation through a two-pronged attack: (1) a tender offer and (2) a proxy fight.

> **Tender offer:** The bidder makes an offer to the target's public shareholders stating:

>> "If you tender your shares to us, we will buy a [certain number of shares] at a [certain price] per share. Once we have a sufficient number of shares, we will use our voting power to remove the current board members and replace them with people who favor a merger with us. In the merger with us, we will cash out all the current shareholders at [certain price] per share."

> **Proxy fight:** The bidder also solicits proxies from the target's public shareholders, stating:

>> "Appoint us as your proxy and we will vote to replace the current board with people who favor a merger with us."

Of course, target's board will also solicit proxies, stating:

>> "The price the bidder is offering to you for your shares is too low. Re-elect us and we will lead the company to a more profitable future, which will result in higher share prices."

If the bidder offers an attractive price in the tender offer and the proposed merger, target's shareholders will react favorably to the tender offer and proxy solicitation. For example, if target's shares are currently trading on the NYSE at $20 per share, the bidder will have to offer a strong premium over the $20 trading price in its tender offer and proposed merger.

There are detailed federal laws that govern tender offers and proxy fights in public corporations.

9A-500 DEFACTO MERGER AND SUCCESSOR LIABILITY:

The requirement for shareholder voting and appraisal rights might make a statutory merger, consolidation, or share exchange burdensome and costly. Clever lawyers might be able to structure the transaction to avoid shareholder voting and appraisal rights.

For example, some jurisdictions do not provide for shareholder voting or appraisal rights when a corporation sells substantially all of its assets. To avoid the shareholder voting and appraisal rights required in mergers, lawyers in these jurisdictions may structure the transaction as a sale of all of target's assets to the purchasing corporation, instead of a merger. Indeed, in these types of assets sales, the purchasing corporation will often also assume all of target's liabilities as part of the terms of the transaction.

Some courts might hold that this transaction is a **defacto merger** – i.e., its substance is that of a merger, even though its form is an asset purchase, so we will treat is as a statutory merger. Shareholders of the target corporation should have voting and appraisal rights just like in a statutory merger. However, **many jurisdictions (including Delaware) do not subscribe to the defacto merger doctrine**.

> ***Note:*** sometimes ***creditors*** of the target will cry defacto merger in an attempt to hold the purchasing corporation liable for target's liabilities after target's sale of substantially all of its assets to the purchasing corporation. When creditors claim there was a defacto merger, they are simply using the term as a substitute for the **successor liability doctrine**.[375]

---

[375] See §9A-404(c), above.

9A-600 APPRAISAL RIGHTS – GENERAL NOTES:

Market out exception to appraisal rights: Some jurisdictions provide that if the shareholder has a "market out" she will not get appraisal rights. In other words, if she can sell her shares on an **active securities market**, there is no need for the corporation to buy her out.

For example, if the corporation's shares are traded on Nasdaq, NYSE, or other stock exchange, the shareholder will not have appraisal rights. Similarly, if the corporation's shares are not listed on an exchange, but still have a large public float and an active over-the-counter market, the shareholder will not get appraisal rights.

The corporation must provide notice to shareholders regarding appraisal rights. When the corporation notifies shareholders of the transaction and their right to vote, it must also notify the shareholders if they have appraisal rights.

Perfecting appraisal rights: The shareholder must take certain actions to perfect her appraisal rights, otherwise she will lose them. The most important actions are (1) notifying the corporation of the intent to exercise appraisal rights and (2) not voting in favor of the proposed transaction.

9A-700 FIDUCIARY DUTIES IN MERGERS AND ACQUISITIONS:

Mergers, consolidations, mandatory share exchanges, and asset sales are like any other transaction as far as fiduciary duties are concerned. Directors, officers, and controlling shareholders have fiduciary duties in these transactions.

Duty of care issues can arise for directors and officers when they are considering and approving these transactions, as we saw in *Smith v. Van Gorkom*, for example.[376] The board of both corporations must carefully consider the transaction, gather adequate information and spend sufficient time deliberating the transaction.

Duty of loyalty issues can arise for directors, officers, and controlling shareholders when they are considering and approving merger and acquisitions transactions.[377] When the directors, officers, or controlling shareholders of a corporation have shareholdings in the other corporation to the merger, sit on its board, serve as one of its executive officers, or otherwise have a private, material financial interest in the transaction, the transaction involves self-

---

[376] See Chapter 6, §6A-204(c).

[377] See Chapter 6, §6A-202 et seq. and §6A-211 et seq.

dealing. In addition, keep in mind that mergers can be used to freeze-out minority shareholders.[378]

Please note that **when a shareholder has appraisal rights in a merger, she might not be allowed to assert her fiduciary duty claim** – appraisal rights might be her only protection. When a shareholder wants to make a duty of loyalty claim against directors or a controlling shareholder in a freeze-out merger context, many courts **require the shareholder to make a prima facie case of fraud or unfairness in the transaction** (i.e., unfair price and unfair dealings). In other words, she cannot merely allege a conflict of interest.[379] If she does not make a prima facie case of fraud or unfairness, her only remedy is appraisal rights.

Fiduciary duties in hostile takeovers are a little more complicated.[380] When a bidder begins a hostile takeover of the target, the target's board has some tools at its disposal to defend against the hostile takeover. For example, many public corporations have a "poison pill" in their **articles of incorporation**. The poison pill is actually called a "rights plan," but the term "poison pill" is more colorful. The board places the rights plan in the articles of incorporation pursuant to its authority to issue shares and define their rights under a blank check preferred provision.[381]

Under a poison pill, once a bidder in a hostile takeover acquires a certain percentage of the target's shares – 5%, for example – all the other shareholders are issued a right to buy more shares in the company for a very low price. Because the other shareholders will exercise this right to acquire more shares, the number of outstanding shares will increase and the bidder's shareholdings will drop from 5% to .05%, for example. In other words, acquiring 5% of the outstanding shares of the company is tantamount to swallowing a poison pill – it destroys your ability to take over the company.

There are other measures a board can take to thwart a hostile takeover. For example, a board might **change the record date for the shareholders' meeting**, taking away the potential acquirer's right to vote any shares it acquired after the record date. The board of the target might **convene the shareholders' annual meeting at an earlier date**, giving the potential acquirer less time to solicit proxies and garner support for her bid to vote out and replace the target's current board.

The terms of the poison pill/rights plan grants the target's board the power to recall it. If the board makes a decision not to recall the poison pill, they are

---

[378] See Chapter 6, §6A-211(d) for discussion of the freeze-out merger.

[379] *Weinberger v. UOP, Inc.*, 457 A.2d 701 (Del. Sup. Ct. 1983).

[380] For a discussion of hostile takeovers, see §9A-404(d), above.

[381] See Chapter 4, §4A-204(a) for a discussion of blank check preferred.

putting a huge impediment in the way of the takeover. What standard should we use to review the board's decision not to recall the poison pill - business judgment rule or fairness?

If we believe the board is defending against the hostile takeover because the price the bidder if offering the shareholders is too low, we would probably apply the business judgment rule. On the other hand, if we believe the board is defending against the hostile takeover because they will lose their jobs when the bidder takes control, we have a duty of loyalty issue. Under the duty of loyalty, the directors are required to prove the fairness of their decision.

Delaware has adopted an intermediate fiduciary duty standard when the target's board adopts some sort of defensive strategy against a hostile takeover:[382]

> The board must be able to articulate **a reasonable belief that a defense** against the hostile takeover was warranted – i.e., that the bid creates some sort of **threat to the shareholders**. Normally, the board will claim the bidder was offering a low price.
>
> The board must then show its **defensive measure was proportionate to the threat**. Normally, as long as the defensive measure does not completely preclude a possible takeover, it will not be disproportionate. In the case of a poison pill, for example, the bidder can still gain control of target's board through a proxy fight and the new board can recall the poison pill.

9A-800 THE ATTORNEY'S ROLE IN MERGERS AND OTHER BUSINESS COMBINATIONS:

The attorneys on both sides of the transaction will draft the relevant documents for the transaction. The attorneys will advise their clients on tax consequences, structuring options, and fiduciary duties related to business combinations. The parties to a merger or other business combination will often first sign a non-binding **memorandum of understanding** (MOU) or non-binding **letter of intent** (LOI) before signing the definitive merger agreement.

The MOU or LOI will spell out, in general terms, the planned transaction. It is usually drafted to be non-binding, but because the parties will exchange sensitive information about their businesses, the MOU or LOI will contain binding **non-disclosure and confidentiality terms**.

---

[382] The leading Delaware case is *Unocal Corp. v. Mesa Petroleum Co.*, 493 A.2d 946 (Del. 1985).

While the parties are negotiating the definitive merger agreement and working out the details of the transaction, the lawyers and financial advisors of the acquirer will engage in an investigation of the target's business. This investigation process is called **due diligence**. The due diligence process, in summary, proceeds as follows:

> The acquirer's lawyers and financial advisors send a **due diligence request list** to the target. The request typically asks the target to produce material contracts, financial statements, descriptions of legal claims, lists of material assets, etc.

> The lawyers and financial advisors go through the information to verify that the target's condition is as the acquirer expects, looking for red flags and other issues that should be negotiated or included in the definitive agreement.

There are numerous things that lawyers look for in the due diligence process but they tend to spend a significant amount of time reviewing the target's **material contracts**. One important issue is whether the material contracts will terminate upon consummation of the contract. Imagine the target has a significant long-term supply contract with an important customer that is crucial to the target's ability to meet future revenue predictions that make the deal worthwhile for the acquirer. The supply contract has the following **anti-assignment clause**:

> Neither Party shall assign, in whole or in part, this Agreement or any of the rights, interests or obligations under it without the prior written consent of the other Party. Any assignment in violation of this clause gives the other Party the right to terminate this Agreement.

What does this anti-assignment contract clause mean for the transaction? First, it means that if we structure the transaction as a sale of all of target's assets to the acquirer, we will encounter an obstacle to the transfer of this important contract. We could ask the customer to waive the clause, but the customer might want to renegotiate more favorable terms.

We could consider structuring the transaction as a **forward merger** so that target merges into acquirer (or the acquirer's subsidiary).[383] A forward merger might avoid the issues associated with the anti-assignment clause because a merger does not technically result in an "assignment" or "transfer" of the contract. However, a court might find there is enough ambiguity in the assignment clause to let the jury decide whether the parties intended the anti-assignment clause to apply when the contractual rights and obligations will

---

[383] See §9A-401(a)-(c), above, for examples of forward mergers.

belong to another party as the result of the merger. This possibility creates uncertainty for the transaction.

Now consider how our analysis might change if the anti-assignment clause were drafted in a slightly different manner, such as:

> Neither Party shall assign, in whole or in part, **by operation of law or otherwise**, this Agreement or any of the rights, interests or obligations under it without the prior written consent of the other Party. Any assignment in violation of this clause gives the other Party the right to terminate this Agreement.

The language "operation by law" might be interpreted to mean assignment by virtue of a merger. To avoid this anti-assignment clause in a merger transaction, we could structure the transaction as a **reverse merger.** In the reverse merger, the target survives the merger, and the acquirer is merged out of existence.[384] With the reverse merger, the target survives and maintains its contractual rights and obligations. It is more likely that a court would find the anti-assignment clause did not apply to the reverse merger.

Often, the anti-assignment clause will have additional language similar to the following:

> Any **Change in Control** of a Party that results from a merger, consolidation, stock transfer or asset sale is deemed an assignment or transfer for purposes of this Agreement.

This type of clause is called a **change-in-control clause**. If the original agreement between target and its customer were drafted properly, it would define "change of control" to include changes in the board, executives, or controlling shareholder of the target. A reverse merger would not circumvent the clause because, even though the target would survive the merger, it would more than likely be under the control of the acquirer's board, executives or controlling shareholders after the consummation of the transaction. In other words, the existence of this change-of-control clause in one or more of target's material contracts would leave us no choice but to negotiate and persuade the respective contracting party to waive the clause.

Typical circumstances that constitute a change of control are a sale of more than 50% of target's stock, a new majority shareholder, the elimination of the current majority shareholder (without a new majority shareholder), a sale of substantially all of the assets, or a change in a majority of the board members.

---

[384] See §9A-401(d)-(e), above, for examples of reverse mergers.

In summary, before the parties can structure and consummate the merger transaction, **the lawyers must carefully review all material contracts for anti-assignment clauses and change of control provisions**.

UNIT 9B

PARTNERSHIPS – FUNDAMENTAL TRANSACTIONS:

See Chapter 5, §5B-201(b), Voting on Extraordinary Matters

UNIT 9C

LLCS – FUNDAMENTAL TRANSACTIONS:

See Chapter 5, §5C-201(c), Voting on Extraordinary Matters

CHAPTER 10
PROTECTING CREDITORS

UNIT 10B
PARTNERSHIPS – PROTECTING CREDITORS:

10B-100 **PARTNERSHIPS – LIMITATIONS ON DISTRIBUTIONS TO PARTNERS:**

    10B-101 GENERAL PARTNERSHIPS:

    10B-102 LIMITED LIABILITY PARTNERSHIPS:

    10B-103 LIMITED PARTNERSHIPS:

10B-200 **PARTNERSHIPS – PIERCING THE VEIL:**

    10B-201 GENERAL PARTNERSHIPS:

    10B-202 LIMITED LIABILITY PARTNERSHIPS:

    10B-203 LIMITED PARTNERSHIPS – PIERCING AND THE CONTROL RULE:

UNIT 10C
LLCS – PROTECTING CREDITORS:

10C-100 **LLCS – LIMITATIONS ON DISTRIBUTIONS TO MEMBERS:**

10C-200 **LLCS – PIERCING THE LIMITED LIABILITY VEIL:**

UNIT 10A

CORPORATIONS – PROTECTING CREDITORS:

10A-100 PROTECTING THE CORPORATION'S CREDITORS – INTRODUCTION:

This unit explores how corporate law protects the interests of the corporation's creditors. To this point in our studies of corporate law, we have discussed the main function of corporate law, which is providing default and mandatory rules for the internal governance of the corporation. We have discussed the specifics of that internal governance dynamic – namely, how corporate law protects shareholders, directors, and officers. Because the corporation's creditors are not part of that internal governance dynamic, they rely mainly on contracts to protect their interests. In addition, there are other state and federal laws that specifically create, define, and limit creditors' rights in general. To a much lesser extent, however, corporate law does indeed provide some protections for the corporation's creditors.

10A-101 THE CORPORATION'S CREDITORS:

A corporation's creditors include **traditional lenders**, such as banks and credit unions. They also include **trade creditors** – the suppliers that sell to the company on credit. In addition, if the company has issued debt securities, the **holders of these debt securities** are creditors of the corporation.[385]

Another creditor category is **any person the corporation pays in arrears**. A company pays in arrears if it pays after it has received the service. For example, if a company pays its employees on October 10 for the work they performed in September, the company pays wages in arrears. If the company pays its wages in arrears, the employees will be creditors. If the company pays its rent in arrears, the lessor will be a creditor. The same is true for utilities companies and other services-providers that the corporation pays in arrears.

Finally, any person who has some other **contractual claim** or **tort claim** against the corporation is also a creditor of the corporation.

---

[385] See Chapter 4, §4A-302 for a discussion of debt securities.

The first line of protection for creditors is the contract. There are various contractual terms that traditional lenders and other creditors negotiate into agreements to protect their interests, but they generally fall into one of the following categories:

> **Guarantors or co-signers:** The contract might require the debtor-corporation to have a guarantor for the obligation or a co-signer.[386] One or more of the shareholders might act as a guarantor or a co-signer. Sometimes parent corporations and sister corporations act as guarantors or co-signers for each other's obligations.

> **Limitations on business:** The contract might prohibit the debtor-corporation from engaging in certain lines of business or certain transactions to maintain an acceptable level of business risk.

> **Limitations on additional debt:** The contract might prohibit the debtor-corporation from borrowing additional money, in order to ensure the corporation does not overextend itself.

> **Limitations on distributions to shareholders:** The contract might prohibit the debtor-corporation from making distributions to shareholders, to better ensure the corporation has sufficient cash to meet its obligations.

These contractual terms are more common in loan agreements, debt securities, and other credit arrangements, where the parties sit down and carefully negotiate these terms. We see them less often in transactions with trade creditors and other contracts that are smaller in scope or size. In addition, tort creditors are not normally in a position to negotiate such terms prior to the transaction that creates the corporation's tort obligation.

Interest rates and pricing is another method that creditors use to protect themselves. **The greater the risk that the debtor-corporation will not be able to meet its obligations, the greater the interest rate or price the corporation will have to pay.**

For example, if there is very little risk a corporation will be able make payments under a loan agreement, a bank will lend money to the corporation at a low interest rate. If the risk is greater, the interest rate will be higher. Similarly, if a supplier that sells on credit believes there is very little risk the corporation

---

[386] A guarantor promises to meet the debtor's obligations only if the debtor fails to meet them. The creditor must first seek performance from the debtor. Only when the debtor fails to meet its obligations can the creditor seek performance from the guarantor. In contrast, each co-signer is a co-debtor, bearing joint and several liability under the contract. The creditor can seek performance from one of the co-signers, some of them, or all of them.

will not pay, it will charge the corporation a lower price. If there is greater risk, the price will be higher.

This relationship between risk and price is one reason corporate law scholars and economists often say that **shareholders pay for their limited liability**. If creditors can look only to the assets of the corporation to satisfy their claims, there is greater risk their claims will be unsatisfied. The creditors will charge the corporation a higher price to compensate themselves for the risk.

10A-103 NON-CORPORATE LAW PROTECTIONS FOR CREDITORS – THE BASICS:

The creditors of a corporation are protected by various state and federal laws that protect creditors in general. Two important creditor-protection doctrines that might be of particular interest to the creditors of a corporation are equitable subordination and fraudulent transfer.

Equitable subordination:

When a corporation is in bankruptcy, the Bankruptcy Code gives the court the power to subordinate any creditor's claim (i.e., to make it last in priority) if the creditor has engaged in **inequitable conduct** that caused injury to the other creditors.[387]

A shareholder of a corporation will often lend money to the corporation, which gives her two separate claims against the corporation: an equity claim and a fixed claim. With respect to her **equity claim** (i.e., her claim as "shareholder"), the shareholder will only receive what remains after the corporation satisfies the creditors' claims. With respect to her **fixed claim** (i.e., her claim as "creditor"), the shareholder is entitled to receive payment with the other creditors.

When a corporation in bankruptcy owes money to one of its controlling shareholders as a fixed claim (i.e., as debt, not equity), a court has the power to subordinate the controlling shareholder's fixed claim if the shareholder has engaged in misconduct that has caused harm to the

---

[387] 11 U.S.C. §510(c) provides, in relevant part:

[T]he court may --

(1) under principles of equitable subordination, subordinate for purposes of distribution all or part of an allowed claim to all or part of another allowed claim or all or part of an allowed interest to all or part of another allowed interest; or

(2) order that any lien securing such a subordinated claim be transferred to the estate.

corporation, such as mismanagement or some other breach of fiduciary duty to the corporation.

Fraudulent transfers:

Sometimes a debtor-corporation will transfer its assets to a third party to protect those assets from its creditors. The third-party transferee is usually a related party, such as a sister corporation, a parent corporation, a shareholder, or the shareholder's spouse or child.

Generally, under the Bankruptcy Code[388] and the Uniform Fraudulent Transfers Act,[389] a court can void such a transfer if:

> (1) It was made with the actual intent to hinder, delay, or defraud creditors; OR

> (2) The debtor did not receive a reasonably equivalent value *and* the transaction left the debtor with assets insufficient to pay its debts as they come due.

10A-104 CORPORATE LAW PROTECTIONS FOR CREDITORS - INTRODUCTION:

State corporate law statutes and the common law of corporations provide three main protections for a corporation's creditors:

Legal limits on distributions to shareholders:

By now, you are familiar with the concept of corporate distributions to shareholders, usually in the form of a cash **dividend**. Corporate law statutes limit the amount a corporation can distribute to its shareholders. The purpose of the limitation is to prevent the shareholders from leaving the corporation with funds insufficient to meet its obligations to creditors.

Piercing the corporate veil:

Judges have created the common-law doctrine of piercing the corporate veil (or **piercing the limited liability veil**). Under special circumstances, a court will ignore a shareholder's limited liability privileges and hold her personally liable for the corporation's obligations.

---

[388] 11 U.S.C. §548(a).

[389] Uniform Fraudulent Transfers Act §4(a).

Protection of creditors during the dissolution process:

As we discussed in Chapter 9, a dissolved corporation must provide notice to creditors and pay off its debts in the liquidation process.[390]

10A-200 CORPORATE LAW PROTECTIONS FOR CREDITORS – LIMITATIONS ON DISTRIBUTIONS TO SHAREHOLDERS

10A-201 DISTRIBUTIONS AND THE RESIDUAL CLAIM:

Imagine you are a shareholder in a corporation. Limited liability protects your personal assets from the corporation's creditors, but the corporation's assets are at risk. What would be a good strategy to better maximize the protection of your overall wealth? You could cause the company to transfer corporate assets to you through a distribution/dividend.

To prevent shareholders from siphoning corporate assets, leaving the corporation with little or nothing to satisfy its debts, state corporate law statutes place limits on the amount a corporation may distribute to its shareholders. These statutory limitations on distributions attempt to balance two competing interests: (1) the **shareholders' legitimate interest in receiving a return on their investment**; and (2) the risk that shareholders will use distributions to divert wealth from creditors to themselves.

Because the shareholders have a right to the residual, we should allow them a right to access the residual. However, delineating how much of the corporation's assets represent the residual is not as simple as it may appear at first blush. When a **company is in liquidation**, it is easier for us to conceptualize and define the residual. In liquidation, the residual is simply the money that remains after liquidating the corporation's assets and paying creditors' claims. Even then, some contingent liabilities, such as tort liability for a defective product, might not arise until years after the corporation's dissolution and liquidation.

When the **company is still a going concern**, it is even more difficult for us to conceptualize and define the exact amount of the residual claim. Take a look at the balance sheet of XYZ Corp. in §10A-201(c), below. Let us assume that this is the balance sheet of a company that is a going concern.

The balance sheet is divided into three large categories: **Assets**; **Liabilities**; and **Owners' Equity**. The balance sheet can be viewed as an equation:

---

[390] See Chapter 9, §9A-300 for a discussion of voluntary dissolution.

Assets – Liabilities = Owners' Equity.

This equation should make sense to you because you already understand that the residual claim (i.e., the equity claim) is what is left over after the company uses its assets to pay off its fixed claimants (i.e., its liabilities).

The **Owners' Equity is the balance sheet's representation of the shareholders' residual claim.** It is only an approximation of the actual residual claim. There are two reasons the Owners' Equity on a corporation's balance sheet does not accurately reflect the actual residual claim:

(1) The assets listed on the balance sheet are not an accurate reflection of the company's assets; and

(2) The liabilities listed on the balance sheet are not an accurate reflection of the company's liabilities.

Let us take a closer look at the balance sheet's representation of assets and liabilities to see why they are only an approximation of the company's true assets and liabilities.

10A-201(a) **ASSETS ON THE BALANCE SHEET:**

Owners' Equity is equal to Assets minus Liabilities. If the Assets on the balance sheet are not an accurate reflection of the company's actual assets, the Owners' Equity will not be an accurate reflection of the company's actual residual. However, **the value of the assets on the balance sheet are not designed to reflect the actual fair market value of those assets.**

In the sample balance sheet in §10A-201(c), below, the company's total assets are $341,000. Of that, the company's **equipment** has a **book value** (i.e., a balance sheet value) of **$27,000**.

The balance sheet tells us that the company paid **$50,000** to acquire its equipment and that the equipment has **depreciated**[391] by **$23,000**, which leaves a $27,000 book value for the equipment.

---

[391] Depreciation is simply the accounting method of allocating the cost of the asset over the life of the asset to represent that the company is gradually using up the asset. For example, if the company purchases equipment for $5,000 and the equipment has a useful life of five years, the company will depreciate the asset on its books by $1,000 each year until the asset has been completed depreciated.

After the **first year**, the book value of the asset will be **$4,000** ($5,000 less $1,000 depreciation).

After the **second year**, the book value of the asset will be **$3,000** ($5,000 less $2,000 depreciation).

After the **third year**, the book value of the asset will be **$2,000** ($5,000 less $3,000 depreciation).

The **book value does not necessarily reflect the actual fair market value** of the equipment. If the company were to sell the equipment, it might receive more than $27,000, and it might receive less. The same holds true for the company's other factory and its land.

In addition, there are **some "assets" that will not appear on the balance sheet** at all. The **balance sheet will not reflect the company's contractual obligations**. If the company has entered into a favorable contract to provide its goods or services, for example, the contract would not appear on the balance sheet. The balance sheet's assets only reflect transactions where the company has already delivered goods or provided services to the customer, and is waiting for the customer to make payment.

> ### Illustration 1:
>
> The company enters into a five-year contract to provide services to its customer. Under the contract, the company will receive hundreds of millions of dollars. **This contract will not be reflected in the balance sheet's assets.**
>
> ### Illustration 2:
>
> The company has provided services to its customer under a contract and is waiting for the customer to pay the agreed price of $1 million. **The $1 million will appear on the company's balance sheet as an asset** in *accounts receivable* until the customer pays.

10A-201(b) LIABILITIES ON THE BALANCE SHEET:

Once again, Owners' Equity is equal to Assets minus Liabilities. If the Liabilities on the balance sheet are not an accurate reflection of the company's actual liabilities, Owner's Equity will not be an accurate reflection of the company's actual residual. Indeed, **many of the company's obligations are not reflected in the balance sheet's liabilities section.**

The company's **contractual obligations are not included in its liabilities on the balance sheet**. If the company has entered into a contract to purchase goods or services, this contract will not appear on the balance sheet as a liability. The balance sheet's liabilities only reflect

---

After the **fourth year**, the book value of the asset will be **$1,000** ($5,000 less $4,000 depreciation).

After the **fifth year**, the book value of the asset will be **$0** ($5,000 less $5,000 depreciation).

This is a simplified example that leaves out some details and nuances, but it provides the important concepts of depreciation.

transactions where the company has already received goods or services, and has not yet paid for them.

Illustration 1:

The company enters into a five-year lease to rent a large manufacturing facility for $500,000 per month. **This contract will not be reflected in the balance sheet's liabilities.**

Illustration 2:

The company has received legal services from a law firm but has not yet paid the agreed $25,000 fee. **The $25,000 will appear on the company's balance sheet as a liability** (a payable or accrued expense) until the company makes payment.

10A-201(c) SAMPLE BALANCE SHEET:

See next page for the sample balance sheet of XYZ Corp.

XYZ Corp.
BALANCE SHEET
as of December 31, 20XX

ASSETS:		LIABILITIES:	
Current Assets:		**Current Liabilities:**	
Cash	25,500	Accounts payable	53,000
Accounts receivable	36,500	Rent payable	3,500
Inventory	15,000	Wages payable	6,000
Pre-paid expenses	2,000	Other payables	1,000
		Current portion of long-term debt	7,000
Total current assets:	79,000		
		Total current liabilities:	70,500
Land, Plant, Equipment:		**Non-current liabilities:**	
Land	45,500	Bank loan	185,000
Factory	250,000		
Less depreciation	60,500	Total non- current liabilities:	185,000
Equipment	50,000		
Less depreciation	23,000		
Total land, plant, equipment:	262,000	**TOTAL LIABILITIES:**	**255,500**
		OWNERS' EQUITY:	
		Common stock	30,000
		Retained earnings	55,500
TOTAL ASSETS:	**341,000**	**TOTAL OWNERS' EQUITY**	**85,500**
		TOTAL LIABILITIES & OWNERS' EQUITY:	**341,000**

10A-202 RULES LIMITING DISTRIBUTIONS:

State corporate law statutes use various tests to limit the amount a corporation may distribute to its shareholders. Each of these tests define, in its own way, **what portion of the residual the shareholders may withdraw** from the corporation so that the corporation's remaining assets are sufficient to meet its obligations.

State corporate law statutes generally use one of the following tests, or some combination, to determine if a distribution to shareholders is permissible:

10A-202(a) EARNED SURPLUS TEST:

Under the earned surplus test, a company may only issue dividends out of *earned surplus.* Earned surplus is a legal term. The accounting equivalent is **retained earnings**. To understand retained earnings and the earned surplus test, we need to take a closer look at the "**Owners' Equity**" portion of the balance sheet.

In a corporation, the Owners' Equity portion of the balance sheet might be called "Stockholders' Equity" or "Shareholders' Equity." The Owners Equity on a balance sheet is often represented by two line items: **Capital** and **Retained Earnings**.

For example, if you look at the balance sheet in §10A-201(c), above, you will see the following in Owners' Equity:

Common stock:	**30,000**
Retained earnings:	**55,500**

Common stock is just another possible version of "**Capital**." It represents **how much capital the shareholders have invested in the corporation**.

In this example, we know that the shareholders have invested **$30,000** in the corporation in exchange for their shares in the corporation. The balance sheet's Owners' Equity section does not tell us how many shares each shareholder owns. For that information, we would need to look at the shareholder ledger.[392]

The **retained earnings** (aka **earned surplus**) simply represent the **profits the company has made over the years** that have not been distributed to the shareholders.

---

[392] See Chapter 5, §5A-201(a) for a discussion of the shareholder ledger.

In this example, the company has **$55,500** in earnings it has retained. However, from this number, we cannot tell how much of the retained earnings are profits from this year and how much are profits from previous years. For that information, we will need to look at the income statements from this year and previous years.

If a jurisdiction has an **earned surplus test** for distributions to shareholders, the corporation may only issue dividends from its retained earnings. In other words, in the example above, the corporation could distribute up to **$55,500** to its shareholders, but no more.

10A-202(b) CAPITAL SURPLUS TEST:

The **capital surplus test** might also be known as the **surplus test** or the **capital impairment test**. By whatever name it takes, it limits dividends to the amount that is in the company's **retained earnings plus its capital surplus.**

You will only see this test in jurisdictions that require corporations to assign a **par value** or **legal value** to the shares it issues. Par value and legal value are arbitrary values that corporations assign to each share of stock. Often, it is just a penny per share or even less. However, do not be confused: par value or legal value does not represent the actual market value of the stock or how much the shareholder paid the corporation in exchange for the stock.

Illustration:

Corporation A issues and sells 10,000 shares to Investor. Each share has a par value of $1.00, and Investor pays $1,000,000 for the 10,000 shares.

The total par value of the shares issued to Investor is $10,000. The remaining $990,000 the Investor paid to the company is called **capital surplus** or **additional paid-in capital**.

Capital surplus (aka **additional paid-in capital**) just represents **how much the corporation received for its shares over and above the par or legal value**.

Owners' Equity on a balance sheet is often represented by two line items: **Capital** and **Retained Earnings**. As we already examined, if you look at the balance sheet in §10A-201(c), above, you will see the following in Owners' Equity:

Common stock:	**30,000**
Retained earnings:	**55,500**

If the corporation were incorporated in a jurisdiction where the law required par value or legal value, the Owners' Equity would have the following three line items, rather than only two:

Common stock:	?
Additional paid-in capital:	?
Retained earnings:	55,500

To determine how much of XYZ Corp.'s capital would be split between common stock and additional paid-in capital, we need more information. Let's assume that the company has issued **10,000 shares** of stock with a **par value of $0.01 per share** and has received **$30,000** from the investors. With those assumptions, the corporation's Owners Equity would appear as follows:

Common stock:[393]	100
Additional paid-in capital:	29,900
Retained earnings:	55,500

If a jurisdiction has the **capital surplus test** for distributions to shareholders, the corporation **may only issue dividends from its retained earnings plus additional paid in capital**. In other words, in the example above, the corporation could distribute up to **$85,400** [55,500 + 29,900] to its shareholders, but no more.

10A-202(c) INSOLVENCY TEST:

In jurisdictions that adopt the insolvency test, a corporation **may not** issue a dividend if either one of the following would apply:

If, after giving effect to the dividend, the **corporation's total liabilities would exceed its total assets;**[394]

OR

If, after giving effect to the dividend, the **company would not be able to pay debts as they come due**.

---

[393] 10,000 shares x $0.01 = $100

[394] The test actually looks at whether the total liabilities plus liquidation rights of preferred shareholders. For the sake of simplification, we are assuming the corporation has no preferred stock.

AFTER THE DIVIDEND, WILL THE CORPORATION'S TOTAL LIABILITIES EXCEED ITS TOTAL ASSETS?

The first part of the test is rather straightforward. It focuses on the company's assets versus its liabilities after giving effect to the dividend.

Illustration:

If you look at the balance sheet in §10A-201(c), above, you will see:

Total assets: 341,000

Total liabilities: 255,500

With respect to this first part of the insolvency test, the company could issue a dividend to its shareholders up to $85,500* because, after giving effect to the dividend, the company's total assets would be 255,500 and the total liabilities would also be 255,500 (which means the total liabilities would not exceed total assets).

> *You might ask how the company could issue a dividend of $85,500 if it only had $25,500 in cash. The cash account is a practical limit on the size of the dividend, not a legal limit in this first part of the insolvency test. The company would not be able to issue a cash dividend larger than its cash account unless it sold some of its assets or received payment on some of its accounts receivable.

One slight wrinkle to this part of the test is that the company is allowed to use the **fair market value of its assets**, rather than the book value of the assets on the balance sheet.[395]

Illustration:

As we said, the company's total assets according to the balance sheet are $341,000. Remember, however, the value of the assets on the balance sheet is not based on the actual market value.[396] The balance sheet value of the company's equipment is $27,000 ($50,000 cost of acquisition minus $23,000 depreciation). If the fair market value of the equipment is actually $40,000, not $27,000, the company's total assets for the first part of the insolvency test is $354,000, not $341,000.

AFTER THE DIVIDEND, WILL THE CORPORATION BE ABLE TO PAY ITS DEBTS AS THE COME DUE?

The second part of the insolvency test focuses on whether the company would be able to pay its bills if it issued the dividend. We cannot completely rely on

---

[395] See 10A-201(a) for a discussion on the difference between the actual fair market value of an asset and its book value on the balance sheet.

[396] See id.

the numbers in the corporation's balance sheet to determine whether issuing the dividend would cause it to be unable to pay its debts as they come due. However, the balance sheet is a good place to start to get a good idea of what debts will be coming due.

The liabilities portion of the balance sheet is divided into **current liabilities** and **non-current liabilities**.

The **total current liabilities** give us our best balance sheet estimate of the company's debts that are coming due. Current liabilities are **the obligations that the corporation will have to satisfy within the next twelve months**. Some of them will come due more quickly than twelve months.

For example, **accounts payable** represents the money the corporation owes to suppliers for credit purchases of inventory or raw materials. Typically, the corporation will have to pay its accounts payable within thirty, sixty, or ninety days, depending on the terms with the supplier.

In addition, other current liabilities, such as **wages payable**, **rent payable**, and **utilities payable** represent what the corporation owes the employees, the lessor, and the utilities company for what it received from them in the previous month. In other words, these current liabilities will normally be paid within five to thirty days.

There are **certain debts that may be coming due that will not appear on the balance sheet**. We discussed earlier that not all obligations appear on the balance sheet.[397] For example, the rent payable number on the balance sheet only represents the rent the corporation owes the lessor for the month that just ended. It does not reflect the rent the corporation will have to pay the lessor for the next twelve months under its lease agreement. The corporation should also take these off-balance sheet debts into consideration in determining whether they will be able to meet their debts as they come due after issuing a dividend.

Illustration:

Imagine the corporation in §10A-201(c), above, has entered into a five-year lease of a storefront, for which it promises to pay $3,500 per month. Over the next 12 months, the company will have to pay $42,000 to the lessor. This $42,000 does not appear on the balance sheet. The only rent that appears on the balance sheet is the $3,500 it owes the lessor for last month's rent.

Now that we understand what debts are coming due, we need to understand whether the company will be able to pay those debts. Of course, **we pay debts**

---

[397] See 10A-201(b), above.

503

with cash. We will also pay the dividend in cash.[398] The most conservative approach would be to see if we would have enough cash, after paying the dividend, to pay the debts as they come due.

> *Illustration:*
>
> The balance sheet in 10A-201(c), above, shows the company only has $25,500 in cash, and at least $70,500 in current liabilities. A very conservative approach would caution against issuing any dividend.

A less conservative approach would look at all of the current assets compared to all of the current liabilities.

> *Illustration:*
>
> The balance sheet in 10A-201(c), above, shows the company has $79,000 current assets and only $70,500 in current liabilities. These numbers suggest the company could distribute as much as $8,500 to its shareholders.

Current assets are the **assets the corporation expects to turn into cash within the next twelve months**.

> For example, **accounts receivable** represents the money customers owe the corporation for sales the corporation made on credit. Typically, the customers will have to pay the corporation within thirty, sixty, or ninety days, depending on the terms of the sale.
>
> **Inventory** represents the goods the company has on hand, ready to sell to customers. Most businesses expect to sell their current inventory in less than twelve months.
>
> **Pre-paid expenses**, on the other hand, reflects cash the corporation has used to pre-pay future expenses. Although, it is listed as a current asset, **it does not represent cash** that the company will receive – instead it represents the value of services the company will receive for the cash it has pre-paid. As such, you should not consider pre-paid expenses as an asset the company can use to pay its debts as they come due.

Also, do not forget that when comparing the current assets to current liabilities, the company should consider its contractual obligations over the next twelve months that do not appear in the balance sheet's current liabilities.

---

[398] It is possible to pay a dividend in something other than cash, such as securities or other corporate assets. These dividends are called dividends-in-kind, and they are less common than cash dividends.

10A-202(d) NIMBLE DIVIDEND TEST:

The nimble dividend test is the most lenient of the dividend standards. It is normally **combined with the capital surplus test or the earned surplus test,** depending on the jurisdiction. It **allows the company to issue a dividend out of the current profits,** even if the corporation could not meet the capital surplus test or the earned surplus test.

For example, if the jurisdiction combines the capital surplus test with the nimble dividend test, the corporation could issue a dividend if it had profits during this accounting period, even if it did not have sufficient retained earnings and additional paid-in capital to pay the dividend. To determine whether a company had profits in the relevant accounting period, one must look at its **income statement**.

Illustration:

Imagine the company's has experienced operating losses over the past several years. As a result, it has a negative owners' equity on its balance sheet:

Common stock:	**100**
Additional paid-in capital:	**5,000**
Retained earnings (loss):	**(25,000)***

*Parenthesis indicates a negative number.

Under an **earned surplus test**, the company would not be allowed to issue a dividend because it had no earned surplus (i.e., retained earnings). Under a **capital surplus test**, the company would also not be allowed to issue a dividend because there is no capital surplus (i.e., additional paid-in capital plus retained earnings is still a negative number).

However, if the law of the state of incorporation adopts the nimble dividend test, the company would be allowed to issue a dividend if it made a profit in the current accounting period. Once again, we would have to look at this periods income statement to determine if the company made a profit.

10A-203 LIABILITY FOR VIOLATING DISTRIBUTION RULES:

Generally, if the board of directors authorizes a distribution in violation of the jurisdictions distribution rules, the **directors will be personally liable** up to the amount of the dividend. In addition, any **shareholder who received the**

dividend knowing it violated the distribution rules will also be liable for the amount of the distribution she received.

10A-300 CORPORATE LAW PROTECTIONS FOR CREDITORS – PIERCING THE CORPORATE VEIL

10A-301 PIERCING THE CORPORATE VEIL – BASIC CONCEPT:

When a court pierces the corporate veil, it disregards the shareholder's limited liability protection and **allows the company's creditor to recover from the shareholder's personal assets**. The court will justify holding the shareholder personally liable for the corporation's debts because the shareholder has somehow abused the privilege of limited liability. The problem in trying to predict when a court will pierce the corporate veil is that it is often difficult to distinguish between when a shareholder has abused the limited-liability privilege and she has abused it.

10A-302 PIERCING THE CORPORATE VEIL – THEORETICAL BACKGROUND:

10A-302(a) UNDERSTANDING WHY JUDGES PIERCE THE CORPORATE VEIL:

Limited liability allows corporations to externalize costs to creditors – both voluntary creditors (i.e., contractual creditors) and involuntary creditors (i.e., tort creditors). By creating limited liability, state legislatures have effectively decided that the **benefits of limited liability to society** – increased economic activity and innovation – outweigh the **costs of limited liability to society** – the ability of shareholders to externalize the costs of doing business in society.

Piercing the limited liability veil is the judicial response to the broad, absolute legislative grant of limited liability. Through piercing, judges protect their territory in the legal system's overall goal of justice. When protecting investors with limited liability would result in an injustice, a judge will pierce the corporate veil.

10A-302(b) UNDERSTANDING LIMITED LIABILITY AND PIERCING – A THOUGHT EXPERIMENT:

To better understand the benefits of limited liability, put yourself through the following thought experiment: Imagine you are asked to invest in a company in a world where there is no limited liability. As you answer the following questions, you will have a clearer sense of how limited liability reduces the cost of capital for a company.

Will you invest in the company without limited liability protection? You might, but because you bear the increased risk of personal liability, the return you expect for your investment will have to compensate you for this increased risk. In other words, you will expect the same return as you would for an investment in a limited liability world, but you will invest less capital for that same return.

What type of co-investors do you want? Wealthy co-investors. If you share the risk of personal liability with your co-investors, you want them to have the financial wherewithal to take responsibility for their fair share of the company's debts, should it ever come to that. Your need for solvent co-investors requires you to bear the costs of investigating the financial condition of each of your co-investors before you invest. It also necessitates you bearing the costs of continuing to monitor their individual financial conditions throughout the life of the venture. By the way, you fellow investors also want you to be wealthy, which may limit your investment opportunities.

What type of dividend policy do you want the company to adopt? A Conservative dividend policy. You want the company to distribute lower dividends and hold on to more cash as insurance for the possibility that your co-investors will not be able to meet their share of any liability for the company's obligations. Holding on to cash is not necessarily a sound business strategy unless the company can put it to good use.

What type of business strategies do you want the company to pursue? Conservative business strategies. The more risk the company takes in business, the greater the personal risk you bear. Of course, higher risk opportunities have the potential for higher return. With more conservative business strategies, you are foregoing the potential for greater returns.

Now, put yourself in the position of a policy maker: You want to promote economic activity. You want to promote innovation. These activities will be good for the economy, and good for the people you represent. You recognize that the costs of personal liability for the investors will result in fewer business ventures. In addition, the business ventures that are established will take fewer risks as a whole. Less risk-taking translates into less innovation in your economy.

You explore the possibility of creating a regime that protects investors with limited liability and you weigh the benefits of limited liability against the costs of limited liability – a more robust, innovative economy versus creditors bearing the costs of greater risk. You understand that creditors are not completely exposed. In many cases, the creditors will be able to structure their dealing with companies to provide themselves with greater protections.[399] They may ask for personal guaranties from the company's investors. They may charge the company more to compensate themselves for the additional risks. In addition, you recognize that most of the creditors will also benefit from limited liability themselves.

You decide to enact laws that protect investors with limited liability. You believe the overall benefits of limited liability will exceed the costs. However, it is not a perfect world. There are some businesses where the costs of limited liability will exceed the benefits, but as an administrative matter, it is too difficult to draft a law that can make such distinctions.

Judges, however, look at the law in the context of individual cases. They believe, rightfully or not, that they have both the ability and the mandate to do justice on a case-by-case basis. Although, the legislative grant of limited liability provides protection in all cases because its overall benefit outweighs the overall costs, judges are resistant to the idea that they should look at the overall benefit of limited liability. Their instinct is to do justice for each case. The **doctrine of piercing the limited liability veil is the judicial attempt to review the benefits and costs of limited liability on a case-by-case basis**.

10A-303 PIERCING THE CORPORATE VEIL – THE TEST:

Piercing the corporate veil is unprincipled.[400] Courts employ a **stink test:** If the judge thinks the shareholder's conduct is an abuse of the limited liability privilege, she will pierce the corporate veil and hold the shareholder personally liable for the debts of the corporation.

Courts have formulated piercing tests and factors that make the doctrine seem more principled, but the decisions are dependent on the judges' subjective feelings about the fairness of the circumstances.

The test: A court will pierce the corporate veil when

(1) There is a **unity of interest** between the shareholder and the corporation, and

(2) Respecting the limited liability veil would promote **injustice**.

---

[399] See §10A-102, above, for a discussion of contractual protections for creditors.

[400] Frank H. Easterbrook & Daniel R. Fischel, *Limited Liability and the Corporation*, 52 U. CHI L. REV. 89 (1985) ("'Piercing' seems to happen freakishly. Like lightning, it is rare, severe, and unprincipled.").

These two elements, plus a possible third element, are discussed immediately below.

10A-304 **UNITY OF INTEREST – THE FACTORS:**

When there is really no real distinction between the shareholder and the corporation, there is a **unity of interest** between them. Court's often express the same concept with different terminology, such as "the shareholder was conducting business in her **individual capacity**," or "the corporation was the shareholder's **alter ego**."

The conceptual problem with the unity of interest factor is that in a closely-held corporation, especially a one-shareholder corporation, a unity of interest between the corporation and the shareholder(s) is a truism. The corporation's separate legal identity is a legal fiction. A corporation is merely a limited liability insurance policy for the shareholders. Virtually all shareholders in closely-held corporations recognize no distinction between their interests and the corporation's interests. As far as they are concerned, they are the corporation and the corporation is them.

Nevertheless, when a shareholder has gone too far in her failure to respect the legal fiction of the corporation's separate personhood, the court might disregard the limited liability that protects that shareholder. The court will usually consider several factors to determine whether there was a unity of interest between the shareholder and the corporation. The court will typically look for the following:

> **The shareholder failed to maintain corporate records or observe corporate formalities.**
>
> Did the corporation appoint officers, create bylaws, hold shareholders meetings and board meetings? Did the corporation keep minutes and records? Did the corporation file its annual reports with the secretary of state and pay its annual renewal fees?
>
> **The shareholder commingled corporate funds and assets with her personal funds and assets.**
>
> Did the corporation and its shareholder have separate bank accounts? Did the shareholder withdraw money from the corporation's bank account for her personal use?

The shareholder undercapitalized the corporation.

Did the shareholder invest any capital into the corporation? If so, was it only a nominal amount? If the shareholder invested very little capital, did the corporation maintain adequate liability insurance?

The shareholder treated the assets of corporation as her own.

Did the shareholder use the company car, building, cell phone, etc. for her personal matters?

The one factor that seems to receive the most attention by the courts and scholars is the first factor: **failing to maintain corporate records or observe corporate formalities**. It is easy to fall into the trap and justify piercing because of the failure to observe corporate formalities. It is easy to rashly conclude, without giving great thought to the matter, that maintaining corporate formalities is the price shareholders pay for limited liability.

However, there is little or no relationship between corporate formalities and the policies that justify piercing of the corporate veil. If piercing the corporate veil serves to protect the corporation's creditors, the factors we use to determine whether we pierce should be relevant to promoting better protection for creditors. However, the observation of corporate formalities provides no obvious protection for creditors. In sharp contrast, the other factors provide more obvious protections for the interests of creditors. Let us examine the other factors to see how they provide improved protections for creditors:

> ***The shareholder comingled corporate assets with her personal funds:*** If the shareholder's bank account and the corporation's bank account are not distinguishable, we are safe in presuming that the shareholder is using the corporation's cash as her own. Effectively, she is receiving distributions from the corporation without regard to the distribution rules, potentially leaving the corporation with less cash to satisfy creditors' claims.

> ***The shareholder undercapitalized the corporation:*** If the shareholder had invested more capital into the corporation, the corporation would have more assets available to pay off the claims of its creditors.

> ***The shareholder treated the assets of corporation as her own:*** The shareholder's use of the company car, cell-phone service, and other corporate assets, without paying market price for their use, effectively drains the corporation of its assets.

Now, compare those factors with the **observance of corporate formalities**:

510

If a corporation holds its annual shareholders meeting, as required by the corporate law statute, are the interests of the corporation's creditors better protected? Probably not.

If a corporation has regular board meetings and keeps copious minutes of those meetings, are the interests of the corporation's creditors better protected? Probably not.

If the corporation makes its annual report to the secretary of state and pays its annual fees, does that provide better protection for creditors? Probably not.

Why, then, should any of these facts be a consideration for piercing the corporate veil?

Some courts have argued that failure to observe corporate formalities is a proxy for other indicia that justify piercing the corporate veil:

> In the context of a close corporation, the failure to follow corporate formalities is important because the trier of the facts may reasonably infer that such conduct springs not from merely innocent, overworked inattention to paperwork by the sole or controlling shareholder, but is indicative of the fact that such shareholder views the business as his or her own individual business so that there is no need to "go through the motions" of complying with formalities . . . [.][401]

However, the failure to observe corporate formalities hardly seems to be an accurate proxy for misconduct, especially in single-shareholder corporations. Corporate formalities are intended for the internal governance of the corporation and the protection of minority shareholders, not the protection of creditors. There is no need to go through with formalities in single-shareholder corporations because there are no minority shareholders to protect.

10A-305 INJUSTICE:

For most courts, unity of interest is not enough to pierce the corporate veil. These courts will only pierce when (1) there is unity of interest, AND (2) adherence to corporate form would **sanction fraud or promote injustice**.

Normally, "fraud or injustice" in this context means some sort of unfairness that is **akin to fraud or deception, or that some compelling public interest**

---

[401] *Laya v. Erin Homes, Inc.*, 352 S.E.2d 93, n. 6 (1986).

justifies piercing. Courts are never really clear about what type of conduct satisfies this element. Most courts say that fraud or injustice must be some wrong in addition to failure to pay the plaintiff-creditor. In any case, courts do not seem to have trouble finding this element when the unity of interest element has been satisfied.

10A-306 CREDIT INVESTIGATION:

In the closely-held corporation, creditors often force shareholders to give up their limited liability by requiring them to personally guaranty the corporation's obligations. In addition, creditors often protect themselves by investigating the credit worthiness of the corporation they deal with. In fact, the ability of creditors to engage in this type of private ordering to protect themselves against the risks of limited liability is one justification for limited liability.

Based on this reasoning, some courts will add a third element to the piercing doctrine:

> The court will not pierce the corporate veil if it would it have been reasonable for plaintiff to have conducted a **credit investigation prior to extending credit to the corporation.**

Courts are conservative in their application of this third element. Normally, it is only reasonable for a creditor to do a credit investigation when the creditor is a sophisticated party that we would expect to conduct a credit investigation as part of its business, such as a bank or, possibly, a commercial lessor.

10A-307 ENTERPRISE LIABILITY:

There is a sub-set of corporate piercing cases that are often referred to as enterprise liability. In these cases, the court pierces the veil between two or more corporations owned by a common shareholder.

Illustration:

Sally is the sole shareholder of three corporations, ABC Inc., LMN Inc. and XYZ Inc.

ABC Inc. is unable to pay its creditors. The creditors might try to use the piercing doctrine to hold Sally personally liable for ABC's debts. They might also use piercing/enterprise liability to hold LMN Inc. and XYZ Inc. liable for ABC's debts.

The underlying concept of enterprise liability is to ignore the form of the shareholder's ownership structure and look at its substance to determine **whether the corporations act as a single enterprise**.

The **factors in the unity of interest element** we discussed above apply to enterprise liability cases as well. However, instead of merely asking whether the shareholder treated corporate assets as her own, for example, we would also ask whether the corporations under the shareholder's control treated each other's assets as their own. In addition, we might look at whether the three corporations shared common directors, executive officers, and other employees. Similarly, if they shared common facilities and other assets, a court might find there was a unity of interest between these three entities.

UNIT 10B

PARTNERSHIPS – PROTECTING CREDITORS:

10B-100 PARTNERSHIPS – LIMITATIONS ON DISTRIBUTIONS TO PARTNERS:

10B-101 GENERAL PARTNERSHIPS:

In contrast to the law governing corporations, there are no restrictions on distributions to general partners. General partners are liable for the debts of the partnership, making it irrelevant whether the assets are with the partnership or with the partners.

10B-102 LIMITED LIABILITY PARTNERSHIPS:

Curiously, RUPA has no restrictions on distributions to the partners of an LLP. One would expect that the limited liability nature of an LLP would warrant legal limitations on distributions to partners similar to those we see in the corporation. In spite of the RUPA approach, some jurisdictions have indeed placed limitations on distributions to the partners of an LLP. For example, Ohio's Partnership Act provides:

> A limited liability partnership shall not make a distribution to a partner to the extent that at the time of the distribution and after giving effect to the distribution, all liabilities of the limited liability partnership exceed the fair value of the assets of the limited liability partnership, other than liabilities to partners on account of their economic interests and liabilities for which the recourse of creditors is limited to specified property. . . .[402]

You will notice that Ohio's approach to distributions to partners in an LLP is the first part of the insolvency test we discussed in 10A-202(c), above.

---

[402] Ohio Revised Code, Chapter 17, §1776.84

514

10B-103 **LIMITED PARTNERSHIPS:**

State limited partnerships statutes have limitations on distributions to the partners of an LP similar to those of corporate law statutes.

10B-200 **PARTNERSHIPS – PIERCING THE VEIL:**

10B-201 **GENERAL PARTNERSHIPS:**

Because general partners are not protected by limited liability, there is no need for a piercing doctrine.

10B-202 **LIMITED LIABILITY PARTNERSHIPS:**

It is possible a court could apply the piercing doctrine to LLPs, although I am not aware of any case where this has happened. However, the piercing doctrine is not as crucial for creditors of an LLP as it is for the creditors of a corporation. Under default liability rules for LLPs, there will usually be one or more partners who bear personal liability for the LLP's obligations,[403] which allows the creditors to recover from the personal assets of one or more partners without having to resort to a piercing argument. Any personal liability claim a creditor makes will be based on whether the partner in question was responsible for the conduct that created the liability or supervised the person whose conduct was responsible for the liability, rather than the traditional piercing arguments. In other words, the existing default liability rules for the partners of an LLP already provide a sufficient basis for holding partners personally liable for the debts of the LLP, and make piercing somewhat redundant.

Many LLP statutes protect all partners from personal liability for the partnership's contractual obligations. These contractual cases might be ripe for a piercing claim, under the right circumstances.

10B-203 **LIMITED PARTNERSHIPS – PIERCING AND THE CONTROL RULE:**

In general, there is no piercing in limited partnerships. If you recall, limited partnerships have at least one general partner and at least one limited

---

[403] See Chapter 3, §3D-403 for a discussion of limited liability and personal liability for partners of an LLP.

partner.[404]   With respect to the general partner, there is no need for piercing because the general partner does not enjoy limited liability.

With respect to limited partners, who are protected with limited liability, piercing seems highly unlikely. Limited partners are passive in the management of the business, which means there is very little possibility they could engage in the type of conduct that would prompt a court to pierce the limited liability veil. To the extent that a limited partner engages in actual control of the business, a creditor of the business seeking to hold the limited partner personally liable would argue the limited partner acted as a general partner. In other words, the creditor would request the court to look past the form of the partner's status as limited partner to the substance of the partner's actual role in the partnership as a general partner. In the LP context, this argument hinges on what approach the relevant statute takes to a limited partner's participation in the limited partnership's business.

In state limited partnership statutes, there is normally a section addressing when a limited partner's control of the partnership's business will result in her being treated as a general partner for the purposes of personal liability. These sections are generally referred to as the **control rule**. A little history is important in understanding the control rule and how it plays a role in holding a limited partner personally liable for the debts of the partnership:

> The 1916 version of the Uniform Limited Partnership Act (**ULPA 1916**) provided that **a limited partner who engaged in "control of the business" had the same liability as a general partner.** It was left to the courts to determine exactly what type of conduct constituted "control of the business," but it was otherwise clear that exercising rights voting similar to those of minority shareholders in corporations would not constitute the control of the business.

The ULPA 1916 approach allowed the creditors of a limited partnership to argue that a limited partner should be liable for the debts of the partnership because of the limited partner's active participation in the business. This version of the control rule made piercing the limited liability veil unnecessary. Indeed, the control rule provided creditors with greater protection than the piercing doctrine. The piercing doctrine requires the creditor to show a unity of interest between the limited partner and the partnership, which is a higher burden than showing mere control of the business.

However, the control rule of ULPA 1916 is no longer the law in most U.S. states. Instead, most limited partnership statutes take one of two approaches:

---

[404] See Chapter 3, §3D-303 for a discussion of limited liability and personal liability for partners of a limited partnership.

The 1985 revised version of the Uniform Limited Liability Partnership (**RULPA 1985**) provided that a limited partner would only be liable as a general partner if two elements were satisfied: **(1) she participated in the control of the business; AND (2) the creditor reasonably believed her to be a general partner.**

Under limited partnership statutes that take the **RULPA 1985 approach**, one might see a creditor make a piercing argument, but only in cases where she could not have a reasonable belief that the limited partner was a general partner. I have not heard of a case where such an argument was made, so it is uncertain whether a court would even entertain this possibility.

The 2001 revised version of the Uniform Limited Liability Partnership (**RULPA 2001**) provided that a limited partner could be active in the control of the business without the fear of personal liability. **No level of control or active participation by the limited partner would subject her to any personal liability as a general partner under the RULPA 2001.**

Under limited partnership statutes that take the **RULPA 2001 approach**, a creditor might make a piercing argument as a last resort, but would need to show more than control of the business by the limited partner. She would need to show a unity of interest between the limited partner and the partnership. Once again, I can only speculate as to whether a court would allow piercing in a limited partnership context.

UNIT 10C

LLCs – Protecting Creditors:

10C-100 LLCs – Limitations on Distributions to Members:

State LLC statutes have limitations on distributions to the members of an LLC similar to those of corporate law statutes. [405] If you understand the different approaches to limiting distributions in corporations, you will be able to understand the same in the LLC context.

10C-200 LLCs – Piercing The Limited Liability Veil:

Piercing the LLC veil is similar to piercing the corporate veil,[406] except maintaining formalities will not be a factor in the unity of interest element. [407] If you recall, LLC statutes do not require formal meetings, minutes, bylaws, appointment of officers, etc.[408] When a court applies the unity of interest test in the LLC context, it should not consider whether the LLC failed to maintain the formalities a corporation would be expected to observe.[409]

---

[405] See §10A-202 et seq., above, for a discussion of limitations on distributions to the shareholders of a corporation.

[406] See §10A-300 et seq., above, for a discussion of piercing the limited liability veil in corporations.

[407] See §10A-304, above, for a discussion of the role of corporate formalities in piercing the limited liability veil.

[408] See Chapter 5, Unit 5C for a discussion of the relaxed approach to formalities in LLCs.

[409] See RULLCA §304(b).

APPENDIX A

ACCOUNTING PRIMER

A-100 **ACCOUNTING TERMS AND CONCEPTS:**

A-101 INTRODUCTION:

A-102 IMPORTANT ACCOUNTING TERMS AND CONCEPTS:

    A-102(a) REVENUE:

    A-102(b) EXPENSES:

    A-102(c) EARNINGS:

    A-102(d) ASSETS:

    A-102(e) INVENTORY:

    A-102(f) DEPRECIATION:

    A-102(g) LIABILITIES:

    A-102(h) OWNERS' EQUITY:

A-200 **FINANCIAL STATEMENTS:**

A-201 THE BALANCE SHEET:

A-202 THE INCOME STATEMENT:

A-203 THE CASH FLOW STATEMENT:

A-204 SAMPLE FINANCIAL STATEMENTS:

    A-204(a) SAMPLE BALANCE SHEET – EXPLANATION:

    A-204(b) SAMPLE INCOME STATEMENT – EXPLANATION:

    A-204(c) SAMPLE CASH FLOW STATEMENT – EXPLANATION:

A-100 ACCOUNTING TERMS AND CONCEPTS:

A-101 INTRODUCTION:

If you practice law in the business world, it will be impossible for you to avoid accounting terminology and concepts. In law school, you learn the language of law, which is very important for your career as an attorney. However, your business clients speak the language of business, which is accounting.

If you do not have a background in accounting, I would suggest you take your school's version of accounting for lawyers. You will find it to be one of the most practical and useful classes of your law school career. Contrary to popular misconceptions, you do not have to be good at math to understand accounting. Basic accounting involves only simple arithmetic that you can do on a calculator. I am notoriously bad at math (I blame it on the fact that my grandparents were first cousins) and I have become been fluent in accounting, after building on what I learned in one course on accounting for lawyers.

The goal of this accounting primer is not to make you an expert in accounting, but to provide an initial introduction for those who have never studied accounting. Naturally, a deep understanding of any subject requires constant exposure to it, but there must always be that first exposure. For those students who are unfamiliar with accounting, please consider this your first exposure. For those students who have already learned some accounting, consider this primer to be a refresher.

A-102 IMPORTANT ACCOUNTING CONCEPTS:

A-102(a) REVENUE:

Revenue is the company's **sales**, represented in a dollar amount. If the company sold 100 widgets to a customer for a price of $10 per widget, the company's revenue for that sale would be $1,000.

Revenue is not profit. To determine profit, you would have to subtract the company's expenses from it revenue.

As far as accounting is concerned, a sale counts as revenue only when it is **accrued**. To put it another way, a sale counts as revenue **when the company has delivered what it has promised**, even if the customer has not yet paid. Compare the following three situations:

Situation 1:

March 10: The company sells and delivers 100 widgets to the customer for $1,000. The customer promises to pay on April 9.

> **Analysis:** This sale is considered revenue on March 10. On March 10, the company records the $1,000 as revenue, even though it has not received any cash for it. (If the customer eventually fails to pay, we will have to make later adjustments to the books).

Situation 2:

March 10: The company enters into a contract with the customer for the company to sell 100 widgets to the customer for $1,000, delivery on April 9.

> **Analysis:** This sale is not considered revenue yet. On March 10, the company may NOT record this contract as revenue. The company cannot record revenues until it has delivered the goods. Upon delivery of the widgets on April 9, the company will record the revenue for the April period, not the March period.

Situation 3:

March 10: The company enters into a contract with the customer for the company to sell 100 widgets to the customer for $1,000, delivery on April 9. The customer prepays $1,000 when it signs the contract.

> **Analysis:** This sale is not considered revenue yet. On March 10, the company may NOT record the $1,000 cash it received as revenue. As we said above, the company cannot record revenues until it has delivered the goods. The cash is in the company's bank account, and the company can spend the cash, but the cash is not revenue, yet. Upon delivery of the widgets on April 9, the company will record the revenue for the April period, not the March period.

A-102(b) **EXPENSES:**

Expenses are the costs of doing business. It is easier to explain expenses with examples.

If I am a **retailer** of shoes, my expenses are:

> My **cost of goods sold**, which includes my costs of acquiring the shoes from a wholesaler

> My **overhead**, which includes all other expenses, such as my rent, utilities, salaries, insurance, property tax, etc.

If I am a **manufacturer** of shoes, my expenses are

> My **cost of goods sold**, which includes my costs of acquiring the **raw materials**, and my **manufacturing overhead**, which are the expenses I incur for processing the raw materials into finished shoes (e.g., factory rent, factory utilities, factory worker salaries, factory insurance, and other expenses attributable to the manufacturing process).

> My **general overhead**, which are the costs of selling my goods and other general expenses (office/store rent, office/store utilities, administrative and sales salaries, and other expenses attributable to the selling process and general administrative work).

Costs are only counted as expenses when they have **accrued**. In the context of expenses, accrual means that the company has **used** (i.e., consumed) the goods or services. The date of actual payment is irrelevant to determining when the cost is an expense

Compare the following two situations:

Situation 1:

March 1 – March 31: The company uses $5,000 of electricity during the month of March. The company pays the electricity bill for March on April 9.

> **Analysis:** March expense. The company would record this as an expense for March, even though it did not pay until April. The expense was paid in April, but it was accrued in March because the company **used** the electricity in March.

Situation 2:

March 10: The company enters 3-year lease for manufacturing space at $10,000 per month. The lease begins on April 1.

> **Analysis:** Not an expense yet. The company will expense $10,000 at the close of each month of the lease. In other words, the $10,000 expense will accrue at the end of each month because the company **uses** the premises each month.

There are some costs you might expect to be considered expenses for the company that are not immediately recognized as expenses.

If the company **purchases assets**, such as manufacturing equipment, computers for the office, delivery vehicles, buildings, etc., the cost of the acquisition of the asset is **not immediately recognized as an expense**. Instead, the company will slowly expense the asset over time. This process is called "depreciation." If the asset is a non-tangible asset, like intellectual property, the process is called "amortization."

Illustration:

The company purchases a delivery vehicle for $30,000.

> ***Analysis:*** Not an expense yet. The company will expense a portion of the $30,000 each year over the useful life of the vehicle (the useful life is probably around 5 years).

Finally, when a company **purchases inventory**, it **does not immediately expense** the cost of the purchase. Instead, it expenses the inventory upon sale of the inventory.

Illustration:

The company operates a retail shoe store. On March 10, it purchases a pair of shoes for $20 from its supplier.   On April 9, it sells that pair of shoes to a customer.

> ***Analysis:*** The company recognizes the expense of acquiring the inventory on April 9, not on March 10.

A-102(c) **EARNINGS:**

Earnings simply mean **profits**. The earnings are calculated by **subtracting the expenses from the revenues.** It is also called **income**.

The important thing to remember about the earnings is that they do not necessarily provide a good picture of the company's cash position. This is because **the revenues and expenses that make up the earnings are not necessarily cash transactions**.

Illustration:

If I sell and deliver on credit, I receive no cash immediately, but I still account for the sale as revenue immediately.

If I receive a cash payment from my customer before I deliver, I have received cash immediately, but I cannot account for this as revenue yet (not until I deliver).

If I pay cash to purchase a piece of equipment to manufacture my goods, I have an immediate outlay of cash that will not be recognized as an expense immediately (the expense will be depreciated over time).

If I prepay my supplier for goods she will deliver later, I have an immediate outlay of cash that will not be recognized as an expense immediately. It will be recognized as an expense only after I have received delivery of the goods and re-sold them to my customers.

A-102(d) ASSETS:

You already have an in intuitive understanding of what an asset is, so don't let the definition confuse you. An asset is property that provides value to the business. Assets can be **tangible property**, such as cash, buildings, vehicles, and equipment. Assets can also be **intangible property** like intellectual property.

However, please keep in mind that **a contract is not an asset** according to accounting rules.

Illustration:

The company enters into a contract to supply widgets to a customer for the next five years. The customer promises to purchase a minimum number of widgets over the next 5 years.

This contract translates into future revenues for the company, but accounting rules do not treat it as an asset.

Making a sale and delivery to a customer will increase asset accounts in one of two ways:

1) If the customer pays in cash upon delivery, our cash increases. Cash is an asset account. Of course, because we delivered product to the customer, our inventory account (asset) will decrease. Unless we are selling at a loss, the increase in the cash account will more than make up for the decrease in our inventory account.

2) If the customer accepts delivery on credit, promising to pay in 30 days, our **accounts receivable** increase. Accounts receivable are assets. Once again, because we delivered product to the customer, our inventory account (asset) will decrease. Unless we are selling at a loss, the increase in accounts receivable will be greater than the decrease in our inventory account.

Finally, the **value of the asset on the company's books is the cost of acquiring the asset**, not the current market value of the asset. Thus, for example:

Illustration:

The company acquired a building for $100,000. Two years later, the market value of the building is $200,000. However, on the company's books, the building's value is listed as $100,000 (less depreciation, which will be discussed in some more detail below).

A-102(e) INVENTORY:

Inventory is **one category of assets**. It represents the goods the company sells. It might be finished goods, such as shoes or handbags. It might be the raw materials for goods the company manufactures, such as leather and buckles for the shoes and handbags.

When the company acquires leather for its shoes, the leather is an asset – raw material inventory. When a piece of leather is finally sold to a customer in the form of a shoe, the cost of that piece of leather is deducted from the inventory account. At the same time, the cost of that leather is recognized as an expense.

A-102(f) DEPRECIATION:

Depreciation is the accounting method of apportioning the costs of the use of an asset to the business operations. If the company buys a piece of machinery to manufacture handbags, the machinery will eventually need to be replaced. In other words, the machinery gets used up a little every day. Depreciation is the accounting concept that **determines the cost of the gradual decline of the asset**.

Depreciation shows up in two ways in accounting:

1) **Determining the value of an asset:** On the company's financial statement, the asset is listed at the cost of acquiring the asset, less the depreciation of the asset over the past several years since the asset was acquired.

2) **As an expense:** The cost of the use of the asset has to be included in the determination of the company's earnings. Thus, the depreciation of an asset over a particular period will be an expense for that period.

A-102(g) LIABILITIES:

Liabilities are the various debts the company owes to creditors. You often hear people say that someone or something is a "liability," implying a liability is something detrimental. However, accounting liabilities are actually good things. A company needs to incur liabilities in order to do business. It must buy on credit and borrow money from banks. Creditors provide a large amount of the capital that a company needs to operate.

Please keep in mind that mere contractual obligations are not accounting liabilities. Attorneys might view contractual obligations as liabilities because we know the company will eventually have to pay or perform. However, accounting rules look at contractual obligations differently: **contractual obligations are not liabilities until the company has received what it bargained for.**

Illustration:

The company signs a contract where is promises to buy 10,000 pairs of shoes over the next 12 months for $20 per pair. The promise to purchase shoes will only turn into an accounting liability each time the supplier delivers the shoes to the company on credit. Indeed, if the company pays cash upon each delivery, this contract will never result in any accounting liabilities.

When a supplier delivers goods to us on credit, we incur a liability called an "**account payable**."

A-102(h) OWNERS' EQUITY:

You are already familiar with the concept of owners' equity. The owners of a business are the residual claimants, which is simply another way of describing the equity claim.

If the company is liquidated and its assets sold, the owners are entitled to whatever remains after the creditors' claims are met. Thus, in accounting, the owners' equity is always the remainder of **the assets minus the liabilities**.

The accounting version of owners' equity is not a completely accurate representation of the true residual claim for several reasons:

The assets are not listed on the accounting books at market value. The market value may be higher or lower than what appears on the company's financial statements.

The company might have contractual obligations that do not show up on the books as liabilities.

A-200 FINANCIAL STATEMENTS:

The financial statements of a company tell part of the story of the company's financial condition. There are three financial statements, and they each play a part in presenting the financial condition of the company:

A-201 THE BALANCE SHEET:

The balance sheet takes stock of the company's **assets and liabilities**. It essentially answers the question: What do we have, what do people owe to us, and what do we owe to other people?

The balance sheet only presents a picture of the company at a particular moment in time. Because the company's assets are changing every day, the balance sheet will never be current.

A-202 **THE INCOME STATEMENT:**

The income statement tells us the profits of a company during a specific period of time. It presents the revenue and expenses of the company for a specific period of time – e.g., 3 months, one year, etc. You can think of it as something akin to your tax return.

A-203 **THE CASH FLOW STATEMENT:**

The cash flow statement tells us how cash was going in and out of the company during a specific period of time – e.g., 3 months, one year, etc. Students with no familiarity with accounting often wonder how the cash flow statement differs from the income statement.

There are two main differences between the cash flow statement and the income statement:

1) **The income statement does not necessarily measure all cash transactions.** As we discussed above, a transaction can qualify as "revenue" even when the company has not yet received cash. Similarly, a transaction can qualify as an "expense" even though the company has yet to make a cash outlay. In each of the respective cases, the company will eventually receive cash or pay cash, but the cash might be received in a different accounting period. If so, the income statements and cash flow statements will differ.

    Similarly, we saw that a company might make a cash payment (prepayment) that would not yet be considered an "expense." The company might also receive a cash payment (advance payment) that would not yet be considered "revenue." Eventually, each transaction will be recognized as an expense or revenue, but it might not happen until the next accounting period.

2) **The income statement does not reflect financing activities:** The income statement measures profit. However, a company may borrow money from a bank or receive investment from new equity investors. The capital they receive from the bank or the investors is not part of the company's "operations" – e.g., it is not revenue from the sale of widgets. It is a separate activity – financing. The cash flow statement will present all cash transactions, whether they are financing or operations. In contrast, the income statement does not reflect any financing activities.

A-204 **SAMPLE FINANCIAL STATEMENTS:**

Please look at the financial statements for an imaginary company, below. Try to work your way through the explanations that follow the financial statements.

See the financial statements on the following page.

BALANCE SHEET OF XYZ CORP.
December 31, 20XX

Assets:

Cash:	50,000
Accounts receivable:	2,000
Pre-paid expenses:	1,500
Inventory:	7,000
Equipment:	30,000
Less depreciation:	5,500
Building:	105,000
Less depreciation:	20,000
Land:	60,000
TOTAL ASSETS:	**230,000**

Liabilities:

Accounts payable:	3,000
Rent payable:	4,000
Wages payable:	8,000
Advance payments:	2,000
Bank loan:	57,000
TOTAL LIABILITIES:	74,000

Owners' Equity:

Capital:	1,000
Additional paid-in capital	99,000
Retained earnings:	56,000
TOTAL OWNER'S EQUITY:	156,000
TOTAL LIABILITIES AND OWNERS EQUITY:	**230,000**

INCOME STATEMENT OF XYZ CORP.
January 1 – December 31, 20XX

Revenues:	345,000
Costs of goods sold:	143,000
Gross profit (loss):	202,000
Other expenses:	
Wages:	102,000
Utilities:	9,500
Depreciation	7,000
Rent	52,000
Advertising	1,000
Interest on bank loan	3,000
Other gains (losses):	(1,500)
Income (loss) before income tax:	26,000
Income tax:	5,000
NET INCOME (LOSS):	21,000

CASH FLOW STATEMENT OF XYZ CORP.
January 1 – December 31, 20XX

Cash flow from operating activities:

Cash from customers:	349,000
Cash used for operations:	310,000
Net cash from operations:	39,000

Cash flow from investing activities:

Cash from investing;	1,000
Cash used for investing:	4,500
Net cash from investing:	(3,500)

Cash flow from financing activities:

Cash from financing;	10,000
Cash used for financing:	6,000
Net cash from financing;	4,000
Net increase in cash:	39,500
Cash at beginning of period:	10,500
Cash at end of period:	50,000

530

A-204(a) SAMPLE BALANCE SHEET – EXPLANATION:

1) The balance sheet presents a **picture of the assets and liabilities of the company at a particular moment in time**. In this case, the moment in time is the last day of the year. The balance sheet is very ephemeral. Indeed, the balance sheet will be out of date immediately on January 1 of the next year with the company's first delivery or receipt of goods or services or the company's first payment or receipt of payment.

Imagine on January 1 of the next year, the company orders raw materials from a supplier and makes a prepayment of $10,000 cash. Many of the balance sheet accounts will change: the **cash account** (asset) will be reduced by $10,000; the **pre-paid expenses account** (asset) will increase by $10,000.

Imagine on January 1 of the next year, the company receives goods it ordered from a supplier on credit for $8,000. Let's assume the goods are shoes that the company plans to sell to its customers. The company has 30 days to pay. With the receipt of the goods, the following changes will occur to the balance sheet: the **inventory account** (asset) will be increased by $8,000 because the company just received $8,000 worth of shoes; the **accounts payable account** (liability) will increase $8,000 because now the company owes $8,000 to the supplier.

Imagine on January 1 of the next year, the company pays the $4,000 rent it owes. With the payment of the rent, the following changes will occur to the balance sheet: the **rent payable account** (liability) will be reduced by $4,000 and the company's **cash account** (asset) will be reduced by $4,000.

2) Notice how the balance sheet presents **Assets, Liabilities and Owners' Equity**. The equation of the balance sheet is **Assets – Liabilities = Owners' Equity**. Actually, the balance sheet presents the equation in a different form: **Assets = Liabilities + Owners' Equity**. The two equations are equivalents, of course.

3) You will notice how the **assets are valued** – at the cost of acquisition, less the depreciation that has accumulated over the years. Thus, we know the company acquired the building in the past for $105,000. According to the balance sheet, the accounting value of the building has decreased $20,000 over the years since the company's acquisition, for a net value of $85,000. In reality, however, the building will likely have a different actual market value. You cannot discern the actual market value of an asset by looking at the balance sheet numbers.

531

4) Owners' Equity is the accounting representation of the residual claim. If the company were to liquidate its assets and pay off its creditors, the owners would receive the remainder. The remainder, or "residual," is the owners' equity. The actual residual might be higher or lower depending on the actual market value of the assets. Remember, the values of the assets listed on the financial statements are not the market values, so the owners may get more or less for the assets if they sold them on the open market.

The Owners' Equity on this balance sheet is divided into **capital** and **accumulated retained earnings.**

Capital refers to the cash the owners have invested in the company. Here, the owners have invested $100,000 in the company. In other words, over the years, investors have given the company $100,000 in exchange for ownership interests. This does not mean that the company still has the $100,000 in cash. Indeed, one look at the balance sheet tells us that the company only has $50,000 cash. The company has used the capital to buy assets, pay salaries, pay suppliers, etc.

Accumulated retained earnings represent the profits of the company. If the company makes a profit, it belongs to the owners. The company may distribute profits to the owners by giving them cash (often called a dividend). If the company does not actually give the cash profit to the owners, it must still credit the owners with the profit on the balance sheet. The accountants will make an entry to increase the Owners' Equity account by the amount of the profit not actually distributed to the owners. Here, we see that the company has accumulated and retained $56,000 of profit over the years. If the company had accumulated $56,000 of losses over the years, instead of profits, the accumulated retained earnings would be negative - i.e., ($56,000).

A-204(b) <u>**Sample Income Statement – Explanation:**</u>

1) Income is simply the profit for the period of time stated on the income statement. Notice how the time frame for the income statement is different from the balance sheet. The balance sheet counts assets and liabilities at a particular moment. The income statement measures profitability over a particular duration. In this case, the income statement is measuring the profitability for an entire year. Profits are measured by **subtracting expenses from revenues.**

2) The **revenues** for this company for the year were $345,000. Remember, not all of this number represents cash received by the company. If, for example, the company delivered goods to a buyer on December 15 and it gave the buyer 30 days credit, the company received no cash, but the sale was still considered revenue.

In addition, the company might have received cash during the period the income statement covers, but the cash would not be revenue for that period. You can imagine a situation where the company received cash during the year for deliveries it made to customers in the previous year. The revenue for those sales would have been recorded in the previous year's income statement.

3) The **expenses** for this company for the year were $325,000. The expenses are normally divided into several different items. The first item is the **cost of goods sold.** The cost of goods sold for a merchandiser (i.e., someone who buys goods from a supplier and then resells them to a customer at a higher price) is the cost of purchasing the goods from the supplier.[410] In this case, the company purchased $143,000 worth of goods from suppliers that it sold to customers. The company might have purchased more than $143,000 worth of goods from suppliers, but the company may only expense the cost of the goods it actually sold to customers. Thus, we know that the company made sales of goods for $345,000, and the goods that it sold cost $143,000 to acquire.

The other expenses, such as wages, utilities, advertising, etc., are often called **overhead.**

4) Not all of the expenses represent a cash outlay for the company. For example, the company might have purchased the goods from a supplier on credit and not paid by the end of the year. The cost of those goods

---

[410] Determining the costs of goods sold for a **manufacturer** is more complicated. You need to determine how much it cost the manufacturer to produce the goods it sold, e.g., the costs or utilities, labor, and raw materials attributable to the manufacturing process.

533

would still be expenses for the year (if the company actually sold them during the year). The company might not have paid its bill for the utilities it used at the end of the year, but those utilities would still be expenses for the year.

_____

A-204(c) **SAMPLE CASH FLOW STATEMENT – EXPLANATION:**

1) The cash flow statement is more straightforward than the income statement. The **cash flow statement only cares about whether cash came in or went out** in the period. It does not care whether the company delivered goods in the period. It does not care whether the company received the goods in the period. In short, **the cash flow statement does not care whether the cash outlay could be considered an "expense," nor does it care whether the cash received could be considered "revenue."** Notice how the time frame for the cash flow statement is the same as the income statement. The cash flow statement measures cash flow over the same period as the income statement.

2) A company can have cash flow from three different sources.

The first possible source is **"operations"** or **"operating activities."** These terms simply refer to the business of the company. If the company sells shoes, its cash flow from operations includes cash it received from customers and cash paid for operating expenses, e.g., inventory from suppliers, utilities, rent, insurance, advertising, etc.

The second source of cash flow is **"investing activities."** When the company buys new equipment or facilities, it is investing in itself. Thus, if it pays $10,000 cash for a new delivery truck, the $10,000 outlay of cash will appear on the cash flow statement under "cash used for investing." The company might want to sell its old delivery truck. If it received cash for the old truck, it would appear on the cash flow statement under "cash received from investing activities." The sale or purchase of a delivery truck would not be considered **operations** because the company does not sell delivery trucks as its business.

The third source of cash flow is **"financing activities."** If the company receives cash capital from owners or from lenders, it shows up on the cash flow statement under "cash received from financing activities." If the company repays the principal of the loan or returns capital to the investors, the transaction would appear on the cash flow statement as "cash used in financing activities."

535

INDEX:

545